MYANMAR'S
MOUNTAIN AND MARITIME
BORDERSCAPES

The **ISEAS – Yusof Ishak Institute** (formerly Institute of Southeast Asian Studies) was established as an autonomous organization in 1968. It is a regional centre dedicated to the study of socio-political, security and economic trends and developments in Southeast Asia and its wider geostrategic and economic environment. The Institute's research programmes are the Regional Economic Studies (RES, including ASEAN and APEC), Regional Strategic and Political Studies (RSPS), and Regional Social and Cultural Studies (RSCS).

ISEAS Publishing, an established academic press, has issued more than 2,000 books and journals. It is the largest scholarly publisher of research about Southeast Asia from within the region. ISEAS Publishing works with many other academic and trade publishers and distributors to disseminate important research and analyses from and about Southeast Asia to the rest of the world.

MYANMAR'S MOUNTAIN AND MARITIME BORDERSCAPES

LOCAL PRACTICES, BOUNDARY-MAKING AND FIGURED WORLDS

EDITED BY SU-ANN OH

YUSOF ISHAK INSTITUTE

First published in Singapore in 2016 by
ISEAS Publishing
30 Heng Mui Keng Terrace
Singapore 119614

E-mail: publish@iseas.edu.sg
Website: <http://bookshop.iseas.edu.sg>

All rights reserved. No part of this publication may be reproduced, stored in a retrieval system, or transmitted in any form or by any means, electronic, mechanical, photocopying, recording or otherwise, without the prior permission of the ISEAS – Yusof Ishak Institute.

© 2016 ISEAS – Yusof Ishak Institute, Singapore

The responsibility for facts and opinions in this publication rests exclusively with the author and his interpretations do not necessarily reflect the views or the policy of the publisher or its supporters.

ISEAS Library Cataloguing-in-Publication Data

Myanmar's Mountain and Maritime Borderscapes : Local Practices, Boundary-making and Figured Worlds / edited by Su-Ann Oh.
    Papers originally presented at a Conference on Myanmar from the Margins, held in Institute of Southeast Asian Studies, 14–15 November 2013.
    1. Internal migrants—Myanmar.
    2. Myanmar—Politics and government.
    3. Myanmar—Boundaries.
    4. Myanmar—Religious life and customs.
    I. Oh, Su-Ann.
    II. Conference on Myanmar from the Margins (2013 : Singapore)
DS528.7 M99   2016

ISBN 978-981-4695-76-3 (soft cover)
ISBN 978-981-4695-77-0 (e-book, PDF)

Cover photo: Watercolour paintings on the front and back covers reproduced with kind permission of Su-Ann Oh

Typeset by Superskill Graphics Pte Ltd
Printed in Singapore by Mainland Press Pte Ltd

Contents

List of Tables vii

List of Figures viii

Acknowledgements ix

Notes on Language, Terminology and Geographical Names xi

Contributors xiii

Abbreviations xix

1. Introduction 1
   Su-Ann Oh

I. Overview of Myanmar's Mountain and Maritime Borderscapes

2. Electoral Sovereignty in Myanmar's Borderlands 39
   Nicholas Farrelly

3. The Maritime Frontier of Myanmar: Challenges in the Early 21st Century 70
   Maung Aung Myoe

II. Territorial Claims and Imagined Boundaries

4. Burman Territories and Borders in the Making of a Myanmar Nation State 99
   Maxime Boutry

5. Ritual and the Other in Rakhine Spirit Cults 121
   Alexandra de Mersan

6. Rohingya Territoriality in Myanmar and Bangladesh: Humanitarian Crisis and National Disordering 146
   Anders Bjornberg

III. Social Organization and Border Economies

7. The Culture and Landscape of the Humanitarian Economy among the Karen (Kayin) in the Borderland of Southeast Myanmar and Northwest Thailand 171
   Alexander Horstmann

8. Navigating Learning, Employment and Economies in the Mae Sot-Myawaddy Borderland 191
   Su-Ann Oh

IV. Mobile Practices and Moving Borders

9. The Spatiality and Borderless-ness of Contentious Politics: Kachin Mobilities as Capability 215
   Karin Dean

10. The Mule Caravans as Cross-Border Networks: Local Bands and their Stretch on the Frontier between Yunnan and Burma 237
    Jianxiong Ma and Cunzhao Ma

V. Identity Construction and the Politics of Belonging

11. "I Want to Stay Forever in You" 261
    Decha Tangseefa

12. Life along the Naf Border: Identity Politics of the Rohingya Refugees in Bangladesh 283
    Kazi Fahmida Farzana

13. Home of the Housekeeper: Will Shan Migrants Return after a Decade of Migration? 306
    Amporn Jirattikorn

14. Moving on: Spaces of Engagement in the Kayah–Mae Hong Son Borderland 323
    Carl Grundy-Warr and Chin Wei Jun

VI. Institutionalized Identity and Border Practices

15. The Chin State-Mizoram Border: Institutionalized Xenophobia for State Control 353
    Bianca Son and N. William Singh

16. Tăi Buddhist Practices on the China-Myanmar Border 369
    Takahiro Kojima

Index 389

List of Tables

2.1	Characteristics of Borderland Constituencies, Sorted by Border Length	41
2.2	Myanmar 2010 General Election Results in Borderland Constituencies	45
2.3	Voter Density (per km^2) by Party Contesting 2010 General Election	56
3.1	Myanmar Waters	71
3.2	The Largest Offshore Gas Projects	86
3.3	Income from Yadana and Yetagun Projects (Sale of Gas to Thailand) US$ Million Fiscal	88
16.1	Number of Priests and Monasteries	373

List of Figures

1.1	Map of Upland, Lowland and Maritime Myanmar	9
1.2	Map of Natural Resources in Myanmar's Border Regions	15
2.1	Map of Borderland Constituencies	40
2.2	Map of People's Assembly 2010 Election Results in Borderland Constituencies	44
2.3	Map of Concentration of Military Installations in Myanmar	59
2.4	Map of Incidents of Armed Conflict in Myanmar (2011–13)	60
2.5	Map of Myanmar's Border and Coastal Trade Zones	61
3.1	Map Showing Location of Three Islands under Dispute	74
3.2	Map Showing Grey Areas between Myanmar, Bangladesh and India	77
3.3	Map Showing Myanmar's Claimed Territorial Waters	78
12.1	Drawing 1: Peaceful Rakhine State in the Distant Past	291
12.2	Rohingya Song 1	292
12.3	Rohingya Song 2	294
12.4	Drawing 2: Life in Rakhine State	296
12.5	Drawing 3: Life in Bangladesh — At the Nayapara Refugee Camp	298
14.1	Part of the Mae Hong Son-Kayah (Karenni) Borderland where We Carried Out our Research	327
14.2	Map Showing Estimated Areas of Kayah State Most Likely Affected by Landmines	338
14.3	Playing Football at a Border Refugee Camp Near Ban Nai Soi	345
16.1	Map of Dehong Prefecture	370
16.2	Map of Məŋ Mau Basin	371
16.3	Migration of 38 Monks and 78 Novices in Ruili from 2004–09	376
16.4	Migration of Ven. V, Abbot of TS Temple	377
16.5	Migration of Ven. S, Abbot of HS Temple	378
16.6	Migration of Mr. T, *Holu* of TL Village	381

Acknowledgements

This book is the product of a conference on Myanmar's borders that took place in November 2013. It was organized and funded by the ISEAS – Yusof Ishak Institute, Singapore with administrative and financial support from Kyoto University, Center for Southeast Asian Studies "Southeast Asian Studies for Sustainable Humanosphere" Research Program, JSPS Asian Core Program "Asian Connections".

The conference, and hence this book, would not have been possible without the assistance of a number of people. Ambassador Tan Chin Tiong, Director of ISEAS, provided institutional support and Ooi Kee Beng helped in the development of the project. My heartfelt thanks go to them for supporting this project.

It was a pleasure to collaborate with Professor Yoko Hayami at the Center for Southeast Asian Studies, Kyoto University who brought invaluable ideas and insights for which I am grateful.

Special thanks go to the various people who contributed to the conference as participants, discussants and moderators, in particular: Terence Chong, Kersten Duell, Lee Hock Guan, Kevin McGahan, Muhammad Arafat Mohamad, Rizwana Abdul Azeez, Song Jiyoung, Moe Thuzar, Bridget Welsh and Wu Keping.

I would also like to express my appreciation to Itty Abraham, Nicolas Lainez, Vatthana Pholsena, Robert Taylor, Moe Thuzar and Tin Maung Maung Than for their excellent and constructive suggestions during the development of the conference and the book. They gave generously of their time and counsel.

My gratitude goes to Betty Tan, Loh Joo Yong and Ramlee Othman for providing superb logistical support for the conference, and Li Ling Ling and Chin Mui Lan for their administrative help. I would also like to extend my thanks to Chiaki Abe and her administrative team at Kyoto University.

Veena Nair provided excellent editing and support for which I am truly grateful.

I would also like to thank the staff at the ISEAS Publishing under the leadership of Ng Kok Kiong for their professional and meticulous work.

Special thanks go to the contributors of this volume, who participated unreservedly and enthusiastically and who generously gave their time and support throughout the various rounds of revision and editing.

Finally, it is with sadness that I write that one of the authors, Bianca Son, passed away in 2014. She had just been awarded her PhD from SOAS and was looking forward to a fine academic career. Her chapter was co-written with a colleague, N. William Singh, who took on the responsibility of completing the revisions.

Su-Ann Oh

Notes on Language, Terminology and Geographical Names

In this volume, "Burma" is used to refer to the country under British colonial rule up until 1989; "Myanmar" is used when referring to the country from 1989 onwards.

"Burmese" is used as an adjective, for example when referring to language and nationality. With regard to the names of ethnic groups, both former and current terms are used and presented as "Burman/Bamar", "Karen/Kayin" and so on.

Authors who have deviated from these conventions have made their preferences known in the endnotes of their individual chapters.

Contributors

Maxime Boutry obtained a PhD in Social Anthropology and Ethnology at the School for Higher Studies in Social Sciences (EHESS, Paris) in 2007, dealing with the appropriation of the marine environment by Burmese fishermen in the Tenasserim Region (southern Myanmar). His research questions the processing of Burmese identity through inter-ethnic relationships, and notably the interactions between Burmese fishermen and Moken (a few thousand sea gypsies inhabiting southern Myanmar and southern Thailand). Taking frontiers as "laboratories" where Burmese societies' adaptations to political, social, economical and cultural changes are shaped, he seeks to detect, through different scales of time and space, forms of continuity in the changes affecting Myanmar. In the meantime, his work fits with an applied anthropology on subjects such as Burmese immigration and human trafficking, as well as a reflection on humanitarian aid since cyclone Nargis struck Myanmar in 2008.

Anders Bjornberg is a doctoral student in Sociology at Binghamton University where his research interests include border studies, state formation, national sovereignty, and the sociology of colonialism. He is currently based in Dhaka, Bangladesh undertaking fieldwork for his dissertation on the sociopolitical dimensions of immigration between Myanmar and Bangladesh under grants from the Fulbright Program and the American Institute of Bangladesh Studies. He came to his current research interests through work experience in refugee resettlement in Chicago, USA where he helped recently arrived refugees and asylees secure social and economic stability.

Chin Wei Jun is a graduate researcher and teaching assistant in the Department of Geography, National University of Singapore. Her current research concerns issues of "homeland" in relation to Karenni refugees.

Karin Dean is a senior researcher at the School of Humanities, Tallinn University, where she teaches undergraduate and graduate courses and supervises Masters and Doctoral students. She is theoretically interested in conceptualizing borders, territorialities, cross-border networks and power relations, and empirically in the political geography of the Kachin in northern Myanmar and beyond, where she has conducted ethnographic research since 2000. She worked as an independent researcher/reporter based in Thailand from 1999 to 2007, and completed a PhD in Geography at the National University of Singapore in 2003.

Nicholas Farrelly is a Fellow in the Coral Bell School of Asia Pacific at the Australian National University (ANU), Canberra, where he is also Director of the ANU Myanmar Research Centre. For the past 15 years, Nicholas has focussed on the study of ethnic minority issues in Myanmar's borderlands. After graduating from the ANU with First Class Honours and the University Medal, he completed Masters and Doctoral theses at Balliol College, University of Oxford, where he was a Rhodes Scholar. In 2006 he co-founded New Mandala, an academic website on Southeast Asian affairs. Based at the ANU, it provides daily analysis of social, cultural and political issues with particular attention to Thailand, Indonesia, Malaysia and Myanmar. From 2013 to 2016, Nicholas held an Australian Research Council fellowship for a study of Myanmar's political cultures "in transition".

Kazi Fahmida Farzana is a Senior Lecturer in the College of Law, Government and International Studies at University Utara Malaysia, Kedah, Malaysia. Her research focuses on refugee studies and forced migration, contemporary political theories particularly citizenship and multiculturalism, politics and humanitarian issues in Myanmar and South Asia. Her works have appeared in journals such as *Austrian Journal of South-East Asian Studies*, *Journal of Muslim Minority Affairs*, and *Asian Geographic*.

Carl Grundy-Warr teaches Geopolitics in the Department of Geography, National University of Singapore. He has edited several books and written numerous papers on border issues and forced displacement.

Alexander Horstmann is an Associate Professor of Modern Southeast Asian Studies at the Department of Cross-Cultural and Regional Studies, University of Copenhagen and relates area studies to Multicultural Studies, Religion and Minority Studies. Topics that he explores are everyday multiculturalism, religious diversity, violence, humanitarianism, and diaspora/exile. His latest book, *Building Noah's Ark: Refugee, Migrants and Religious Communities* (2015) is concerned with the use of religion by refugee-migrants as a material and spiritual resource. Fieldwork for this project on humanitarian cultures was done in conjunction with the project cluster "Streams of Knowledge along the Thai-Burmese Border Zone: Multiple Dimensions of People, Capital and Culture", coordinated by Decha Tangseefa (Bangkok). A research grant by the Thailand Research Fund for this project is gratefully acknowledged. Further contributions on this topic appeared in *Journal of Refugee Studies, Moussons (Social Sciences Research on Southeast Asia), Journal of Borderlands Studies, Austrian Journal of Southeast Studies (ASEAS)*.

Amporn Jirattikorn is a Lecturer at the Department of Social Sciences and Development at Chiang Mai University, Thailand. She received her PhD in Anthropology from the University of Texas, Austin in 2008. Amporn's research interests are in the areas of media flows and mobility of people across national boundaries, focusing particularly on the movement of Shan migrants from Myanmar into Thailand. Amporn's recent publications have centred on the construction of migrant identities through media consumption, ethnic media production in Myanmar, and the formation of Shan nationalist consciousness.

Takahiro Kojima is an Associate Professor of Southeast Asian Studies at the Department of International and Cultural Studies, Tsuda College. His first experience living in Myanmar was from 1999 to 2003. He went as a Japanese language teacher, and then studied Burmese at Yangon University of Foreign Languages for two years. During this period, he became a Theravada Buddhist monk twice. This experience led him to start academic research as a PhD student at Kyoto University in 2003. Initially he researched Buddhism and state in contemporary Myanmar, until 2005. After that he carried out fieldwork in a village of Dehong Prefecture, Yunnan, China, located on the China-Myanmar border, concerning religion and society among the Tai people from 2006 to 2007. He was awarded his doctorate from Kyoto University in 2010.

Cunzhao Ma is a local scholar in Zhihua village in Fengyi township in Dali city, western Yunnan Province, China. His specialty is local history studies, especially the history of the Hui and local caravans in western Yunnan. He has conducted long-term research on the oral history of muleteers since 2002, and has three books about caravans and local history published recently by Yunnan University Press and Hong Kong University of Science and Technology.

Jianxiong Ma is an Associate Professor of Anthropology in the Division of Humanities at the Hong Kong University of Science and Technology. His books include *The Lahu Minority in Southwest China: A Response to Ethnic Marginalization on the Frontier* and *Reinventing Ancestor: Ethnic Mobilization in China's Southwest Frontier and the Historical Construction of Lahu (in Chinese)*. His present research focuses on the historical formation of the Sino-Burma frontier and ecological conditions of cultural diversity and ethnicity in southwest China, especially in Yunnan Province.

Alexandra de Mersan is an Associate Professor at the National Institute for Oriental Languages and Civilizations (INALCO) school in Paris. She did her PhD in Anthropology on Arakanese society of Myanmar in 2005. Since then, she has been conducting research mostly on Buddhism and spirit cults, Buddhist statuary, mobility and migration, Arakan and the building of the nation.

Maung Aung Myoe received his PhD in Political Science and International Relations from Australian National University. He was a visiting fellow at the Institute for Defence and Strategic Studies (IDSS) and a post-doctoral fellow at the Asia Research Institute (ARI), National University of Singapore. Since 2010, he has been working at the International University of Japan. He teaches Foreign Policy Analysis and Southeast Asian International Relations. His research interests cover civil-military relations, foreign policy analysis, and politics and foreign relations in Myanmar. His recent publications include *Building the Tatmadaw: Myanmar Armed Forces since 1948* and *In the Name of Pauk-Phaw: Myanmar's China Policy since 1948*; both were published by the Institute of Southeast Asian Studies (ISEAS) in 2008 and 2011 respectively.

Su-Ann Oh is a Visiting Fellow at the ISEAS – Yusof Ishak Institute who graduated from the London School of Economics and completed her doctorate at the University of Oxford. Her research focuses on forced migration, education, identity, Myanmar and the Thai-Burmese borderlands. She is currently writing a book on education in the refugee camps in Thailand. She is also on the board of directors of Room to Grow Foundation which provides basic necessities to unparented children on the Thai-Burmese border (http://roomtogrowfoundation.org/).

N. William Singh teaches Sociology at Pachhunga University College (Mizoram University), Aizawl, India. He did his research at Jawaharlal

Nehru University (JNU), New Delhi and Freie Universität, Berlin. He was a Junior Research Fellow, University Grants Commission (UGC) and a German Academic Exchange Service (DAAD) Fellow. His PhD thesis submitted to JNU was entitled "Nature and Dynamics of Civil Society: Young Mizo Association of Mizoram". He has published his research works in reputable journals and as chapters in edited volumes of Routledge Press. He has presented papers in several International Conferences — South Korea, Vienna, Berlin, Hong Kong, New Delhi and also at national seminars in India. He has organized a conference on social dynamics and interfaces between tradition and modernity in Aizawl. His forthcoming book, *Becoming Something Else: Society and Change in India's Northeast*, will be released by Cambridge Scholars Publishing, United Kingdom (UK). At present, he is editing his PhD thesis for publication and writing a biography on Laldenga entitled "The Art of Dissent and Peacemaking: Laldenga of Mizoram".

Bianca Son Suantak completed her PhD in the Department of History, University of London's School for Oriental and African Studies (SOAS) in 2013. Her dissertation is entitled "The Making of the Zo: The Chin, the Lushai and the Kuki of Burma and India". During her studies, Bianca taught Research Methods for Historians as well as writing workshops. She also organized and convened three international academic conferences held in Thailand, SOAS and Vienna in 2009, 2011, and 2013 respectively. She contributed articles regularly to Chin and Zo organizations in Myanmar and in India.

Decha Tangseefa is an Assistant Professor at the Faculty of Political Science, Thammasat University, Bangkok. His research interests are political theory, cultural studies, and critical international studies, especially relating to migration and the border. He has contributed to major anthologies and journals in Thai and English. Apart from teaching at Thammasat University, he has also been working with civil society on the Thai-Burmese borderland. From 2008 to 2011, he taught in a college in a refugee camp on the border. In the past few years, he has been working with the Shoklo Malaria Research Unit, University of Oxford scientists and their global networks helping with social science aspects of malaria mass drug administration. Currently, he is working on two English manuscripts. The first is a co-authored book on the Mae Sot special economic zone. The second, a single-authored book, is entitled *Human, Animal, and Thing: Paradox of Security along the Thai-Burmese Borderland*.

Abbreviations

ABSDF	All Burma Students' Democratic Front
ADRA	Adventist Development and Relief Agency
AFPFL	Anti-Fascist Peoples Freedom League
ALTSEAN	Alternative ASEAN Network
BSPP	Burma Socialist Programme Party
CBO	Community Based Organizations
CIDKP	Committee for Internally Displaced Karen People
CNF	Chin National Front
CPB	Communist Party of Burma
DKBA	Democratic Karen Benevolent Army
DoF	Department of Fisheries
EC	European Commission
EIP	English Immersion Programme
FBR	Free Burma Rangers
IDP	Internally Displaced Person
INGO	International Non-Governmental Organization
ITLOS	International Tribunal for the Law of the Sea
KBC	Kachin Baptist Convention
KED	Karen Education Department
KHRG	Karen Human Rights Group
KIA	Kachin Independence Army
KIO	Kachin Independence Organization
KNG	Kachin News Group
KNLA	Karen National Liberation Army
KNLP	Kayan New Land Party
KNPLF	Karenni Nationalities People's Liberation Front
KNPP	Karenni National Progressive Party
KNU	Karen National Union
KNWO	Karenni National Women's Organization
KRC	Karen Refugee Committee
KSDC	Karenni Social Development Centre
KSWDC	Karenni Social Welfare and Development Centre
LMTC	Leadership and Management College

MAF	Myanmar Armed Forces (*Tatmadaw*)
MHIP	Mizo Women's Association
MN	Myanmar Navy
MNDAA	Myanmar National Democratic Alliance Army
MNF	Mizo National Front
MNFF	Mizo National Famine Front
MOE	Ministry of Education
MOGE	Myanmar Oil and Gas Enterprise
MOI	Ministry of Interior
MPSI	Myanmar Peace Support Initiative
MZP	Mizo Students' Association
NGO	Non-Governmental Organization
PAMRA	Peace Accord MNF Returnees Association
PDP	People's Democratic Party
PLA	Patriotic Liberation Army
SEZ	Special Economic Zone
SHRF	Shan Human Rights Foundation
SLORC	State Law and Order Restoration Council
SPDC	State Peace and Development Council
TBBC	Thailand Burma Border Consortium
TBC	The Border Consortium
UMEHL	Union of Myanmar Economic Holding Limited
UN	United Nations
UNCLOS	United Nations Convention on the Law of the Sea
UNFC	United Nationalities Federal Council
UNHCR	United Nations Commissioner for Refugees
USDP	Union Solidarity and Development Party
VSO	Voluntary Service Overseas
WAMY	World Assembly of Muslim Youth
WH	Wide Horizons
YMA	Youth Mizo Association

1

Introduction[1]

Su-Ann Oh

Often viewed as marginal spaces at the edge of a nation, borders are in fact sites of social, political and cultural change that impact local and national politics. This edited volume underscores this relationship by drawing attention to the significance of the frontier regions in defining and exemplifying many of the dilemmas that beset Myanmar. As van Schendel and de Maaker assert, "[t]he making of borders cannot be separated from attempts to define nations" (2014, p. 3).

The border is often understood as the "line of physical contact between states" (Paasi 1999b, p. 13). In everyday parlance and in the field of international relations, borders are taken to be stable features that separate one nation state from another (Minghi 1963, p. 407), created by and negotiated between state agents, and codified in maps.

This book takes a different approach. It conceptualizes borders — and boundaries — as social practice — processes rather than objects (Berg and van Houtum 2003; Baud and van Schendel 1997), verbs rather than nouns (van Houtum 2011, p. 50) — that are constantly being enacted.

> The production and reproduction of boundaries is part of the institutionalization of territories — the process in which their territorial, symbolic and institutional 'shape' is determined (Paasi 1991). Therefore boundaries manifest themselves in numerous social (economic, cultural, administrative and political) practices and discourses that may be simultaneous and overlapping (Paasi 1999a, p. 670).

Boundaries may be viewed as constituting

> lines of separation or contact [that] may occur in real or virtual space, horizontally between territories, or vertically between groups and/or

individuals. The point of contact or separation usually creates an 'Us' and an 'Other' identity, and this takes place at a variety of sociospatial scales (Newman and Paasi 1998, p. 191).

Looking at this obversely, we can say that the act of creating boundaries is the act of constructing figured or symbolic worlds. Practice theory is used in this introductory chapter to frame local practices of border-, boundary- and world-making while referencing larger structures and sociohistorical production. This enables us to consider Myanmar's frontiers not just as entities defined by the border but as spaces where symbolic worlds emerge from local context, partly transforming widely circulating models of nation, identity and culture, and vice versa. The chapters in this volume, by providing compelling studies of local practice — spiritual, religious, economic, intimate, cultural and imaginary, for example — relating to territorial claims, social organization, mobility, and identity (in individual and institutionalized forms) help us understand these life worlds and the ways in which non-state actors challenge and/or circumvent the state's attempts to control their relations with material and non-material space.

The elaboration of these local practices in the context of border spaces is significant because Myanmar's border regions share commonalities that, besides the presence of national borders, distinguish them from the heartlands in three ways. First, as this introductory chapter and Section I of the book describe, Myanmar's border zones are situated in the mountainous and maritime regions of the country while the heartlands are located in the lowlands. This alerts us to the differences wrought by geography, topography and ecology in these three zones, and their contribution to the creation of distinct historical and political ideologies, institutions and identities. For this reason, this volume includes chapters that consider the seas that Myanmar shares with Thailand, Bangladesh and India. Further, this reminds us of the transboundary and transnational nature of these geographical features: mountains do not conform to state borders, rivers change course, oceans are fluid and continuous.

Nevertheless, geography alone does not determine the course of history. Myanmar's borderlands, unlike the seas and the heartlands, have been shaped by decades of armed and other forms of conflict, resulting in a space that is militarized, fragmented, precarious and regulated by multiple authorities. Since the signing of ceasefire agreements, they have been characterized by the ambiguity of "not war, not peace" (Grundy-Warr and Dean 2011). Combined with the opening up of the economy, which has introduced diverse actors (including foreign corporations), these regions (and the seas) are experiencing new forms of conflict and instability on top of those which have plagued them for decades.

By considering Myanmar's border regions as a whole, this book uses them as tools to problematize deep-seated divisions and recent changes in the country, enabling us to investigate the dialectic relationship we posit exists between the borderlands and the hinterland. Further, by treating the country as a common demonimator, this book provides context to the borders, going some way to countering the criticism of border studies as a field populated by isolated case studies (Sidaway 2011, p. 974). In doing so, it contributes to the growing body of work on Southeast Asian (see Horstmann and Wadley 2006; Miyazaki 2004; Rajaram and Grundy-Warr 2007; Horstmann 2011*c* among others) and Asian borderlands (see van Schendel and de Maaker 2014; Cons and Sanyal 2013 on South Asia).

SOCIAL PRACTICE THEORY, BORDERS AND THE MYANMAR NATION

This chapter grounds the practice of boundary- (and border-) making in practice theory as proposed by Bourdieu (1972) and developed by other scholars. In essence, practice theory holds that social practice is relational, situated and "sited", that is, it only acquires meaning when understood in context (space) (Schatzki 2002) and in history (time) (Holland and Lave 2009). In the first instance, the production of figured worlds, identities and cultural artefacts happens locally through practice. The figured world is the socially produced and culturally constructed "realm[s] of interpretation in which particular characters and actors are recognized, significance is assigned to certain acts, and particular outcomes are valued over others" (Holland et al. 1998, p. 52). "Orders are arrangements of entities (e.g., people, artifacts, things), whereas practices are organized activities. Human coexistence thus transpires as and amid an elaborate, constantly evolving nexus of arranged things and organized activities" (Schatzki 2002, p. xi).

Cultural production generated in and around these encounters — a ritual (de Mersan's chapter, this volume) or a song (Decha Tangseefa and Farzana's chapters, this volume), for instance — usually has relatively limited translocal currency. Sociohistoric production, in contrast, occurs over a longer time span and in multiple, local institutional arrangements or are represented in artefacts that circulate widely through extended, translocal networks (Wortham 2006). These then become installed as collective and powerful social formations that have significance in many local spaces and timescales. In a nutshell, socially produced identity and worlds emerge "historically, locally and interactionally" (Wortham 2006, p. 10).

There is a dialectic relationship between shorter timescales and longer timescales: the latter are collectively mediated through and changed by processes at a particular time and space, and vice versa, just as the interaction between individuals and social life is relational and dialogic. Thus, local practice and production result from the dynamic interaction of two types of history materialized in the present: "history-in-person" (where the past is brought to the present through persons) and history in institutions (historically institutionalized struggles) (Holland and Lave 2009, pp. 4–5). In other words, encounters between persons are dependent on past relations (class, gender, ethnic and so on) in the "embodied histories-in-person of the two people and in the sociohistorically produced, collectively recognized discourses, practices, policies and artifacts that constitute the institutional arrangements (supposedly) governing relations" in a specific space (Holland 2010, p. 274).

Tensions and contestations occur as sociohistoric formations are brought into spaces of local practice, become established and dominate the social order. Conversely, social formations sometimes lose their power when actors articulate new worlds. These manifest in contentious local practice that may be collectively or individually enacted.

To illustrate practice theory in understanding Myanmar's borders, we take the issuing of Myanmar's border passes as an example of local practice. Myanmar issues border passes to people who seek to enter its territory through official overland channels. However, local practice surrounding these institutionalized arrangements differs throughout the borders and depends on local context and diplomatic relationships with neighbouring countries. For example, in 2010, Thai citizens were issued a border pass at the Myawaddy (Myanmar)-Mae Sot (Thailand) border allowing travel around Myawaddy for a day on a single entry pass, whereas at the Muse-Ruili border, Chinese citizens could obtain single or multi-entry passes valid for a year of travel around Mandalay and Myitkyina and the rest of the country depending on their residential status (whether they lived around the border or not) (Ishida 2013, pp. 317–20). Who is issued these passes, the area of travel permitted, the duration of stay and whether these passes may be used multiple times differed according to location in Myanmar (and time) (ibid.).

The symbolic functions of the practice of issuing border passes are: to mark the beginning of the state's jurisdiction and sovereignty, to demarcate territory and to establish the "imagined political community" (Anderson

1991, pp. 6–7) or symbolic world that is called "Myanmar". The practice of issuing border passes is but one of a host of practices enacted at the country's frontiers in order to "produce, express and reproduce" (Paasi 1999a, p. 670) territoriality and nation.

Over time, these local practices normalize the existence of the border and inscribe certain notions of history, territory and identity within and vice versa. This stems from the Westphalian concept of sovereignty, according to which, every political state must have a definite territorial boundary which ought to correspond with differences of culture and language. Thus, the boundaries of a state serve to contain territory and identity while simultaneously communicating the limits of state power and expressing national identity (Newman and Paasi 1998). The Burmese state attempts to corral nation and people within boundaries of territory that it defines through symbolic, political and discursive practices and structures (see Paasi 1996). Burman/Bamar cultural identity is used to define national identity and the ideological character of the state through cultural (Lewis 1924; Berlie 2008), social (Callahan 2003; Salem-Gervais and Metro 2012), political and spatio-territorial (Ferguson 2014; Lambrecht 2008) practices.

Going back to the example of border passes, we observe that local communities may or may not engage in the practice of acquiring border passes. Indeed, they were crossing the river into Myawaddy from Mae Sot long before the existence of state borders. While large numbers of people walk across the Friendship Bridge and obtain official border passes to enter Myanmar, equally large numbers cross under the bridge without doing so. At the same time, many who obtain border passes do not adhere to the conditions of the pass. This is contentious to state practice and institutional arrangements with regard to the border. Thus, the bridge and the river can be viewed as the site of history-in-person and historically institutionalized struggles.

> What is important to the study of the ontology of borders is hence not the item of the border per se, but the objectification process of the border, the *socially constituent power practices attached to a border that construct a spatial effect* and which give a demarcation in space its meaning and influence (van Houtum 2011, p. 50, emphasis added).

In other words, power is represented and manifested in spatial formations through social practice: the border (or specifically the bridge and river in this example) represents "temporary stand-offs in a perpetual transformative … socio-spatial power struggle" (van Schendel 2002, p. 658, citing Swyngedouw 1997, p. 169). Over time, certain practices gain dominance and become institutionalized while others disappear. As such, we need to study the practice of border-making over the long durée (Baud and van Schendel 1997).

Local contentious practices regarding the border can take on a myriad of forms, combining over a period of time to generate sociohistoric production. Besides circumventing border checkpoints, local communities have moved border markers and/or occupied territory in defiance of state-demarcated boundaries. The Kachin Independence Organization (KIO) and the Karen National Union (KNU), like the Myanmar state, cleave to the notion that physical territory is inextricably bound to identity and belonging but their idea of where the physical and sociopolitical boundaries lie differs greatly from that of the Myanmar state. The practice that these groups have of using the border as an escape valve subverts the state's authority imbued in the border. In such circumstances, the border — a political and symbolic marker of the sovereignty and territory of the Myanmar state — also limits the state's jurisdiction. Thus, counter-insurgency operations in these regions are less effective because insurgents and civilians can flee across the border into neighbouring countries and operate from bases there.[2] In doing so, they thwart the sovereignty of the state, both in escaping its reaches and in appropriating its resources.

Local practices become contentious when they rub up against the state's construction of space and social life. These are evidenced by inter-state disputes over border markings, the inadequate reach of state jurisdiction and authority at the borders, the diversity of cultures, languages and identities and the conflict of interests between border communities. Nevertheless, territory has become indispensable to everyday definitions of nation, identity and belonging (Abraham 2014, pp. 1–18). This conception has become so naturalized that it is often forgotten that it is a recently imported construct. With the exception of Vietnam, pre-colonial polities in Southeast Asia based their administration on the control of labour, not land (Steinberg 1987, p. 30). Thus, until the nineteenth century, the modern concept of national boundaries did not exist. While local people had concepts of territoriality that were understood in terms of flexible geographic boundaries and a range of rights governing resources therein, they "were not much concerned with the demarcation of frontiers" (Steinberg 1987, p. 5). For example, the Moken, sea nomads in the Andaman Sea, view territory as ancestral estates, resource nodes and cultural-economic units that are based on kin networks, rather than as spaces with demarcations (Sopher 1977, p. 61). To them, the "inalienable gift of territory is not just an economic resource but more of an affirmation of social relations" (Chou 2013, p. 56, citing

Weiner 1985, p. 210). Moreover, for them, territory and identity cannot be so easily uncoupled from mobility.

> Their social relationships of maritoriality ownership and rights are firmly anchored in the seascape via movement rather than that based upon permanent settlements delineated by borders and boundaries. The seascape is perceived as life- and living-spaces not hampered by state-defined borders and boundaries (Chou 2013, pp. 49–50).

Thus, groups living in Myanmar's frontiers have constructed complex, multi-layered and shifting forms of allegiance and identity (Decha Tangseefa 2006; Horstmann 2011*a*; Sharples 2012; Prasert Rangkla 2014; Oh 2012; Ardeth Maung Thawnghmung 2012; Grundy-Warr and Dean 2003; Dudley 2001, 2006, 2010; Farzana 2011; Pinkaew Laungaramsri 2006; Amporn Jirattikorn 2008, 2010, 2011) within symbolic worlds that reference international neighbours, border processes, the state, ethno-nationalism, communism, war, displacement, suffering (Horstmann, this volume) and fear (Grundy-Warr and Chin, this volume).

In addition, while often thought of as "ethnic" enclaves, the borders of Myanmar are also populated by a host of diverse peoples with contested and relational identities such as Chinese migrants (Toyota 2003; Chang 2014*b*) and traders (Chang 2013, 2014*a*) on the Chinese border, Burmese "economic" migrants on the Thai border (Arnold and Hewison 2006; Arnold and Pickles 2011; Campbell 2012; Pearson and Kusakabe 2012; Lyttleton 2014, pp. 110–42; Nobpaon Rabibhadana and Hayami 2013; Boutry and Ivanoff 2009; Lee 2007) political dissidents (O'Kane 2005; Amporn Jirattikorn 2008), activists (Simpson 2013, 2014) and sea nomads (Ivanoff 2008).

As these examples demonstrate, those communities living in the border regions construct figured worlds and corresponding boundaries that do not necessarily match those formulated by the state. There is no universal way in which people relate to space, identity and affiliation. For these reasons, we turn to an examination of the distinct historical, geographical, social and political context of Myanmar's border spaces.

MYANMAR'S MOUNTAIN AND MARITIME BORDER REGIONS

Upland, Lowland and Maritime Myanmar

The striking thing about Myanmar is that it is surrounded by a "highland horseshoe that encompasses the Irrawaddy basin on the west, north and east" (Lieberman 2010, p. 333) (see Figure 1.1). This area is distinguishable from the inner regions of the country by its higher elevation where the highest peak (5,152 metres) is in Kachin state and the lowest (less than 700 metres) is in the two borderland constituencies in Rakhine state, as observed by Nicholas Farrelly (this volume). In this upland belt, altitude combined with distance from Naypyitaw and poor road conditions contribute to the "friction of terrain" (Scott 2009, p. 47) and isolation from the capital of the country.

This highland horseshoe has been identified as part of an upland region known as Zomia (van Schendel 2002, pp. 653–57) and the Southeast Asian massif (McKinnon and Michaud 2000), a transnational area characterized by its elevation, ecological conditions, sparse population, historical isolation, language affinities, religious commonalities, cultural traits, ancient trade networks and marginal position vis-à-vis surrounding states (van Schendel 2002, pp. 653–54).[3] Leach (1954), in his work on upland swiddeners, contended that what set people apart in the highland zones had less to do with their language and culture than their framework of political ideas, and this was greatly influenced by the altitude they lived at and hence the hold that the state (and its political and cultural influences) had over them. In fact, he contended that geography may have had more influence over identity in pre-British Burma than language, religion or dress.

This argument was further developed by James Scott (2009) who observed that lowland wet-rice agriculturalists almost always lived in states, also known as padi states, while upland swiddeners lived beyond the reach of these states (see also Renard 1987, pp. 255–71). He argues that the conventional view of highlanders as backward, uncivilized, primitive and barbaric was a construct of the lowland padi kingdom, and that the traits that these adjectives describe are actually distinctive agricultural, religious and social features that hill societies cultivated to escape lowland state authority. Scott's main contribution is that hill societies cannot be understood as entities separate from valley societies or through the ideology of valley societies. Rather, padi states and their highland counterparts were mutually constitutive.

This argument can also be used to describe the relationship between the lowlands and the sea. As Figure 1.1 illustrates, lowland Myanmar is bounded by the Indian Ocean in the south where a string of islands leading to the island of Sumatra divides the upper part of the ocean into the Bay of Bengal and the Andaman Sea. The body of water belonging to Myanmar is shaped roughly like a wrench. Like the highland horseshoe, the wrench is part of another Zomia, or more precisely a "watery Zomia" (Scott 2009, p. xiv) that stretches from the Indian Ocean to the Pacific Ocean.

INTRODUCTION

FIGURE 1.1
Map of Upland, Lowland and Maritime Myanmar

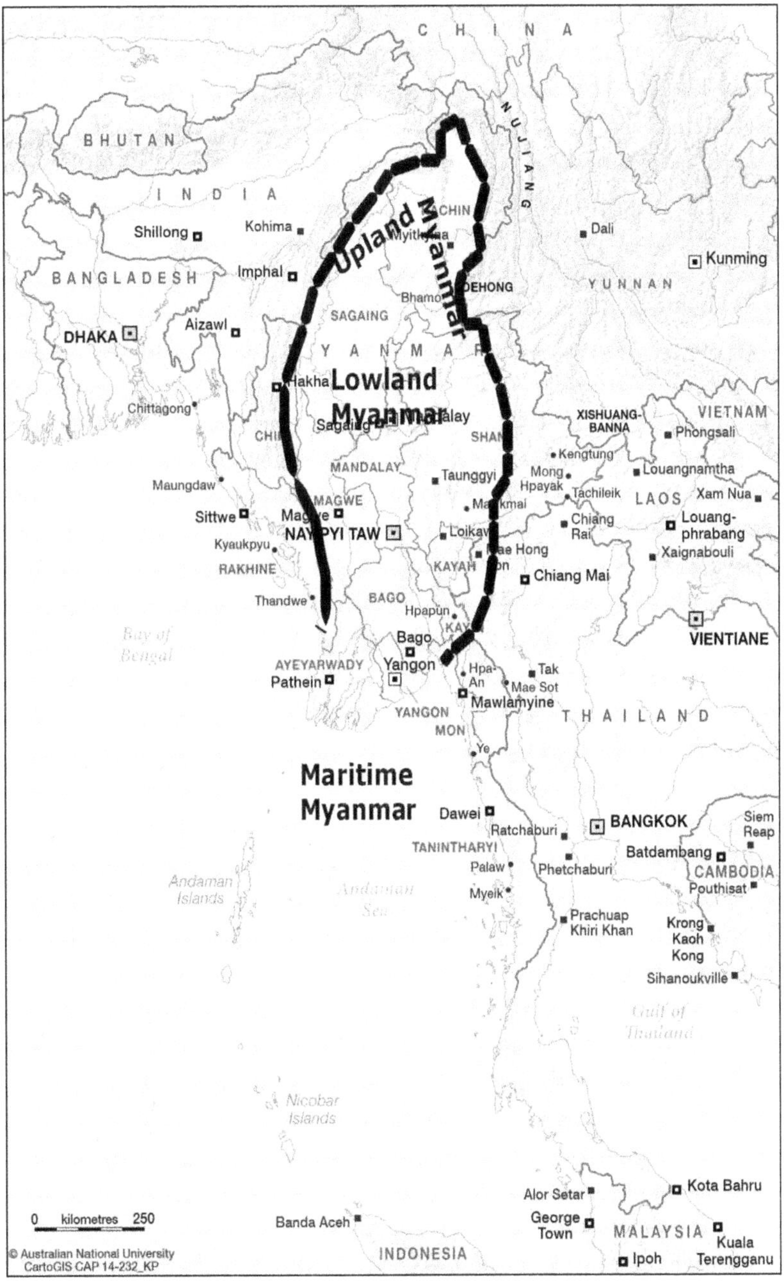

Source: CartoGIS, College of Asia and the Pacific, The Australian National University.

We are used to thinking of the sea as empty and uninhabited. However, until recently, the Andaman Sea and the other seas in Southeast Asia were inhabited by sea nomads whose mobility was inhibited only by the elements. Of the Moken, whose principal residential and (shell)fishing grounds are located in southern Myanmar and Thailand, Boudier et al. assert that "[s]cattering, dissimilation, adapted technology, the ideology of non-accumulation and living on the fringes of the 'great' societies are what make the Moken true Zomians" (2015, p. 105). "Their nomadism is seen as a consequence of their perpetual flight and as a succession of historical accidents. Nomad culture, personified today through the Moken, remains a tuber culture. It is the 'rice of the Moken'..." (Bourdier et al. 2015, p. 106).

Like mountain Zomia, marine Zomia is defined by its geography (or rather hydrography), ecology, trade networks, mobile practices and transnationalism. Lowlanders have similar perceptions of mountain and marine Zomians, characterizing them as backward, uncivilized and marginal to the lowland state; for example, the Moken have been described as "irresponsible and dominated potential vagabonds" by the Thais and the Burmese (Bourdier et al. 2015, p. 104). Zomians, on the other hand, have viewed the padi states as a cultural force threatening to dominate and change their lifestyle. Mountain swiddeners and marine nomads alike have developed political, social and cultural practices around the fear of slavery, in order to protect their freedom of movement and preserve their distinctive identity.

The perceptions that each group has of the other are in fact the result of a process whereby boundaries are made, reinforced and perpetuated, through spatial, ideological and identity practices. In fact, these boundaries are not as clear-cut or as fixed as we are led to believe. Throughout history, these separate societies have engaged in collaboration and conflict. For example, up to the middle of the twenty-first century, the sea nomads' mobile lifestyles

> were highly valued by the power-holders of the early Malay states of the western Malay region and by the various sultanates that arose in coastal Borneo, the southern Philippines and eastern Indonesia. They were in fact the key players and the building blocks for the sustenance of sedentary communities that developed around the Bay of Bengal (Chou 2013, p. 44, citing Benjamin 1986, p. 16).

Paradoxically, as states emerged, the sea nomads became progressively marginalized by padi states. This example shows that (cultural) boundaries are nuanced and mutable, a fact that Boutry (this volume) explores in the relationship between the Burman/Bamar and the Moken in the littoral zone.

Armed Conflict, Militarization and Border Development
The physical and social landscapes in the border regions have also been deeply affected by decades of armed conflict and structural violence. Figure 2.3 in Farrelly (this volume) shows the highly contested space in the highland horseshoe: there is a high concentration of militarized zones controlled by various non-state armed groups, pro-government militias and the Burmese Army. These spaces have been, and continue to be, sites of armed conflict, militarization and displacement, and their spatial configuration remains unsettled despite recent ceasefire agreements and current peace negotiations.

The significance of internal boundaries in Myanmar cannot be overstated. Since independence, the country has experienced insurgency from groups of ethnic and other ideological persuasions, among them the Kachin, Karen/Kayin, Karenni/Kayah, Wa, Shan, Chin, Mon, Pa-O (see Gravers and Ytzen 2014, pp. 165–72), the All Burma Students' Democratic Front (ABSDF) and the Communist Party of Burma (CPB). The prevalence of armed conflict (Kramer 2010; Smith 1991; South 2003, 2008; Tin Maung Maung Than 2005), militarization (Fink 2008) and ethno-nationalist sentiment (Gravers 2014; Sadan 2013) has created a border landscape of patchwork military installations littered with landmines and displaced people (Decha Tangseefa 2006, Grundy-Warr 2002; Dudley 2001; Farzana 2011; Jacquet and O'Loughlin 2012; Lang 2002; Hull 2009).

This space may be described as a giant game of Othello or Reversi where the state has sought to penetrate rebel-held areas, referred to as "black" zones, to transform them into "brown" areas where contestation takes place, thence into government-controlled or "white" zones and to prevent them from turning back into "black" zones (Smith 1991, p. 259). The ground is constantly shifting as territory is seized and allegiances (and names) are changed. Along the southeastern border, the Democratic Karen Buddhist Army (DKBA) — now called the Democratic Karen Benevolent Army — split from the Karen National Liberation Army (KNLA) and became proxies of the Burmese Government. On several occasions, some battalions have rejoined the KNLA or independently fought against the *Tatmadaw* (Myanmar Army) despite the ceasefire agreement.

Armed conflict continues to erupt periodically between the *Tatmadaw* and the Kachin Independence Organization in northern Myanmar, after a fourteen-year ceasefire was broken in 2011. In early 2015, the Myanmar National Democratic Alliance Army (MNDAA) in the Kokang Self-Administered Zone in northern Shan state near the Chinese border began a military campaign to claim what they believe to be Kokang land from the *Tatmadaw*.

The mutually constitutive nature of the state and these regions is worth highlighting. The military junta and military-backed Myanmar Government created a narrative of the border regions that characterized them as unruly, backward and ethnic (Lambrecht 2008, p. 153), posing a threat to national security and unity. This imaginary has been upheld and shaped by practices involving territorial control, security discourses and development. For instance, the Burmese state used a multi-pronged strategy to territorialize these conflict-ridden regions: forcing the rank-and-file of the Myanmar Army to live off the land, thereby creating competition with local insurgents for local resources (Jannuzi 1998, p. 203; Karen Human Rights Group, KHRG 2008a), forcibly relocating people to strategic villages, confiscating food, destroying crops, forcing people into portering (KHRG 2006), undertaking "border development" (Lambrecht 2008; KHRG 2007, p. 3) and adapting Colonial Waste Land laws to suit the purposes of the *Tatmadaw* at the local level (Ferguson 2014). The latter has enabled the army to profit from national and international business interests once it was more thoroughly entrenched (Ferguson 2014).

These territorialization and counter-insurgency strategies are institutionalized boundary-making practices which, when viewed at the national scale, have clear socio-spatial consequences.

> Geography... plays an important role in creating differential experiences of oppression... the geographical bounded-ness of non-Burman communities in the ethnic states acts to make ethnicity more ascriptive. That is, while non-Burman status might not be immediately apparent in an urban centre in the central heartland, the military has been free to conduct violent campaigns against communities in the ethnic states, knowing that these campaigns will target those most suspect (in its eyes) as citizens (Walton 2013, p. 19).

The insurgent activities of non-state armed groups adds to the precariousness and ambiguity of these regions, resulting in multi-scalar territorialities of "overlapping spaces of dependencies and constellations of power" (Paasi 1999b, p. 86) which are much more pronounced than in the heartlands.

Local communities responded by planting landmines, hiding crops and other objects that the army or non-state armed groups would appropriate, moving their farms to concealed locations, fleeing into the jungles, to IDP camps and/or across the border, joining insurgent groups, and/or complying with forced relocation while enacting everyday forms of resistance (KHRG 2008b, p. 6; KHRG 2009, p. 6). These local contentious practices of fleeing, hiding, dissembling and resisting have produced sentiments, discourses, artefacts, rituals and identities (as elaborated upon by the authors in this volume) that spring from these specific material, affective, economic and political landscapes.

On the Chinese and, particularly, the Thai side of the border, access to better economic opportunities, international NGOs, technologies, knowledge and ideologies, and kin and other networks has provided fertile ground for the development of a civil and political society that references the local political and affective landscape while connected to trans- and international networks. On the Thai-Burmese border, in particular, there is a plethora of organizations and collectives working on human rights, democracy (Oo Sai Thet Naing 2012), humanitarianism (Horstmann 2011b, 2015, this volume; Desaine 2011 for the Kachin border), migrant workers' rights (Arnold and Hewison 2006, pp. 171–77), the environment (Simpson 2013, 2014), and (ethno-) nationalism (Rajah 2002) through advocacy, education, health and other activities, some of which involve unauthorized cross-border endeavours.

This non-state sanctioned movement of goods, people and knowledge subverts state power, circumvents state sanctions and challenges state authority. To counter this, the state attempts to regulate existing or emergent mobility practices. However, this control is neither uniform nor standardized. First, within state regulatory frameworks, different sets of regulations are applied to distinct spaces. For example, part of the Myawaddy border next to Thailand is controlled by non-state armed groups working as proxies of the Burmese state (the Democratic Karen Benevolent Army (DKBA) for example) that regulate border movement in ways that differ from their Burman/Bamar counterparts. Second, even within the state apparatus, local officials interpret border controls differently from central headquarters. Other parts of the border are manned by the Karen Nation Union (KNU), a non-stated armed group that has waged war against the Burmese state for decades. In other words, there exist multiple regulatory authorities whose practices are based on state regulations, custom, ideology or religion. Clearly, the borders are intersections of multiple competing authorities (Abraham and van Schendel 2005) whose individual and institutional practices create anxieties for states (Rajaram and Grundy-Warr 2007).

Ceasefires, Natural Resource Extraction and Special Economic Zones

Myanmar is blessed with natural resources, and a large proportion of them are found in the border areas (see Figure 1.2). The seas are replete with natural gas and fish stocks, the rivers meandering through the highlands have been earmarked for hydropower projects, and there are substantial tracts of land being used for logging, mining, agri-business and industry, particularly in the terrestrial border regions. Most of the approved foreign direct investment in Rakhine state on the Bangladeshi border is in oil and gas projects (Transnational Institute, TNI 2013, p. 24), such as the Shwe Gas Project at the Kyaukphyu Special Economic Zone (SEZ).

Ceasefires in the border regions have played a significant role in enabling the state to assert its hegemony over swathes of the highland border areas. It does this by co-opting those non-state armed groups who have agreed to ceasefire agreements. In return for acting as state proxies, these non-state armed groups are permitted to control territory, grant concessions for natural resource extraction and agri-business, and carry out rent-seeking activities.

The state's industrial and commercial plans for these regions may be viewed as a redefinition of space from one of war to one of resource extraction, production (Dean 2002, pp. 131–41; Woods 2011) and governance (Maclean 2007). Besides granting concessions for resource extraction, long-term land use and associated infrastructure, the state also uses special economic zones (SEZ) as a spatio-economic strategy to territorialize the borderlands. At present, three large SEZs are being built at Dawei in Tanintharyi Region, Kyaukphyu in Rakhine state, and at the port of Thilawa just south of Yangon. The first two are located in the borderlands. It is interesting to note that of the seven further SEZs planned, five will be located in ethnic borderlands: Karen/Kayin State (Hpa-an, Myawaddy and Three Pagoda Pass), Shan State and Arakan/Rakhine State. The other two will be situated in Naypyitaw and Mandalay (TNI 2013, p. 29).

With regards to marine resources, Maung Aung Myoe's chapter alerts us to the fact that the hydrocarbon reserves in the Andaman Sea generate the greatest source of external revenue for Myanmar. Combined with revenue from fish stocks, Myanmar's preoccupation with its maritime borders has shifted from securing territory from non-state armed groups to protecting natural resources from external actors. This shows that borders have strategic value in allowing states to lay claim to resources and to exploit the differentials they create, a feature that local residents and groups have long capitalized on.

INTRODUCTION 15

FIGURE 1.2
Map of Natural Resources in Myanmar's Border Regions

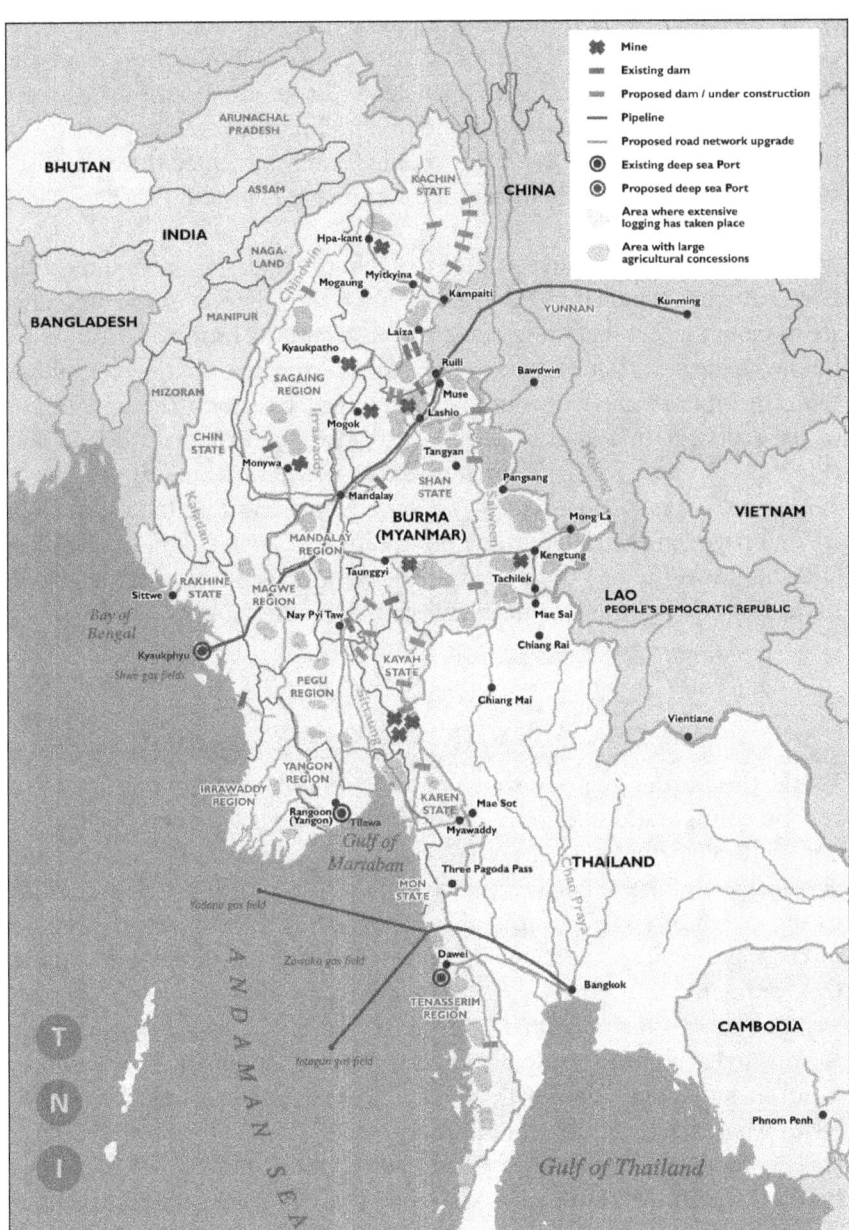

Source: Reproduced with the kind permission of Transnational Institute.

Nevertheless, these benefits are not evenly distributed. New land laws, land seizures, inadequate compensation, the destruction of local livelihoods, economies and the environment from industrial pollution negatively affect certain communities while the state, military conglomerates, local and foreign companies, related state agencies and sometimes non-state armed groups profit in the name of development. The multi-scalar practices of these actors have "simultaneously extended and fragmented the centralised state control of spaces where natural resources are located" (Maclean 2007, p. 249).

These conflicts are not confined to the border areas; the economy of the border regions is in flux like the rest of the country. However, the difference stems from the fact that these industrial projects have only become possible following the new round of ethnic ceasefires. Given new political complexes, the transitional political economy in the border regions, the opening up of the economy to a diversified range of actors, and changes to land laws (Fink 2015), these forms of territorial claims will continue to increase in Myanmar (Ferguson 2014, p. 307). Consequently, new boundaries will be created between the rich and the poor, capitalist owners and the landless, and the powerful and the disenfranchised which "make it necessary for us to rethink the borders in a way that is neither Cartesian nor linear" (Bourdier et al. 2015, p. 20).

ASSYMETRIES AND LOCAL PRACTICE

While the border regions share many similarities, each one possesses unique configurations of ethnic, political, economic, geographical, social and cultural attributes, so that some border areas are more vibrant, volatile or vocal than others. For this reason, studies of local practice are critical to understanding the nuances and complexities therein and the type of forces these regions exert on the fabric of society, economy and politics in Myanmar.

Due to space constraints, this edited volume does not cover all the regions in each of the borders. In particular, the Laotian-Burmese frontier is not included due to a dearth of scholarly research (although see Walker 1999). Moreover, even along one border, there is a host of variables that shape specific locations. The Thai-Burmese border, for instance, is characterized by the sea and the confluence of Malay, Thai and Burmese communities at its southern end, while its more northern sites are influenced by the endeavours of a multiplicity of economic actors and regulatory authorities in the mountainous, terrestrial and riparian border spaces in Mon, Karen/Kayin, Karenni/Kayah and Shan States.

Given the profusion of factors, I limit my observations about the diversity found along the borders and in the border regions to two features: the presence of armed conflict and the gravitational pull of next-door neighbours.

At first glance, it appears that the non-state armed ethnic groups operating from the border areas have similar goals and grievances. However, they behave differently from one another, depending on their geographical location, moral tenets, ideological concerns, size and access to resources. Not all groups are fighting for independence/autonomy or ethno-nationalist reasons; some (particularly those in Shan State) have access to more resources through the trade in drugs and gems; others operate from Myanmar's borders but engage in warfare in neighbouring countries (Gravers and Ytzen 2014, pp. 165–72).

These groups are also placed in different administrative categories by the state, which in turn has implications for their involvement in the national reconciliation process. The complexity of this process is beyond the scope of this introduction, suffice to say that this has made the peace negotiations between the non-state armed groups and Naypyitaw a labyrinthine and monolithic endeavour involving many armed groups and requiring unilateral agreements. In addition, the diversity of interests and bargaining power has made the "nationwide" ceasefire agreement a misnomer. First, not all groups are involved in the negotiations and second, only slightly more than half of the fifteen involved in peace negotiations signed the agreement in 2015. Notably, some of the groups which refused to sign are based along the Chinese border (the Kachin Independence Army, the Wa State Army and the Shan State Army-North) and have the largest militias in the country.

Interestingly, the littoral region is unusual in that there has been no armed conflict along ethnic lines. Instead, patron-client relationships and exogamous marriage (see Boutry, this volume) between Burman/Bamar and the Moken have been instrumental in integrating these two communities socially, culturally and economically. This serves as a useful reminder that scholarship on Myanmar and its borders may be understood in ways that go beyond armed conflict and ethnicity.

The second feature I consider is the relationship that the border regions have with neighbouring countries. While all border communities gravitate towards the countries next door, the extent to which they may gain access to resources on the other side of the border varies. For instance, there is more international aid available in and through Thailand than in the other neighbouring countries. Also, China and Thailand are economically better off than Bangladesh and Laos, and therefore able to provide better economic opportunities and infrastructure. Moreover, the nature and strength of relationships forged at the borders differ. Some groups, such as the Kachin, have had much success in deepening and exploiting kin and other networks on the other side of the border. The Chin, on the other hand, face various forms of discrimination from the Mizo, a kin group, in bordering Mizoram, India. As Son and Singh (this volume) describe, the Young Mizo Association (YMA) has constructed Mizo hegemonic space as one upheld by Christian tenets and that is free from alcohol. The YMA carries out collective local practices of discrimination, and in doing so, it "create[s] cultural forms as means to gain some limited control over their own construction" (Holland and Lave 2009, p. 20). Over time, the production and reproduction of mediated practices of discrimination produce, institutionalize, and disperse a sociohistoric discourse, one in which the Chin are portrayed as immoral bootleggers and rapists. This example highlights the complexities of local contentious practices of boundary- and identity-making which coincide with the state border.

The uneven access to resources on the other side of the border means that migrants and the displaced are better able to acquire aid, insert themselves into local, transnational and international networks, and develop counter-hegemonic movements in some borders rather than others. This becomes clear when we compare the chapters on the Thai border (Grundy-Warr and Chin, Horstmann, Oh, Decha Tangseefa) with those on the Indian and Bangladeshi ones (Son and Singh, Bjornberg, Farzana). It would seem that migrants are more likely to move to the eastern rather than the western borders in search of sanctuary, solidarity and employment, if they have the means to do so.

At the macro level, the diplomatic and economic relationship that Myanmar has with neighbouring countries plays a role in the weight that Myanmar places on individual border regions. India, China and Thailand have substantial political clout with Myanmar and the two latter countries dominate Myanmar's external trade. Myanmar is more likely to settle border disputes, skirmishes and migration issues expediently with these partners than it would with Bangladesh and Laos, its less economically successful and powerful neighbours.

Given these disparities, I posit that, combined, the borderlands pull the country in different directions and at different speeds. This may result in uneven and asymmetrical development, which would have real implications for the country as a whole. I argue that how this unfolds is revealed by examining local practices — which is the main focus of this book.

STRUCTURE OF THE BOOK

As a whole, this book is consciously comparative despite the fact that not all the papers are. There have been few attempts to assemble studies on Myanmar's borders in a holistic manner and to understand how borders interact with one another, although see Boutry (2011), TNI (2013), Dean (2007, 2011), Grundy-Warr (2002), Grundy-Warr and Dean (2003). Thus, the aim is to examine the patterns, trends, anomalies and contradictions emerging in the different border areas so as to obtain insights and pose questions about their relationship with the hinterlands and about these frontiers.

These trends are discerned through an examination of the range of socio-spatial practices and formations employed by various local actors. As there are more studies on practices related to the control of physical space — using territorialization strategies such as warfare, landmines, land laws, sedentarization and enclosures, infrastructure, industrial, extractive and productive projects — this book includes social practices which reside in other spheres. The four practices — territorial claims, social organization, mobility, and identity construction (through individual and institutionalized forms) — are taken up in Sections II to VI. Section I of the book sets out the context of Myanmar's mountain and maritime border spaces. As the reader will notice, the book is structured so that the analysis may be grounded in social practices rather than geography. Nevertheless, there is some overlap between the two.

I. Overview of Myanmar's Mountain and Maritime Borderscapes

This section serves as an introduction to Myanmar's border regions. Nicholas Farrelly's chapter begins by setting out the four ways in which the borderland constituencies are different from the heartlands: isolation from the rest of Myanmar, strong links to neighbouring countries, mountainous terrain and the main origin of Myanmar's diaspora. Having laid out the context of the borderlands, he combines data on voting behaviour in the 2010 general elections with that on conflict and military deployments and cartographic representation in the border constituencies to "clarify ideas of marginality, contestability, belonging and dissent in the new electoral system" (Farrelly, Chapter 2 in this volume). According to Farrelly, whether electoral sovereignty can be established in Myanmar depends very much on the borderlands. These regions — home bases of the major ethnic resistance movements — have persistently pursued autonomy or disavowed national political institutions, have had partial involvement in the electoral process, and have experienced major obstacles to integration into the national project. Clearly, rather than being peripheral, the transactions, negotiations and contestations that occur in the border regions are central to our understanding of Myanmar's social, economic and political landscape.

Scholarship on borders and boundaries in Myanmar, like elsewhere, tends to focus on the terrestrial borders; less research has been conducted on riparian and maritime borders. Maung Aung Myoe's chapter aims to partially address this gap. He begins by providing us with an overview of the maritime disputes between Myanmar, Thailand, Bangladesh and India. Some maritime boundary disputes with Thailand and India have been resolved but those with Bangladesh remain delimited. Besides state level disputes over maritime boundaries, there is an emerging politics of resource (hydrocarbon and fish stocks) control between central and local/regional governments, for the first time in Myanmar at least since 1962. The chapter describes the challenges posed by domestic contenders and foreign entities to the Myanmar state's authority over and management of the maritime frontier, highlighting the many actors involved in contesting and transgressing Myanmar's water boundaries and the land-based techniques and ideologies the state uses to territorialize the marine.

II. Territorial Claims and Imagined Boundaries

The three essays in this section show how, in the minds of the Burmese, belonging is undeniably tied to the notion of territory and hegemony, whether this relates to the Burman, people who have been designated *kala* (people from the West (South Asia) or foreigner) or the Rohingya. Too often, discussions about Burmese nationals of South Asian descent are reduced to religion and/or ethnicity. Thus, this approach gives us a broader way of perceiving and situating notions of belonging, their associated practices and their intimate ties with imagined territories. This in turn leads us to consider what we mean by borders and borderlands — not just the normative institutions and physical spaces that have been designated by the state, but the imagined and cognitive boundaries that exist in the collective consciousness.

Maxime Boutry begins his chapter by questioning the assumption that sectarian violence in Myanmar is about the threat that Islam poses to Buddhism. Instead, he hypothesizes that Myanmar's Muslims are perceived as a threat to Burman/Bamar *and* Arakanese/Rakhine hegemonies on what they consider their respective territories. This leads him to consider

Burmanization, identity and territory so as to analyse how Burman/ Bamar hegemony has manifested in the borderlands and to what extent. Interestingly, the Burman/Bamar along the Tenasserim maritime border are "both Zomians in flight from the oppressive centre (having found greater freedom of practice in conquering a pioneer front) and vectors for the Burmanization of local traditions and practices" (Bourdier et al. 2015, p. 21). Boutry shows how these Burman/Bamar have integrated with the Moken, so that the Burmanization process has been adapted and reformulated by patron-client relationships and exogamy, "leading to a blurring of state-formulated racial and ethnic categories" (ibid.). The uniqueness of Boutry's work is that, instead of focusing on ethnic minorities, he looks to the practices surrounding Burman/Bamar identity and Burmanization to unpack the complex dialectics of borderscapes, identity and imagined territories — something that has received little attention in the literature on Myanmar.

Turning to the western border of Myanmar, Alexandra de Mersan poses insightful questions about what rituals say vis-à-vis current social and political circumstances in Rakhine State. This is particularly salient, given the periodic outbreaks of sectarian violence between Buddhists and Muslims since 2012. Her work shows how Burman/Bamar and Rakhine hegemony, enacted in spirit (*nat*) rituals, is spatially located since spirits are ethnically represented and territorially bound. Variations in rituals, and the decline in invitations to and (non) appearance of *kala* spirits signal the changing orientations and perceptions of the Rakhine, particularly in relation to the 'other'. Alexandra de Mersan's research on spirits (*nats*) in this section draws upon Bénédicte Brac de la Perrière's observation that the Burmese kings of old, in making a *nat* a cultural hero tied to a specific region,

> territoralised the link of the *nats* to the communities that depend on them. In doing so, the Burmese kings changed the very nature of the ties of identity in these communities: probably quite diverse before their Burmesization, community identity seems now to be defined as a form of local particularism, limited to a defined territory that is part of a national expanse... In fact, the essence of this policy has consisted in using the *nats* alone to fuse, on the local level, autochthony and sovereignty (Brac de la Perrière 1996, p. 58).

These rituals are social practices that provide us with a window into collective cognitive maps of territory, hegemony and belonging in the figured worlds that exist in Rakhine State. They reiterate the constant (re)production of the link between discursive, normative and spatial boundaries.

Anders Bjornberg's chapter on the Rohingya underlines the way in which territory is ingrained in notions of belonging at a different scale. He describes how both Myanmar and Bangladesh view the Rohingya as an aberration who have to be excised from the territory of the nation state. Arguing that the Rohingya pose an ideological and symbolic threat to "contemporary constructions of nationalism" (Chapter 6 in this volume) instead of a military one in both countries, Bjonberg provides examples of how both nations seek to reconfigure the historicity and identity of the Rohingya in ways which deny their political and cultural claims to citizenship. The Rohingya, in their movement across state-defined borders, their place-making and their narratives (see Farzana, this volume) are creating spaces that challenge Bangladesh and Myanmar's notion of nation, territory and boundaries, creating a subaltern critique of the territoriality-identity-belonging trinity.

III. Social Organization and Border Economies

This section examines the organized activities of refugees, migrants and humanitarian actors (these groups are not mutually exclusive) which reconfigure notions of jurisdiction and legitimacy, undermining the spatial boundaries and sovereignty of the Myanmar Government. Both chapters demonstrate how the Thai-Burmese border landscape — in its tangible and intangible forms — is shaped by borderlanders' organized proactive and defensive responses to shifting power structures and alliances of the state, non-state armed groups and corporations through practices that have created and reside in the humanitarian and education spheres. Sturgeon calls this "landscape plasticity", "[a] combined spatial and temporal knowledge," which "gives [borderlanders] a certain resilience in negotiating with state agents..." (2011, p. 25).

The multiple and overlapping domains of power and the multi-scalar activities of diverse actors have transformed this space into a tumultuous, turbulent and troubled landscape. Political repression in Myanmar, the lack of public social welfare, the existence of a war economy, and the dominance of a neoliberal capitalist economy on the Thai side of the border, has produced a humanitarian economy and an economy of intimacy (Lyttleton 2014, pp. 110–42) that strive to mitigate the insecurity, deprivation, ambiguity and precariousness that prevails in this region.

Alexander Horstmann's chapter is a detailed study of the emergence and spread of the humanitarian economy on the Thai-Burmese border. Steeped in notions of Karen/Kayin nationalism, culture and suffering, this industry has enabled the Karen/Kayin (and Karenni/Kayah) to establish a niche in providing alternative underground support in health care, education and social welfare in an effort to counter or mitigate the effects of political and socio-economic disparities in the region. This has, in turn, shaped the economy, infrastructure and materiality of the border.

Su-Ann Oh expands on the humanitarian economy by contrasting its institutions and cultural norms with those of the neoliberal capitalist economy that prevails on the Thai side of the border. By analysing the schooling, training and employment of Burmese migrants on the Thai border, she reveals the values, social practices and institutional affiliations of the humanitarian economy, and demonstrates how they contrast with those of the neoliberal capitalist one. She concludes with foreboding: as the political shifts in Myanmar herald the flight of donor funding to Myanmar and away from the border, those who are left in the humanitarian economy become even more vulnerable to the vagaries of donor fatigue and fancies.

IV. Mobile Practices and Moving Borders

The mobility of people, goods and ideas highlights the way in which border actors negotiate various regulatory authorities, thereby reconfiguring power relations ingrained in normalized spatial arrangements. The mobile practices described in these chapters invite us to observe networks and technologies that transcend the physical moorings of the territorial border and to consider its spatial, social, affective and virtual dimensions, showcasing the diversity of mobile practices at different sites on the Chinese Thai border. The authors demonstrate how actors negotiate various authorities, thus providing insights into the power relations amongst these parties. This is often manifested in the form of border performances (Coplan 2012) and games (Andreas 2009) where state actors, local authorities and local communities exploit, negotiate or circumvent local and central regulations to further their own interests.

Karin Dean contends that in order to better problematize the contentious politics of the Kachin, one has to take into account networks that span "space, scales and positionalities" (Chapter 9 in this volume) including Internet-based communication technology. By focusing on the hyper-movement of information about the Kachin conflict across the Internet, she posits that Kachin mobilities, including the movement of information, are part of a continuity of flows across space and time and best conceptualized as capabilities that have been produced collectively for different purposes. In this way, Dean draws our attention to the way in which mobilities, framed as capabilities, construct meaning and connect the Kachin in contentious politics.

To a certain extent, this is akin to Bowen's identification of mobility and "Islam as a transnational public space". "[T]ransnational Islam creates and implies the existence and legitimacy of a global public space of normative reference and debate, and that this public space cannot be reduced to a dimension of migration or of transnational religious movements" (Bowen 2004, p. 880). What Dean describes applies to other Myanmar-related contentious politics (ethnic such as the Karen/Kayin or ideological such as the National League for Democracy) and exemplifies the tension between the Burmese political regime and Myanmar-related "communities that recognise and act according to cultural notions that transcend the categories of the territorial state" (Kalir et al. 2012, p. 13).

Jianxiong Ma and Chunzhao Ma's chapter forms the historical backdrop to Dean's work by describing how mule caravans tapped into extensive networks across local political structures and different cultural systems, acting as a mechanism for mobility and social networking across the Chinese Empire and the Burmese kingdom. In their highly detailed account of the social structure and operations of mule caravans, they weave local politics, social boundaries, patronage, cross-border networking, cultural practices and long-distance travel into a fascinating account of the circulation of people, mules, goods and capital. Since the border began where their networks ended, one can say that the travels and networks of the humble mule caravans played a role in shaping the frontier between China and Burma. These cyclical journeys that took place up until recently also provide an example of alternative conceptions and practices of mobility that mapped space through kin networks, patronage, and resource units. In addition, these trading practices constituted a transnational popular realm that enjoyed an informal oppositional power (based on economic rather than political force) against "national" states while incorporating various state agencies (Chang 2009, pp. 566–67). "In consequence, the interacting force embraced different scales (local, regional, national, and transnational) of geopolitical and geosocial entities" (Chang 2009, p. 568).

V. Identity Construction and the Politics of Belonging

The fifth section of the book examines the way that stateless, displaced and migrant communities fashion identity and belonging to counter state discourses and hegemonic Burman/Bamar identity. It also considers how neighbouring country communities define these communites. The chapters draw our attention to the discursive, cultural, contextual and moral ways in which identity and the politics of belonging are enacted and performed in relation to Myanmar's borders and borderlands and the figured worlds that these represent.

All four chapters deal explicitly with how displaced people of ethnic origin (Karen/Kayin, Rohingya, Shan and Karenni/Kayah) construct their identity and belonging through the idea of "home", envisaged through (others') memory, imagination and the affective landscape. As Liisa Malkki writes

> …now, more than perhaps ever before, people are chronically mobile and routinely displaced, and invent homes and homelands in the absence of territorial, national bases — not in situ, but through memories of, and claims on, places that they can, or will, no longer corporeally inhabit (Malkki 1992, p. 24).

The importance of possessing and expressing cultural identity and belonging in Myanmar cannot be overstated. Although the cultural scripts produced are effectively the weapons of the weak, these communities feel the necessity to create and express them regardless. This is because political and social life is heavily ethnicized in Myanmar, and the establishment and codification of a cultural identity often marks the difference between survival and extinction.

Decha Tangseefa focuses on meaning-making surrounding the creation of songs by young Karen/Kayin refugee camp residents. He asserts that "music is used as a discursive fabric", woven from a variety of discourses — "nation, home, homeland, religion, natural beauty of their homeland, mother, family and friendship" (Chapter 11 in this volume) — to enable young refugees to maintain a way of life that is no longer possible. Indeed, the performance of these songs serves the purpose of reaffirming and re-imagining identity and belonging. It also provides the means by which the intangible and invisible may be expressed and shared, even if they are not heard, acknowledged or understood beyond the camps.

This is also the case for the Rohingya, as described in Farzana's chapter. The Rohingya living in camps in eastern Bangladesh use drawings, songs and narratives to legitimize their claims of belonging in the face of state resistance and opposition. They have also invoked notions of "desh" (homeland) and historical origins in Rakhine State rather than territorial warfare in recent years to assert these claims.

Indeed, as Newman and Paasi wrote, the construction of an identity narrative is itself a political action (1998, p. 195). In this way, the Rohingya (and the Karen/Kayin) use locally produced cultural artefacts to counter external actors' constructions of them, enacting a (cultural) politics of belonging that repudiates state and external discourses (as detailed in Bornberg, this volume).

These sentiments are echoed in Amporn Jirattikorn's chapter on the Shan who live in Chiang Mai, Thailand. Jirattikorn uses the cultural politics of belonging to situate their ambivalence towards "home" and return within the wider framework of current social, economic and cultural circumstances in Myanmar. The upshot of it is that many Shan migrants find themselves in a state of residential limbo: they do not feel a sense of cultural belonging to their homeland and border hometowns, nor do they have permanent and legitimate claims to stay in Thailand.

In their chapter, Carl Grundy-Warr and Chin Wei Jun argue that the process by which the borders are becoming incorporated into the country's political economic transformation have to be in the forefront of discussions of the everyday lives of borderlanders and, in their particular study, displaced Karenni/Kayah's prospects for return. Commercial and industrial disputes (as opposed to military conflict in the past) in the Thai-Burmese borderland has led to land and resource dispossession, making Karenni/Kayah refugees wary about returning. Although there appears to be some optimism for a decent life on the Karenni/Kayah border, the fear, mistrust and suspicion that has emerged from militarization, business interests and displacement underscore the unequal political and economic power that dominates this landscape. The Karenni refugees' ideas about return, which encompasses home and belonging, are intimately tied to the local context and its affective landscape.

VI. Institutionalized Identity and Border Practices

This final section considers the everyday politics of identity and belonging through institutionalized practices at the Indian and Chinese borders respectively. Together, these two papers remind us that micro-level perceptions shape border processes and formations and that we cannot take for granted the nature of these perceptions, since they are embedded in wider economic and political circumstances in both countries.

In describing the institutionalization of xenophobia towards the Chin by the Mizo on the Indian side of the border, Bianca Son and N. William Singh draw our attention to the way in which external actors play a role in the politics of belonging. The Young Mizo Association (YMA) in Mizoram on the Indian side of the border, configures economic, political, moral and discursive space through social practices that undermine the position of the Chin in Mizoram society, and which relegate them to an inferior position in the Mizo world. The paradox between self-proclaimed kinship and institutionalized discrimination provides a fascinating look into the production of cultural boundaries that serve to reproduce state borders.

In contrast, Takahiro Kojima's chapter on the local ritual and healing practices of a non-state sanctioned Buddhist sect on the Chinese border highlights the intermingling of the spiritual, the material and the national. Despite the state's attempts to institutionalize a particular form of Buddhism (in both Myanmar and China), certain Buddhist sects and their practices continue to operate and maintain their spiritual legitimacy on the Chinese-Burmese border. Chinese villagers invite Burmese monks and "layreaders" (*holu*) of the same sect to move to their villages to take up residence in vacant village temples. This has created an amalgamation of spiritual and cultural practices which Chinese villagers view as meaningful, potent and appropriate. Here, state borders are ignored in the sacred realm but exploited in the mundane: Burmese monks and layreaders are willing to move across the border because the Chinese economy is doing much better than the Burmese one, enabling them to collect more alms and improve their standard of living.

The chapters in this and the previous section ask us to consider the ways in which sociocultural and moral constructions of identity and everyday practices by individuals and in institutions are used to build legitimacy and credibility in creating belonging and exclusion.

CONCLUSION

This edited volume presents Myanmar's border spaces as entities that share geographical and political histories, instead of as discrete, disparate units attached to a national border. While these geographical features are not the sole determining characteristic of these domains, they alert us to the fact that mountain and maritime Myanmar have more in common with each other than with the lowlands, particularly in regard to their relationship with the state and to their connections with international neighbours. Moreover, examining the boundaries — geographical and constructed — of these regions provides us an entrée into the figured worlds located therein: how they are given meaning and shape, and how they vie for dominance in the social order. The elaboration of this continuous contentious process brings us closer to an understanding of the relationship between Myanmar's border domains and its heartlands.

The other objective of this book is to reflect on our perceptions of the sea so as to provide alternative ideas of what a border is and how it shapes national concerns. This requires us to consider maritime frontiers as more than spaces to be territorialized, exploited or secured. Human endeavours on the sea are stymied or facilitated by waves, tides, winds, currents and the stars, engendering means of travel, forms of navigation, belief systems and lifestyles that are vastly dissimilar from those on land. By paying attention to these nuances, we can begin to work towards a richer and more refined conceptualization of territory/maritoriality, borders/boundaries, identity and belonging/life worlds, which would provide us with a better framework for studying Myanmar's borders.

Notes
1. I would like to thank Itty Abraham, Vatthana Pholsena, Karin Dean, Nicholas Farrelly, Robert Taylor and Wu Keping for offering insightful comments on conference papers and proceedings. My gratitude goes to Nicolas Lainez, Itty Abraham, Karin Dean and Alexander Horstmann for reviewing the various drafts of this chapter. I am also thankful to Nicholas Farrelly and the ANU College of Asia and the Pacific for providing Figure 1.1 in this chapter. Finally, a big thank you goes to Veena Nair for her meticulous editing and invaluable help.
2. The Myanmar military began systematically applying the 'Four Cuts' in the Irrawaddy Delta against Karen/Kayin and Communist insurgents in the late 1960s. This strategy, aimed at eliminating sources of food, finance, recruits and intelligence for insurgent groups from their families and local villagers (Smith 1991, p. 259), enabled the state to penetrate rebel-held areas and to push the insurgents from the Delta and Bago Yoma into the more remote border areas. As a result, the territory that insurgent armies controlled shrank and became centred on relatively well-defined territories. In the case of the KNU, this region bordered Thailand. At this point, the Myanmar Army realized that the Four Cuts strategy was futile. However, the Four Cuts campaign was re-instated along the border areas (Kachin State, Shan State, Karenni State, Karen State, Mon State and Tenasserim Division) in early 2011 following a resurgence of armed conflict by ethnic ceasefire groups who resisted joining the Border Guard Force (Wai Moe 2011).
3. Zomia is a term coined by Willem van Schendel to designate a place in highland Asia that exists as a political and historical entity distinct from the usual divisions of Asia: Central, South, East, and Southeast. There is some debate over the exact geographical span of Zomia and of these Asian highlands. Van Schendel has extended Zomia from the western Himalayan Range through the Tibetan Plateau and all the way to the lower end of the peninsular Southeast Asian highlands to include southern Qinghai and Xinjiang within China, and a portion of Central Asia, encompassing the highlands of Pakistan, Afghanistan, Tajikistan, and Kyrgyzstan. James Scott's definition of Zomia is closer to that of the Southeast Asian mainland massif and refers to places whose altitude is above 300 metres (Michaud 2010).

References

Abraham, Itty, and Willem van Schendel. "Introduction: The Making of Illicitness". In *Illicit Flows and Criminal Things: State, Borders and the Other Side of Globalization*, edited by Willem van Schendel and Itty Abraham. Bloomington: Indiana University Press, 2005, pp. 1–37.

Abraham, Itty. *How India Became Territorial: Foreign Policy, Diaspora, Geopolitics*. Stanford: Stanford University Press, 2014.

Amporn Jirattikorn. "Pirated Transnational Broadcasting: The Consumption of Thai Soap Operas among Shan Communities in Burma". *Sojourn: Journal of Social Issues in Southeast Asia* 23, no. 1 (2008): 30–62.

——. "Shan Noises, Burmese Sound: Crafting Selves through Pop Music". *South East Asia Research* 18, no. 1 (2010): 169–89.

——. "Shan Virtual Insurgency and the Spectatorship of the Nation". *Journal of Southeast Asian Studies* 42, no. 1 (2011): 17–38.

Anderson, Benedict. *Imagined Communities: Reflections on the Origin and Spread of Nationalism* (Revised and extended edition). London: Verso, 1991.

Andreas, Peter. *Border Games: Policing the U.S.-Mexico Divide*. Ithaca and London: Cornell University Press, 2009.

Ardeth Maung Thawnghmung. *The 'Other' Karen in Myanmar: Ethnic Minorities and the Struggle without Arms*. Lanham: Rowman and Little Field, 2012.

Arnold, Dennis and Kevin Hewison. "Exploitation in Global Supply Chains: Burmese Migrant Workers in Mae Sot, Thailand". In *Transnational Migration and Work in Asia*, edited by Kevin Hewison and Ken Young. London: RoutledgeCurzon, 2006: 165–90.

Arnold, Dennis and John Pickles. "Global Work, Surplus Labour, and the Precarious Economies of the Border". *Antipode* 43, no. 5 (2011): 1598–624.

Baud, Michiel and Willem van Schendel. "Toward a Comparative History of Borderlands". *Journal of World History* 8, no. 2 (1997): 211–42.

Benjamin, Geoffrey. "Between Isthmus and Islands: Reflections on Malayan Palaeo-Sociology". National University of Singapore, Department of Sociology Working Paper Series no. 71 (1986).

Berg, Eiki and Henk van Houtum. "A Border is not a Border. Writing and Reading Borders in Space". In *Routing Borders between Territories, Discourses and Practices*, edited by Eiki Berg and Henk van Houtum. Aldershot: Ashgate Publishing, 2003, pp. 1–10.

Berlie, Jean. *The Burmanization of Myanmar's Muslims*. Bangkok: White Lotus Press, 2008.

Bourdier, Frédéric, Maxime Boutry, Jacques Ivanoff, and Olivier Ferrari. "Introduction". In *From Padi States to Commercial States: Reflections on Identity and the Social Construction of Space in the Borderlands of Cambodia, Vietnam, Thailand and Myanmar*. Amsterdam: Amsterdam University Press, 2015, pp. 15–42.

Bourdieu, Pierre. Esquisse d'une théorie de la pratique [Outline of a Theory of Practice]. Paris: Éditions du Seuil, 1972.

Boutry, Maxime and Jacques Ivanoff. "La monnaie des frontiers. Migrations birmanes dans le sud de Thaïlande, réseaux et internationalisation des frontières" [The Currency of the Borders: Burmese Migration in the South of Thailand, Networks and Internationalization of Frontiers]. In *Carnet de l'Irasec*. Bangkok: Research Institute on Contemporary Southeast Asia (IRASEC), 2009.

Boutry, Maxime. "Les Frontières <mouvantes> de Birmanie" [The 'Moving' Frontiers of Burma]. Moussons 17 (2011).

Bowen, John R. "Beyond Migration: Islam as a Transnational Public Space". *Journal of Ethnic and Migration Studies* 30, no. 5 (2004): 879–94.

Brac de la Perrière, Bénédectine. "The Burmese *Nats*: Between Sovereignty and Autochthony". *Diogenes* 44, no. 174 (1996): 45–60.

Callahan, Mary. "Language Policy in Modern Burma". In *Fighting Words: Language Policy and Ethnic Relations in Asia*, edited by Michael E. Brown and Sumit Ganguly. Cambridge: Massachusetts Institute of Technology (MIT) Press, 2003, pp. 143–76.

——. *Political Authority in Burma's Ethnic Minority States: Devolution, Occupation and Coexistence*. Washington, D.C.: East–West Center, 2007.

Campbell, Stephen. "Cross-ethnic Labour Solidarities among Myanmar Workers in Thailand". *Sojourn: Journal of Social Issues in Southeast Asia* 27, no. 2 (2012): 260–84.

Chang, Wen-Chin. "Venturing into "Barbarous" Regions: Transborder Trade among Migrant Yunnanese between Thailand and Burma, 1960s–1980s". *The Journal of Asian Studies* 68, no. 2 (2009): 543–72.

——. "The Everyday Politics of the Underground Trade in Burma by the Yunnanese Chinese since the Burmese Socialist Era". *Journal of Southeast Asian Studies* 44, no. 2 (2013): 292–314.

——. "By Sea and by Land: Stories of Two Chinese Traders". In *Burmese Lives: Ordinary Life Stories under the Burmese Regime*, edited by Wen-Chin Chang and Eric Tagliacozzo. New York: Oxford University Press, 2014a, pp. 174–99.

——. *Beyond Borders: Stories of Yunnanese Chinese Migrants of Burma*. New York: Cornell University Press, 2014b.

Chou, Cynthia. "Space, Movement and Place: The Sea Nomads". In *The Sea, Identity and History: From the Bay of Bengal to the South China Sea*, edited by Satish Chandra and Humanshu Prabha Ray. Singapore: Institute of Southeast Asian Studies (ISEAS), 2013, pp. 41–66.

Cons, Jason and Romola Sanyal. "Geographies at the margins: borders of South Asia — introduction". *Political Geography* 35 (2013): 5–13.

Coplan, David B. "Border Show Business and Performing States". In *A Companion to Border Studies*, edited by Thomas M. Wilson and Hastings Donnan. Chichester: Wiley-Blackwell, 2012, pp. 507–21.

Dean, Karin. *Tackling the Territorial Trap: Kachin Divided by the Sino-Burmese Boundary*. Doctoral dissertation, National University of Singapore, 2002.

——. "The Sites of the Sino-Burmese and Thai-Burmese Boundaries: Transpositions Between the 'Conceptual' and Life-worlds". In *Borderscapes: Hidden Geographies and Politics at Territory's Edge*, edited by Prem Kumar Rajaram and Carl Grundy-Warr. Minneapolis: University of Minnesota Press, 2007, pp. 183–200.

———. "Spaces, Territorialities and Ethnography on the Thai-, Sino- and Indo-Myanmar Boundaries". In *Ashgate Research Companion to Border Studies*, edited by Doris Wast-Walter. Farnham: Ashgate Publishing, 2011, pp. 219–44.

Decha Tangseefa. "Taking Flight in Condemned Grounds: Forcibly Displaced Karens and the Thai-Burmese In-between Spaces". *Alternatives: Global, Local, Political* 31, no. 4 (2006): 405–29.

Desaine, Lois. "The Politics of Silence — Myanmar NGOs' Ethnic, Religious and Political Agenda". In *Carnet de l'Irasec*. Bangkok: Research Institute on Contemporary Southeast Asia (IRASEC), 2011.

Dudley, Sandra. "Displacement and Identity: Karenni Refugees in Thailand". Doctoral dissertation, University of Oxford, 2001.

———. "Re-shaping Karenni-ness in Exile: Education, Nationalism and Being in the Wider World". In *Exploring Ethnicity in Burma*, edited by Mikael Gravers. Copenhagen: Nordic Institute for Asian Studies (NIAS) Press, 2006, pp. 77–106.

———. *Materialising Exile: Material Culture and Embodied Experience among Karenni Refugees in Thailand*. Oxford and New York: Berghahn, 2010.

Farzana, Kazi Fahmia. "Music and Artistic Artefacts: Symbols of Rohingya Identity and Everyday Resistance in Borderlands". *Austrian Journal of South-East Asian Studies* 4, no. 2 (2011): 215–36.

Ferguson, Jane M. "The Scramble for the Waste Lands: Tracking Colonial Legacies, Counterinsurgency and International Investment through the Lens of Land Laws in Burma/Myanmar". *Singapore Journal of Tropical Geography* 35, no. 3 (2014): 295–311.

Fink, Christina. "Militarization in Burma's Ethnic States: Causes and Consequences". *Contemporary Politics* 14, no. 4 (2008): 447–62.

———. "Re-envisioning Land Rights and Land Tenure". In *Myanmar: The Dynamics of an Evolving Polity*, edited by David I. Steinberg. Boulder: Lynne Rienner, 2015, pp. 243–66.

Gravers, Mikael and Flemming Ytzen, eds. *Burma/Myanmar — Where Now?* Copenhagen: Nordic Institute of Southeast Asian Studies (NIAS), 2014.

Grundy-Warr, Carl. "Geographies of Displacement: The Karenni and the Shan across the Myanmar-Thailand Border". *Singapore Journal of Tropical Geography* 23, no. 1 (2002): 93–122.

——— and Karin Dean. "The Boundaries of Contested Identities: 'Kachin' and 'Karenni' Spaces in the Troubled Borderlands of Burma". In *Routing Borders between Territories, Discourses and Practices*, edited by Eiki Berg and Henk van Houtum. Aldershot: Ashgate, 2003, pp. 75–96.

——— and Karin Dean. "Not Peace, Not War: The Myriad Spaces of Sovereignty, Peace and Conflict in Myanmar/Burma". In *Reconstructing Conflict Integrating War and Post-War Geographies*, edited by Scott Kirsch and Colin Flint. Farnham: Ashgate, 2011, pp. 91–114.

Holland, Dorothy. "Symbolic Worlds in Time/spaces of Practice: Identities and Transformations". In *Symbolic Transformation: The Mind in Movement through Culture and Society*, edited by Brady Wagoner. Hove: Routledge, 2010, pp. 269–83.

Holland, Dorothy and Jean Lave. "Social Practice Theory and the Historical Production of Persons". *Actio: An International Journal of Human Activity Theory* 2, no. 1 (2009): 1–15.

Holland, Dorothy, William Lachicotte Jr, Debra Skinner, and Carole Cain. *Identity and Agency in Cultural Worlds*. Cambridge, MA: Harvard University Press, 1998.

Horstmann, Alexander. "Sacred Networks and Struggles among the Karen Baptists across the Thailand-Burma Border". *Moussons* 17 (2011*a*): 85–104.

——. "Sacred Spaces of Karen Refugees and Humanitarian Aid across the Thailand-Burma Border". *Austrian Journal of South-East Asian Studies (ASEAS)* 4, no. 2 (2011*b*): 254–71.

——. "Borderlands and Border Studies in Southeast Asia". *Austrian Journal of South-East Asian Studies* 4, no. 2 (2011*c*): 203–214. <http://www.seas.at/our-journal-aseas/browse-issues/aseas-42/> (accessed on 1 January 2015).

——. "Secular and Religious Sanctuaries: Interfaces of Humanitarianism and Self-Government of Karen Refugee-Migrants in Thai Burmese Border Spaces". In *Building Noah's Ark for Migrants, Refugees, and Religious Communities*, edited by Alexander Horstmann and Jin-Heon Jung. New York: Palgrave Macmillan, 2015, pp. 129–56.

—— and Reed L. Wadley, eds. *Centering the Margin: Agency and Narrative in Southeast Asian Borderlands*. Asian Anthropologies Series 4. Oxford and New York: Bergahn, 2006.

Hull, Stephen. "The 'Everyday Politics' of IDP Protection in Karen State". *Journal of Current Southeast Asian Affairs* 28, no. 2 (2009): 7–21.

Ishida Masami. "Epilogue: Potentiality of Border Economic Zones and Future Prospects 2013". In *Border Economies in the Greater Mekong Subregion*, edited by Masami Ishida. Basingstoke: Palgrave Macmillan/ Institute of Developing Economies-Japan External Trade Organisation (IDE-JETRO) 2013, pp. 299–331.

Ivanoff, Jacques. "Change, Resistance or Cultural Permanence among the Sea Faring Populations". In *Southern Ethnic Dynamism: the Andaman Littoral and Marine Populations*. Bangkok: Chulalongkorn University Social Research Institute (CUSRI)/Research Institute on Contemporary Southeast Asia (IRASEC), 2008, pp. 95–112.

Jannuzi, Frank, S. "The New Burma Road (Paved by Polytechnologies?)". In *Burma Prospects for a Democratic Future*, edited by Robert I. Rotberg. Washington, D.C.: Brookings Institution Press, 1998, pp. 197–208.

Jaquet, Carine and Conor O'Loughlin. "Redefining Humanitarian Space: The Kachin IDP Crisis in Myanmar". In *Humanitarian Exchange Magazine* 55 (2012) <http://www.odihpn.org/humanitarian-exchange-magazine/issue-55/redefining-humanitarian-space-the-kachin-idp-crisis-in-myanmar> (accessed 1 June 2015).

Kalir, Barak, Malini Sur, and Willem van Schendel. "Introduction Mobile Practices and Regimes of Permissiveness". In *Transnational Flows and Permissive Polities Ethnographies of Human Mobilities in Asia*, edited by Barak Kalir and Malini Sur. Amsterdam: University Press Amsterdam, 2012, pp. 11–26.

Karen Human Rights Group (KHRG). *Surviving in Shadow: Widespread Militarization and the Systematic Use of Forced Labour in the Campaign for Control of Thaton District*. Location undisclosed: KHRG, 2006.

——. *Development by Decree: The Politics of Poverty and Control in Karen State*. Location undisclosed: KHRG, 2007.

——. *Growing Up under Militarisation: Abuse and Agency of Children in Karen State*. Location undisclosed: KHRG, 2008a.

——. *Village Agency: Rural Rights and Resistance in a Militarized Karen State*. Location undisclosed: KHRG, 2008b.

——. *Cycles of Displacement: Forced Relocation and Civilian Responses in Nyaunglebin District*. Location undisclosed: KHRG, 2009.

Kramer, Tom. "Ethnic Conflict in Burma: The Challenge of Unity in a Divided Country". In *Burma or Myanmar? The Struggle for National Identity*, edited by Lowell Dittmer. New York: World Scientific 2010, pp. 51–81.

Lang, Hazel J. *Fear and Sanctuary: Burmese Refugees in Thailand*. Ithaca: Cornell University Press, 2002.

Lambrecht, Curtis W. "Oxymoronic Development: The Military as Benefactor in the Border Regions of Burma". In *Civilizing the Margins: Southeast Asian Government Policies for the Development of Minorities*, edited by Christopher R. Duncan. Singapore: National University of Singapore (NUS) Press, 2008, pp. 150–81.

Leach, Edmund R. *Political Systems of Highland Burma: A Study of Kachin Social Structure*. London and Cambridge: Harvard University Press, 1954.

Lee, Sang Kook. "Integrating Others: A Study of a Border Social System in the Thailand-Burma Borderland". Doctoral dissertation, National University of Singapore, 2007.

Lewis, James L. "The Burmanization of the Karen People: A Study in Racial Adaptability". Doctoral dissertation, University of Chicago, 1924.

Lieberman, Victor. "A Zone of Refuge in Southeast Asia? Reconceptualizing Interior Spaces". *Journal of Global History* 5 (2010): 333–46.

Lyttleton, Chris. *Intimate Economies of Development: Mobility, Sexuality and Health in Asia*. Abingdon: Routledge, 2014.

MacLean, Ken. "Spaces of Extraction: Governance along the Riverine Networks of Nyaunglebin District". In *Myanmar: The State, Community and the Environment*, edited by Trevor Wilson. Canberra: Australian National University (ANU) Press, 2007, pp. 246–70.

Malkki, Liisa. "National Geographic: The Rooting of Peoples and the Territorialization of National Identity among Scholars and Refugees". *Cultural Anthropology* 7, no. 1 (1992): 24–44.

McKinnon, John and Jean Michaud. "Presentation: Montagnard Domain in the Southeast Asian Massif". In *Turbulent Times and Enduring Peoples: The Mountain*

Minorities of the South-east Asian Massif, edited by Jean Michaud. Richmond: Curzon Press, 2000, pp. 1–25.

Michaud, Jean. "Editorial — Zomia and Beyond". *Journal of Global History* 5 (2010): 187–214.

Minghi, Julian V. "Boundary Studies in Political Geography". *Annals of the Association of American Geographers* 53, Issue 3 (1963): 407–28.

Miyazaki, Koji, ed. *Dynamics of Border Societies in Southeast Asia. Proceedings of International Symposium. Research Institute for Languages and Cultures of Asia and Africa*. Tokyo University of Foreign Studies, 2004.

Newman, David and Anssi Paasi. "Fences and Neighbours in the Postmodern World: Boundary Narratives in Political Geography". *Progress in Human Geography* 22, no. 2 (1998): 186–207.

Nobpaon Rabibhadana and Yoko Hayami. "Seeking Haven and Seeking Jobs: Migrant Workers' Networks in Two Thai Locales". *Southeast Asian Studies* 2, no. 2 (2013): 243–83.

Oh, Su-Ann. "Identity and Inclusion Education in Refugee Camps in Thailand". In *Refugee and Immigrant Students: Achieving Equity in Education*, edited by Florence E. McCarthy and Margaret Heather Vicker. Charlotte: Information Age Publishing, 2012, pp. 65–88.

O'Kane, Mary. *Borderlands and Women: Transversal Political Agency on the Burma–Thailand Border*. Victoria: Monash University Press, 2005.

Oo Sai Thet Naing. "Popular Education, Cross-border Civil Society and Possibilities for Democracy in Burma". Doctoral dissertation, University of Technology, Sydney, 2012.

Paasi, Anssi. "Deconstructing Regions: Notes on the Scales of Spatial Life". *Environment and Planning A* 23 (1991): 239–56.

———. *Territories, Boundaries and Consciousness*. Chichester: John Wiley, 1996.

———. "Boundaries as Social Practice and Discourse: The Finnish⊠Russian Border". *Regional Studies* 33, no. 7 (1999*a*): 669–80.

———. "The Political Geography of Boundaries at the End of the Millennium: Challenges of the De-territorializing World". In *Curtains of Iron and Gold: Reconstructing Borders and Scales of Interaction*, edited by Heikki Eskelinen, Ilkka Liikanen and Jukka Oksa. Aldershot: Ashgate, 1999*b*, pp. 9–24.

Pearson, Ruth and Kyoko Kusakabe. *Thailand's Hidden Workforce: Burmese Women Factory Workers*. London: Zed Books, 2012.

Pinkaew Laungaramsri. "Women, Nation, and the Ambivalence of Subversive Identification along the Thai-Burmese Border". *Sojourn: Journal of Social Issues in Southeast Asia* 21, no. 1 (2006): 68–89.

Prasert Rangkla. "Karen Ethno-nationalism and the Wrist-tying Ceremony along the Thai–Burmese Border". *Journal of Southeast Asian Studies* 45, no. 1 (2014): 74–89.

Rajah, Ananda. "A 'Nation of Intent' in Burma: Karen Ethno-nationalism, Nationalism and Narrations of Nation". *The Pacific Review* 15, no. 4 (2002): 517–37.

Rajaram, Prem Kumar and Carl Grundy-Warr, eds. *Borderscapes: Hidden Geographies and Politics at Territory's Edge*. Minneapolis: University of Minnesota Press, 2007.
Renard, Ronald D. "Minorities in Burmese History". *Sojourn: Journal of Social Issues in Southeast Asia* 2, no. 2 (1987): 255–71.
Sadan, Mandy. *Being and Becoming Kachin: Histories Beyond the State in the Borderlands of Burma*. Oxford and London: Oxford University Press and The British Academy, 2013.
Salem-Gervais, Nicolas and Rosalie Metro. "A Textbook Case of Nation-Building: The Evolution of History Curricula in Myanmar". *Journal of Burma Studies* 16, no. 1 (2012): 27–78.
Schatzki, Theodore R. *The Site of the Social: A Philosophical Account of the Constitution of Social Life and Change*. University Park: Penn State University Press, 2002.
Scott, James C. *The Art of not being Governed: An Anarchist History of Upland Southeast Asia*. New Haven: Yale University Press, 2009.
Sharples, Rachel. "Spaces of Solidarity Karen Identity in the Thai-Burma Borderlands". Unpublished doctoral dissertation, RMIT University, 2012.
Sidaway James D. "The Return and Eclipse of Border Studies? Charting Agendas". *Geopolitics* 16, no. 4 (2011): 969–76.
Simpson, Adam. "Challenging Hydropower Development in Myanmar (Burma): Cross-Border Activism under a Regime in Transition". *The Pacific Review* 26, no. 2 (2013): 129–52.
———. *Energy, Governance and Security in Thailand and Myanmar (Burma): A Critical Approach to Environmental Politics in the South*. Farnham: Ashgate, 2014.
Smith, Martin, J. *Burma: Insurgency and the Politics of Ethnicity*. London: Zed Books, 1991.
Sopher, David. *The Sea Nomads: A Study of the Maritime Boat People of Southeast Asia*. Singapore: National Museum Publication, 1977.
South, Ashley. *Mon Nationalism and Civil War in Burma: The Golden Sheldrake*. New York: RoutledgeCurzon, 2003.
———. *Ethnic Politics in Burma: States of Conflict*. Abingdon: Routledge, 2008.
Steinberg, David J., ed. In *Search of Southeast Asia: A Modern History*. Honolulu: University of Hawaii, 1987.
Sturgeon, Janet C. *Border Landscapes: The Politics of Akha Land Use in China and Thailand*. Seattle: University of Washington Press, 2011.
Tin Maung Maung Than. "Dreams and Nightmares: State Building and Ethnic Conflict in Myanmar (Burma)". In *Ethnic Conflicts in Southeast Asia*, edited by Kusuma Snitwongse and W. Scott Thompson. Singapore: Institute of Southeast Asian Studies (ISEAS), 2005, pp. 65–108.
Toyota, Mika. "Contested Chinese Identities among Ethnic Minorities in the China, Burma and Thai Borderlands". *Ethnic and Racial Studies* 26, no. 2 (2003): 301–20.
Transnational Institute (TNI). "Developing Disparity. Regional Investment in Burma's Borderlands". Amsterdam: Transnational Institute (TNI) and Burma Centrum Netherlands (BCN), 2013.

van Houtum, Henk. "The Mask of the Border". In *The Ashgate Research Companion to Border Studies*, edited by Doris Wastl-Walter. Farnham: Ashgate, 2011, pp. 49-61.

van Schendel, Willem. "Geographies of Knowing, Geographies of Ignorance: Jumping Scale in Southeast Asia". *Environment and Planning D: Society and Space* 20, no. 6 (2002): 647-68.

van Schendel, Willem and Erik de Maaker. "Asian Borderlands: Introducing their Permeability, Strategic Use and Meanings. Special issue on Asian Borderlands". *Journal of Borderland Studies* 29, no. 1 (2014): 3-10.

Wai Moe. "Naypyidaw Orders New 'Four Cuts' Campaign". In *The Irrawaddy*, 4 March 2011 <http://www2.irrawaddy.org/article.php?art_id=20880> (accessed 1 June 2015).

Walker, Andrew. *The Legend of the Golden Boat: Regulation, Trade and Traders in the Borderlands of Laos, Thailand, China, and Burma*. Richmond: Curzon Press, 1999.

Walton, Matthew J. "The 'Wages of Burman-ness': Ethnicity and Burman Privilege in Contemporary Myanmar". *Journal of Contemporary Asia* 43, no. 1 (2013): 1-27.

Weiner, Annette B. "Inalienable Wealth". *American Ethnologist* 12, no. 2 (1985): 210-27.

Woods, Kevin. "Ceasefire Capitalism: Military-Private Partnerships, Resource Concessions and Military-State building in the Burma-China Borderlands". *Journal of Peasant Studies* 38, no. 4 (2011): 747-70.

Wortham, Stanton. *Learning Identity: The Joint Emergence of Social Identification and Academic Learning*. New York: Cambridge University Press, 2006.

Section I

Overview of Myanmar's Mountain and Maritime Borderscapes

Electoral Sovereignty in Myanmar's Borderlands

Nicholas Farrelly

INTRODUCING THE BORDERLANDS

Myanmar's ongoing political reorganization offers opportunities to understand national geography and sovereignty in new ways. This chapter is the first scholarly effort to comparatively examine the political, cultural and economic characteristics of Myanmar's borderland constituencies. Under the 2008 Constitution, 330 elected constituencies are represented in Naypyitaw's Lower House (*Pyithu Hluttaw*) with fifty-two of those constituencies sharing a land border with Myanmar's neighbours: Bangladesh, India, China, Laos and Thailand. These constituencies in Chin State (6 constituencies), Kachin State (9 constituencies), Kayah State (3 constituencies), Kayin State (4 constituencies), Mon State (1 constituency), Rakhine State (2 constituencies), Sagaing Region (6 constituencies), Shan State (16 constituencies) and Tanintharyi Region (5 constituencies) are the focus of this chapter (see Figure 2.1 and Table 2.1).[1] While previous Myanmar governments have been described as "isolationist" or "insular", the administration that was headed by President Thein Sein has actively embraced the regional community and sought new international connections. As Myanmar relished its first opportunity to chair the Association of Southeast Asian Nations (ASEAN) in 2014, this analysis helps illuminate a range of important political and geopolitical forces in borderland areas. From such a perspective, the borderland constituencies are ideal sites for seeking answers to questions about the relationships and disjunctures that define Myanmar's diverse political terrain.

FIGURE 2.1
Map of Borderland Constituencies

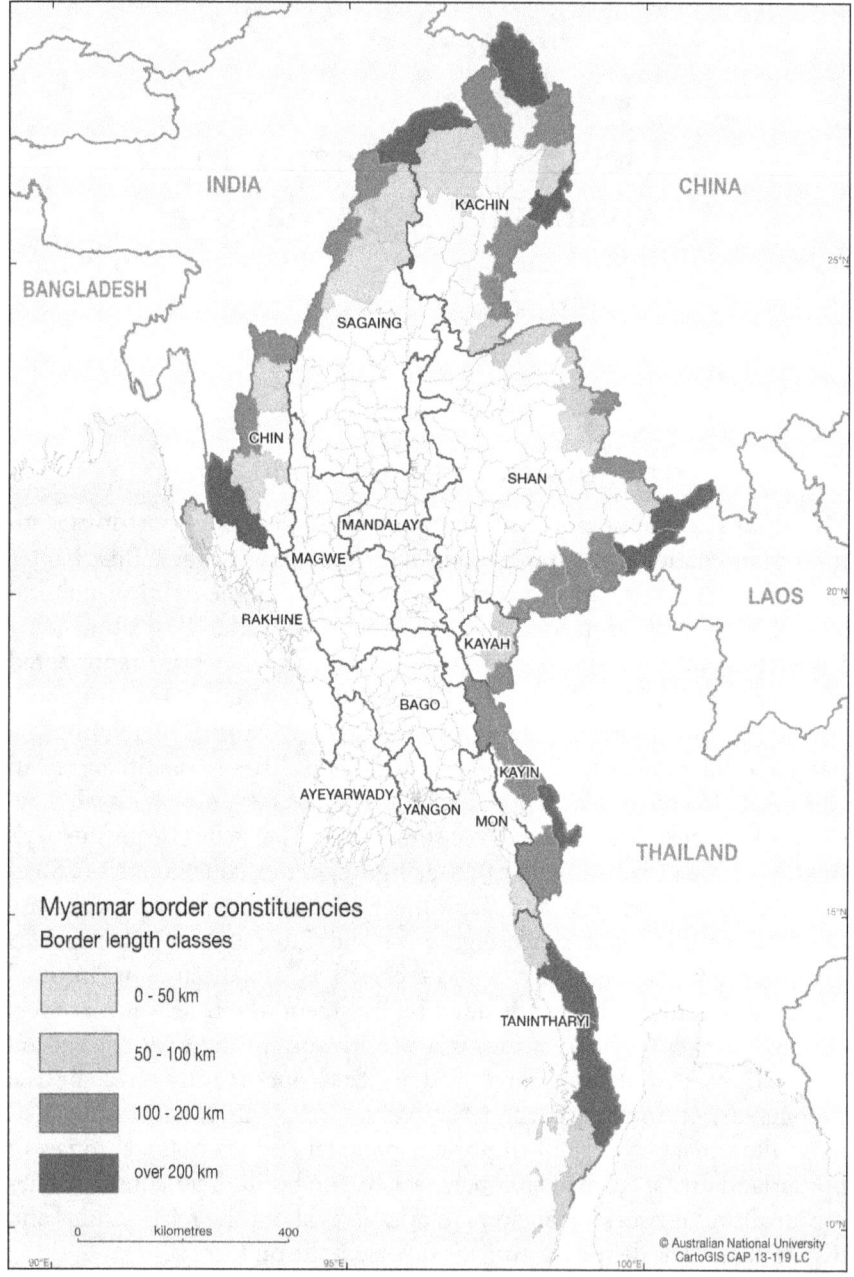

TABLE 2.1
Characteristics of Borderland Constituencies, Sorted by Border Length

Constituency	Area (km²)	Principal road	Major border crossing	Significant road	Mountain pass	Border length (km)
Hkamti	9,538.51	n	n	0	0	2
Tanai	15,337.10	n	n	0	0	10
Homalin	13,162.00	n	n	1	0	21
Madupi	5,718.56	n	n	1	0	29
Tedim	3,434.23	n	n	1	0	29
Ye	2,889.30	n	n	0	0	37
Pangsang	3,671.67	n	n	1	0	39
Buthidaung	2,445.35	n	n	1	0	46
Falam	2,832.90	n	n	1	0	46
Tsawlaw	4,289.37	n	n	3	1	48
Bawlakhe	2,128.77	y	n	0	0	51
Mongmao	2,197.00	n	n	2	0	52
Hopang	1,681.18	y	n	2	0	58
Namhkan	1,482.86	y	n	0	0	58
Namphan	2,065.09	n	n	1	0	59
Yebyu	4,363.06	n	n	0	0	61
Mansi	3,496.09	y	n	1	0	63
Laukkaing	596.78	n	n	3	0	65
Shadaw	2,674.60	n	n	2	0	66
Mongla	2,113.30	n	n	1	0	74
Kawthoung	2,688.25	n	y	0	0	80
Bokpyin	6,268.03	n	n	2	0	94
Muse	2,442.62	y	y	1	0	95
Maungdaw	1,928.63	n	n	2	0	98
Konkyan	1,326.39	n	n	1	0	107
Momauk	2,976.63	n	n	1	0	108
Monghsat	5,676.71	n	n	3	0	111
Mongton	5,460.19	y	n	2	0	116
Pangwaun	1,529.25	n	n	6	0	121
Mese	1,854.03	n	y	2	0	126
Hpapun	7,519.82	n	n	1	0	137
Mongpan	6,043.33	y	n	3	0	142
Tamu	1,736.67	n	n	3	0	146

continued on next page

TABLE 2.1 — *cont'd*

Constituency	Area (km²)	Principal road	Major border crossing	Significant road	Mountain pass	Border length (km)
Hlaingbwe	4,782.45	n	n	2	0	154
Lay Shi	4,073.77	n	n	4	0	159
Mongyang	3,107.63	n	n	7	0	159
Thantlang	4,212.05	n	n	2	0	165
Kyainseikgyi	8,341.31	n	y	2	1	170
Lahe	5,282.80	n	n	2	0	181
Khaunglanhpu	7,075.87	n	n	1	5	182
Puta-O	6,709.25	n	n	2	3	182
Waingmaw	5,985.11	n	n	2	4	188
Tonzang	4,409.46	n	n	5	0	198
Paletwa	10,626.50	n	n	4	0	215
Dawei	7,028.57	n	y	0	1	221
Tachileik	3,989.16	y	y	2	0	222
Chipwi	4,143.82	n	n	3	7	227
Nanyun	8,513.25	n	n	3	1	268
Mongyawng	5,428.35	n	n	8	0	293
Myawaddy	3,265.02	y	y	4	0	337
Nawngmun	9,744.11	n	n	0	9	337
Tanintharyi	12,359.60	n	n	2	1	367

From the swamps of the south to the Himalayan peaks of the far north, the borderlands are Myanmar's most diverse and broken country: mountainous, often forested, and with sparse populations scattered across countless small villages and some hundreds of more sizeable towns. What the borderland constituencies all have in common is an international border, which brings them into close contact, both now and in the past, with neighbouring peoples (Farrelly 2012a, pp. 130–33). In a manner of speaking the borderlands are a "laboratory of continuity" (Boutry 2011, p. 21) that has "shaped the Burmese societies' adaptations to political, social, economical and cultural changes". In many cases, connections across the international frontier are intense, deeply personal and relatively immune to the vicissitudes of national polity formation. Around Myanmar's borders the frontier meanders for 6,000 kilometres, although the precise length is a matter of some dispute. The shortest international border shared by one of the borderland constituencies is less than two kilometres (in Khamti, Sagaing Region) while the longest is over 300 kilometres (Tanintharyi, Tanintharyi

Region). The constituencies of the borderlands also differ greatly in terms of population density, economic conditions and their integration with what could be generically described as Myanmar's national "mainstream". Some borderland areas are among the most economically precarious in the country, although some are also sites for the accumulation of great, and often illicit, wealth (see Buchanan et al. 2013, pp. 46–47; Chit Su 2013). In some constituencies the adjoining international frontier is peripheral even to local concerns, with few people ever visiting. In other cases, such as the "border towns" of Myawaddy in Kayin State or Muse in Shan State, the political economy of the constituency is constantly reshaped by the border, which serves as a hub for the almost continuous movement of people and trade. Even with the peace agreements brokered by the Thein Sein government since it took power in 2011, some borderland constituencies are also the sites of ongoing conflict, usually predicated on ethnic fault lines. There are still regular periods of violence and instability.

To help explain these conditions, my comparative treatment of electoral influences across the borderland constituencies describes the fluidity of political control during the current period of flux and uncertainty. This is a somewhat unconventional analysis because it seeks a national level picture drawing on a wide range of information sources that became available in the wake of Myanmar's November 2010 general election (see the results in Figure 2.2 and Table 2.2). This was the first election in Myanmar for twenty years, and it saw twenty-three "national race" political parties (out of forty) contest seats at the local (state or region) and national (lower house or upper house) levels. In borderland constituencies such ethnic political parties were most often defeated by the Union Solidarity and Development Party (USDP), the successor to the former military dictatorship, which won thirty-four of the forty-seven constituencies that were contested (voting was cancelled in five borderland constituencies due to security issues). In four of the constituencies that were won by the USDP in 2010 (Konkyan, Lahe and Laukkaing in Shan State, and Myawaddy in Kayin State) no other party competed. A further six seats in the borderlands were won by the Shan National Democratic Party, with two seats for the National Unity Party and Chin Progressive Party, and one each for the Phalon-Sawaw Democratic Party, the Wa Democratic Party and the All Mon Region Democracy Party. Furthermore, elections were cancelled in five constituencies, all in the eastern-most portion of the Shan State, where a tense situation prevailed in the lead-up to the vote. Overall, by winning 72 per cent of seats in the borderlands, the USDP fared slightly worse than it did across the country as a whole where it won 78 per cent of seats. The result in the borderlands

FIGURE 2.2
Map of People's Assembly 2010 Election Results in Borderland Constituencies

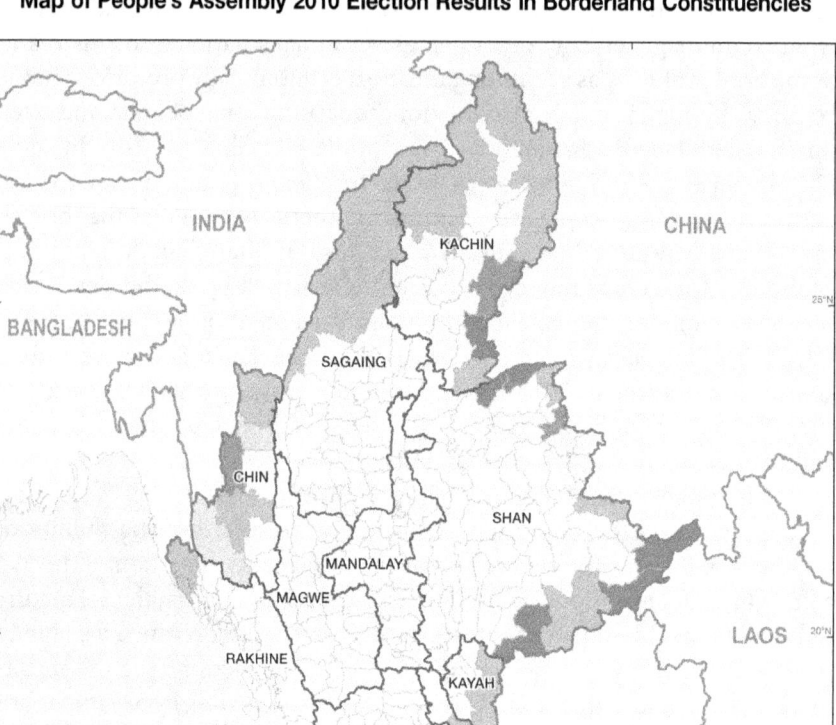

TABLE 2.2
Myanmar 2010 General Election Results in Borderland Constituencies

Constituency	Winning Party	Winning vote	Losing vote	Area (km²)	Voter density
Bawlakhe	Union Solidarity and Development Party	4,524	449	2,128.77	2.34
Bokpyin	Union Solidarity and Development Party	20,746	10,281	6,268.03	4.95
Buthidaung	Union Solidarity and Development Party	51,985	47,802	2,445.35	40.81
Chipwi	Union Solidarity and Development Party	4,957	3,181	4,143.82	1.96
Falam	Chin Progressive Party	8,975	7,122	2,832.90	5.68
Hlaingbwe	Phalon-Sawaw Democratic Party	30,540	17,955	4,782.45	10.14
Homalin	Union Solidarity and Development Party	23,132	19,762	13,162.00	3.26
Hopang	Wa Democratic Party	17,582	294	1,681.18	10.63
Khaunglanhpu	Union Solidarity and Development Party	3,308	3,177	7,075.87	0.92
Kawthoung	Union Solidarity and Development Party	29,350	14,491	2,688.25	16.31
Hkamti	Union Solidarity and Development Party	9,037	2,376	9,538.51	1.20
Konkyan	Union Solidarity and Development Party	0	0	1,326.39	0.00
Kyainseikgyi	Union Solidarity and Development Party	8,673	3,372	8,341.31	1.44
Lahe	Union Solidarity and Development Party	0	0	5,282.80	0.00
Laukkaing	Union Solidarity and Development Party	0	0	596.78	0.00
Lay Shi	Union Solidarity and Development Party	5,827	1,163	4,073.77	1.72
Mansi	Union Solidarity and Development Party	7,595	6,159	3,496.09	3.93
Madupi	Union Solidarity and Development Party	8,436	7,910	5,718.56	2.86
Maungdaw	Union Solidarity and Development Party	137,691	68,523	1,928.63	106.92

continued on next page

TABLE 2.2 — cont'd

Constituency	Winning Party	Winning vote	Losing vote	Area (km²)	Voter density
Mese	Union Solidarity and Development Party	2,603	244	1,854.03	1.54
Momauk	Shan Nationals Democratic Party	10,715	10,551	2,976.63	7.14
Monghsat	Union Solidarity and Development Party	16,853	2,433	5,676.71	3.40
Mongla	Elections Cancelled	0	0	2,113.30	0.00
Mongmao	Elections Cancelled	0	0	2,197.00	0.00
Mongpan	Shan Nationals Democratic Party	3,929	3,319	6,043.33	1.20
Mongton	Union Solidarity and Development Party	8,716	3,225	5,460.19	2.19
Mongyang	Union Solidarity and Development Party	2,697	940	3,107.63	1.17
Mongyawng	Shan Nationals Democratic Party	9,409	5,413	5,428.35	2.73
Muse	Shan Nationals Democratic Party	22,380	18,648	2,442.62	16.80
Myawaddy	Union Solidarity and Development Party	0	0	3,265.02	0.00
Namhkan	Shan Nationals Democratic Party	21,350	15,462	1,482.86	24.83
Namphan	Elections Cancelled	0	0	2,065.09	0.00
Nanyun	Union Solidarity and Development Party	12,189	7,445	8,513.25	2.31
Nawngmun	Union Solidarity and Development Party	3,153	630	9,744.11	0.39
Paletwa	Chin Progressive Party	12,629	6,129	10,626.50	1.77
Pangsang	Elections Cancelled	0	0	3,671.67	0.00
Pangwaun	Elections Cancelled	0	0	1,529.25	0.00
Hpapun	Union Solidarity and Development Party	5,185	2,959	7,519.82	1.08
Puta-O	Union Solidarity and Development Party	20,284	5,671	6,709.25	3.87

Shadaw	Union Solidarity and Development Party	1,563	184	2,674.60	0.65
Tachileik	Shan Nationals Democratic Party	22,255	20,756	3,989.16	10.78
Tamu	Union Solidarity and Development Party	23,424	10,165	1,736.67	19.34
Tanai	Union Solidarity and Development Party	7,260	4,734	15,337.10	0.78
Dawei	Union Solidarity and Development Party	28,119	14,531	7,028.57	6.07
Tanintharyi	Union Solidarity and Development Party	20,482	19,101	12,359.60	3.20
Thantlang	National Unity Party	12,075	8,295	4,212.05	4.84
Tedim	Union Solidarity and Development Party	12,446	10,320	3,434.23	6.63
Tonzang	Union Solidarity and Development Party	6,948	5,055	4,409.46	2.72
Tsawlaw	Union Solidarity and Development Party	1,083	1,037	4,289.37	0.49
Waingmaw	National Unity Party	12,652	10,663	5,985.11	3.90
Ye	All Mon Region Democracy Party	34,605	15,983	2,889.30	17.51
Yebyu	Union Solidarity and Development Party	17,452	14,377	4,363.06	7.30

was considered further evidence of the lacklustre transition to representative democracy: the 2010 election was neither free nor fair.

This judgement needs to be understood in the context of the history of conflict and resistance in borderland areas. For its part, the Myanmar Government has substantive concerns about security in the borderlands and seeks to manage its interactions with borderland peoples to mollify their long-standing calls for autonomy. In this vein, the 2008 constitution provides a level of self-governance in three borderland areas: Kokang (centred on the town of Laukkaing), Naga (Lahe) and Wa (Hopang). It is still too early to determine exactly what impact those exceptional arrangements in the so-called "Self-Administered Zones" will have on the distribution of power in Myanmar's borderland constituencies, and whether further concessions to local autonomy will be offered. The Wa, a powerful, well-funded and well-armed group, have indicated they seek greater self-governance (Hla Hla Htay 2013). The whole situation is complicated by the fact that "[s]wathes of Burma's borderlands have been run for decades as fiefdoms by ethnic militias fighting on-off wars with the Burmese army" (Roughneen 2013). Some of those wars, such as the one with the major Kachin armed group, the Kachin Independence Army, have yet to be meaningfully resolved. Disputes over sovereignty are widespread and have often appeared intractable. To explain the contested distribution of contemporary political power, this analysis of the fifty-two borderland constituencies draws on cartographic and electoral insights, and material garnered from field research, including in 2014 in Myanmar's Parliament.[2] Taken together the electoral dynamics of these constituencies at the furthest peripheries of Myanmar help clarify ideas of marginality, contestability, belonging and dissent in the new electoral system.

The data for a study of this nature comes from a variety of sources. First, there is the electoral information and the delineation of constituency boundaries, as drawn from the Myanmar Electoral Commission and the Alternative ASEAN Network on Burma (ALTSEAN). This basic information structures the arguments and analysis in ways that offer some ready and novel comparisons, especially in the original mapping products that have been produced for this purpose. Second, there is information on conflict and military deployments curated from a number of official sources, and from data collected by the U.S. Campaign for Burma. The third source of information has been generated specifically for this chapter through a geographical analysis, based on cartographical details at a fine resolution. The judgements about characteristics of constituencies offered in this chapter, and in the maps included as appendices, are informed by that computational Geographic Information System work undertaken in the Australian National University (ANU) College of Asia and the Pacific. The integration of these sources, combined with my experience researching in Myanmar's borderlands for more than a decade, and more recently in the Myanmar Parliament, offers a new appraisal of the political and social context facing Myanmar today. This is not, however, a study of elections or of the parliament but rather, of the geography that informs them. Analysing the contemporary electoral terrain through such an array of techniques and concepts presents Myanmar's borderlands as a specific zone of study that can help to illuminate a range of concerns about the country's political evolution.

Using a comparative national-level approach, this chapter argues that re-imagining Myanmar's borderlands requires the consideration of electoral sovereignty as a contestable concept. That sovereignty is a new, partial and inconsistent addition to a political landscape previously defined by military, ethnic and ideological determinations. To make this argument, the chapter begins with a description of the conceptual and methodological basis for this research. Next, the chapter identifies some of the common characteristics of the borderland constituencies. What follows are specific discussions of how such sovereignty is directly linked to population distribution, ethnic complexity, military deployments and popular enfranchisement. Each section builds towards the argument that Myanmar's borderlands are undergoing a process of deliberate and incremental integration as part of a national political system that may, over time, enjoy the endorsement of borderland peoples. Given the partial and relatively superficial participation of borderland peoples in the 2010 election it is too early to claim that electoral sovereignty has displaced the long-term dynamic of disenfranchisement and central government dominance in borderland areas. Now in the aftermath of the 2015 general election, the borderland constituencies will benefit from further considered analysis of the new electoral terrain with the NLD in charge. Further studies of these constituencies may start from the "ground up", emphasizing the character of local politics across the entire borderlands. For now, a national-level analysis helps to explore Myanmar's borderland transformations from a useful distance, and also from "above".

CONCEPTUALIZING POSITION AND POLITICS

The Myanmar borderlands, in their full diversity, have rarely been examined in any systematic fashion. Instead a variety of different approaches have been taken, each of which offers a set of valuable insights about these areas. For a start, the study of borderlands in Myanmar has emphasized ethnic categories (see Lieberman 1978, pp. 455–62; Grundy-Warr and Wong 2002, pp. 98–101; Sturgeon 2004, pp. 463–67). Speaking generally, this longstanding approach has its roots in colonial practice, and the scholarship that formed around it (see Temple 1910; Carrapiett 1929) and since that period there have been good reasons for continuing to work with ethnic categories (for an outstanding example see Robinne and Sadan 2007). Myanmar's major ethnic groups, large-and-small, are well-known to scholars and analysts, and have formed the basis for ongoing academic discussions. Among the works that have generated sustained interest in Myanmar's borderland peoples it is worth acknowledging *Political Systems of Highland Burma: A study of Kachin social structure* (1954), by Edmund Leach, the 2009 book,

The Art of Not Being Governed: An Anarchist History of Upland Southeast Asia, by James C. Scott, and, most recently, *Being and Becoming Kachin: Histories Beyond the State in the Borderworlds of Burma* (2013) by Mandy Sadan. Such books — read by audiences far beyond the boundaries of Myanmar Studies or Southeast Asian Studies — have become well-known contributions to methodological and conceptual debates.

The borderlands themselves have proved a popular category for analytical attention. Edmund Leach, the renowned anthropologist of the Kachin, authored a 1960 essay on the "frontiers of Burma", and more recently there have been important contributions by scholars such as Walker (1999), Grundy-Warr and Dean (2003) and Woods (2011). Such studies inevitably focus on one or other borderland sites, with the preponderance of work exploring more accessible areas of the Myanmar-Thailand and Myanmar-China borderlands. Studies of the Myanmar-India borderlands (such as Jacob 2010; Farrelly 2009*a*) have been rarer, although there are substantial studies of northeast India that are often read alongside more general works on interstitial Southeast Asia (such as Thant Myint-U 2011; Lintner 2012). Until the recent spike of interest associated with Muslim-Buddhist violence, far less attention has been paid to the Myanmar-Bangladesh borderlands although there are still some important scholarly works in that region (see Van Schendel 2004). Given its relative inaccessibility, and the physical barrier of the Mekong River, the border between Laos and Myanmar is arguably the least well-understood. Nearby areas of the eastern Shan State generate sporadic academic interest. Among all of the border areas it was the Myanmar-Thailand frontier that was most commonly studied during the later years of military dictatorship in Myanmar when other types of research were often judged impractical. The proliferation of writing on "the border" during these years has left a healthy reservoir of historical, political and cultural information (see Falla 1991; Thornton 2006; Farrelly 2009*b*; Lee 2012). In almost all cases, the study of Myanmar's borderlands has been determined in a particularistic framework, somewhat divorced from the broader environment of borders and their many transgressions.

For the study of Myanmar's borderlands as a whole — if such is to prove a desirable style of research — a different approach can be justified. That approach requires an awareness of the myriad local histories and societies, but also an effort to offer more abstract insights about the nature of geography, politics, community and control. The challenge of finding an adequate role for theory in such a discussion introduces the need for a subtle approach to the prevailing ambiguities and inconsistencies. In this case it is reasonable to infer a plurality of borderlands, distinctive in their social and cultural characteristics, yet shaped by similar experiences of marginality, linkage and struggle. Myanmar's borderlands, as a set of discrete spheres for study, may well defy ready navigation and it is fair to surmise that any single set of sources cannot adequately capture the local situations. Even the definition of the borderlands is open to interpretation. For some, the borderlands deserve a narrow delineation, including only those areas in direct and immediate contact with the frontier. In such calculations it would be just the border towns and hamlets that are deemed integral to the borderlands. This chapter takes a different approach, defining the borderlands based on the fifty-two lower house constituencies of Myanmar's *Pyithu Hluttaw* that have a connection, short or long, with an international border. This is a consciously maximalist interpretation of borderlands, one that ultimately covers almost one-third of Myanmar's territory. The borderland is thus expansive, stretching, in some cases, more than a hundred kilometres from the border.

WHAT DO THE BORDERLAND CONSTITUENCIES HAVE IN COMMON?

While it is clear that there are great differences across the borderlands, and these would usually be emphasized early in any analysis, it is worth describing four of the ways that the constituencies are similar. First, there is the lack of easy connection to the rest of Myanmar. The density of road and rail links is low in such areas, with only 9 principal roads and 100 secondary roads across the 52 borderland constituencies. There are also 33 mountain passes, the majority in the far north, concentrated in the constituencies of Nawngmun, Chipwi, Khaunglanhpu and Waingmaw, all in Kachin State. Among the borderland constituencies there are 9 major border crossings but a very large number of informal border crossings, probably more than 1,000. In some cases, the relevant authorities from the neighbouring country police those crossings (see Ball 2004, 2013). It is commonplace, as a result, to see Thai Border Patrol Police or Chinese People's Liberation Army personnel stationed at these ad-hoc crossings. Only 3 of the constituencies, in Mon State and Tanintharyi Region, are serviced by rail, and there are only 14 borderland constituencies that have at least one small airport. This compares to the 141 constituencies in the rest of the country that have a railway, and the 54 constituencies that have airports. There are, for reference, no major airports in the borderlands. Twenty-one of the borderland constituencies have major rivers flowing through them. Previously, the Myanmar Government's preoccupations in the borderlands were defined by security concerns. With large areas of the borderlands under the control of anti-government forces, most of the infrastructure is ramshackle and under-utilized. For this reason the density of roads or bridges of any type, while difficult to judge in a rigorous fashion, suggests that most people outside the major towns in the borderlands are still dependent on small trails, some of which are only fit for passage during the dry season. This borderland infrastructure deficit often makes it easier to visit places like Chiang Mai or Mangshi in neighbouring countries than Yangon, Naypyitaw or Mandalay. Often there are locally mandated systems for approving international travel across the borders for work, education or healthcare. Infrastructure development is underway but is mostly limited to a small number of constituencies along the Thai and Chinese borders.

Second, in the borderland constituencies there are generally strong links to adjacent areas of neighbouring countries where they can benefit from political, economic and cultural support. Compared to their ties with central Myanmar, for many borderland constituencies it has been links with Bangladesh, India, China, Laos and Thailand that are significantly stronger. The cultural and historical ties of many borderlands peoples are relevant. For instance, adjacent to the Shan State borderland constituencies there are hundreds of thousands of Shan-speaking peoples in northern Thailand and southwestern China. The flows of people that have led to this division of the Shan population have not stopped and even today Shan from the Shan State seek new lives across the international frontiers (Farrelly 2009*b*, 2012*a*). Among *Pyidaungsu Hluttaw* representatives the most common second language, after English, is Thai. It is spoken well by at least a dozen members of the 2011–15 legislature.[3] Robust international links are one of the inevitable outcomes. In other places, such as the Chin State, major dialect and cultural variations on the Myanmar side of the border are matched by complicated conditions in Mizoram, the ethnic Chin homeland in northeast India. In fact, in any direction, the blending and blurring of peoples across the borderlands ensures that there are unexpected connections between people who nowadays carry different citizenship. The inconsistency of these connections means it is unreasonable to generalize about the variety of ways that "international", sub-ethnic links are formed.

Third, across the borderlands isolation caused by the sparse infrastructure in the borderlands is reinforced, in a number of ways, by the mountainous terrain. Perhaps the most startling statistics on the borderland constituencies emerge from comparing elevation range. What sets them apart from other areas of the country is that, in general, the range of elevation in the borderlands is much greater. In Myanmar's borderlands, the lowest variation in elevation is found in the two borderland constituencies in Rakhine State, where it is less than 700 metres.[4] At the upper end of the spectrum is Nawngmun in Kachin State where the elevation range is an astounding 5,152 metres. The average range for borderland constituencies is 1,994 metres. For the 330 constituencies in the country as a whole, including the borderlands, the average is 890 metres, an average brought down considerably by the 77 constituencies where the elevation range is less than 100 metres. Based on these Geographic Information System calculations it is also possible to analyse the relative "slopeynesss" of different areas. The average slopeyness of the borderland constituencies has been calculated with a figure of 5.97 based on the steepness of the terrain across the entire set of borderlands constituencies. For the country as a whole, including the borderlands, it is only 2.36. The borderland constituencies are also an average of 568 kilometres from Naypyitaw, with the closest being Bawlakhe in Kayah State only 168 kilometres as the crow flies (but much further by road). This contrasts with the furthest constituency from Naypyitaw, Kawthoung in Tanintharyi, which is 1,099 kilometres from Myanmar's new capital. The national average is 351 kilometres. In summary, it is a much longer and more difficult journey from borderland constituencies to Naypyitaw than it is from other parts of the country.[5]

Fourth, peoples from all parts of Myanmar's borderlands have travelled far from their home areas in search of security and prosperity. There are no good figures on the size of Myanmar's diaspora, but given how many people from the Kayin, Mon, Kachin, Shan, Chin and Rohingya populations have left Myanmar during the twentieth and twenty-first centuries, it is likely that borderland peoples are disproportionately represented in the diaspora.[6] Some have made it as far as Bangkok or Kunming, while there are those, particularly from among the ethnic minorities who have settled elsewhere. Some have made their way to countries like the United States, United Kingdom and Australia. This diaspora presents a different challenge for analysis of borderland politics, and one that is entirely inconsistent and ambiguous. In many cases diasporic populations originally from the borderlands have links to ethnic resistance movements and have continued their activism from abroad. Among this cohort there are significant numbers who sought to downplay the importance of the 2010 election and only reluctantly accepted the prospect of political transition in the country under the leadership of President Thein Sein from 2011 to 2016.

Inevitably, there are some areas outside the borderlands that share all four of these characteristics, yet rarely in such a comprehensive way. The expansive definition of borderlands that I have introduced in this chapter can adequately reconcile that situation. Indeed, by some assessments the entire country deserves an interstitial status, caught uneasily between the giants of India and China, and encouraged to accept influences not only from Thailand and from Bangladesh, but also from the maritime cultures that have developed around the Bay of Bengal and the wider Indian Ocean region. Myanmar fits between a number of different systems of politics, culture, language and society, and has a history of blending and integrating their influences. It is thus reasonable that the borderlands described here also lurch beyond the immediate realm of "the border" to entangle towns and villages far from international frontiers. What they share is a status as borderland constituencies on Myanmar's new political map where some power has been devolved to the voters across the length and breadth of the country. This new delineation of the national geography upends some expectations of the ways that ethnicity conflates with politics, and suggests that we need to be more familiar with the institutional mechanisms that are being used to reshape Myanmar politics.

ELECTORAL SOVEREIGNTY CONSIDERED

The two things that matter for this analysis are the inconsistent range of electoral sovereignty and the scope of the democratic franchise. As the Myanmar people went to the polls in 2010, a new era of public participation in the political process offered some tentative glimpses of what elections may mean for Myanmar's "normality" (Holliday 2013, pp. 93–94). It is those elections that provide an early opportunity to begin conceptualizing Myanmar's borderlands around the idea of electoral sovereignty: an idea that has its genesis in the modest popular contestation that has emerged in politics since the promulgation of the 2008 Constitution. To fully appreciate the subtleties of this process, electoral sovereignty cannot be taken as a categorical status, determined by the inclusion of people who were excluded by the authoritarian system. Electoral sovereignty is, instead, muddled by the fact that in the borderlands the political and the geographical are entwined. The space for political activity has grown at the same time that information on the political processes and sentiments relevant to all of Myanmar's borderlands have become newly available.

So what is the current status of electoral sovereignty in Myanmar's borderlands? To answer this question I introduce data and analysis about population distribution, ethnic complexity and military deployments, before turning to a discussion of the partial enfranchisement of people in Myanmar's borderlands.

Population and Voter Distribution

There are few matters more important to an understanding of electoral sovereignty in Myanmar's borderlands than the number and density of voters in the 330 lower house constituencies. The number of voters is a reasonable indication of political participation and also of the shape of the political geography. Overall, Myanmar's borderlands have the electorates with the lowest populations and where the numbers of voters, at least at the 2010 poll, were also lowest. Such a firm statement is complicated by the fact that population figures in Myanmar are unreliable, a situation only partially rectified by the release of data from the 2014 census. It remains difficult to determine with any confidence how many people live in each of the borderland constituencies. Critics of the census have tended to focus on its conduct in borderland areas (see Transnational Institute 2014). Nonetheless some initial analysis of the high and low voter turnout from 2010 suggests that comparing population and voter distribution between densely populated areas, with very large numbers of voters, and sparsely populated parts of the country is a meaningful exercise. As Chit Win (2013) shows, the number of votes required to win a seat in the borderlands was lower in almost all cases than in non-borderland constituencies. His preliminary data indicates that the lowest number of votes was required in Kayah State with only 7,292.79 votes cast per elected seat, followed by the Chin, Kachin and Kayin states, and then Tanintharyi Region, and the Shan, Mon and Rakhine states. By contrast in Ayeyarwaddy Region, a part of the country that could be considered the antithesis of the borderlands, there were 102,747.55 votes cast per elected *Hluttaw* seat. In general, the flattest, most ethnically homogenous and most Bamar-dominated areas required the largest number of votes to win a seat in the lower house of the *Hluttaw*.

When the contrasting size of constituencies is taken into account, to help understand voter density, the comparison between the borderlands and the rest of the country is even starker. With the cancelled elections excluded from consideration, the voter density across the entire country is 643 per constituency, yet in the borderlands it is only 8.6 (see Table 2.3). This is an astonishing difference and indicates that not only are borderland areas less densely populated but that they are also over-represented, with respect to the number of voters at least. Across the country the average constituency size

TABLE 2.3
Voter Density (per km²) by Party Contesting 2010 General Election

Political party	All Myanmar		Borderlands only	
	Mean	Seats won	Mean	Seats won*
All Mon Region Democracy Party	44.09	3	17.51	1
Chin National Party	3.34	1		0
Chin Progressive Party	3.72	2	3.72	2
Independent	8.33	1		0
Inn National Development Party	56.36	1		0
Kayin People's Party	4.56	1		0
National Democratic Force	6308	8		0
National Unity Party	18.98	13	4.37	2
Phalon-Sawaw Democratic Party	20.16	2	10.14	1
Rakhine Nationals Progressive Party	79	9		0
Shan Nationals Democratic Party	7.23	18	10.58	6
Union Solidarity and Development Party	577	259	7.4	34
Unity and Democracy Party of Kachin State	0.15	1		0
Wa Democratic Party	6.44	2	10.63	1
TOTALS	**510**	**330**	**9.19**	**47**

*Note that elections were only contested in forty-seven of the fifty-two borderland constituencies at the 2010 general election, with voting in the constituencies of Pangsang, Pangwaun, Namphan, Mongla and Mongmao in Shan State cancelled.

is 2,346 square kilometres yet in the borderlands it is almost twice the size at 4,380 square kilometres. The 52 borderland constituencies therefore make up 32.64 per cent of the national territory. These contrasts help to explain how the township boundaries, on which the constituencies are based, are only a very general guide to the optimal delineation of electorates. It is true that in some borderland areas voters were discouraged from participating in the 2010 election, and so there are good reasons to expect that such numbers will increase over time. Yet the formation of constituencies, based as they are on township boundaries, means that there are wild distortions in their size, importance and connectivity. The borderlands constituencies are, in general, among the largest, least dense and most ethnically diverse constituencies in the country. For now, they may also be "over-represented" in Myanmar's legislatures due to the way that the electorate boundaries have been demarcated.

Ethnic Complexity

It is well understood that Myanmar's modern political geography is delimited on ethnic lines: there are seven Bamar-majority regions and seven ethnic minority-majority states. Inevitably, these groups of people have moved around over the decades and by now it is not possible to simply focus on the supposedly dominant ethnic group in any given area. In some notionally "ethnic" places, such as the Shan, Kachin and Mon states, the number of Bamar residents, and voters, is significant. Likewise in Tanintharyi Region, which is defined as Bamar-majority, there are important populations of Mon and Kayin. In the borderlands of Rakhine State, voter registration is an especially fraught issue because of the presence of large numbers of non-Rakhine Muslims, many of whom were enfranchised in the 2010 election by virtue of their identity cards (see Ei Ei Toe Lwin 2013). The complexity of the ethnic landscape has not been fully assessed, and it will take the 2014 census, and perhaps a further census in the decade ahead, and subsequent analysis of all data, to determine more effectively the distribution of ethnic groups and its implications for electoral sovereignty.

The complexity of ethnic distribution is especially relevant to the variety of ways that electoral sovereignty has been claimed in borderland areas. In many places there are relatively few voters, and in 2010 they opted to support the USDP. In such constituencies where there was little electoral competition, the USDP polled well, securing relatively large margins of victory. Among the 52 constituencies examined in this chapter, there are only 7 that could be considered close contests in 2010, where the margin of victory was less than 5 per cent (Momauk, Khaunglanhpu and Tsawlaw in Kachin State; Madupi in Chin State; Tachileik in Shan State; Tanintharyi in Tanintharyi Region, and Buthidaung in Rakhine State). There were a total of 29 such constituencies around the country. In more stable political systems these might be considered "marginal" seats. In the borderlands, the USDP won 5 of these closely contested constituencies. At the other end of the spectrum there were 3 constituencies that saw a margin of victory greater than 80 per cent. These were Bawlakhe and Mese in Kayah State, won by the USDP against meek National Unity Party competition, and Hopang in the Shan State which was won by the Wa Democratic Party with more than 90 per cent of the vote. In Hopang the USDP did not contest the election against the two local Wa candidates.

In all cases, the ethnic character of these contests, whether they had close results or not, needs to be examined closely. The USDP has consistently run "ethnic" candidates in these borderland areas. Now that they are all living together in the USDP guesthouse in Naypyitaw, it is very apparent that this strategy of ethnic inclusion paid dividends. Naypyitaw had anticipated that a contest for control of borderland areas would shape the outcome of the 2015 election. Looking close at a broader range of borderlands seats where there were real contests in 2010 leads to some further conclusions. Importantly, in the 2010 election voters in the borderlands tended to support the USDP over the explicitly "ethnic" alternatives. To illustrate this point it is helpful to describe the situation in one of the few constituencies where the USDP did not win. In this case it was up against the Shan Nationals Democratic Party's Zaw Tun, a twenty-six-year-old Shan farmer contesting the constituency of Momauk. This was the most fiercely contested election in any of the borderland constituencies, with a final margin of less than 1 per cent. Against the USDP's Yone Mu, who is ethnic Chinese, there were, in the final count, only 164 votes separating the candidates. It is not surprising that this contest generated claims of electoral impropriety (Democratic Voice of Burma 2010).

Military Deployments

A careful examination of the deployment of the Myanmar Government's Army, Navy and Air Force units indicates, somewhat unsurprisingly, that there are very significant numbers of military personnel in border areas, and adjacent constituencies (see Figure 2.3). The fact that Myanmar's borderlands have long histories of instability and insurgency explains some of these deployments. From the south, where the New Mon State Party/ Mon National Liberation Army has long opposed Myanmar rule (South 2003, pp. 35–49), to the far north where the Kachin Independence Army/ Organization has fought since 1961 (Farrelly 2012*b*, pp. 55–56), there are significant pockets in Myanmar's borderlands where ethnic resistance movements have flourished. Ready re-supply and sanctuary in neighbouring countries, especially Thailand and China, has given the most significant armed groups certain operational advantages (see Figure 2.4 for details on recent conflict hotspots). From the key Kachin, Wa, Shan, Kayah, Kayin and Mon rebel bases it is usually only a short walk to the neighbouring country. In some cases members of the *Hluttaw* elected in 2010 have strong professional and family links to non-government armed groups. Earlier in their lives, some have even been charged with crimes related to their armed insurgency. While China and Thailand have often tolerated the presence of these armed groups, and have benefited from servicing their economic and political requirements, there is increasing hesitancy about the role these bases play.

FIGURE 2.3
Map of Concentration of Military Installations in Myanmar

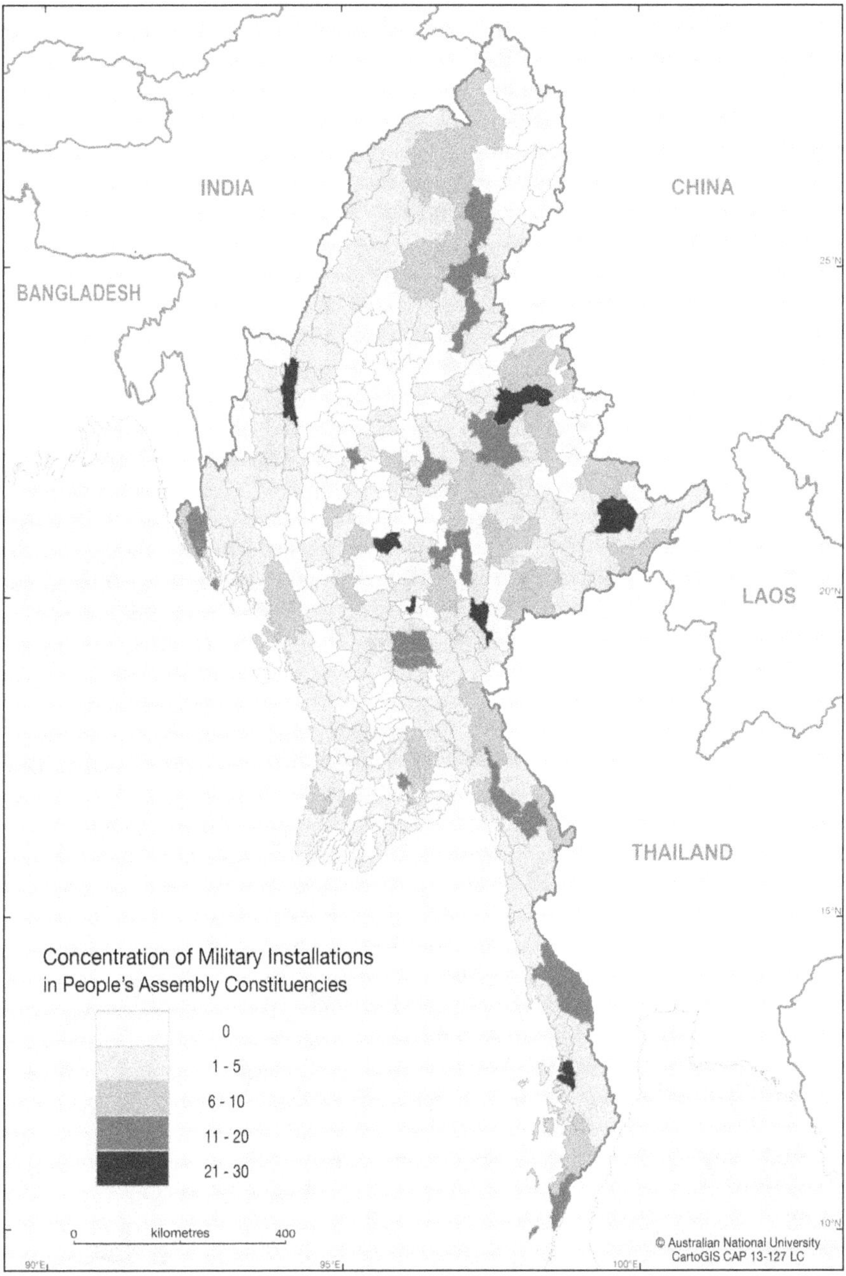

Concentration of Military Installations
in People's Assembly Constituencies

- 0
- 1 - 5
- 6 - 10
- 11 - 20
- 21 - 30

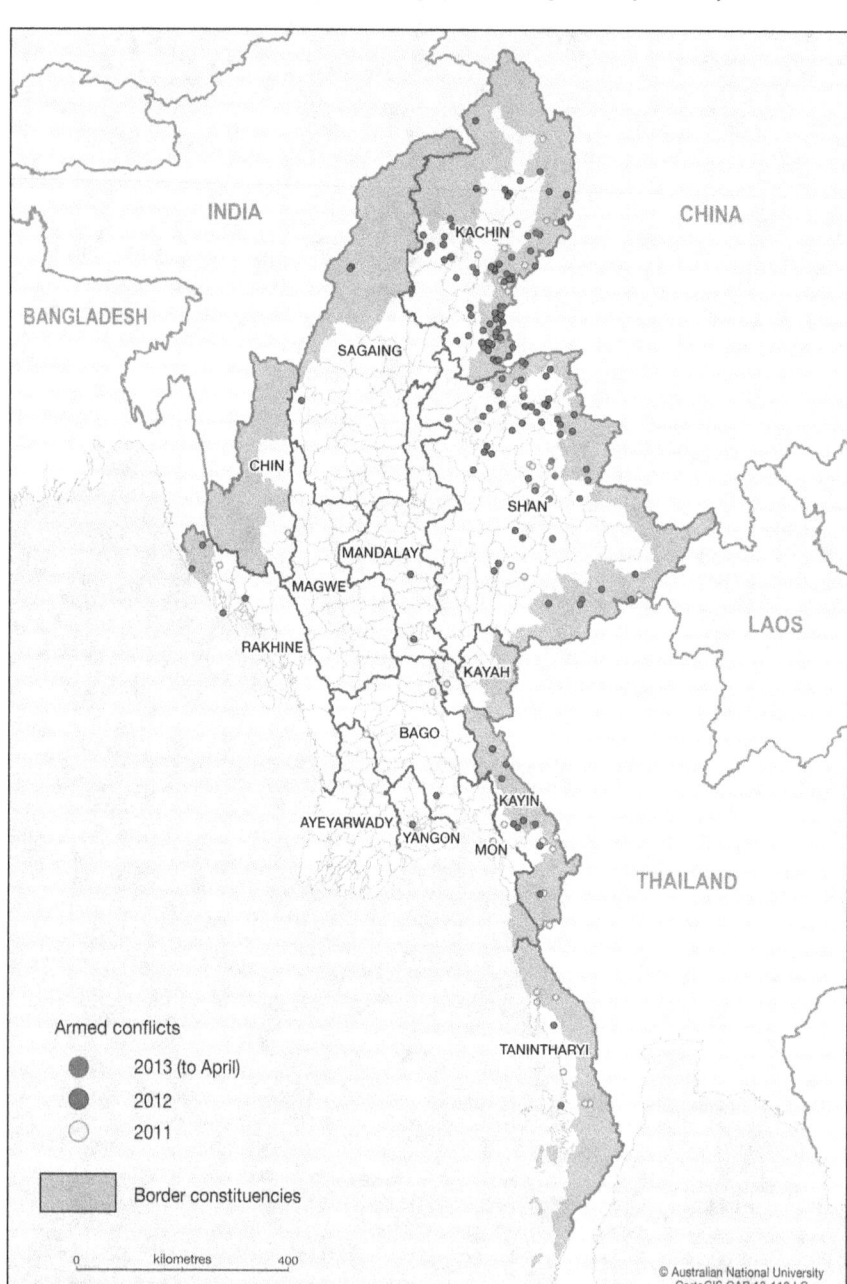

FIGURE 2.4
Map of Incidents of Armed Conflict in Myanmar (2011–13)

ELECTORAL SOVEREIGNTY IN MYANMAR'S BORDERLANDS 61

FIGURE 2.5
Map of Myanmar's Border and Coastal Trade Zones

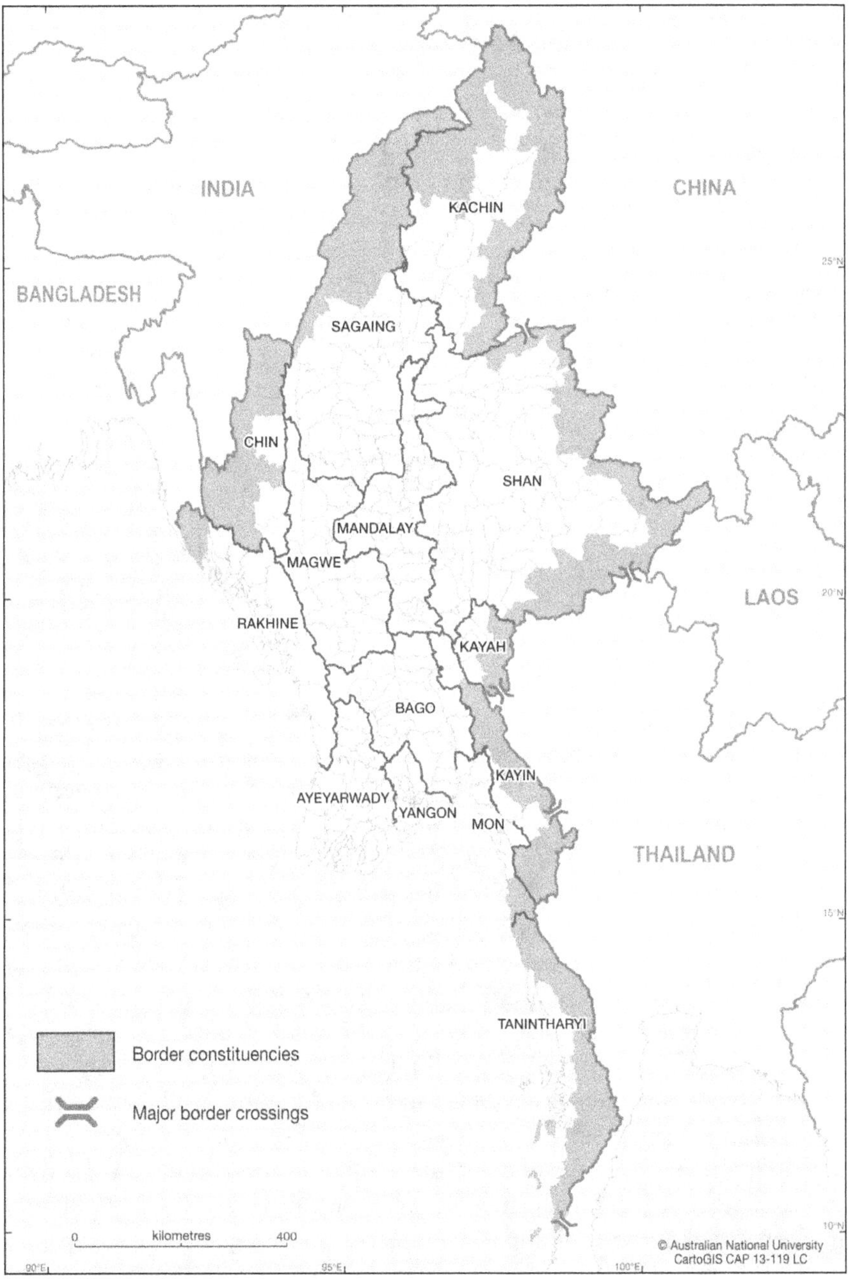

Taking the constituencies immediately adjacent to the borderlands into consideration demonstrates that there are at least two dozen significant military bases along the borders with Thailand and China, with a number also close to the Indian and Bangladesh borders. In other cases, the border areas are near strategic communication or transportation nodes (see Figure 2.5). In some parts of the country the deployment of Myanmar Army personnel has begun to be unwound, with forward deployed forces retreating to their bases under the auspices of new ceasefire agreements. A further process of incremental decentralization and civilianization is an important trend in the borderlands. It is apparent that the fundamental challenge for the government is to convince ethnic armed groups of the overall integrity of the electoral process. In parts of the borderlands where government control has been enforced by roaming Myanmar Army units and by the fixed outposts they have established at strategic locations, it will be difficult to persuade local people that the changes occurring are in their best interests. Scepticism of the Myanmar Government and its army is very strong across the borderlands, and will require careful, long-term management. If such military deployments remain a significant part of borderland life, electoral sovereignty will be diminished and incomplete.

POPULAR ENFRANCHISEMENT

This chapter has discussed how the 2008 Constitution provides the people of Myanmar with strong indications that they will be enfranchised to choose their own leadership at the regional and national level. The 2010 general election was the first opportunity to see this process in action and while it was a disappointment for those seeking democratic transformation, it had a more profound impact on the reshaping of the national political geography. That new geography is predicated on the 330 townships at the lower house level of the national legislature. These constituencies should serve to enfranchise Myanmar's people in ways that change some of the most fundamental preconceptions about Myanmar politics. To provide a framework for understanding the limitations of electoral sovereignty in the fifty-two constituencies of Myanmar's borderlands I will explore three key obstacles to popular enfranchisement in these areas.

First, there is the issue of constituency size. In this context it is prudent to be aware that vast disparities between electorate size and population have emerged. In general, the electorates with the largest populations are in densely populated urban areas; they are also the smallest. The largest electorates by population have over 300,000 people, while the smallest has around 1,000. Many of the electorates with the lowest populations are in the borderlands, especially in Kayah, Chin, Kachin and Shan states. There is a noticeable and concomitant "devaluing" of the votes of those who live in Myanmar's flatlands, particularly in Ayeyarwady, Magwe and Mandalay.[7] Reconfiguring this system could have the effect of disempowering ethnic minority peoples in remote borderland areas. The alternative would be to find more equitable ways of representing the majority Bamar population. The vast distances in some sparsely populated constituencies are a further issue for the consolidation of electoral sovereignty. When Thomas Kean (2013) from *The Myanmar Times* asked one Kachin State *Hluttaw* representative about the challenges he faces meeting constituents, he said:

> Kawnglanghpu is very hard to reach, because you have to walk twenty days to reach the edge [of the township] and if you tour around the villagers and come back, you have to take at least two months so I couldn't go back yet…There are no proper roads, just jungle tracks, lots of leeches and wild animals. Not many people want to go there; only my relatives are willing to accompany us.

Until there are better transportation links, these remote towns and villages will remain isolated and easy to ignore. In this case the elected representative suggested "the central government couldn't reach our people" (Kean 2013). With steep, broken terrain the logistical challenge for many borderland constituencies is yet to be fully understood in the national political conversation.

Second, there is the general issue of ensuring that political campaigns can be undertaken freely in borderland areas in ways that fully enfranchise those eligible to vote. The legacy of ethnic conflict in most of the places discussed in this chapter is clearly relevant and there are expectations that violence will continue in some places. Such violence needs to be seen in the context of the deployment of significant government security forces to the borderlands. These forces, usually consolidated in the major towns, dampened the prospect of non-USDP political success in the 2010 election and in 2015 they will again serve both political and security functions. The future of fuller electoral sovereignty in ethnic areas will rely on integration of the diverse peoples that live in these places, irrespective of their histories of resistance to central government control. Adequate funding for political campaigns will be required to ensure that candidates can travel to remote villages to support their political agendas. In 2010 it is apparent that the campaigning in many borderland constituencies was particularly inadequate and partial. The need to count votes from such areas is a further logistical, financial and administrative challenge. In some areas literacy in Burmese may be a final obstacle to the active political participation of borderland peoples.

Third, there is the challenge of garnering acceptance for the 2008 Constitution among ethnic minorities and their leaders. While there is no opinion polling or other evidence that can be used to make the point, it appears likely that Myanmar's borderland constituencies are among those parts of the country where dissatisfaction with the current political process is highest. In 2010 many political contests were conducted under conditions where the spectre of further violence was all too apparent. It is inevitable that people were anxious. During visits to the Kachin and Rakhine borderlands in early 2014 there was widespread hesitation about the value of the current political transformation. Some queried whether anything had changed. Even today many people in the borderlands embrace their marginal status in Myanmar, using it as further justification to call for more radical changes to the structures of governance and power. Their integration into the national mainstream has remained incomplete, with education, media and other forms of mass engagement only arriving in many areas during recent decades. Given the country's history it is inevitable that disaffection from the national "mainstream" will be a significant issue for many years to come. Many borderland people feel that they may need to take advantage of any future opportunities to opt out of the Myanmar political process through further armed struggle or popular boycotts.

It is that persistent threat to secede or otherwise disavow the institutions of Myanmar's national politics that diminishes the chance of electoral sovereignty being fully consummated in the borderlands. The partial character of electoral involvement, and the major obstacles to the further enmeshment of borderland peoples, will be the fundamental challenge for future Myanmar governments. It is from the borderlands that the major ethnic resistance movements draw their strength and it is from these same regions that so much of Myanmar's economic potential will emerge. Providing sufficient incentive for the inclusion of all Myanmar peoples in the national political system has been a long-term problem. Any future Myanmar government, even one spearheaded by Aung San Suu Kyi's National League for Democracy, will face the conundrum of managing such histories of conflict, intolerance and distrust. Arguably the most damaging threats to Myanmar's nascent democracy are those that will ferment alongside the dissatisfaction and grievance of the frontiers. Expanding electoral sovereignty to all of these areas, providing a basis for political competition, and implementing protocols for peaceful and tolerant discussion, will be preoccupations for a generation to come.

CONCLUSIONS ON BORDERLAND POLITICS

Unresolved debates about constituency formation and electoral process hint at the challenges being generated for Myanmar's political parties and the borderland peoples they seek to represent. If we assume that the political configuration is likely to continue being re-shaped then the lessons that can be drawn from the border areas are especially important. The borderlands are crucial to the formation of a new political consensus about Myanmar's political institutions. If, as seems likely, the peoples of the borderlands do not respond positively to the processes of integration underway then the 2008 Constitution, and its framework for political participation, will require revision. In 2014 discussion of constitutional review became bolder: major changes seem likely. Those changes will be an important part of the country's transformation, with sentiments in the borderlands helping to motivate the necessary reforms. Nonetheless, the borderland constituencies will require sustained attention in ways that the "ethnic" areas more generally, may not. It is in the borderlands that isolation from the centralizing force of Myanmar society is most apparent. And not only are many of the people of the borderlands isolated from central Myanmar, they are often separated, by geography and sometimes by instinct, from each other. Where strong connections exist in Myanmar's borderlands they tend to pull, inconsistently, towards the neighbouring nation states. That so many people from these areas have sought sanctuary and economic opportunity in Thailand, China, India and Bangladesh is a strong indication of the vibrant ties that exist.

Experiences of democratic government in three of those countries — Thailand, India and Bangladesh — imply that, in the long-term, the integration of ethnic minority peoples will be a contested process. Among the neighbours, and in areas adjacent to Myanmar, there are recent histories of sporadic local-level political strife under conditions where there are regular and predictable elections. The traumatic experiences of northeast India suggest that vibrant democratic institutions do not necessarily neuter the appeal of resistance to central government rule. The Indian Government has struggled to generate a political or economic structure that adequately resolves the long-held claims for autonomy and independence in that region (see the discussion in Farrelly 2009b). It is possible that the overall picture of political inclusion in Myanmar will prove more benign, yet that would counter decades of practice and prejudice. The implications of today's incomplete electoral sovereignty in Myanmar's borderlands are stark in a context where political negotiation has historically been accompanied by violence and retribution. To adequately include the peoples of the borderlands in Myanmar's new quasi-democratic system will require new imagination.

Indeed, integrating Myanmar's diverse peoples into a system that gives them sufficient voice in the national conversation will be a permanent conundrum. From the perspective of ethnically Bamar powerbrokers in Naypyitaw, it will not be possible to acquiesce to all of the demands of borderland leaders and instead there will be a need to design more adequately a system that recognizes the complexity of the ongoing discussions about population, ethnic classification, military deployments and popular enfranchisement. Yet bringing all of Myanmar's peoples together in the one system is an historic opportunity. For now it is the proxies of the USDP who ran for election in the borderlands who are taking on representative responsibilities in Naypyitaw. Many of these technocratic representatives, often drawn from the ranks of schoolteachers and local officials, were not re-elected. They may well be replaced by politicians who present a much more aggressive attitude towards the development of their local areas. Until then, the current phase of nascent democratization offers a chance for rethinking how Myanmar society interacts with its borderlands. The fifty-two constituencies discussed in this chapter are crucial. For now, the prevailing deficit of electoral sovereignty is matched by the paucity of investment in borderland infrastructure and the types of connections, physical and emotional, that will need to be built between these areas and central Myanmar. Without that infrastructure — in its political, economic and cultural forms — Myanmar will struggle to find the right balance between local difference and national solidarity.

Notes

1. The borderland constituencies relevant to an analysis of the upper house of Myanmar's Parliament (the *Amyotha Hluttaw*) are beyond the scope of this chapter. For reference, the upper house has 168 elected constituencies of which forty-four constituencies share an international border. The two houses constitute the *Pyidaungsu Hluttaw* (Union Assembly) which meets on a regular basis as the country's supreme legislative body.
2. This chapter benefits from the outstanding technical support of Lauren Carter, Kay Dancey and Karina Pelling in the ANU College of Asia and the Pacific. Their cartographical skills proved invaluable for the analysis offered here. Chit Win also has my thanks for sharing his insights about electoral politics in Myanmar's borderlands, especially with respect to the background of some key Members of Parliament. The production of this chapter was supported by an Australian Research Council DECRA fellowship.
3. This is not a scientific count but is based on discussions with *Pyidaungsu Hluttaw* representatives during field research from January to April 2014 in Naypyitaw. Some MPs speak fluent Thai, usually as a result of strong cultural and economic connections on the other side of the border. Naturally, those legislators with such

language skills usually represent parts of Shan, Kayah, Kayin or Mon State, or Tanintharyi Region.
4. Although, in this sense, elevation range can prove a deceptive measure: these areas of Rakhine State are divided from the rest of Myanmar by significant mountains elsewhere in Rakhine State. Poor road conditions add to their isolation. To travel overland from Maungdaw to Naypyitaw requires around thirty hours of continuous motorized travel in 2014's road conditions.
5. With these observations in mind I have previously sought to create a more scientific "isolation index" for Myanmar. That work will be presented at a future opportunity once some of its current inadequacies can be rectified through computational techniques, or otherwise.
6. Interactions with members of the Myanmar diaspora in Singapore, Malaysia and Thailand suggest that peoples from the borderlands are significantly over-represented among the populations that have migrated in the past generation. There is a chance that the data on migration that will emerge from Myanmar's 2014 census will help to clarify the rough outlines of the Myanmar population outside the country, perhaps with some appreciation of "ethnic" breakdown.
7. I am grateful to Chit Win for his efforts to analyse the numbers relevant to the observations made in this paragraph. His forthcoming work will present a fuller appraisal of the variety of ways that constituency sizes have been distorted in Myanmar's current electoral geography.

References

Ball, Desmond. *The Boys in Black: The Thahan Phran (Rangers), Thailand's Para-military Border Guards*. Bangkok: White Lotus, 2004.

———. *Tor Chor Dor: Thailand's Border Patrol Police*. Bangkok: White Lotus, 2013.

Boutry, Maxime. "Les frontieres <mouvantes> de Birmanie" [The 'Moving' Frontiers of Burma]. *Moussons. Recherche en Sciences Humaines Sur l'Asie du Sud-Est*, no. 17 (2011): 15–23.

Buchanan, John, Tom Kramer and Kevin Woods. "Developing Disparity: Regional Investment in Burma's Borderlands". Amsterdam: Transnational Institute and Burma Centre Netherlands, 2013.

Carrapiett, William James Sherlock. *The Kachin Tribes of Burma*. Yangon: Government Printing, 1929.

Chit Su. "Chin State Facing Food Shortage after Rains". In *The Myanmar Times*, 14 October 2013 <http://www.mmtimes.com/index.php/national-news/8483-chin-state-facing-food-shortage-after-rains.html> (accessed 26 October 2013).

Chit Win. "Unpublished Data Associated with PhD Project". Canberra: Australian National University, September 2013.

Democratic Voice of Burma (DVB). "Electioneering Scandals Plague USDP", 21 October 2010 <http://www.dvb.no/elections/electioneering-scandals-plague-usdp/12334> (accessed 26 October 2013).

Ei Ei Toe Lwin. "Rakhine Parties Clash Over ID issue". In *The Myanmar Times*,

15 October 2013 <http://www.mmtimes.com/index.php/national-news/8492-rakhine-parties-clash-over-id-issue.html> (accessed 26 October 2013).

Falla, Jonathan. *True Love and Bartholomew: Rebels on the Burmese Border.* Cambridge: Cambridge University Press, 1991.

Farrelly, Nicholas. "'AK47/M16 Rifle — Rs. 15,000 each': What Price Peace on the Indo-Burmese Frontier?" *Contemporary South Asia* 17, no. 3 (2009a): 283–97.

———. "Tai Community and Thai Border Subversions". In *Tai Lands and Thailand: Community and State in Mainland Southeast Asia*, edited by Andrew Walker. Singapore: Nordic Institute of Asian Studies (NIAS) Press, 2009b, pp. 64–83.

———. "Exploitation and Escape: Journeys Across the Burma-Thailand Frontier". In *Labour Migration and Human Trafficking in Southeast Asia: Critical Perspectives*, edited by Michele Ford, Lenore Lyons and Willem van Schendel. Oxford: Routledge, 2012a, pp. 130–48.

———. "Ceasing Ceasefire? Kachin Politics Beyond the Stalemates". In *Myanmar's Transition Openings, Obstacles and Opportunities*, edited by Nick Cheesman, Monique Skidmore and Trevor Wilson. Singapore: Institute of Southeast Asian Studies (ISEAS), 2012b, pp. 53–71.

Grundy-Warr, Carl, and Elaine Wong Siew Yin. "Geographies of Displacement: The Karenni and the Shan across the Myanmar-Thailand border". *Singapore Journal of Tropical Geography* 23, no. 1 (2002): 93–122.

Grundy-Warr, Carl and Karin Dean. "The Boundaries of Contested Identities: 'Kachin' and 'Karenni' Spaces in the Troubled Borderlands of Burma". In *Routing Borders between Territories, Discourses and Practices*, edited by Eiki Berg and Henk van Houtum. Aldershot: Ashgate, 2003, pp. 75–96.

Hla Hla Htay. "UWSA Flexes Muscles in Bid for Legitimacy". In *The Myanmar Times*, 28 May 2013 <http://www.mmtimes.com/index.php/national-news/6916-wa-flexes-muscles-in-bid-for-legitimacy.html> (accessed 7 October 2013).

Holliday, Ian. "Myanmar in 2012: Toward a Normal State". *Asian Survey* 53, no. 1 (2013): 93–100.

Jacob, Jabin T. *The India-Myanmar Borderlands: Guns, Blankets and Bird Flu.* Bordeaux: Science Politique Relations Internationales Territoire, 2010.

Kean, Thomas. "In Myanmar's Parliament, Far from Home". In *The Myanmar Times*, 14 January 2013 <http://www.mmtimes.com/index.php/national-news/3735-in-the-hluttaw-far-from-home.html> (accessed 26 October 2013).

Leach, Edmund R. *Political Systems of Highland Burma: A Study of Kachin Social Structure.* London: The Athlone Press, 1954.

———. "The Frontiers of 'Burma'". *Comparative Studies in Society and History* 3, no. 1 (1960): 49–68.

Lee Sang Kook. "Scattered but Connected: Karen Refugees' Networking in and Beyond the Thailand-Burma Borderland". *Asian and Pacific Migration Journal* 21, no. 2 (2012): 263–85.

Lieberman, Victor B. "Ethnic Politics in Eighteenth-Century Burma". *Modern Asian Studies* 12, no. 3 (1978): 455–82.

Lintner, Bertil. *Great Game East: India, China and the Struggle for Asia's Most Volatile Frontier*. New Delhi: Harper Collins, 2012.
Robinne, Francois and Mandy Sadan, eds. *Social Dynamics in the Highlands of Southeast Asia: Reconsidering Political Systems of Highland Burma*. Leiden: Brill, 2007.
Roughneen, Simon. "Sanctioned Firms Listed Among Burma's Top Taxpayers". In *The Irrawaddy*, 17 September 2013 <http://www.irrawaddy.org/economy/sanctioned-firms-listed-among-burmas-top-taxpayers.html> (accessed 6 October 2013).
Sadan, Mandy. *Being and Becoming Kachin: Histories beyond the State in the Borderworlds of Burma*. Oxford: Oxford University Press, 2013.
Scott, James C. *The Art of not being Governed: An Anarchist History of Upland Southeast Asia*. New Haven: Yale University Press, 2009.
South, Ashley. *Mon Nationalism and Civil War in Burma: The Golden Sheldrake*. London: RoutledgeCurzon, 2003.
Sturgeon, Janet C. "Border Practices, Boundaries, and the Control of Resource Access: A Case from China, Thailand and Burma". *Development and Change* 35, no. 3 (2004): 463–84.
Temple, Richard Carnac. "The People of Burma". *Journal of the Royal Society of Arts* 58, no. 3003 (1910): 695–711.
Thant Myint-U. *Where China Meets India: Burma and the New Crossroads of Asia*. London: Faber and Faber, 2011.
Thornton, Phil. *Restless Souls: Rebels, Refugees, Medics, and Misfits on the Thai-Burma Border*. Bangkok: Asia Books, 2006.
Transnational Institute (TNI). "Ethnicity without Meaning, Data without Context: The 2014 Census, Identity and Citizenship in Burma/Myanmar". Amsterdam: Burma Centrum Nederland and Transnational Institute, 2014.
Van Schendel, Willem. *The Bengal Borderland: Beyond State and Nation in South Asia*. London: Anthem Press, 2004.
Walker, Andrew. *The Legend of the Golden Boat: Regulation, Trade and Traders in the Borderlands of Laos, Thailand, China and Burma*. Honolulu: University of Hawaii Press, 1999.
Woods, Kevin. "Ceasefire Capitalism: Military–Private Partnerships, Resource Concessions and Military–State Building in the Burma–China Borderlands". *Journal of Peasant Studies* 38, no. 4 (2011): 747–70.

3

The Maritime Frontier of Myanmar: Challenges in the Early 21st Century

Maung Aung Myoe

Myanmar, geographically located at the junction of South, Southeast, and East Asia, shares common maritime boundaries with Bangladesh in the northeast of the Bay of Bengal, with Thailand and India in the Andaman Sea. From the mouth of the Naf River to Kawthaung (Bayint Naung Point), Myanmar has a 2,228-kilometre (1,385-mile) coastline. The coastline consists of three sections: the Rakhine coastline of 713 kilometres (443 miles), the Ayeyarwady Delta coastline of 437 kilometres (272 miles), and the Tanintharyi coastline of 1,078 kilometres (670 miles). On land, the coastline is shared by six administrative states or regions in Myanmar, namely, Rakhine State, Ayeyarwady Region, Yangon Region, Bago Region, Mon State and Tanintharyi Region. After the declaration of the Territorial Sea and Straight Baseline in 1968, Myanmar promulgated its Territorial Sea and Maritime Zones Law in 1977, prior to the conclusion of the 1982 United Nations Convention on the Law of the Sea (UNCLOS). Myanmar then signed the UNCLOS and ratified it on 21 May 1996, after which it came into effect on 20 June 1996. In accordance with Article 76 (paragraph 8) of the UNCLOS, on 16 December 2008, Myanmar submitted information on the limits of the continental shelf beyond 200 nautical miles from the baselines to the Commission on the Limits of the Continental Shelf. Myanmar has 29,043 square nautical miles of internal waters and 9,895 square nautical miles of territorial waters (please see Table 3.1 for more details). There are 852 big and small islands in Myanmar waters.

This chapter describes the challenges posed by domestic contenders and foreign entities on the Myanmar state's authority, management and

TABLE 3.1
Myanmar Waters

No.	Myanmar Waters	Square Nautical Miles
A	Internal Waters (shore to baselines)	29,043.6380
B	Territorial Sea Waters (baseline to TS line)	9,895.1860
C	Contiguous Zone (TS line to CZ line)	9,879.7018
D	Exclusive Economic Zone (CZ line to Exclusive Economic Zone line)	92,392.1250
	TOTAL MYANMAR WATERS	**141,210.6508**

Source: Ministry of Defence

control of the maritime frontier, highlighting the many actors involved in making and unmaking the frontier in Myanmar waters. In addition, it looks at the emerging politics of resource control between the central and local/regional governments, for the first time in Myanmar at least since 1962. Using two types of natural resources located in Myanmar waters as examples — fish stocks and hydrocarbon reserves — this chapter describes and analyses the way in which the exploitation of natural resources affects local and central politics, people's livelihoods and the forms of collusion between business and government. Moreover, it examines why and how the Myanmar state makes use of its maritime frontier, in terms of both location and resources, to its political advantage. It ends by arguing that, within the last two decades, the Myanmar state has been increasingly capable of managing its water frontier and effectively making use of it in its conduct of foreign relations. Moreover, the geopolitical significance of its maritime frontier will make Myanmar an important player in East Asian regional politics.

CHALLENGES IN THE MARITIME FRONTIER

Since the Myanmar Government rarely publicizes challenges in Myanmar maritime frontiers, it is difficult to know the real extent of the problems. In fact, there are many issues, and some are serious, that the Myanmar Government needs to address in the context of security in its maritime frontier. These include the lack of law and order (in the form of insurgency) in the coastal waters, maritime territorial dispute with Thailand, human trafficking (including the Rohingya issue), illegal, unreported and unregulated (IUU) fishing, and so on. Until March 2012, this included Myanmar's maritime territorial dispute with Bangladesh, which was settled by the decision of the International Tribunal for the Law of the Sea (ITLOS) on 14 March 2012.

Historically, like their counterparts on land, state institutions have been weak in enforcing the maritime frontier. Both local challengers and external entities have always contested the state authorities in Myanmar waters. Until recently, it appeared that anti-government organizations operated in coastal waters and its adjacent areas. Even when an area is clear of insurgent activities, there are attempts by some insurgent organizations to (re)establish their operation bases. One example is the Ayeyarwady Delta region. As the delta is politically and militarily important, both state security forces and insurgents have tried to maintain their presence. In fact, the *Tatmadaw* (Myanmar Armed Forces) initiated a number of military operations to clear insurgents in the delta and to make it a hard-core support base for government security forces.

According to statistics provided by the *Tatmadaw*, a total of 1,015 state security personnel (soldiers, polices, and people's militias) lost their lives in the twelve years between 1962 and 1974, to make the delta an insurgent-free area (South West Command 1995). Yet, at least a couple of times in the past, some insurgent organizations have tried to infiltrate the delta and to (re)establish strongholds. In the 1970s, this was accomplished by the anti-government forces of the Patriotic Liberation Army (PLA), the military wing of former Prime Minister U Nu-led People's Democratic Party (PDP), later renamed the People's Patriotic Party (PPP). On 23 September 1972, a special PLA unit of about thirty-four men ventured across the Gulf of Martaban to Ayeyarwady Delta, via Ranong (in Thailand), to (re)establish their foothold and operation bases. However, the attempt failed utterly in the face of the *Tatmadaw*'s counter-insurgency (Smith 1999, p. 291; Tin Maung Win 2000; A Tatmadaw Researcher 1991, pp. 101–05).[1] The *Tatmadaw* launched a military operation codenamed "Htaw Paing" from 27 September to 21 October 1972, and captured all the infiltrators, dead and alive. A similar attempt was made almost twenty years later. In 1991, several Karen National Liberation Army (KNLA) troops infiltrated the Ayeyarwady Delta to (re)establish strongholds. In October 1991, it was recorded that 345 KNLA insurgents infiltrated Bogale Township, Ayeyarwady Division. The *Tatmadaw* launched "Operation Mone-Daing" on 3 October, under the supervision of the South West Command, and No. 11 Light Infantry Division to carry out a zoning operation. The Air Force also provided troop transportation and strafing with its gunships. About

34,000 villagers were mobilized for this operation. By the end of October, 247 insurgents were killed and six captured alive. This was followed by a mopping-up operation. By the end of the year, the *Tatmadaw* had killed 317 insurgents and captured twenty-five alive; three had surrendered.

Probably since the early days of its post-colonial era, various anti-government organizations, most of which are armed illegally, have operated in Myanmar's coastal waters. Various reports produced by the government indicated that insurgents collected "protection money" from, or taxed, local villagers and business people for their business activities in Myanmar (coastal) waters, which included illegal trade. A recent publication by a former student activist revealed this fact. In the aftermath of the 1988 uprising, soon after the military takeover of the state, many student activists went to the Myanmar-Thai border and took up arms against the newly constituted military government. They formed the All Burma Students' Democratic Front (ABSDF) and engaged in armed struggle against the military government, which came to power in September 1988. The ABSDF had a military column for maritime operations, basically to collect protection money mostly from Thai fishing boats, which had permission to fish in Myanmar waters (Htet Aung Kyaw 2013, pp. 219–20). Other insurgent groups are also involved in the collection of protection money (or what they call revenue) from fishing trawlers. For example, in late 1993, the combined group of various insurgent groups collected between 5,000 baht to 30,000 baht (US$140–US$840) per boat, depending on size. It appeared that various anti-government armed groups operated in Myanmar waters (Htet Aung Kyaw 2013, pp. 319–20). These facts testify to the general state of weak law and order in the maritime frontier. Local people are subjected to political contestation between the government and anti-government forces.

Acting on the intelligence provided by the Indian military in April 1998, a *Tatmadaw* column conducted an operation on Christie Island, the maritime boundary between Myanmar and Thailand, to capture an arms stockpile. The column seized a few dozen mostly outdated rifles and ammunition, but at the same time it found fifty-eight civilians who did not know that the island was a military restricted zone. While the forces understood that these people were innocent civilians collecting wood and bamboo from nearby villages, they were ordered by the Commander-in-Chief Office to eliminate all the civilians. The list of victims included an infant, children, women including a pregnant woman, and men. A few weeks later, a Myanmar naval task force arrested twenty-two Myanmar and Thai nationals fishing illegally in nearby waters. Once again, all twenty-one persons were killed and the fishing trawler was sunk.

Maritime Disputes with Thailand

Myanmar and Thailand share a maritime boundary in the Andaman Sea that is 142 nautical miles long.[2] An agreement to delineate the maritime boundary was signed on 25 July 1980 and was ratified on 14 February 1982 but the sovereignty over three islands at the mouth of the Pakchan River has remained unresolved (see Figure 3.1). Although there were no specific meetings or negotiations on the issue of the three islands, it was brought up from time to time at various meetings. The two countries finally declared the three islands a "no man's land" and the issue has remained a source of tension, which led to a series of naval confrontations and clashes in late 1998 and again in 2003. So far the problem of the three islands remains unsettled. Due to this undemarcated maritime boundary, there are several naval clashes in the disputed area. The latest one occurred on 21 September 2013 when the Royal Thai Navy claimed that a Burmese gunboat opened fire on a Thai fishing trawler in the waters claimed by Thais (Maung Aung Myoe 2012).

FIGURE 3.1
Map Showing Location of Three Islands under Dispute

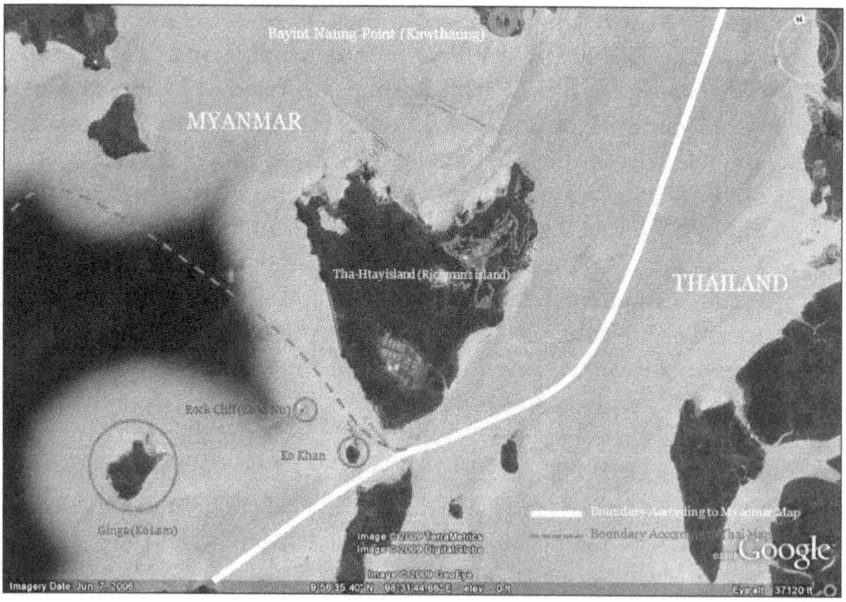

Source: Adaptation of image downloaded from Google Maps.

Maritime Dispute with Bangladesh

The Myanmar-Bangladesh boundary measures approximately 168.5 miles (271 kilometres), including the Naf River boundary of about 39.8 miles (64 kilometres). While the land and river boundary had been demarcated in accordance with the international law of state succession, the maritime boundary demarcation remained problematic until March 2012 when the International Tribunal for the Law of the Sea (ITLOS) passed a judgement (see Maung Aung Myoe 2012). The judgement, dated 14 March 2012, brought a win-win situation for both countries. However, due to the application of the method of adjusted equidistance line for demarcation, to reach an "equitable solution" to address the issue of concavity of the Bangladesh coastline, there appeared a grey area, "where the adjusted equidistance line used for delimitation of the continental shelf goes beyond 200 nm off Bangladesh and continues until it reaches 200 nm off Myanmar (International Tribunal for the Law of the Sea 2014, paragraph 464)." The judgement stated:

> The grey area arises as a consequence of delimitation. Any delimitation may give rise to complex legal and practical problems, such as those involving transboundary resources. It is not unusual in such cases for States to enter into agreements or cooperative arrangements to deal with problems resulting from the delimitation.
>
> Accordingly, in the area beyond Bangladesh's exclusive economic zone that is within the limits of Myanmar's exclusive economic zone, the maritime boundary delimits the Parties' rights with respect to the seabed and subsoil of the continental shelf but does not otherwise limit Myanmar's rights with respect to the exclusive economic zone, notably those with respect to the superjacent waters.
>
> There are many ways in which the parties may ensure the discharge of their obligations in this respect, including the conclusion of specific agreements or the establishment of appropriate arrangements. It is for the Parties to determine the measures that they consider appropriate for this purpose (International Tribunal for the Law of the Sea 2014, paragraphs 472, 474, and 476).

In simple terms, in the grey area, as part of its Exclusive Economic Zone, Myanmar has the right to explore and exploit natural resources, both living and non-living, of the waters superjacent to the seabed, of the seabed, and its subsoil as well as the airspace above the water. However, for Bangladesh, as part of its continental shelf, it has rights related only to the seabed and subsoil. Now, with the judgement passed by the Permanent Court of

Arbitration on 7 July 2014 on the India-Bangladesh maritime boundary dispute, there is an overlapping grey area between Myanmar, Bangladesh and India, with implications on negotiations among the three countries for sharing natural resources. Since the area is known for hydrocarbon resources, the three countries need to establish appropriate arrangements for exploration and exploitation (please see Figure 3.2 for more details).

Baselines in Myanmar Territorial Waters
Myanmar claimed a system of straight baselines and declared that its territorial sea would henceforth extend 12 nautical miles (nm) seaward from these straight baselines. Myanmar's twenty-one straight baseline segments extend for a total of 826.4 nm, starting from the southern point of Oyster Island (known as Mayu Island) on the Rakhine Coast and terminating at the western point of Murray Island on the Tanintharyi Coast.[2] None of the base-points is situated on the mainland and all are on islands along the coast. The baselines appear to depart from the general direction of the coastline and islands that are not in the immediate vicinity of the coast are used as turning points. In addition, a single baseline segment across the Gulf of Martaban, between Alguada Reef (Pathein Light) and western point of Long Island, India extends 222.3 nm in length, setting the record as the longest single straight baseline segment in the world. The consequence of this extraordinary claim is that at one point along the Gulf of Martaban, the distance from the land mass to the baseline is 132 nm (Prescott and Schofield 2005, p. 654) (please see Figure 3.3 for more details).

While normal baselines account for a majority of the baselines around the world, international law does allow coastal states to apply straight baselines where particular geographical circumstances or features exist. Article 7 of the 1982 UNCLOS states:

> 1. In localities where the coastline is deeply indented and cut into, or if there is a fringe of islands along the coast in its immediate vicinity, the method of straight baselines joining appropriate points may be employed in drawing the baseline from which the breadth of the territorial sea is measured.
> 2. Where because of the presence of a delta and other natural conditions the coastline is highly unstable, the appropriate points may be selected along the furthest seaward extent of the low-water line and, notwithstanding subsequent regression of the low-water line, the straight baselines shall remain effective until changed by the coastal State in accordance with this Convention.
> 3. The drawing of straight baselines must not depart to any appreciable

FIGURE 3.2
Map Showing Grey Areas between Myanmar, Bangladesh and India

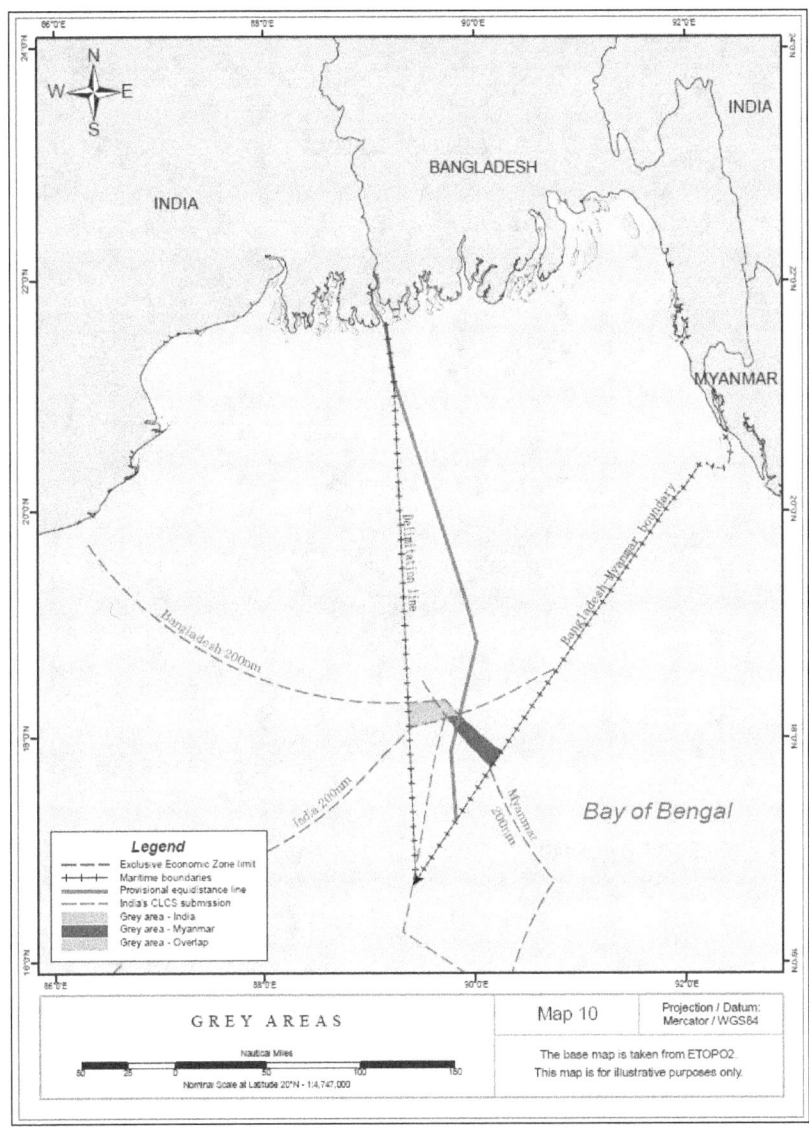

Source: Reproduced with the kind permission of the Ministry of Defence, Myanmar.

extent from the general direction of the coast, and the sea areas lying within the lines must be sufficiently closely linked to the land domain to be subject to the regime of internal waters.

FIGURE 3.3
Map Showing Myanmar's Claimed Territorial Waters

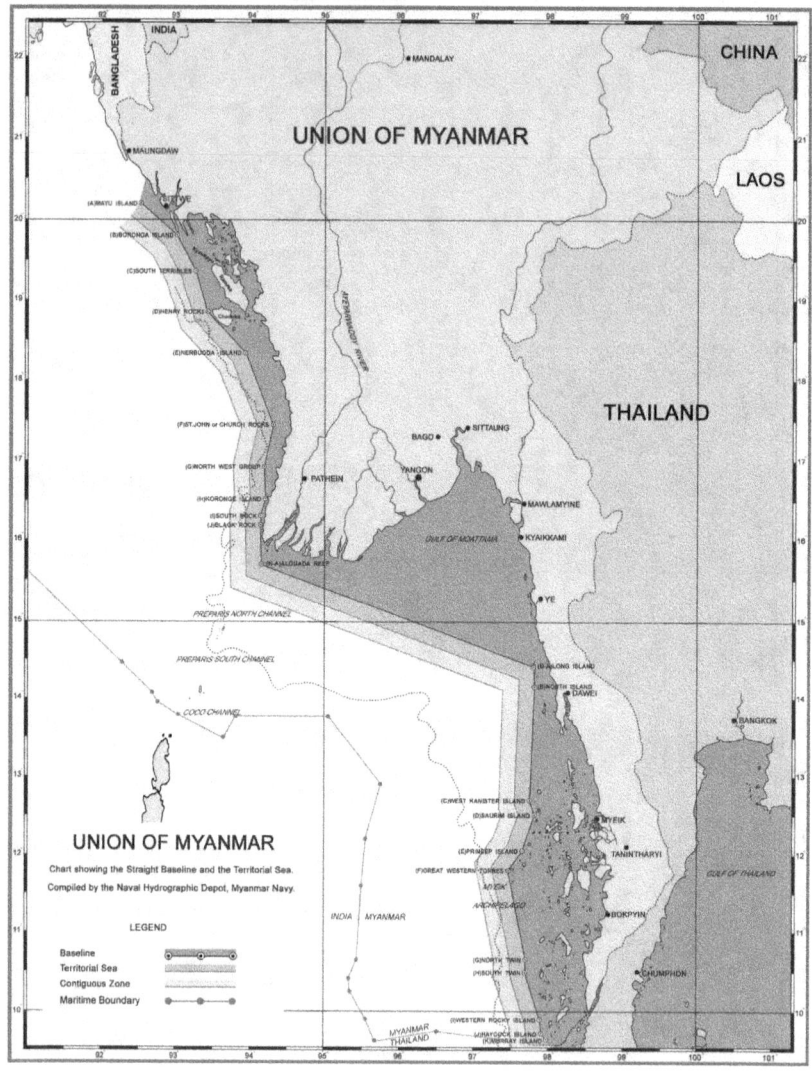

Source: Reproduced with the kind permission of the Ministry of Defence, Myanmar.

Article 7 is not without controversy. It remains unclear how many and how deep the indentations need to be to constitute a "deeply indented and cut into" coastline. It also fails to come up with how many and how close islands need to be to one another in order to form a "fringe" of islands. There are other points that may be subject to different interpretations. For example, what is meant by the term "highly unstable" and what angle constitutes the divergence to an "appreciable extent" from the general direction of the coast? Because of this, many coastal states have liberally or flexibly interpreted Article 7 and claim their straight baselines, sometimes resulting in excessive claims. Hence, there are numerous cases of international protests on straight baseline claims and the United States leads the field in this regard, protesting against any practices that it deems excessive or contrary to the provisions of UNCLOS. Victor Prescott and Clive Schofield explained that

> a group of countries have vested interest in avoiding significant reductions in the areas of the high seas and international seabed [and] this group includes the United States of America and perhaps some other major naval powers that want their navies and surveillance aircraft to operate without hindrance over the largest area of seas possible, [and] it is no coincidence that the country with the most effective navy and air force has been most diligent in protesting against straight baselines that obviously breach the rules in Article 7 (Prescott and Schofield 2005, p. 142).

The United States (U.S.) asserts that no baseline segment should exceed 48 nautical miles in length (United States Department of State 1987, p. 14). However, the U.S. position is by no means universally accepted. There are twenty-three countries, which have more than 50 nautical miles in some segments on their straight baselines. Of these, sixteen have been the subject of objections by the United States (Prescott and Schofield 2005, pp. 654–55).

The straight baselines claimed by the Myanmar Government drew protests from some countries, most notably the United States in 1982, as they were considered not to be in compliance with the 1958 Convention or the 1982 Law of the Seas. As mentioned earlier, Myanmar set the record by drawing a single straight baseline of 222.3 nm across the Gulf of Martaban and claims an extra of about 14,300 sq nm (or 49,000 sq km — an area similar in size to Denmark) as internal waters which, otherwise, would be part of the territorial sea or the high seas (United States Department of State 1992, p. 24). Moreover, in Myanmar's case, there is an opinion that the straight baselines have been used even where the coastline is not deeply indented and where there is not a fringe of islands along the coast in its immediate vicinity, and the baselines depart to an appreciable extent from the general direction of the coast. The United States has not only protested against Myanmar's straight baselines but has also declared the right of operational assertion (United States Department of State 1992, p. 26).

During the political turmoil in late 1988, the sighting of a U.S. naval fleet of five warships, including the aircraft carrier Coral Sea, within Myanmar territorial waters on the morning of 12 September 1988 became a cause for concern for the *Tatmadaw*. When the military authorities lodged a complaint and sought an explanation from the U.S. embassy for this brief but threatening presence of U.S. warships, the latter explained that it was for the evacuation of U.S. embassy staff in Myanmar. Myanmar authorities pointed out that 276 people, including some U.S. embassy staff, had been evacuated on the evening of 11 September on a chartered flight.[3]

In recent years, the U.S. Navy has conducted operational assertions against Cambodia, Vietnam, and the Philippines in Southeast Asia. This has alerted the Myanmar Government to the possibility of similar acts by the U.S. Navy in its waters. The Myanmar Navy established three naval regions in Heingyi (at the mouth of the Ayeyarwady River), Yangon and Heinze (Long Island) and located two naval flotillas to maintain security in the territorial waters enclosed by the Gulf of Martaban. During the Cyclone Nargis crisis in May 2008, Myanmar appeared to be acutely worried about the prospect of operational assertion by the United States. Myanmar is unlikely to step back from its straight baselines system and to redraw the baseline in the Gulf of Martaban. Therefore, this area could be a potential flashpoint in the future.

THE POLITICAL ECONOMY OF FISHING

Myanmar's maritime frontier is endowed with two particular types of natural resources: fish and hydrocarbon (in the form of oil and gas). Myanmar's marine fishery consists of three distinct fishing zones, namely, onshore, inshore and offshore. Since 1994–95, the Department of Fisheries (DoF) has regulated the onshore area as inshore fisheries of marine fisheries in compliance with the Myanmar Fishery Law. Accordingly, the inshore area starts from the lowest tide level to about 8 fathoms in depth (approximately 8–16 kilometres from shore). As for offshore fishing management, the DoF had divided the Myanmar coastal line into 150 blocks of fishing grounds measuring 30×30 nautical miles each by using latitude and longitude lines. These blocks were located in four designated fishing areas, Rakhine, Ayeyarwady, Mon and Tanintharyi, which encompass 40, 44, 14 and 52 blocks respectively. According to the DoF, in 2011, there were 28,350 small-scale fisheries boats registered with the government for inshore fishing, of which 15,100 (53 per cent) were non-motorized.[4] Moreover, there were 2,450 offshore vessels, 400 (16 per cent) of which were owned by foreigners.

The Department of Fisheries does not permit Myanmar vessels to engage in deep-sea fishing and, restricts their fishing activities to inshore waters. Deep-sea fishing grounds are allocated to foreign vessels that have been granted a permit by the DoF. Local fishermen complain that foreign vessels do not comply with the regulations and capture large volumes of fish illegally in inshore waters which are reserved for Myanmar vessels. Adding to this problem is what is known as the "special right" to fish granted to the Union of Myanmar Economic Holding Limited (UMEHL), a business owned by the military. In other words, special fishing rights are reserved for foreign vessels and those vessels operated by or under the UMEHL as it is very profitable.

The military government in Myanmar, after taking over the state as the State Law and Order Restoration Council (SLORC), and subsequently renaming itself the State Peace and Development Council (SPDC) in November 1997, declared on 18 September 1988 that it would change the country's economic system from a centrally-planned economy into a market-based one. With regard to marine fishing, the Myanmar Government enacted the Law Relating to the Fishing Rights of Foreign Fishing Vessels on 2 April 1989 and the Myanmar Marine Fisheries Law on 25 April 1990. Meanwhile, during the visit of General Chavalit Yongchaiyudh of Thailand to Myanmar in December 1988, the Myanmar Government promised the Thai general that it would grant fishing rights to Thai trawlers. Hence, 241 Thai fishing trawlers were legally fishing in Myanmar waters by mid-1989. Despite official permission to fish in Myanmar waters, there were problems with illegal fishing. Cases of arrests of Thai fishermen operating illegally in Myanmar waters were not uncommon. Between September 1988 and 1992, the Myanmar Government seized 231 illegal Thai fishing trawlers with a total of 2,346 crew members. The government estimated that the amount of fish seized with the trawlers was worth well over 345 million kyat (about US$50 million) (Maung Aung Myoe 2002, p. 127).

In 1989, the Myanmar Government issued permits to Thai trawlers to fish in designated areas. The permit fees varied from US$8,000 to US$12,000 per month. A permit was issued to a single trawler and was subject to annual renewal. Soon afterwards, the Myanmar authorities discovered that many Thai trawler operators had been cheating. Between late 1989 and early 1993, a total of 83 Thai fishing trawlers were fined more than US$1.5 million for violation of fishing contracts (Maung Aung Myoe 2002, p. 127). However, illegal fishing in Myanmar waters has persisted due to the corruption and the lack of monitoring and surveillance by law enforcement authorities. There have been several reports of Burmese naval officers taking bribes from Thai trawlers in exchange for turning a blind eye to illegal fishing. Myanmar protested to the Thai Government about Thai trawlers fishing in restricted zones as well as duplicating and making forged permits. Illegal fishing has become a major source of tension between the two countries since the Myanmar Navy has become more effective in patrolling Myanmar waters and pursuing illegal trawlers. While illegal fishing mainly occurs around the Tanintharyi coastal area, the Rakhine coastal area also has the same problem, although illegal fishing by foreign vessels has rarely been reported there. It appears that most illegal fishing activities are carried out by local fishermen on the Rakhine coast. In these cases the issue is either overlooked or resolved through negotiations and bribes. Nevertheless, between 1993 and 2000, out of 582 Thai citizens arrested for various charges, more than 450 were for illegal fishing (Maung Aung Myoe 2002, p. 127). Between 1988 and 2003, the Myanmar Navy seized a total of 3,157 illegal fishing boats of various sizes, including 923 foreign boats, and commodities on board worth nearly 9,900 million kyat (around US$1,414 million). The arrest of people involved in illegal fishing was particularly high in the period between 1988 and 1993.[5]

Some people knowledgeable about illegal fishing around the Tanintharyi coastal area argue that these figures do not reflect the reality and scale of illegal fishing. Corruption is rampant and the extortion of protection money is not uncommon. The situation is worse than official figures reveal. In early January 2009, the Independent Mon News Agency (Burma News International 2009) reported that Myanmar authorities seized at least one illegal fishing boat per day in Myanmar waters and that about one hundred more were operating without official permits, but obtained "unofficial tickets" through bribery. Boat owners paid between 50,000 and 60,000 baht (US$1,400 to US$1,680) per month for unofficial fishing rights, depending on the size of the boat. Those boats that failed to obtain unofficial fishing tickets were seized but they were released once they paid the bribe. The report quoted an interview with a man who had negotiated with a local Myanmar Navy officer for the release of a fishing boat and its crew by paying for three motorbikes and various commodities worth 150,000 baht. The same report stated that despite the Myanmar Government's ban on shellfish harvesting, and a sentence of twenty years imprisonment if caught, illegal activities have continued and that a boat could catch, on average, enough shellfish to make a profit of 60,000 baht, and sometimes up to 150,000 baht as reported by Burma News International (2009). Thus, it could be argued that illegal fishing has been going on at a fairly large scale in Myanmar waters and the Myanmar Government appears to be unable to resolve it.

Another issue related to illegal fishing is the unregulated exploitation of marine resources. As mentioned earlier, Myanmar's marine fisheries are comprised of inshore and offshore fisheries. Inshore fishery is carried out within five nautical miles from the shore on the Rakhine coast and ten nautical miles on the Ayeyarwady and Tanintharyi coasts. This fishing is usually carried out by passive fishing gear such as gill nets, drift nets, long lines, and traps. Offshore fishery is carried out in the area extending from the outer limit of the inshore fishing zone. The main fishing gear involved here are bottom trawls, purse seine, surrounding net, drift nets, and long nets. Until the late 1980s, the marine products taken were mostly for domestic consumption. However, since the early 1990s, the Myanmar Government has promoted the production and export of marine products.

Between 1988 and 2008, marine fish production tripled, the volume of marine products export increased seventy times, and the export earnings grew from US$10 million in 1988 to US$561 million in 2008.[6] Yet it is important to note that by 2003, marine fish production had already passed Myanmar's Maximum Sustainable Yield (MSY) of 1.05 metric tons (tonnes) per year. In 2008, marine fish production (amounting to 1.679 tonnes) was far beyond the MSY. The situation is far more alarming since the official figures are much lower than the actual amount caught by legal and illegal fishermen. In 2011, it was reported that marine capture fisheries amounted to 2.15 tonnes, which is more than twice the level of MSY.[7] If the government fails to address this issue, Myanmar's fishery resources will be depleted in the near future.

Until the early 1990s, the primary role of the Myanmar Navy (MN) had been restricted to patrolling rivers and inshore waters and to supporting the army in counter-insurgency operations. Due primarily to the nature of these missions and to financial limitations, the MN maintained a very modest fleet of mostly small and lightly armed boats. Yet it never lost sight of coastal surveillance and the protection of territorial waters, which was reflected in the procurement of a small number of corvettes and coastal patrol crafts. Yet, for all practical purposes, the MN was primarily a coastal navy and its effective patrols never extended beyond the country's brown waters. In 1988, the MN's order of battle included four ageing corvettes — Yan Taing Aung, Yan Lone Aung, Nawarat and Nagakyay (which were decommissioned in 1995), two offshore patrol vessels (OPVs) — Indaw and Inya, seven coastal patrol boats (CPs) — PGM 411-414, 421-423, twelve river patrol boats (PRBs) and a few landing crafts. There were neither torpedo boats nor minesweepers in the MN. The MN envied the navies of neighbouring countries for their frigates, corvettes, and missile crafts.[8]

In 1990, the Myanmar Navy, along with the Army and the Air Force, began a major naval procurement programme.[9] The MN is apparently interested in building up its blue-water capabilities although it has a long way to go in this area. Yet the MN argues that it needs to protect the country's Exclusive Economic Zone and, that it is under pressure from naval force modernization programmes in neighbouring countries. Illegal fishing in Myanmar waters, most prominently by Thai trawlers, is a concern for the MN. For better patrol over Myanmar waters, including the Exclusive Economic Zone, the MN expanded naval regional command, from three to five, and flotilla, from just one to three, from 1988 onwards. With frigates, corvettes, and many more Fast Attack Crafts (FACs), the MN is now capable of providing more effective patrol over Myanmar waters.

Myanmar's coastal and offshore waters have been heavily exploited since the opening of these areas to extensive fishing, particularly by Thai trawlers in the early 1990s. Several signs of over-fishing are visible and there is considerable concern, particularly among local environmentalists and fishing communities whose livelihoods depend on coastal waters. The trawl fishing practised by Thai trawlers is considered particularly destructive to the natural marine environment. There is clearly an urgent need to manage coastal fisheries. At the alarming rate of marine fish stock depletion, as the yearly catch exceeds the MSY, local communities along the coastline will face serious threats to their livelihood. Their household income will be dramatically affected. Local fishing communities and fishery businessmen are complaining about "unfair" fishing rights for Thai trawlers and their illegal fishing activities. In a press interview on 14 December 2012, the Secretary of the Myanmar Fisheries Federation told the press that "Myanmar should not continue permitting Thailand or other countries to work in the country's seafood fisheries industry. Only national entrepreneurs should be allowed to work in the industry" (*The Nation* 2012). Another official from the federation stated that "fishing boats from Thailand officially registered in Myanmar did a lot of illegal fishing in the country's waters for years. They exploited a lot. Although the two countries share mutual friendship, that's the truth. We discussed the issue based on these facts." In the past, this kind of information was unlikely to appear and the Myanmar press and the authorities were likely to ignore it. However, nowadays the government cannot afford to ignore these concerns. Moreover, the Myanmar Fisheries Federation backed a plan to ensure that sufficient fishing grounds are left open to villagers in Rakhine State and Tanintharyi and Ayeyarwady regions as reported by *The Myanmar Times* (2012). According to current fisheries laws, regional governments are allowed to rent and tender fishponds and rivers to business people. This right may soon be extended to marine fishing, as regional governments are also responsible for the livelihood of local communities along the coastline.

HYDROCARBON EXTRACTION AND GEOPOLITICS

Hydrocarbon is the other important natural resource in Myanmar's maritime frontier. Oil and gas production in Myanmar come from seventeen sedimentary basins: fourteen onshore and three offshore. The three offshore basins are Rakhine, Moattama, and Tanintharyi — all situated along the coastline of Myanmar. While onshore production began in the colonial era, starting in 1887, mostly in central Myanmar, offshore production is a recent phenomenon. Onshore oil and gas production was organized into forty-eight blocks; its offshore counterpart has fifty-two blocks, divided equally between shallow and deep waters.[10] All the offshore productions are Production Sharing Contract (PSC) blocks. In early 2009, it was estimated that offshore blocks had the potential to produce up to 392.932 mmbbl (million barrels) of crude oil and 131.967 tcf (trillion cubic feet) of natural gas. The Myanmar Government invited foreign investment in the oil and gas production sector and many foreign firms engaged in this line of business. For about twenty years, from 1989 to 2010, the oil and gas sector drew the largest amount of foreign direct investment (FDI) in Myanmar.[11]

By making use of its maritime resources, especially gas, the Myanmar Government managed to secure political and diplomatic support from China, India, and Thailand and, to a lesser extent, Russia. As mentioned earlier, there are fifty-two offshore blocks in the Myanmar Exclusive Economic Zone. Oil and gas companies from fifteen countries invested in the exploration of oil and gas in Myanmar. The cumulative amount of investment in Myanmar's oil and gas sector up to the end of March 2011 was US$4,236.13 million, of which US$3,780.33 million was in offshore projects.[12]

From China, three big energy companies, namely, CNOOC, CNPC and SINOPEC invested in Myanmar's oil and gas sector. PTTEP from Thailand, Essar Oil, GAIL and NOGC Videsh from India, Petronas from Malaysia, Nippon Oil from Japan, and Daewoo from South Korea are heavy investors in offshore oil and gas.

There are four large-scale offshore gas production projects in Myanmar (please see details in Table 3.2). The first offshore gas project in Myanmar is the Yadana project, located in M-5 and M-6 blocks, with an estimated investment of US$1.2 billion.[13] The PSC agreement was signed in July

TABLE 3.2
The Largest Offshore Gas Projects

No.	Project	Location	Blocks	Partners	Percentage (%)	Reserves (tcf)
1.	Yadana	Moattama Offshore	M-5 M-6	1. TOTAL (France)* 2. UNOCAL (US) 3. PTTEP (Thailand) 4. MOGE (Myanmar)	31.24 28.26 25.50 15.00	6.975
2.	Yetagun	Tanintharyi Offshore	M-12, M-13, M-14	1. Petronas (Malaysia)* 2. Nippon (Japan) 3. PTTEP (Thailand) 4. MOGE (Myanmar)	40.75 19.40 19.40 20.45	4.16
3.	Shwe	Rakhine Offshore	A-1 A-3	1. Daewoo (Korea)* 2. KOGAS (Korea) 3. GAIL (India) 4. ONGC Videsh Ltd. (India) 5. MOGE (Myanmar)	51 8.5 8.5 17 15	4.8 to 8.6
4.	Zawtika	Moattama Offshore	M-9	1. PTTEP (Thailand)* 2. MOGE (Myanmar)	80 20	1.7 to 10.7

* Chief Operator
Source: Ministry of Energy

1992 and the sale of gas agreement — for thirty years — in February 1995. Part of this project included the construction of a gas pipeline from the production site to power plants in Thailand. The Yadana Gas Project is one of the most controversial natural gas development projects in the world as it has been marred by accusations of serious and widespread human rights abuses committed by pipeline security forces on behalf of the companies, including forced labour, land confiscation, forced relocation and so on. The gas field is located in the Andaman Sea, approximately 60 kilometres off the nearest landfall in Myanmar. The field reportedly contains more than 5 trillion cubic feet (140 billion cubic metres) of natural gas, with an expected field life of thirty years. The project is also to transport natural gas through a pipeline from offshore blocks in the Andaman Sea to Thailand and is operated by Total (France), Chevron (United States), PTTEP (Thailand), and the Myanmar Oil and Gas Enterprise (MOGE). The project involved the construction of a 346-kilometre long subsea, from the production site to Daminseik, and a 63-kilometre long onshore pipeline, from Daminseik to the Thai border.[14] Lawsuits were filed against the companies involved in the project.

The second offshore gas project is Yetagun, with US$642 million in investments, located in the Andaman Sea southeast of Yadana field, in M-12, M-13 and M-14.[15] The project began in 1996 and production began in 2000. Again, the sale of gas agreement was signed in March 1997 with Thailand as the importer. The field is developed and operated by Premier (replaced by Petronas in 2002), in partnership with MOGE, PTTEP and Nippon Oil. The Yetagun gas field is estimated to contain a reserve of 3.2 trillion cubic feet (91 billion cubic metres).[16] Again the gas from the field is transported through a 272-kilometre long pipe, of which a 230-kilometre long section is undersea with the rest onshore, where it links with the Yadana pipeline. A pipeline was laid from Nat-Ein-Taung to Ratchaburi in Thailand.

The third project is the Shwe gas project off Rakhine coast, located at blocks A-1 and A-3. A PSC agreement was signed in August 2000 and it is estimated to be the largest offshore gas production project in Myanmar. In January 2004, with the approval of the Myanmar Government, a consortium of South Korean and Indian companies, together with China's state-owned CNPC and Myanmar's state-owned MOGE, announced plans to develop this massive natural gas field. The export of gas agreement, lasting thirty years, was signed in December 2008 and the gas is exported to China via a 793-kilometre long cross-country pipeline between the site and Kumming via Kyaukphyu. Moreover, China is also involved in the construction of a parallel oil pipeline that will connect Myanmar's coastline with China's Yunnan province, reducing China's dependence on the strategically vulnerable Malacca Straits for shipping oil.

Another large-scale gas production project, known as Zawtika (Offshore Technology 2013), is located in M-9 and in the small northeast part of M-11. The production sharing contract agreement was finally signed in November 2003, between MOGE and PTTEP of Thailand, for the exploration. The Myanmar Government approved Zawtika field development plan in February 2011. In this US$2 billion project, the PTTEP holds an 80 per cent stake in the project which is still in the process of development, as reported on the PTTEP website (2013).

The sale of gas from Yadana and Yetagun fields generated a large amount of revenue. Between 1998 and 2010, Myanmar generated an income of nearly US$11.4 billion from the sale of gas to Thailand, US$5,516.835 million from Yadana and US$5,882.985 million from Yetagun. Moreover, it is estimated by the Myanmar Government that these four projects will generate income of nearly US$75 billion for Myanmar in total. The Yadana project will generate a total income of US$28.2 billion between 2011 and 2027, of which Myanmar will receive US$18.5 billion.[17] The Yetagun project will generate a total income of US$18.3 billion in the same period and Myanmar will receive US$11.8 billion.[18] In the case of the Shwe project, the whole project will generate US$48.4 billion in the period between 2013 and 2042, of which Myanmar will receive US$31 billion. The Zawtika project is also estimated to provide the total income of US$24.8 billion for the same period, of which Myanmar will benefit from a sum of US$13 billion (Ministry of Energy) (please see Table 3.3 for more details).

Faced with international pressure and economic sanctions by the United States and its allies, in the aftermath of the 1988 uprising, the military government in Myanmar attempted to break international isolation and to keep its economic lifeline open by making use of its natural resources and geographical location, particularly its maritime frontier. The exodus

TABLE 3.3
Income from Yadana and Yetagun Projects (Sale of Gas to Thailand)
US$ Million Fiscal

Year	Income from the whole project		Income of Myanmar		Total
	Yadana project	Yetagun project	Yadana project	Yetagun project	
1998	52.162	–	20.289	–	20.289
1999	287.629	–	79.104	–	79.104
2000	495.355	122.270	152.595	34.566	187.161
2001	522.931	295.285	189.766	93.353	283.119
2002	493.657	313.800	203.771	110.382	314.153
2003	559.396	491.910	278.871	206.287	485.158
2004	586.795	511.084	355.254	240.692	595.946
2005	662.415	989.292	407.425	482.117	889.542
2006	899.156	1190.430	552.522	751.219	1303.741
2007	985.920	1356.182	656.531	918.887	1575.418
2008	1329.495	1626.438	901.820	1103.561	2005.381
2009	1215.236	1390.580	824.193	921.771	1745.964
2010	1238.478	1542.905	894.694	1020.150	1914.844
TOTAL	9328.625	9830.176	5516.835	5882.985	11399.82

Source: MOGE Financing Table, 2012.

of anti-government activists to border areas, mounting military pressure from various insurgent forces, international pressure and condemnation for crushing the uprising, and imminent bankruptcy rendered the SLORC government desperate to find a way out of these troubles. It was important for the SLORC to prevent Thailand from supporting or helping Myanmar exiles and activists (or to turn a blind eye to other countries helping them). It was reported that the Myanmar Government had only about US$25 million in its foreign exchange reserve, which would have run out in a couple of weeks. The SLORC immediately passed a foreign investment law on 30 November 1988, less than forty-five days after the military takeover. The cash-strapped military government was so desperate to earn foreign exchange that it sold off part of the Myanmar embassy compound in Tokyo at the price of US$325 million.[19] When Thai General Chavalit visited Myanmar in 1989, the SLORC quickly signed an agreement to grant Thai trawlers fishing rights in Myanmar waters. This was done for both political and economic reasons. He was the first foreign dignitary to visit Yangon, breaking Myanmar's diplomatic isolation. With the help of the Thai Government, the SLORC government opened reception camps on the Thai side of the border to repatriate Burmese activists who had ventured into the jungles for refuge.

Key players in Myanmar's offshore oil and gas sector come from China, Thailand, Malaysia, India, South Korea and Japan, among other countries. Through the use of resource and pipeline diplomacy, the SLORC/SPDC government managed to secure political support from these countries, while generating income. According to some observers, even Russia was given some kind of privilege and incentive to invest in Myanmar's oil and gas sector as the Myanmar government tried to win Russian support in the UN Security Council; Russia's veto allows Myanmar to reduce its over-reliance on China.[20]

The Myanmar military leadership is quite aware of the country's geopolitical position in the East Asian region. It is convinced that China is interested in having access to the Indian Ocean. Being aware of China's concern for U.S. containment strategy, the Myanmar leadership is able to make use of its geographical location (and its maritime frontier). Myanmar, in the mind of the military leadership, is the backdoor to and outlet for the backward provinces of China. Myanmar's geographic position is an important exit and safe passage for trade-dependent energy-importing China, especially in the context of growing U.S. dominance in Southeast Asian waters where the Malacca chokepoint controls the vital sea-lane of communication. Moreover, it is increasingly clear that there is competition for dominance in the Western Pacific between the United States and China. Rising China has publicly declared its intention to own a blue-water navy by 2049. One cannot overlook the debates among informed observers on the issue of U.S.-China conflicted relations and the discussion of China's Anti-Access and Anti-Denial (A2/AD) concept and the U.S. AirSea Battle Doctrine in the Pacific waters. The confluence of mutual interests — China to have strategic footholds in and economic benefit from Myanmar and Myanmar to secure Chinese political support — may be observed in the way Chinese investment in Myanmar (particularly in the energy sector) is encouraged and managed. The construction of gas and oil pipelines is a good example. With stakes in Myanmar's gas in the Shwe gas field and the oil and gas pipelines, the Myanmar Government expected China's political and diplomatic support at various international forums.

The construction of gas/oil pipelines does not come without problems. Local villagers along the lines are affected and there are complaints about inadequate or lack of compensation. In some cases, land was forcibly confiscated for the project and villages were relocated. The construction of gas pipelines is done at considerable social and environmental cost. Resources and revenue distribution has recently become an issue as the 2008 constitution in Myanmar allows state and regional governments to raise revenue. Local communities question the use of revenue generated from resources that they share in their respective regions. Rakhine people bitterly complain that they do not benefit from the sale and transportation of gas from Rakhine state and from its offshore sources.

CONCLUSION

In the last twenty years, Myanmar has witnessed several transformations in its water frontier. Exploitation and depletion of natural maritime resources, which was previously unheard of, has become a reality. Many multinational corporations are operating in Myanmar waters to extract natural resources. In recent years, the Myanmar Government has been planning to establish special economic zones, namely Kyaukphyu, Thilawa and Dawei, in Myanmar's water frontier. Another noticeable transformation in Myanmar's maritime frontier in the last twenty years is the increasingly effective patrol over Myanmar waters by the Myanmar Navy.

While Myanmar's land borders are full of exciting issues that characterize the complex relations between territory, sovereignty, identity and resources as well as mobility and migration, its maritime frontier has faced issues which have more to do with the political economy of resource control and revenue distribution. Weak law and order is also a defining feature in Myanmar's coastal waters. The political economy of the maritime frontier in Myanmar highlights the importance of control over maritime resources by state-owned enterprises involved with multinational corporations or the foreign business community. Along the coastline, we now begin to see the emergence of three special economic zones where many foreign companies are expected to invest and with which local people will continue to compete for natural resources. How to share revenue from the exploitation of natural resources in Myanmar's maritime frontier is an important topic among major stakeholders, including regional governments and local communities. For instance, local people question the distribution of revenue generated from the sale of gas from the Shwe gas project off the Rakhine coast. Myanmar state-owned enterprise, MOGE, entered a Production Sharing Contract (PSC) agreement with India and Korea based on cooperation and they signed a sale of gas agreement with China based-CNPC.

One interesting point to note in the Myanmar maritime frontier, unlike its land counterpart, is that the politics and the protection and use of natural resources in the sea is less ethnicized. The most notable issue that takes up the ethnic dimension is the oil and gas exploration off the Rakhine coast. Some local Rakhine activists raise the issue of resource and revenue sharing between the central and local governments. One possible reason for the relative absence of ethnicization of issues along the Myanmar maritime frontier, compared to the land frontier, is that the government has maintained relatively better maritime security presence since the late 1970s. Because of the lack of institutionalized ethnic-based insurgency in Myanmar's water frontier, issues related to maritime resources are less ethnicized. Ethnic based insurgents operate mostly on a sporadic basis. In the case of most insurgent organizations along the terrestrial frontier of Myanmar, they are considerably institutionalized and maintain military bases.

In terms of actors in the Myanmar maritime frontier, state institutions, such as the *Tatmadaw*, Police Force, and various non-state organizations are contesting the control of political space, with the former becoming increasingly dominant. While there are occasional challenges from forces external to Myanmar, the state has remained the most important player in the maritime frontier. In the case of the control over maritime natural resources, there are several players: state-owned enterprises, multinational corporations (particularly Asian business giants), military-owned businesses, regional governments and local people. While the state remains the most important actor in the control and regulation of the exploitation of maritime resources, the control mechanism is now jointly managed with multinational corporations. Nevertheless, the Myanmar Government understands the importance of control over and management of the maritime frontier, including natural resources, as it allows the Myanmar Government to adjust its foreign policy orientation, primarily serving as a geopolitical pivot for rising China and emerging India, in addition to generating revenue. In this context, critics may say that naval modernization in Myanmar is not merely to protect Myanmar territorial waters but also to protect special economic interests, including those of the Asian corporate giants, or the business empire of the state or its key institutions, most notably the *Tatmadaw*, at the expense of local people's livelihoods.

While the resources in and location of Myanmar maritime frontier are certainly a divine dividend for Myanmar, it is not without limits and constraints. Mismanagement and irresponsible use of these resources will deny Myanmar the path to its development and prosperity. In the context of the emerging geopolitical situation, especially in the state of rising China and shifting U.S. interest from Europe to Asia-Pacific, the maritime frontier places Myanmar on the stage of regional politics, if not global, and offers the country an important role to play in regional politics. It is now up to Myanmar to make full use of this opportunity.

Notes

1. On 12 February 1998, a Thai warship attacked the Yan-Naing-510 and fired twenty-five rounds of artillery in disputed waters. On 25 March 2003, around Kawthaung waters, Myanmar's naval vessel Yan-naing 517 was chased by about thirty fishing boats. When it received a distress call, the Myanmar Navy sent two warships to the scene. In the meantime, the Thai Navy also sent a warship and fired at the Yan-Naing 517, but left when it saw the two Myanmar warships approaching.
2. The baselines on the Rakhine coast measure 304.8 nautical miles, on the Gulf of Martaban 222.3 nautical miles and along the Tanintharyi coast 299.3 nautical miles. The straight baselines run the entirety of Myanmar's coastline with the exception of about a 30 nm-long stretch of normal baselines extending southwards from the terminus of the country's land boundary with Bangladesh at the mouth of the Naf River.
3. The U.S. embassy had repeatedly requested permission from the Myanmar authorities to land C-130 military aircraft in Yangon for evacuation purposes. The Myanmar authorities had rejected this request by explaining that such an activity might not only lead to further confusion among the general public but would also send the wrong signal to regional neighbours. The next day, the U.S. embassy issued a statement that sightings of the U.S. fleet in Myanmar territorial waters was just a rumour. However, the truth was that the U.S. fleet was stationed within Myanmar's territorial waters.

4. Source: Department of Fishery.
5. Source: Ministry of Defence.
6. Source: Department of Fishery.
7. Author's compilation.
8. Source: Ministry of Energy.
9. In that year, it commissioned three ex-Yugoslav PB-90-class coastal patrol boats (UMS 424-426). A year later, it placed an order for ten *Hainan*-class FAC-SCs (Fast Attack Craft - Submarine Chaser) from the PRC – UMS 441-450. In March 1994, the MN signed another procurement contract with the PRC for a delivery of six *Houxin*-class FAC-Ms (Fast Attack Craft — Missile). With the technical assistance and weaponry from the PRC, the MN also locally built six 50-metre long FAC-Gs (Fast Attack Craft — Gun) between 1995 and 2006. Moreover, the navy built four FAC-Ms (UMS 557-560) in its naval dockyard and commissioned them in 2004. The naval dockyard also built four River Patrol Crafts in the 1990s. In the same period, the Myanmar Shipyard built two Burma PGM-type coastal patrol crafts. The MN also built and commissioned two 77-metre long corvettes (UMS-771 and UMS-772) and two frigates (F-11 Aung Zaya and F-12 Kyan Sithar), with the assistance of the PRC, in recent years. Besides, it also procured two more frigates (Jianghu-II Class Type 053H1) from China in 2012. The third frigate is under construction. Several locally built coastal patrol crafts (45/47m and 50m long) were commissioned in recent years. Two FAC-M (UMS 561 and 562) were commissioned in 2008, four FAC-G (UMS 563, 564, 565, and 566) in April 2013, four FAC-M (UMS-567, 568, 569 and 570) and one FAC-Stealth (UMS-491) in December 2012. There have been some reports that the MN is building a few more frigates in its dockyards.
10. For shallow waters, 7 blocks in the Rakhine offshore area, 11 blocks in Moattama, and 8 blocks in Tanintharyi. For deep waters, 18 blocks in the Rakhine offshore area and 8 blocks in the Moattama and Tanintharyi offshore areas (Source: Ministry of Energy).
11. Source: Ministry of Energy.
12. Ibid.
13. Ibid.
14. A new MOGE-operated pipeline carrying gas from the Yadana field to Yangon was inaugurated in 2010 and will double the amount of gas for local consumption.
15. Source: Ministry of Energy.
16. Ibid.
17. The total income from Yadana, from the start to 2027, is estimated at US$37.5 billion and Myanmar will receive US$24 billion (Source: Ministry of Energy).
18. The total income from Yetagun, from the start to 2027, is estimated at US$28.2 billion and Myanmar will receive US$17.7 billion (Source: Ministry of Energy).
19. Speech of Lieutenant General Khin Nyunt at No. (3/93) Refresher Course for Senior Military Officers at the National Defence College (30 November 1993).
20. Three Russian companies are operating in one offshore and three onshore blocks (Source: Ministry of Energy).

References

A Tatmadaw Researcher. *A Brief History of Myanmar and the Role of the Tatmadaw 1948–1988*, 3 volumes. Yangon: News and Periodical Enterprise, 1991.

Burma News International. "Thai Fishing Boats Seized Daily by Authorities in Southern Burma", 7 January 2009 < http://www.bnionline.net/index.php/news/imna/5647-thai-fishing-boats-seized-daily-by-authorities-in-southern-burma.html> (accessed 15 October 2013).

Htet Aung Kyaw. *Marathon Journey of a Rebel Student* (Written in Myanmar Language). Yangon: Dawei Watch Publishing House, 2013.

International Tribunal for the Law of the Sea (ITLOS). Paragraphs 464, 472, 474 and 476 of the "Dispute Concerning Delimitation of the Maritime Boundary between Bangladesh and Myanmar in the Bay Of Bengal", 14 March 2012 <https://www.itlos.org/fileadmin/itlos/documents/cases/case_no_16/C16_Judgment_14_03_2012_rev.pdf> (accessed 15 October 2013).

Maung Aung Myoe. *Neither Friend nor Foe*. Singapore: Institute of Defence and Security Studies (IDSS), 2002.

Maung Aung Myoe. "Myanmar's Maritime Challenges and Priorities". In *Maritime Challenges and Priorities in Asia*, edited by Joshua H. Ho and Sam Bateman. London: Routledge, 2012.

Myanmar Times. "Fisheries Body Approves Common Use Fishing Grounds Plan", 29 October 2012 <http://www.mmtimes.com/index.php/business/ 2729-fisheries-body-approves-common-use-fishing-grounds-plan.html> (accessed 15 October 2013).

Offshore Technology. "Zawtika Project, Gulf of Martaban, Myanmar", <http://www.offshore-technology.com/projects/zawtika-gulf-martaban-myanmar-burma/> (accessed 15 October 2013).

Prescott, Victor and Clive H. Schofield. *The Maritime Political Boundaries of the World*. Leiden: Martinus Nijhoff Publishers, 2005.

PTT Exploration and Production Public Company Limited. "Zawtika Project", 31 December 2013 <http://www.pttep.com/en/ourBusiness_EAndPprojectsDetail.aspx?ContentID=18> (accessed 15 October 2013).

Smith, Martin. *Burma: Insurgency and the Politics of Ethnicity*. London: Zed Book, 1999.

Soe Sandar Oo and Myat Nyein Aye. "Fisheries Body Approves Common Use Fishing Grounds Plan". In *Myanmar Times*, 29 October 2012 <http://www.mmtimes.com/index.php/business/ 2729-fisheries-body-approves-common-use-fishing-grounds-plan.html> (accessed 15 October 2013).

South West Command Headquarters. *Historical Development of South West Command HQ and the Ayeyarwady Division (Document BR7181)*. Pathein: Southwest Command Headquarters, 1995.

The Nation. "Myanmar Fisheries Federation not Keen on Thai Collaboration", 14 December 2012 <http://www.nationmultimedia.com/aec/Myanmar-fisheries-federation-not-keen-on-Thai-coll-30196067.html> (accessed 15 October 2013).

Tin Maung Win. *The Politician and Politics.* Thailand: Khit Pyaing Press, 2000.

United States Department of State: Bureau of Oceans and International, Environmental and Scientific Affairs. *Developing Standard Guidelines for Evaluating Straight Baselines, Limits in the Seas* no. 106. Washington D.C.: U.S. Department of State, 1987.

———. United States Department of State: Bureau of Oceans and International, Environmental and Scientific Affairs. *United States Responses to Excessive National Maritime Claims, Limits in the Seas* no. 112. Washington D.C.: U.S. Department of State 1992.

Section II

Territorial Claims and Imagined Boundaries

4

Burman Territories and Borders in the Making of a Myanmar Nation State

Maxime Boutry

How do Burman people perceive and live the borderlands? It has been a few decades since academics started working on Burmanization to explain the national construction of the Union of Myanmar's "geo-body" — the search for a homeomorphism between a territory defined by national borders and a national "identity" (Thongchai Winichakul 2005) — and notably the power struggles between the central state and ethnic areas partly under the control of insurgent armed groups. Walton (2013) even recently discussed the "wages of Burmanness", an ill-defined national Burman identity resulting from the Burmanization process that, if substituted for the creation of an inclusive national identity, could hinder the development of a democratic Union and the place of ethnic minorities within it.

Nonetheless, only a few studies deal with the perception of a Burman identity by the Burmans themselves, or at least Burman discourses of identity relative to their relationship with other minorities (see Boutry and Ivanoff 2008; Boutry 2015). How do Burmans represent their geographic or imagined territories and define their borders? It seems "easier" to find strong identity markers defining "limited social spaces" (for example, the Moken or Khumi social space) than "extended social spaces", such as the Burman or Tai ones.[1] Among other reasons, extended social spaces tend to be assimilated to structures of a larger scale such as kingdoms or states, while limited social spaces are deprived of such power structures. The fact that limited social spaces are mainly viewed as in danger of being assimilated by extended ones (Moken assimilated by Burman through Burmanization, for example) explains the greater focus given to studying "disappearing" or "changing" identities on the part of minorities. Yet, nobody seems to find interesting the possible changes occurring within the majority in contact with minorities. Numbers lay down the law. Yet, is it not necessary to try understanding Burman identity when talking of Burmanness or Burmanization? Or are these concepts only political constructions aimed at controlling populations?

From some examples taken along the Myanmar littoral zone, I would like to draw attention to how borders (administrative but also based on identity as we will see) contribute to the different facets of Burman identity.[2] Firstly because expressions of this identity may be easier to spot when in tension with other environments (ecological, cultural, linguistic, etc.) and secondly, because this may alert us to where homeomorphisms between a dominant Burman identity and the conception of a national territory are possible.

BUDDHISM AND TERRITORY IN BURMAN REPRESENTATIONS

Besides Burmese language, the easiest statement about Burman identity may be the practice of Burman Buddhism.[3] From the narratives of the intrinsic link between the Burman "race" and Buddhism (Rozenberg 2008, p. 36) to the specificities of Burmese practices of Buddhism (Brac de la Perrière 2006), this is the most obvious marker among the Burman and at the same time serves as a field for making Burman identity and Burmese nationhood tally with each other through the territorialization process — that is the Burmanization of Myanmar. Hence, U Nu's policy of instituting Buddhism as the national religion (Lehman 1967, p. 96) and the Buddhization effort targeted at the Union's borderlands (Holmes 1967, p. 137).

The question to ask is whether Buddhism is sufficient to explain Burman identity. What are the discourses produced around this and lived through Buddhism when interacting with the "other"?

The long conflict between Rakhine Buddhists and Rohingya Muslims and the way it has grown since June 2012 into a generalized Muslim-Buddhist animosity throughout the country is enough to question the capacity Buddhism has to bond Burman and other borderland populations. Buddhist principles definitely unify the Burman. The answer "I'm a pure Buddhist" (*but-da' bha-tha sit-sit*) is the most common response to the question "from which race are you?" Yet, Buddhism in practice also divides the Burman: in every village where there is more than one monastery, villagers are generally divided into equivalent competing groups. Hostile discourses toward other Buddhist populations, especially Rakhine, but also Mon (and Thai) abound, despite their shared histories, religion or language.[4] "If you cross the path of a Rakhine and a snake, kill the Rakhine first" is a well-known saying among the Burman. Or another saying of the mother of one of my male assistants: "you can marry any girl from any origin or religion but don't fall in love with a Rakhine." Indeed, the Arakanese and Burmese kingdoms were regularly in conflict, the latter often having tried and succeeded at different periods to expand its influence over Rakhine, especially by King Bodaw Hpaya in 1785 not long before the British annexed it in 1826. It was at that time that Buddhism came to be endorsed by the Burmese kingdom, following the way paved by Alaung Hpaya, Burmese king of the eighteenth century, who projected himself as an "Embryo Buddha" whose fate was to unify all Buddhist territories (Lieberman 1978, p. 475). Even if other historians (see Leider 2011) contest Lieberman's theory on the "Embryo Buddha" concept, the intrinsic relationship underlined between Buddhism (as part of a cosmological order), kingship and territory remains a daily reality. Interestingly, Bodaw Hpaya, whether a universal ruler or not, hastened to bring the then symbol of Arakan's sovereignty, the Maha Muni Buddha, to the Burmese capital of Amarapura with 20,000 prisoners in 1785. This enduring symbol (the statue is still in Mandalay) of animosity between Burman and Rakhine still comes up in Rakhine discourses, notably through the popular belief that the true Maha Muni Buddha statue is still in Rakhine, and more exactly in Kyauk Taw (a Rakhine town) as the Burmese king could not simply have moved it from its plinth. To build further on this argument, I say that the conception of an endangered Buddhism partly unifies Burman and Rakhine against Myanmar's Muslims — notably through religious movements like the "969" — only because it is linked to a perceived threat against their respective territories.[5] This appears quite clearly in the simplifications brought by the Rakhine conflict in categorizing its diverse populations: many Kaman, a Muslim population recognized as a Myanmar ethnic group and whose common language is Rakhine, have been relegated to the Muslim category and share the same internally displaced persons (IDP) camps in Sittwe township. Mara Ma Gri, another ethnic group practising Buddhism but whose physical traits as well as language (a Chittagonian dialect) are similar to the Rohingya, are now emphasizing amongst themselves the necessity of speaking Rakhine even at home in order to be integrated into the sole emerging legitimate population on Rakhine territory, the Rakhine.[6] Finally, Hindus living in the few Rakhine IDP camps around Sittwe have been told to integrate into their Hindu divinities' altar a Buddha statue, distributed by local Buddhist religious groups (interviews with Hindu households in IDP camps 2014).[7] The current conflict created the opportunity of a Rakhinization of Rakhine State in the same way that the Burman government tried to Burmanize Myanmar national territory. This Rakhinization process characterized by the equation "Rakhine identity = Rakhine language + Buddhism + Rakhine State" is explicit as can be seen by the August 2014 request by Rakhine leaders to the Union to study a law aimed at gathering all Rakhine State Muslims (even those who have not yet been displaced by the conflict) in a temporary Muslim area awaiting relocation to a third country (*Irrawaddy Magazine* 2014).

I have dealt mostly with Rakhine representations of the conflict so far to better emphasize the resemblances it has with their Burman neighbours, those resemblances that keep them apart. Indeed, when looking at how the long-standing conflict between Rakhine and Rohingya has been revived, how it has spread to other, mostly Burman, parts of Myanmar and how previous conflicts between the Burman and Muslims in Myanmar occurred, one common pattern emerges. In 1997, anti-Muslim riots in Mandalay began after reports of an attempted rape of a girl by Muslim men, although this was later disproved and led to speculation that the regime may have orchestrated the incident. On 28 May 2012, the brutal rape and murder of a Rakhine woman by a group of "illegal Bengalis" (as qualified by the government) led to recurrent conflicts between the two communities all over Myanmar. In late April 2013, anti-Muslim rioting broke out in Okkan, a city about 100 kilometres from Yangon, after an altercation between a Buddhist monk and a Muslim woman. On 28 May 2013, the Shan town of Lashio was the theatre of another conflict after a Muslim man had become embroiled in a dispute with a female petrol vendor, a twenty-six-year-old Buddhist. Finally, in August 2013, a similar conflict occurred in Htan Gone village after rumours circulated that a young Muslim man had attempted to rape a Buddhist woman. The gendered representation of the conflict is striking and it may not be a coincidence. The threat to Buddhist women — whether Burman or Rakhine — represented by Muslim men is closely linked with the unavoidable religious conversion of women marrying Muslims. I assert here that rather than a threat to Buddhism — which is the message conveyed by the 969 movement — it is perceived as a threat to the Burman and Rakhine hegemonies on their respective territories, a view that will be explained in the following paragraphs.

THE GENDERED REPRESENTATION OF TERRITORIALIZATION

My argument builds on the gendered differentiation made during the Burman territorialization process by which female identity is socialized by males. Buddhism operates a gendered differentiation within the religious order and in everyday life. Nash (1962, p. 290) remarked the "favored place of the male in Buddhist doctrine [who] have *pon* (in this case a sort of glory) just because they are men, and women do not or almost do not." Besides, Rozenberg (2004, p. 513) notes that "strictly speaking, women who adopt a religious life in Burma or elsewhere cannot be called 'nuns' since they do not receive any valid ordination, though the term is widely used for lack of a better way of referring to them." In fact, as Than Myint-U (2004, p. 34) remarked about Burmese kingdoms, this gender differentiation operates in the wider Burman social order, whose key pillars, the Army and the Buddhist Sangha, "were all male". While talking about social order, cosmological representations reinforce the gendered relationship between socialization and the territory, where the guarantors of social order would be male, while the appropriated territory would be female. This is what Sortho (1967) recalls in his analysis of the origins of the *dewatau sotāpan* cult — a Mon cult resembling the cult of the Thirty-Seven Lords — where the chthonic deities are always female:[8]

> The Indian earth-god Visundhara reached South East Asia as a goddess, Visundharior Dharani, whom the Mons call a bau: literally a 'grandmother' or 'ancestress'. The term recurs as the designation of one of the two principal classes of spirit which current reckoning acknowledges: the male kalok or lineage spirits, ancestral house-protectors whose cult descends in the male line, and the bau, village spirits who convey the right to territory (Sortho 1967, p. 132).

In Burman society, very close to Mon, this would translate into the spirit *Min Mahagiri* who, despite not being a lineage spirit, is indeed the male guardian of the household (*ein-twin" nat*), while *shin-ma* (literally, owner/lord — female) are female protectors of the territory. Other famous deities are *Popa Medaw* (guardian of the Popa Mount), *Naing Karaing Medaw* also called the Lady of Pegu (the last capital of the Mon country), or locally acknowledged *nat* such as *Ma Shin Ma* worshipped in the Tenasserim region (at the extreme south of Myanmar), whose shrine is in the town of Tenasserim. In Rakhine as well, "where most of the *nat* connected with the territory are female" (de Mersan 2009, p. 311). Other *shin-ma* thought to control the land are *Kra Zam*, "the lady guardian spirit of Mrauk U" and her sister *Mra Swan*, "the guardian of Parein", both "considered as superior *nat* of the territory" (de Mersan 2009, p. 315).

Regarding "Burmanization", the Burman territorialization process, Buddhism and spirit cults work on building the same representation. The Burman king, as in other Hinduized states, was regarded as a *cakravartin* (universal ruler) and incipient Buddha (Hall 1960, pp. 93–94; Leach 1960, p. 7; Sortho 1967, p. 135). As Hall (1960, p. 41) puts it, "he aspired to become a Buddhist Saviour, a Maitreya, who would extend the blessings of the Law to the whole world, and restore the Golden Age." Hence, the chief or king's task was to bring social order in his realm, to which rights had been acquired as "dowry from his spouse" (Sortho 1967, p. 133). Looking again through the lens of the cult of the thirty-seven *nat*, the king's alliance to his enemies' sisters is a recurrent strategy for taming external elements and appropriating territories. For example, in the myth of Min Mahagiri, a Pyu spirit, or in the myth of Ko Thein Shin, a Shan prince, the Burman king marries the sister of each hero, either in order to kill him (Min Mahagiri) or to subjugate him (Ko Thein Shin). This always results in the king's spouse's inability to survive her brother's death and her consequent death (Brac de la Perrière 2002, pp. 31–48). Yet the cults of the dead heroes, whose legends all make them sons of *naga* females (de Mersan 2009, p. 313) instituted by the king, remain to legitimate his sovereignty over the conquered territories. Indeed, in most of Southeast Asia, ophidian beings "are a representation of autochthonous principles and, as such, symbolize legitimate sovereignty over the land for the kings who marry them" (Brac de la Perrière 2002, p. 49). The royal features characteristic of the *cakravartin* status also authorized royal polygyny (Leach 1960, p. 57), which, from the perspective of acquiring new territories, would have been necessary.

Interestingly, Burman society in its reproductive ideal is mainly endogamous, a principle probably inherited from the Indian culture of castes repudiating an alliance with inferior groups (Leach, op. cit., p. 66). As noted by Than Myint-U about Burman society, historically, "marriage tended to be endogamous within the circle of one's *a-myo*. ... Marriage outside of one's group was permitted, but often actively discouraged, both by royal decree and probably as well by local custom" (Than Myint-U 2001, p. 29). This partial rule regarding alliances, where exogamy is the privilege of the king, is in fact a distinct characteristic of Burman identity. For Brac de la Perrière (2002, 2007 and 2008), Burmanization as the elaboration of Burman hegemonic identity through the cult of the thirty-seven *nat* (directly linked to monarchy), serves to localize particularisms for the purpose of subordinating them. This forms part of the Burman process of ethnicity itself. My argument here is that this process of stretching Burman identity over territories is not only the privilege of the kings (or the modern rulers) and that the cult of the thirty-seven *nat* is not only a symbol of the hegemonic and legitimate Burman rule over their territory but also takes place at the edges of Burman territory whose borders move in time and space.

TERRITORIALIZING BORDERLANDS

The transition process between a *mandala* pattern, with the borderlands shifting in tandem with its ruler (Leach 1960, p. 52; Lieberman 1987, p. 186) and according to allegiances to other societies, and the state where new forms of hegemony are reorganized within the geographically defined borders on the map, really began with British colonization. Later, with the post-war emergence of the region's nation states, borders emerged more widely as geographical lines, replacing frontier zones between "interpenetrating political systems" (Leach 1960, p. 50). In these inter-penetrating zones, populations on both sides manipulated identity traits. Lieberman (1978, p. 457) suggests that the most visible traits (such as hairstyle, dress) were manipulated by the Mon and Burman, for example, depending on whether they wanted to be assimilated into the coastal or interior realms. Similarly the Burmese king Tabin Shwei Hti used to dress in a Mon fashion, and was considered as such by his subjects, to follow the prophecy that only Mon kings could rule Pegu. However, in the new era of nation states, borders are defined in order to separate geographic entities, forging new differences between social, cosmological, cultural, ethnic and national entities in the borderlands, even though these dimensions have traditionally overlapped. The post-colonial process of nationalization generated new spaces within these different borders, changing the character of borderlands: some were left almost "virgin" to Burman colonization dynamics, such as the Ayeyarwady Delta under British rule or, more recently, the Tanintharyi Region. Others were subjected to the reaffirmation of the local population's identity, as in Kachin, Shan or Mon States, notably in a resistance process against coercive military rule spanning the past fifty years. Such a historical process impacted the way the Burman (attempted to) undertake the assimilation of their borderlands.

PATRON-CLIENT NETWORKS AND THE TERRITORIALIZATION OF BORDERLANDS

As a corollary of the economy-oriented policies of the British, the Ayeyarwady Delta underwent a period of intense exploitation in the nineteenth and twentieth centuries, drawing millions of Burman from central Myanmar to the delta, to what was still a "rice frontier" (Adas 1974). The gradual populating of the Ayeyarwady Delta took place in three stages from 1858 to 1941 (Adas 1974) and was mainly initiated by the British who wanted to develop the production of this area. As explained by O'Connor (1995, p. 971), in the early era (AD 700), Mon, Khmer, Cham and Pyu ruled the southern part of mainland Southeast Asia. These ethnic groups were garden-farmers in the highlands or flood-managing farmers in the lowlands. People living in the northern part of Southeast Asia, such as the Thai, Vietnamese and Burman specialized in wet rice agriculture and were known to be skilled irrigators. These peoples expanded southward and conquered three of the largest rice bowls of Asia: the Mekong, the Chao Phraya and the Irrawaddy River deltas. During the first stage of the Burman conquest of the Irrawaddy Delta, the rice economy of Lower Burma grew rapidly, thanks to the existence of large areas of virgin land and to the great number of migrants from Upper Burma. It then became an expanding pioneer front, to which Dao The Tuan and Molle's description about the Chao Phraya Delta (Thailand) applies perfectly:

> As a consequence of [the] gradual colonisation and 'artificialisation' of the region, the delta society has much of the features attributed to frontier societies: a certain degree of independence from the grip of the central state, a propensity to evade social conflicts or responding to bankruptcy by moving further away, and the formation of villages with migrants from different origins and backgrounds, therefore with little 'social glue'. At the same time, the integration to the wider economy and national sphere was provided by the marketing of the rice production surplus (Dao The Tuan and Molle 2000, p. 17).

In other words, the deltaic pioneer fronts were a place of migration, without sufficiently developed traditional villages or kinship units to bring social control and means of empowerment to individuals in these "loosely structured" societies. However, as further pointed out by Dao The Tuan and Molle on the Chao Phraya Delta:

> While the ... society can be considered loosely structured with regards to corporate communities, it is not deprived of strong 'structural regularities'

centred on flexible, voluntary patterns of relationships between individuals. Social control is apparent in issues such as money borrowing or land rental contracts (Dao The Tuan and Molle 2000, p.17).

The establishment of strong patron-client relationships among new villages correlates with the pioneer front's development in terms of production as well as referring spatially to what is called the "rice frontier" (Adas 1974). Scott notes the main preconditions for promoting the patron-client network in three points: the persistence of marked inequalities in wealth, status, and power which are accorded some legitimacy; the relative absence (or collapse) of effective, impersonal guarantees — such as public law — for physical security, property, and position, often accompanied by the growth of semi-autonomous local centres of personal power; and the inability of either kinship units or the traditional village to serve as effective vehicles of personal security or advancement (Scott 1972, p. 8).

Patron-client networks arose in a structurally loose social context, far from the state's control, meaning that the patron could seldom rely on outside support to maintain his power and wealth and thus relied mostly on his local clients' networks, peasants or fishermen. Because Burman society is a Hinduized one, building its political organization on "charismatic kingship" personified by a "divinely inspired monarch" (Leach 1960, pp. 56–57), local patron-client relationships may be considered a key social institution (Scott 1972, p. 13; Lieberman 1987, p. 187). Social bonds are embedded in this relationship and elites may be considered the guarantors of social integrity and identity, and at the same time, the main vectors of territorialization. The critical role of patrons in Burmanizing new spaces lies in the intrinsic relationship between social position and religious accomplishment which characterizes Burman society: the greater the merit a lay person is believed to have acquired through religious exchange, the greater his influence (*oza*), the greater the respect due to him and the greater his social standing (Schober 1989, p. 103).

The relationship between social position — inducing a social order — and religious accomplishment — base of a cosmologic order — is generated through the offerings made to

> beings who belong either to the sacred domain beyond the social hierarchy of lay people or to individuals thought to be superior to the person making the offering. ... On the other hand, food given to those below one's own station in life, even if it is given in a ritual context, is considered an expression of one's loving kindness (*metta*) and compassion (*karuna*) for less fortunate ones and dependents. In return for this kindness, obligations

must be repaid. On account of the dependency thus created, the recipient comes under the influence and power of his benefactor whom he owes gratitude (*kyei: zu: shin*) and in whose dominion of power he now exists (Schober 1989, p. 105).

As such, patrons are also the instigators of the Buddhization of new spaces — carried out by erecting pagodas as well as building schools and monasteries in new settlements. I would even say that patron-client networks represent a minimal unit of territorialization and that, in order to do so, have the same privilege as kings in the matter of "taming" this territory whose female character (symbolic or actual) needs to be won over.

The Ayeyarwady Delta was mostly unpopulated so the Burman populations had to "create society from nothing". It begs the question: how do patron-client networks operate in other, already populated, borderlands?

Leaving the old delta borderland, now fully integrated into the territory of Burman hegemony, I shall go further south, where another pioneer front is still in the process of being Burmanized: the Tanintharyi region and the numerous islands of the Myeik (Mergui) Archipelago. The Myeik Archipelago lies along the southern part of the Tenasserim coastline, on a north-south axis. It extends in the north to the littoral town of Dawei and to the south as far as Phuket in Thailand. Its islands are inhabited, and have been so since at least the seventeenth century, by the Moken, a population of sea nomads of Austronesian origins. Despite the current international border administratively separating the twin towns of Kawthaung (Myanmar) and Ranong (Thailand), the Myeik Archipelago can be incorporated into the wider Malay Peninsula region, including the southern provinces of Thailand and the north of Malaysia. Geographically, the Tenasserim marks the fusion between Myanmar and Malaysia, according to its ecological similarities to the latter country (White 1997, pp. 27–28). Ethnically, the Malays were, besides the Moken, in the majority of those frequenting the islands of the Myeik Archipelago. Even though the border was negotiated between Siam and the British Empire in the nineteenth century (*The Geographer* 1966), the entire region remained a transnational borderland with limits situated inside the national territories that designated cultural and geographic elements more than administrative ones. Consequently, a cultural border existed between paddy states and thalassocracies (maritime realms), rice culture and commerce as well as continental and insular Southeast Asia. This border separated central and lower Burma from the Malay Peninsula, including the south of Moulmein and the Myeik Archipelago, this in spite of the national official border.

Since the beginning of the 1980s, however, the Myeik Archipelago has become a refuge for numerous Burman, mostly coming from Lower Burma, and thus the theatre of an appropriation process of the marine and insular environment, involving both the Burman and the Moken. The main migration of the Burman toward the Tanintharyi Division occurred in the 1990s during a politically tense era, just after the 1988 protest and the elections of 1989. The remote archipelago, despite the hundred-year-old administrative border, was still out of the sphere of control of the Burman central government. On the continent, the Karen were struggling to protect their sovereignty over an imagined Kawthoolei and the Mon were also involved in conflicts with the central state (South 2003, pp. 36, 198).[9] The hundreds of islands composing the Myeik Archipelago offered a way to escape from state control. But the Burman colonization of this region has been shaped in great part by economic issues and state affairs: the Thai fishing industry, also profiting from the remoteness of the archipelago, was exploiting much of its marine resources, and most of the goods produced in the region were going directly to Thailand's economy without benefiting Myanmar. Thailand had already started to "fill" its peninsular borderland (from Kra Buri to Sungai Kolok) with workers from the northeastern part of the country (Isaan) in order to develop copper mining and fishing industries, and rubber and palm oil plantations. In doing so, the Thai nation state was stretching control over its borderlands in the same way Myanmar would soon do. Indeed, in the 1990s, the Myanmar Government under Prime Minister Khin Nyunt decided to privatize the fishing industry (Boutry 2007, p. 393) in an attempt to boost exports and take back control of its own resources, especially in the south. Myanmar realized the potential of the border as a politico-economic source of services such as according fishing rights to a Thai trawling fleet in reward for the return of some students who had fled repression in 1988 to take refuge in south Thailand.[10] The international border had to become effective and so was begun the Burmanization of the borderland.

When the Burman first came to settle in the islands in the 1980s (see Boutry 2014, pp. 154–57) to take advantage of the products found in the archipelago (pearls, birds nets, fish) they were another "minority" among ethnic minorities. Despite being at the forefront of the dominant colonizing population of the country, they could not behave as such but rather had to appropriate the necessary know-how, cultural, mythical and ritual elements in order to adapt to an insular way of life — far from the landmarks of a sedentary, paddy cultivating society. Beginning with the move of a few pioneers coming from Lower Burma (Moulmein notably) in the 1980s,

Burman entrepreneurs went through the city of Myeik and progressively penetrated the archipelago towards the southern islands. While the Moken preceded them, fleeing the first Burman settlements, the nomads' insular territory began to shrink, reduced to a corner at the international border in the south. Added to other factors — such as a deficit in Moken men, the Burman advance into the archipelago led to mixed Moken and Burman settlements.[11]

I have already analysed elsewhere the pioneering processes which led to the creation of these communities (Boutry 2014, 2015) and the resulting implications in the making of a Burman insular identity, halfway between "social segmentation" and ethnic differentiation (Boutry and Ivanoff 2008, p. 30). Here I will retain only the most important facts. The Burman progressively took the place of the traditional *tokè*. *Tokè* is a term of Chinese origin employed from south Myanmar to Indonesia, including Thailand and Malaysia, which designates a patron-entrepreneur relationship. Traditionally, the *tokè* has been central to the preservation of the Moken nomadic way of life. The relationship between the *tokè* and his Moken group lies in the necessity of the nomads in acquiring rice, the basis of their diet and the paradox of an insular population that only cultivates the cereal for ritual purposes (Ivanoff 2004). So the Moken exchange their products collected on the strands or by diving (for pearls, Mother-of-pearl and shells) with the *tokè* for rice, clothes and other consumable goods. The founding myth of the ethnic differentiation of the Moken is the Gaman epic poem (Ivanoff 1985). Gaman is the Malay civilizing hero who will lead the transition from yams to rice for the Moken.[12] The epic poem conveys Islam's beginnings in Southeast Asia that, linked to slavery, will lead to the "nomad choice" (Ivanoff 1998, p. 337): to "roam" in the islands, "eat and spew out the sea" on board the *kabang* (the traditional Moken boat) and to be eternally dependent upon sedentary societies to supply rice in exchange for their products. So the *tokè* is the organic link connecting the Moken to the "rest of the world". Practically, the *tokè* was more often of Chinese origin, of Sino-Burman or Sino-Thai origins.

Starting from the 1980s, the Burman progressively replaced the former *tokè* and took this pivotal role in the relationship between Moken flotillas and the "outside" world. At this time the alliances contracted by the Burman with the Moken were as much opportunistic as strategic for the Burman. Indeed, a Moken group traditionally gives away one of its girls for marriage to the *tokè* to ensure his fidelity. However, from the Burman perspective of profiting from insular resources, it was also a way to acquire, on the one hand, legitimacy in the insular territory and its resources and, on the other, better knowledge of this new environment. These intermarriages between Burman men and Moken women are significant enough to consider in the Burmanization process of borderlands, given the proportion of these alliances in the different settlements of the Myeik Archipelago and, above all, the critical role of the Burman-Moken households in shaping insular social space.

"Marrying" a New Territory
Prior to Burman migration toward the Myeik Archipelago, most of the Moken intermediaries, the *tokè* to whom they used to give a wife, stayed on the littoral and only a few moved with the Moken flotillas. Along with Burman migration, the first islands to be colonized in the north (near the city of Myeik) presented much of the characteristics of the littoral: relatively flat, suitable for agriculture (paddy, rubber plantation) and principally sheltering communities practising coastal fishing (with traps and small nets). Further to the south, the topography is quite different as the islands become hilly, left unprotected from the heavy winds and waves of the monsoon, leaving only narrow beaches to settle down in. In this totally estranged environment, the Burman needed to rely on a knowledge they could only acquire from the Moken. Despite the fact that most of the Burman pioneers who settled in the southern half of the archipelago had a Burman wife on the continent, they contracted alliances with the Moken. These alliances were facilitated by the fact that the Moken traditionally give a wife of their subgroup to their intermediary in exchange for their fidelity and protection. Thus, Burman pioneers implicitly became Moken *tokè*, while still acting as patrons or *kye'zu'shin* since *metta* (loving kindness) can be dispensed to any interlocutor independently of his religion (Morgan 1965; Nakamura 1968, p. 19). The Burman pioneers, in their role of patron transformed into *tokè* for the Moken, initiated a cultural exogamy first seen as a strategic necessity to appropriate the know-how and acquire legitimacy on the islands, while indirectly aimed at Burmanizing the territory. Indeed, most of these Burman entrepreneurs built pagodas and schools, primarily in order to legitimize their settlements in the eyes of the regional authorities. With an acknowledged Buddhist marker on the territory and a school diffusing the Burman language (to Burman and Moken children), the authorities from the Tanintharyi Division see clear markers of Burman appropriation of the territory they can transform into officially administered settlements, hence extending the geo-body of the nation.[13] However, what allows us to characterize these alliances as a pattern of cultural exogamy is that intermarriages induce a hierarchy among the insular Burman (based

notably on their potential to enlist the Moken workforce in their business), profitable for the one married into the Moken founder ancestor's lineage (Boutry 2011, p. 118).

Traditionally, Moken society is divided into subgroups identified with a couple of founder ancestors who were linked to the main island of residence during the monsoon.[14] These ancestors (male *ebab* and female *ibum* in Moken) are materialized by two spirit poles (*lobung*), renewed at each passage between the dry season and the monsoon during the *bo lobung* ritual. These spirit poles (together with other ritual elements such as cemeteries, spirit houses) mark out the archipelago. Thus, the Moken relationship to their territory is intrinsically linked to the couple, a structure that is transposed to the relationship between the Burman *tokè* and their Moken wife, hence the Moken group. Moreover, in the settlements of the south of the Myeik Archipelago, village headmen are, with no exception, Burman men married to Moken women. Those are also the main drivers for the migration of whole Burman families to their villages, who generally begin to work for these patrons. In this particular situation, exogamy becomes a deontic structure of Burmanization.

CONFLICTING IDENTITIES IN IDENTIFIED TERRITORIES

I now turn to the fate of the Burman living in Mon State, so as to compare the Burmanization process in places that have already been territorialized.

Out-migration is affecting Mon State, as has been the case for decades in many other borderlands. It is difficult to obtain reliable figures, but among the estimated 2.3 million Myanmar migrants in Thailand, people coming from Mon State would amount to around 600,000 individuals (International Office for Migrations 2013, p. 8). The fact that out-migration is so widespread in the region results in a lack of a viable local workforce: rubber tappers, miners, paddy field labourers, fishermen, etc. Hence, absentee Mon labour is replaced by a Burman workforce (and marginally by the Mon coming from other areas such as those surrounding Bago town) coming mainly from the Bago and Ayeyarwady regions, and to a lesser extent from the Dry Zone and the Sagaing Region. Wages offered to labourers in Mon State (around 4,000 kyat (US$3)/day) are at least twice the wages a daily worker may earn in the Ayeyarwady Region or the Dry Zone. Yet it is not enough for Mon workers compared to the wages they earn in Thailand (around

300 baht/day, which is 9,000 kyat/day for unskilled jobs). In Ye township alone, at least fourteen migrant clusters are recorded, mainly composed of Burman but also of Mon and Kayin ethnic groups, representing a total population of approximately 10,000 individuals.[15]

Only a few in-migrants who arrived many years ago settled in Mon villages and eventually married Mon or Kayin women. In-migrants generally have restricted access to resources. First, most of them cannot obtain a family list (*ein-htaung-su" sa-yin"*), which is necessary to obtain an identity (ID) card.[16] Besides, the need to obtain authorization from local landowners and authorities to settle is also a way to limit the clusters' expansion. Second, they generally do not have access to land ownership in the region, which is partly related to the first point. Only a few in-migrant settlers have been able to buy residential land in their cluster even though it is less likely to happen given the skyrocketing land prices in 2014. This strategy of limiting access to regional resources (administrative, economic) seems to be a way of regulating the necessary influx of in-migrants to Mon country.

Intermarriages between the Mon and the Burman are uncommon despite the intermingling of communities because even though both populations share the same identity markers, they have different notions of "imagined territory". Also, the Burman cannot understand Mon Buddhism, which differs in its pronunciation of Pali. As in the case of Burman social space, Mon Buddhism refers to a territory, a link explicitly made as in the commemoration held in most Mon pagodas in 2014 for the 200th anniversary of the collapse of Hamsavati/Hanthawaddy (Bago), the last Mon capital. To understand its importance, it is worth noting that all the *hinta* statues — or *hamsa*, the mythical goose of Hindu mythology — found in the pagodas or at the entrance of Mon villages and symbolizing the late Mon capital, are oriented in the direction of Bago.

Relying on Burman monks to hold Buddhist ceremonies is widespread in the migrant clusters. However, the impossibility of penetrating the Buddhist sphere of the Mon continues to relegate the Burman to the impermanent status of guest in this region. Burman people interviewed in migrant clusters often feel like "lower-class citizens" and the Mon consider the "Burman [...] good to use [at work]" (*khaing lop kaung"-de*), as they are more "submissive" and "cheaper" than Mon workers (interviews with Burman migrants and Mon patrons in Ye township 2014).[17] Otherwise, interactions between the two communities are strictly restricted to the economic sphere. Burman workers work for Mon patrons but these Mon patrons are unwilling to let their daughters marry Burman men.

CONCLUSION: PLURAL BORDERS IN THE MAKING OF A UNIFIED MYANMAR NATION STATE

My point is not to state that identity is bound to a territory, but that identity is fluid and expressed differently in relation to territory. Hence, the actual borders of Myanmar for the Burman may not be the national borders, but the borders of an imagined territory where Burman identity is hegemonic. Yet, these imagined territories within the state also affect the construction of a unified Myanmar nation state since it is almost impossible for most Burman migrants in Mon State, for example, to obtain identity papers.

On the contrary, Burman pioneers who started to exploit the Myeik Archipelago's resources, by interacting with the Moken and intermarrying with them found a way to extend their hegemony on the islands through integrating the nomads' imagined territory, where lands (the sea strands where villages are built) are a female domain, while the sea and the forest are the domain of the Moken males. In terms of identities, while the Burman migrants in Mon State see themselves as "invitees" (*ei'-the*), the Burman in the Myeik Archipelago often refer to themselves as Burman "islanders" (*bama kyun"-tha"*). This comparison shows explicitly the difference between an identity border acting as a limit for the Burman in Mon State but working as a catalyst for Burman "islanders" to stretch Burman identity over Myeik insular territory. In other words, Burman migrants and the Mon have competing representations of territorialization (as a construct of a "male" hegemonic identity over a "female" territory) while Burman "islanders" and Moken could negotiate their own imagined territories through intermarriage. In practice, while Burman migrants in Mon State do not have access to citizenship, Burman "islanders" have managed to obtain family registration lists (the most important document needed to obtain national registration cards and other official papers) produced in the nearest township (Kawthaung for instance) in which their Moken wives and mixed children are listed.

Here again the Myanmar populations' representations of territories — that is, a space in which they consider themselves hegemonic — have an actual impact on the construction of the Myanmar nation state. In the case of the Tenasserim, the rising concern over the Thai-Myanmar border and access to the marine resources fostered the integration of the Tanintharyi region into the confines of the Union of Myanmar, notably symbolized by its new function within the international economy, and defined as "the new oil bowl of Myanmar".[18] However, these events revealed a second kind of border, a Burman cultural border between two ways of life: a continental paddy cultivation-centred sedentary one, and an insular maritime and nomadic (or at least highly mobile) one. By integrating this border, the Burman pioneers of the Myeik Archipelago both succeeded in stretching Burman social space and national Burmese territory. Intermarriages with the Moken became even more "acceptable" — given the endogamous tendency of Burman society — since it "affects" only a small number of Burman fishermen. A few pioneers "sacrificed" Burman sociocultural markers (endogamy and purity) in order to integrate the territory into the Burman sphere of influence — through a developing fishing economy and an administrative network — that eventually serves to reinforce the international border with Thailand through transborder trade. And as discussed above, the few Burman pioneers married to Moken women are the first drivers of an all-Burman migration to the islands. Thanks to these pioneers, the Burmese nation state managed to stretch its geo-body to the south more effectively during the past twenty years than the two-and-a-half centuries the region has been officially within the country's administrative borders. The Burman are now always more numerous than before on the islands, coming as whole families (working in fisheries and developing parallel commercial activities such as supplying the villages with provisions, selling alcohol and even proposing karaoke in the islands for the fishermen).

However, this particular case cannot be used to resolve the wider national construction process. Indeed, how would diverse populations share a national territory — even in a federal structure — if rights to citizenship depend on the relationship between ethnic identity and territory? Similarly, it is unlikely that the Burman and Rakhine, despite their alliance against the Muslim threat, would consider themselves as belonging to the same national territory, an opinion reinforced by the current Rakhinization process of Rakhine State.

Notes

1. Limited social spaces referring here to the concept of «espace social restreint» developed by Condominas (1980). The Moken are an Austronesian population of sea nomads living between southern Myanmar and southern Thailand. Their population size is around 3,000. The Khumi are part of the Chin family, and represent a small population living in the south of Chin State, in the vicinity of Paletwa township. They have a relatively small population of between 50,000 and 80,000 individuals.
2. The findings in this article are based on fieldwork conducted at different times in various locations, starting with a four-year study on the populations in the Myeik Archipelago between 2003 and 2007, regular fieldwork in the Ayeyarwady Delta

since 2008, some fieldwork in southern Thailand from 2007 to 2009, in Mon State in 2014 and in Rakhine State between 2012 and 2014.
3. It is difficult to make rational use of the English terminology regarding this country and its dominant population. As pointed out by Houtman (1999, p. 53), "though the regime ostensibly claims to distinguish [through the use of Myanmar] between Burmese [nationality] and Burman [ethnic belonging], this distinction only works in the English language, but in Burmese it in fact ends up saying that Burma and Burmese are Burman". In this chapter, I opted for functional reasons to use the term Burman when dealing with ethnic groups (and identity) and use Burmese when talking about historical, political and religious processes. Therefore, the government is termed Burmese for it is composed mainly of the Burman. The spirit cult comprising of the thirty-seven *nat*, is also termed Burmese so as to keep the sense that most worshippers are Burman but the cult itself has various influences (Mon, Karen, etc.).
4. The Thai are also historical enemies of the Burmese due to the attack of the Burmese King Hsinbyushin (1736–76) on the Thai capital Ayutthaya in 1767 (Sunait Chutintaranond and Than Tun 1995, p. 58).
5. The 969 movement, led by the monk U Wirathu, arose in the aftermath of the Rakhine conflicts in 2012. The core message of this virulent strain of religious nationalism is that Buddhists must unite against a growing Muslim threat.
6. Mara Ma Gri is the Rakhine exonym for the Barua population that can also be found in Bangladesh.
7. Interview with Hindu households living in internally displaced persons (IDP) camps by Maxime Boutry, Sittwe Township, Rakhine State, Myanmar, 25 January 2014.
8. A Burmese spirit (*nat*) possession cult.
9. In June 1949 the Karen National Union (KNU) declared to the world the formation of the Karen Free State of "Kawthoolei". However, from this period until 1995 and the taking of KNU's headquarters at Manerplaw, the entire Karen region has collapsed, "quashing dreams at independence of a prosperous free-state of Kawthoolei" (Smith 1994, p. 44).
10. This happened between 1988 and 1991 under the Thai prime minister's new political orientations toward Myanmar, known as "Chatichai's buffet (i.e., eat all you want) government" (Pavin Chachavalpongpun 2005, p. 65), which favoured loose forms of control over the borderland since the Burmese Government was in negotiation with its Thai counterpart to profit from this resource-laden region.
11. One of the main reasons of this deficit is the employment in the 1980s of Moken men on compressor diving boats which resulted in many deaths. Other risky work commissioned by Chinese and Burmese entrepreneurs such as the use of fishing explosives contributed to deaths in the Moken male population.
12. Gaman provoked the Moken flight toward the sea by committing adultery with the queen's younger sister, Ken. The queen condemned Ken and her people to be drowned (*lemo* in Moken), giving the ethnonym *(le)mo ken* (Ivanoff 1985, pp. 97–124).

13. Regions were called Divisions prior to 2010.
14. While the Moken roam the islands, living on their boats during the dry season (approximately from October to April/May), during the monsoon they settle in temporary villages based on the islands of their ancestors.
15. Data from fieldwork by the author in Ye township, May 2014.
16. Even if the Burman (whether in the Ayeyarwady Delta or in the Dry Zone) can legally obtain an identity card, most farmers living in the countryside never undertook the registration process. Many individuals also lost all their papers during cyclone Nargis which struck the delta in May 2008.
17. Interviews with Burmese migrants and Mon patrons in Ye township by Maxime Boutry, Mon State, Myanmar, May 2014.
18. The hinterlands of the Tanintharyi Division are mainly exploited by Myanmar joint-ventures operating with Thai investments in producing palm oil.

References

Adas, Michael. *The Burma Delta: Economic Development and Social Change on an Asian Rice Frontier, 1852–1941*. Madison: University of Wisconsin Press, 1974.

Bountry, Maxime. "L'appropriation du domaine maritime: des enjeux revisités" [The Appropriation of the Maritime Realm: Revisited Stakes]. In *Birmanie Contemporaine* [Contemporary Burma], edited by Gabriel Defert. Bangkok/Paris: Research Institute on Contemporary Southeast Asia (IRASEC)/Les Indes Savantes, 2007, pp. 389–410.

——. "Les *frontiers* de Leach au prisme des migrations birmanes, ou penser la société en mouvement" [The Frontiers of Leach seen through Burman Migrations, or How to Think of Society in Movement]. *Moussons, Recherche en Sciences Humaines sur l'Asie du Sud-Es*t [Monsoons, Research in the Humanities of Southeast Asia] 17 (2011): 105–25.

——. "The Maung Aye's Legacy: Burmese and Moken Encounters in the Southern Borderland of Myanmar (1997–2007)". In *Burmese Lives: Ordinary Life Stories Under the Burmese Regime*, edited by Wen-Chin Chang and Eric Tagliacozzo. Oxford: Oxford University Press, 2014, pp. 147–73.

——. *Trajectoires littorales de l'hégémonie birmane (Irrawaddy, Tenasserim, sud Thaïlande)* [Littoral trajectories of Burman Hegemony (Irrawaddy, Tenasserim and South Thailand)]. Bangkok/Paris: Research Institute on Contemporary Southeast Asia (IRASEC)/Les Indes Savantes, 2015.

—— and Jacques Ivanoff. "De la segmentation sociale à l'ethnicité dans les suds péninsulaires? réflexions sur les constructions identitaires et les jalons ethniques à partir de l'exemple des pêcheurs birmans du Tenasserim" [From Social Segmentation to Ethnicity in Peninsular South]. *Aséanie* 22 (2008): 11–46.

Brac de la Perrière, Bénédicte. "Sibling Relationships in the nat Stories of the Burmese Cult of the 'Thirty-Seven'". *Moussons, Recherche en Sciences Humaines sur l'Asie du Sud-Est* [Monsoons, Research in the Humanities of Southeast Asia] 5 (2002): 31–48.

——. "Les rituels de consécration des statues de Bouddha et de naq en Birmanie.

Adaptation de Formes Rituelles Indiennes?" [Consecration Rituals of Budddha and nat Statues in Burma]. In *Rites Hindous, Transferts et Transformations* [Hindu Rituals, Transfers and Transformations], edited by Gérard Colas and Gilles Tarabout. Paris: Ecole des Hautes Etudes en Sciences Sociales, Collection Purusārtha, 2006, pp. 201–35.

———. "To Marry a Man or a Spirit? Women, the Spirit Possession Cult, and Domination in Burma". In *Women and the Contested State: Religion, Violence and Agency in South and Southeast Asia*, edited by Patricia Lawrence and Monique Skidmore. Notre Dame: University of Notre Dame, 2007, pp. 208–28.

———. "De l'élaboration de l'identité birmane comme hégémonie à travers le culte birman des trente-sept seigneurs" [On the Elaboration of Burman Identity through the Burman Cult of the Thirty-Seven Lords]. *Aséanie* 22 (2008): 95–119.

Condominas, Georges. *L'espace social. A propos de l'Asie du Sud-Est* [The Social Space. About Southeast Asia]. Paris: Flammarion, (Coll. "Sciences"), 1980.

Dao The Tuan and François Molle. "The Chao Phraya Delta in Perspective: A Comparison with the Red River and Mekong deltas, Viêt Nam". *International Conference The Chao Phraya Delta: Historical Development, Dynamics and Challenges of Thailand's Rice Bowl*. Bangkok: Bangkok Kasetsart University, 2000.

de Mersan, Alexandra. "A New Palace for Mra Swan Dewi. Changes in Spirit Cults in Arakan (Rakhine) State". *Asian Ethnology* 68, no. 2 (2009): 307–32.

Geographer (The). *International Boundary Study, no. 63, Burma-Thailand Boundary*. Washington, D.C.: Office of the Geographer, Bureau of Intelligence and Research, 1966.

Hall, Daniel George Edward. *Burma*. London: Hutchinson University Library, 1960 [1950].

Holmes, Robert. "Burmese Domestic Policy: The Politics of Burmanisation". *Asian Survey* 7, no. 3 (1967): 188–97.

Houtman, Gustaaf. "Mental Culture in Burma Crisis Politics: Aung San Suu Kyi and the National League for Democracy". Tokyo: Research Institute for Languages and Cultures of Asia and Africa (ILCAA), Monograph Series 33, 1999.

International Office for Migration (IOM). *Assessing Potential Changes in the Migration Patterns of Myanmar Migrants and their Impacts on Thailand*. Bangkok: The Asian Research Centre for Migration, 2013.

Irrawaddy Magazine. "For Burma's Rohingya, a Permanent Segregation?", 28 August 2014 <http://www.irrawaddy.org/burma/burmas-rohingya-permanent-segregation.html> (accessed 29 August 2014).

Ivanoff, Jacques. "L'épopée de Gaman: histoire et conséquences des rapports Moken/Malais et Moken/Birmans" [The Epic of Gaman: history and consequences of the Moken-Malay and Moken-Burman relations]. *Asie du Sud-Est et Monde Insulindien* XVI, no. 1–4 (1985): 97–124.

———. "Manger du riz ou ne pas manger du riz? Le choix moken (Archipel Mergui)" [To Eat or Not to Eat Rice? The Moken Choice (Mergui Archipelago)]. *Techniques et Culture* 31–32 (1998): 331–46.

———. *Les naufragés de l'histoire. Les jalons épiques de l'identité* [The Shipwrecked of History. The Epic Stakes of Identity]. Paris: Les Indes Savantes, 2004.
Leach, Edmund. R. "The Frontiers of 'Burma'". *Comparative Studies in Society and History* 3, no. 1 (1960): 49–68.
Lehman, Frederic K. "Ethnic Categories in Burma and the Theory of Social Systems". In *Southeast Asian Tribes, Minorities, and Nations* 1, edited by Peter Kunstadter. Princeton: Princeton University Press, 1967, pp. 93–124.
Leider, Jacques. "Kingship by Merit and Cosmic Investiture: An Investigation into King Alaungmintaya's Self-Representation". *Journal of Burma Studies* 15, no. 2 (2011): 165–88.
Lieberman, Victor B. "Ethnic Politics in Eighteenth-Century Burma". *Modern Asian Studies* 12, no. 3 (1978): 455–82.
———. "Reinterpreting Burmese History". *Comparative Studies in Society and History* 29, no. 1 (1987): 162–94.
Morgan, Kenneth W., ed. *The Path of Buddha. Buddhism Interpreted by Buddhists*. New York: The Ronald Press, 1965.
Nakamura, Hajime. "El problema del individualismo en Oriente" [The Problem of Individualism in the Orient]. *Estudios Orientales* 3, no. 1 (1968): 1–26.
Nash, Manning. "Burmese Buddhism in Everyday Life". *American Anthropologist* 65, no. 2 (1962): 285–95.
O'Connor, Richard A. "Agricultural Change and Ethnic Succession in Southeast Asian States: A Case for Regional Anthropology". *The Journal of Asian Studies* 54, no. 4 (1995): 968–96.
Pavin Chachavalpongpun. *A Plastic Nation: The Curse of Thainess in Thai-Burmese Relations*. Lanham: University Press of America, 2005.
Rozenberg, Guillaume. "How Giving Sanctifies: The Birthday of Thamanya Hsayadaw in Burma". *The Journal of the Royal Anthropological Institute* 10, no. 3 (2004): 495–515.
———. "Être birman, c'est être bouddhiste" [Being Burman is Being Buddhist]. In *Birmanie Contemporaine* [Contemporary Burma], edited by Gabriel Defert. Bangkok: Research Institute on Contemporary Southeast Asia (IRASEC), 2008, pp. 29–52.
Schober, Julian S. "Paths to Enlightenment: Theravada Buddhism in Upper Burma". Doctoral dissertation, University of Illinois, 1989.
Scott, James C. "The Erosion of Patron-Client Bonds and Social Change in Rural Southeast Asia". *The Journal of Asian Studies* 32, no. 1 (1972): 5–37.
Shorto, Harry L. "The Dewatau Sotapan: a Mon Prototype of the 37 Nats". *Bulletin of the School of Oriental and African Studies* 30 (1967): 127–41.
Smith, Martin. *Ethnic Groups in Burma Development, Democracy and Human Rights*. London: Anti-Slavery International, 1994.
South, Ashley. *Mon Nationalism and Civil War in Burma. The Golden Sheldrake*. New York: RoutledgeCurzon, 2003.
Sunait Chutintaranond and Than Tun. *On Both Sides of the Tenasserim Range: History of Siamese-Burmese Relations*. Bangkok: Institute of Asian Studies Monographs, 1995.

Than Myint-U. *The Making of Modern Burma*. Cambridge: Cambridge University Press, 2000.

Thongchai Winichakul. *Siam Mapped. A History of the Geo-body of a Nation.* Chiangmai: Silkworm Books, 2005.

Walton, Matthew J. "The 'Wages of Burman-ness': Ethnicity and Burman Privilege in Contemporary Myanmar". *Journal of Contemporary Asia* 3, no. 1 (2013): 1–27.

White, Walter Grainge. *The Sea Gypsies of Malaya: An Account of the Nomadic Mawken of the Mergui Archipelago with a Description of their Ways of Living, Customs, Habits, Boats, Occupations, etc.* Bangkok: White Lotus Press, 1997 [1922].

5

Ritual and the Other in Rakhine Spirit Cults[1]

ALEXANDRA DE MERSAN

CONTEXT

In June 2012, the Rakhine State (Arakan)[2] was the scene of violent conflict between Buddhists and Muslims. Ever since then, there have been other outbreaks of violence with attacks on mosques and Muslim-owned houses in different parts of the region, notably in Mrauk U, around the town of Thandwe, Yangon and Meiktilla.

This conflict in Rakhine State raises the question of "strangeness" in the sense of belonging to groups at the margins of society, or of being an outsider. I will attempt here to provide an interpretation of the Rakhine concept of the strangeness of the outsider in relation to rituals dedicated to spirits.

Mrauk U is considered by the Rakhine as their cultural and historical heartland. Shortly after the outbreak of the events in Rakhine State, many inhabitants took part in a ceremony whose purpose was to relocate the statue of the palace guardian spirit so that the image faced the West, in the direction of the enemy. Also, many of the inhabitants whose houses had not caught fire in the course of the confrontations that spread through Sittwe (June/July 2012), the capital of Rakhine State, claimed that the guardian spirit of the town had protected them from the flames and from the enemy. This chapter will consider the conflict from the perspective of ritual.

Focusing on ritual is important. I have previously demonstrated how the former Burmese authorities in Rakhine State have relied on spirit cults, to exercise political control over the state (see de Mersan 2009, pp. 319–20,

323–26). In today's context of violence, rituals also allow us to take a step back so as to better understand the situation. Based on the assumption that there is a direct link between rituals and the society that develops them, my main question is "What do rituals have to say about the current social and political situation?". As we shall see with territorial cults, rituals are expressions of social relationships based on territory between different communities.

DIFFERENT NAMES FOR THE MUSLIMS OF RAKHINE STATE

Based on fifteen years of anthropological research in and on Rakhine State (see de Mersan 2005, 2009, 2010, 2012), this chapter reflects, above all, the points of view and beliefs of the Rakhine, a term which nowadays mostly means the Buddhist Rakhine. Although almost all Muslims of Rakhine State are known in the international media or by non-governmental organizations (NGOs) and other non-state actors as "Rohingya", the word was largely unknown to the majority of Buddhist Rakhine until the conflict in 2012, and was consequently never used except by a few learned men in specific contexts.[3] The Rakhine do not speak of "Muslims" but of *kala*. The term has been used for a long time in daily life to indicate "people from the West" or "foreigner". It designates people of Indian origin whatever their religion, whether Hindu or Muslim.[4] Nowadays, it is usually pejorative and tends to refer only to Muslims. This has not always been the case.[5]

The figure of *kala* has to be understood through the categorizations within which the Rakhine think, reflecting their beliefs and conceptions of selfness and otherness. The evolution of this figure has to be taken in a socio-historical perspective in order to understand its meaning and role through territorial cults. In short, *kala* belongs to a local category of "other", which a focus on ritual helps to define.

RAKHINE STATE AT THE MARGINS OF MYANMAR STUDIES

The Rakhine consider themselves a specific group (*lu myo*) distinct from the Burmese. They see themselves as a historical, religious and cultural community, as direct descendants of their own former Buddhist kingdom, inheritors of this land blessed by the Buddha, whose duty is to maintain the dispensation (*sasana*) (de Mersan 2012). After decades of political and social instability, the kingdom was conquered by the Burmese king Bodawpaya in 1785. Then, forty years later Arakan fell under British colonial rule from 1825 to 1948.

Despite colonization having lasted longer in Arakan than in Upper Burma, few studies or articles were published on the Rakhine compared to the Burmese. At the end of the nineteenth century, the Rakhine were seen by the British as an archaic, decaying Burmese race, as reflected in its language and religion, and which would inevitably blend into the Burmese stock or fall under Indian influence (Houghton 1897, p. 454; Spearman 1879, p. 151).

Until the 2012 conflict, in the world of Myanmar studies, Rakhine State was something of a marginal subject.[6] There is a relationship between the level of violence over claims for political recognition and the degree of national or international attention that arises when such violence occurs. Armed groups in Rakhine State were fewer and weaker than those in other states, such as those at the Thai border, for example.

The Rakhine State (like the Mon State) was created in 1974. While this gave official recognition to the cultural and historical differences between the Rakhine and the Burmese, its effect was only symbolic. Moreover, it further encouraged a process in which the Rakhine scholarly and intellectual elite were actively involved in the preservation and maintenance of their differences from the dominant Burmese, something that continues to this day. It is also important to stress the fact that recognition as an ethnic group implies an implicit "autochthony".

KALA THROUGHOUT RAKHINE HISTORY

Without going into details, it is my understanding that starting with British colonization, the subjects of the former kingship who were organized into hierarchized socio-economic classes, became levelled down into a more general community, and were categorized into specific races or ethnic groups in the course of the nineteenth century. This conception of the group emerged in the context of progressive local penetration by, and adoption of, European ideas of races and nations locally, in which "territory" was a fundamental aspect of self-identity.[7] This then resulted in the territorial definition or the assignment of groups, which were then undergoing this process of ethnicization/racialization, while British dominion was being mapped. The creation of frontiers became a problem when those drawn and established by the colonial administration took effect between Burma proper and British India in the 1930s.

Leach (1960, p. 50) reminded us that "frontiers" are not always well established, depend on the scale one chooses to consider, and are the outcome of the dynamics of interaction among groups. Arakan was the buffer zone between India and Southeast Asia. Throughout history the region between Chittagong and Arakan was also made up of continuous relationships and of commercial and cultural exchanges as is the case in most buffer zones. Historians like Jacques Leider (2004, p. 385) have demonstrated the strategic and economic importance of the Chittagong area for the prosperity of the Buddhist kingdom of Arakan which, as a matter of fact, was at its peak when it controlled the port of Chittagong in the seventeenth century. The Chittagong region belongs to the social, economic and political history of Arakan.

There were *kala* in Arakan before the British conquest. The regional presence and influence of populations from the West are ancient, but the degree to which they were recognized varied according to each period. During the Kingdom of Mrauk U (fifteenth to eighteenth century) many were captured in Bengal and, if not sold as slaves to the Dutch, brought by force to work the paddy fields. There were also Muslim poets at the court and Muslim traders in the royal city, but we do not know if they settled in the region. Although the presence of *kala* is ancient and doubtless heterogeneous, it is still difficult to evaluate their number and, above all, their role and contribution to the former kingdom of Arakan (see Leider 1998, pp. 190, 202–06 and d'Hubert and Leider 2011).[8]

First accounts from Westerners at the beginning of the colonial period describe a diversified and stratified society, and mention the presence of Indian-speaking groups whether Hindu or Muslim, with different rituals or cultural practices, who no doubt had a long history there, predating colonization. They point to different types of *kala* populations: pagoda slaves, fishermen, peasants, merchants, ritual specialists or astrologers. The word "Rohingya" refers to Muslims, who at that time were also called "*yakhine kala*". My hypothesis is that this name qualified a specific socioeconomic group (and not Muslims as a whole) in connection with a court elite, possibly of ritual specialists who were deported to Ava, among other members of the court.[9]

Although *kala* lived in Arakan before colonization, thousands of Indians settled in the region during the colonial era, finding work mostly in the rice paddies developed by the British authorities, but also in carrying paddy for trade.[10] We should not assume any continuity either in denominations or in culture between these old *kala* groups and the "new" migrants (as of the 1840s) who are linked to colonialism. From the earliest colonial administrative reports the former wanted to be differentiated from newcomers. However, neither the earlier nor the later migrants were described much during the British period; this was probably because they seemed more familiar, and Buddhism appears to have had much more appeal (if not fascination) for Westerners.

One of the main issues for nearly a hundred years has been the place of "Indians" (as they were called in colonial reports) in the country, who at least since the 1930s "became the symbol of colonialism, of foreign exploitation" (Tinker 1990, p. 40) and who fought to obtain some form of recognizable status within the Burmese nation.[11] There were outbreaks of violence in the 1930s against both migrant and settler Indians, especially in Rangoon in 1938, because of the hiring of Indian coolies rather than local workers ("natives"). As the report from the Commission of Enquiry on Violence noted, it was not a religious conflict, but mostly economic. What is unknown at this stage of research is: how did this violence reach Arakan? Neither do we know exactly how strong the communal tensions due to the nationalist movement that had existed in Rakhine State since the 1920s had been, and the history of this nationalism has yet to be written in detail.[12] This would help our understanding of the development of Rohingya identity. Indeed I argue that it needs to be understood in conjunction with the parallel development of Rakhine nationalism over time.

Hostility Develops during World War II
There were major confrontations between Muslims of Indian origin and the Rakhine, as the former had fought for the British against the Burmese/Rakhine during World War II, and the latter had fought against the British. They provoked massive population movements in 1942 when many Muslims fled southern Rakhine State to take shelter in the far north, near the Indian border (later East Pakistan), while Rakhine Buddhists left their villages near Maungdaw and Buthidaung in the northern part of the region to settle in the south and east.

Confrontations continued after World War II, in 1948, 1978, 1983 and 1990, with many *kala* taking refuge in Bangladesh, whenever a new constitution was drafted (as in 1947 and 1974) or when elections were held (whether consecutive or not to the adoption of these constitutions). This indicates to what extent race and ethnicity are connected to notions of citizenship (and foreigners), and the way it is considered appropriate that populations should participate in the life of the nation (see Yegar 2002, pp. 17–70). Also, these traumatic conflicts, which were never discussed nor resolved, had the consequence of creating lasting distrust between the followers of different religions.

Although it is impossible to evaluate true numbers because of the lack of any census or other form of reliable data since 1931(!), the regular settling or resettling of populations since Burma's independence from what was East Pakistan before becoming Bangladesh in 1971 is also a major aspect of the contemporary problem. Thus, the reasons explaining the antagonism towards *kala* also include the large number of migrants during the colonial period and alleged illegal immigration thereafter. Whether justified or not, the Rakhine have the feeling that invasions by populations from the West have been occurring for a long time. Many are seen as strangers, foreigners, undesirable, and nowadays as disloyal guests.

I argue that *kala* became marginalized and then (absent) foreigners in Rakhine social, cultural and political space through a process of ethnification that started during colonial times and was later consolidated by the creation of the Rakhine State. The idiom of Buddhism in the 1990s stressed this point, developing a growing conception of religion as an essential marker of ethnicity (see below).

"ISLAM" AND "STRANGER" ARE OFTEN SYNONYMOUS

It is important to bear in mind from this short historical overview that *kala*, in Rakhine State but also in most of the rest of Myanmar, have always been thought of as outsiders or guests, despite their sometimes lengthy presence. The words "Islam" and "foreigner" are often considered synonymous. This is underscored by the fact that there were few conversions to Islam. Most Muslims of Rakhine State are descendants of Indian immigrants, who took Rakhine wives, and had children who were Muslim as well. Although there is a lack of quantitative data, it appears that there are fewer interfaith marriages today compared to the past, and the fear for the decay of Buddhism (*sasana*) may have become more real to the Rakhine.

This perception of Islam as foreign is expressed by the words the Rakhine use to talk about Muslims, the most common of which is the word *kala*. Another word the Rakhine use as a synonym is "Bengali" (that is, from Bengal). In that case, it emphasizes their recent and thus implicitly illegal settling in Rakhine State.

Finally, we must stress the fact that fear of Islam is real, and that it reinforces this feeling of Muslims as foreigners. The idea that they aim to conquer the region, to dominate and control it, is widespread. Fear has been further nurtured by aftershocks from the 9/11 World Trade Center attack.

Since then, Myanmar has received images of Islam mostly as a religion of disorder, radicalism, terrorism and conquest. Since the outbreaks of violence in 2012, many DVDs or pictures (which are often compilations of the very worst examples of radical Islam) have been circulated, keeping this fear alive.

IMPORTANCE OF THE IDIOM OF BUDDHISM

This state of mind exists side-by-side with a sometimes reified idea that the Rakhine have of their own history and culture. This idea reached its zenith during the 1990s up until 2007 at a time when the Burmese military junta promoted Buddhism, to both strengthen its authority and legitimize its power. This emphasis on religion in national politics became problematic in the Rakhine State. Indeed, confronted by this process of "Myanmar-ification" as described by Houtman (1999, pp. 59–156), the Rakhine could only express their ethnicity or their national specificity without fear of censorship or repression by adopting the same tools as the junta. The strengthening of this distinct historical community has not ceased over the past fifteen years, and continues through the reference to Buddhism in such tangible forms as in collective undertakings that unite all social actors around Buddhist donations (de Mersan 2012, pp. 109–10). But unlike other multiethnic regions of the country (Robinne 2008), Buddhism cannot serve as a unifying factor here. It even creates borders by following lines of differentiation. This has led the inhabitants to define them according to religion transformed into essential ethnic criteria based furthermore on an increasingly racial concept of ethnic groups (Houtman 1999, p. 71; Rozenberg 2008; Robinne 2015).

However, the consolidated "ethnification" of Rakhine society appeared detrimental to other groups of Rakhine State such as the Muslim populations, whose long-standing local residence and even amicable relations with Buddhists were downplayed and often negated. The ethnification process prevents them from thinking as a plural society in terms of multiculturalism, or from accepting diversity or hybrid identities.

KALA AT THE MARGIN OF RAKHINE STATE

Antagonism had reached such a level by the 1990s when I started working in Rakhine State, that there was a tendency to deny and even erase any Indian presence and influence in Rakhine culture, and for the Rakhine to throw all Muslims together into one basket. At that time India still had a positive value, but this was mostly based on ancient links or influence on Arakan art, religion and literature (see Gutman 1976). Already infrequent references to and mentions of a more complex and multi-faceted history vanished. Indeed, apart from a few articles written in the 1950s and before the Ne Win military coup, there was no mention of a contemporary *kala* or Muslim presence and influence in books and other publications about the Rakhine State. The only exception would appear to be the group known as Kaman who sought refuge in the kingdom of Arakan in the seventeenth century, and are considered to be fully "Arakanized".

On one aspect more directly linked to the Buddhist narrative, or what may be called more socially controlled narratives, the figure of *kala* tends to disappear completely at the beginning of the current century. This can be observed through legends and stories I recorded that were related to some Buddhist sites. In two of them, one of the protagonists is the daughter of a defeated Bengali monarch who was given to the king of Arakan as tribute for his conquest. In one, this aspect of the story has been deleted from its most recent versions. In others, it was said that the king of Arakan rejected the "gift" because the daughter was insufficiently beautiful, or to be more explicit, the people disliked her because she came from Bengal. Both cases reveal a marginalized presence of *kala*, if not the progressive disappearance of this traditional figure from the Rakhine cultural and social landscape.

This contrasts with the position of *kala* in daily life. There is a real lack of studies and anthropological studies on the various populations of Rakhine State including those labelled *kala*. However, before the conflict started, there were many interrelationships between the Rakhine and "them". These relations that differed according to place of residence, were in many places mostly ones that could be qualified as interdependence among neighbours (for example, between rice-growing peasants and livestock breeders) or between business partners, and often hierarchical (as between producers, merchants and carriers, unskilled labourers and their employers) in favour of the Rakhine, *kala* usually occupying a subaltern social position. There were many interpersonal, even friendly relationships, but not being valued; they were seldom mentioned in discussions when people were questioned about them. Finally, although these relationships were based on economic and social interactions, to my knowledge, there were no common collective celebrations or rituals (*pwe*) shared by them. This situation in the late 1990s has to be understood in the light of the historical perspective.

However, *kala* appeared at the margin of society, but in a different position. There are two kinds of discourses: one socially controlled especially with a political purpose, and another one expressed implicitly in practices or domains which are not invested, and which would temper the former one. Stated briefly, a "nationalist" narrative and discourse would deny or minimize any effective relationship. It is produced by the authorizing, legitimizing agents and guardians of Rakhine traditions, that is, among the well-educated (learned people and the elite). As previously noted, this is inseparable from both the policies of the former junta and the Rakhine need for ethnic distinction from the Burmese in their struggle for recognition of their own political rights, which is based on cultural differentiation (see de Mersan 2015). A look at rituals dedicated to spirits, however, provides a different perspective on these issues.

EPISTEMOLOGICAL PRECAUTIONS WHEN DISCUSSING RITUAL

In the context of violent situations as in Rakhine State, documents need to be treated with caution. This may be particularly true of data relating to ritual and this also raises the question of the status of ritual in society, its significance and its eventual functions. Critics frequently make use of these kinds of data to draw conclusions for their own ends. This is underlined by the fact that analyses of ritual are often rare, as many anthropologists have found, seldom going beyond saying that "it is tradition" and that people are doing what they or their forefathers have always done. Rituals are always changing even though they are practised regularly, as in the case presented here. They may have many variations due to factors such as place, social actors, climatic conditions, socioeconomic or political conditions and so on. No doubt these constant adjustments are integral conditions for their perpetuation. However, accumulated observations of the same ritual and its variations make it possible to extract a kind of structure or general framework.

Also, despite such difficulties, it is still possible to consider data from ritual as an expression of something whose contextual transformation says something precisely about the context. It is a fact that rituals that people perform (whatever definition is given to ritual compared to other forms of social activity) have an effect on society, or have a meaning which aims at something which takes on this form. Rituals encompass a society's values (at least partially), and as such constitute a kind of narrative both about the society or the group that produces them.[13] Here, as we shall see, ritual dedicated to spirits embodies a discourse at the margins of society and which, as such, if not opposing, at least challenges socially dominant narratives within Rakhine society. I will focus here on territorial cults.

RITUALS AND SPIRIT CULTS

In Rakhine dialect, the word *nat* refers to a wide range of entities: divinities from the Buddhist cosmology, territory spirits and so on. In Rakhine State, as in many places in Southeast Asia, spirits (*nat*) are the lords and owners (*rhan*) of the land (de Mersan 2009, p. 311; Lehman 2003). They possess and control the land, an area over which they have jurisdiction. The transformation of a local or place-related force into a tutelary spirit is a pre-condition of any human settlement. Inhabitants living on its domain then enjoy its protection, so long as they act and behave properly. Then, as for any relationship, it also has to be nurtured, which is the aim of an annual collective ceremony.

Spirit cults indicate the importance of territory in the constitution of local groups and reflect the social organization among the Rakhine that is based on it. These cults are above all like celebrations of specific localities.

In Rakhine State, as in many other societies in Southeast Asia, rituals such as territorial cults "are often privileged places to build and express the political relationships within the group and between groups" (Schlemmer 2012, p. 21). As such, they legitimize control of that territory and promote its fertility. This is the case as far as they share a common ritual language. At the beginning of my study on the subject in Rakhine State, I was expecting to observe common practices among inhabitants of a same place (village, quarter or town) on spirit cults, whatever their religion or ethnicity.[14] This was not the case because where I observed these rituals, Muslims and Buddhists had already become physically and ideologically separated.[15] However, I lack historical information to show this apart from a few past references to cults common to the different groups, such as from Sittwe during colonial times, where Buddhists, Hindus and Muslims performed rituals in a common setting, or in Mrauk U before the 1990s in a cult dedicated to a spirit known as *motoshiri*. In any case, indications are that these populations no longer share a common ritual language (whereas, as we shall see, the Rakhine still do with other groups, such as the Marma or Hindus).

Even if *kala* or Muslims were not to be found among participants or devotees of these cults, the figure of *kala* was present in territorial cults.

TERRITORIAL CULTS

The Rakhine pay homage to spirits individually whenever they consider it necessary to ask for protection, help or support, but also possibly to inform the spirit of a new household event (a birth, a death, etc.). They also pay homage collectively in the annual ceremony dedicated to the guardian spirit of the village (*nat pwe*, *rwa rhan pwe*) during which they make offerings to the spirit so as to obtain good fortune, health, wealth, and protection from dangers and enemies. The village tutelary spirit (mostly female) is often indissociable from her brother spirit, called "Madjya", who is connected with wildness (and the forest as opposed to the civilized and socialized part of the village).[16] This pair of sibling nat represents figures of autochtony as they were originally the "power of the place".

Briefly put, the annual ceremony consists of inviting and pleasing this tutelary spirit. This is done through songs and dances performed by ritual specialists: musicians and mediums. Songs and dances are part of the offering.

Although dedicated to the owner of the village, many spirits are in fact invited. Spirits manifest themselves when entering the medium's body during this celebration. In other words, one after the other, the spirits possess a medium. The idea is that the ceremony's success depends on the number of spirits who respond to the invitation: the more the better. Their attendance means that they honour and pay homage to the village's tutelary spirit (in these cases it is subordinate to the locality as a value). Above all, they represent those groups with whom the Rakhine interact most frequently in daily life. It is about sustaining relationships of a more or less neighbourly type.

Songs (*nat khran*) recited ritually during this three-day long ceremony are like lists of spirits, who are invited one by one. These incantations then also describe the spirits' "physical" appearance, as "lords" or, more often, as "ladies", or the characteristics of their domain, possibly their journey to attend the ceremony, and so on.

The oral literature repertory, although very rich, is not well known, because it belongs to a domain of practices on which society places little value. Indeed, the elite, scholars and intellectuals are contemptuous of it and often relegate it to the field of superstition and to the uneducated (de Mersan 2009, pp. 311–12).[17] As a consequence, spirit cults have been less subject to the production of narratives by the elite and/or by nationalists, in their efforts to defend Rakhine particularism and the preservation of tradition, in the face of primarily hegemonic Burmese culture. There have nevertheless been examples in recent history of attempts to influence this domain. This also suggests that ritual space (that is, space created by ritual) attracts a broader range of interactions.

ETHNIC *NAT*

Many spirits are invited to attend the annual ceremony. Contrary to the Burmese cult of the Thirty-Seven Lords, which has a pantheon, genealogies, and spirits with known and established biographies sometimes merging with historical characters (see Temple 1906; Brac de la Perrière 1989, pp. 15–47), biographies or other details are scarce in Rakhine State. Among them, most are spirits of places socialized by human activities: rivers (because of fishing or boat traffic), paddy fields, the country (*praññ*), towns, villages, houses, and so on.

Invitations are also addressed to spirits who are considered non-Rakhine — mostly "Indian" (*kala nat*), "Burmese" (*bama nat*) and "Chin" (*khyan: nat*) spirits. This ethnic differentiation means a spirit whose domain is supposed to be inhabited mostly by *kala*, Burmese, or Chin people, or, it would sometimes appear, whose founders were *kala*, Burmese or Chin. There are no spirits labelled as Rakhine because, as owner or master (*rhan*) of the land, there is no need to qualify them as such. From the Rakhine point of view, this is self-evident.

In brief, "Burmese" guest spirits are considered as living in central Burma proper, and to have Pagan or Burmese cultural and historical roots. Some are also associated with a Rakhine village or another that is said to have been founded or inhabited by Burmese (who may have arrived during British colonization).

Chin spirit domains are those of people living in the upper reaches of the main rivers (Lemro, Kaladan, Mayu) in Rakhine State. They are usually characterized by their livelihood (shifting cultivation), and are associated with the forest, drinking rice-beer, traditional dances and attire.

There are two kinds of *kala nats*. Some are spirits whose domain is somewhere near the actual border or in Bengal or India (Naf River, Chittagong, Dhaka, Delhi) while others are in Rakhine State. In some villages of Rakhine State, the guardian spirit is said to be *kala*. As far as I understand, in these cases, the founder of the place was supposed to have been *kala*. *Kala nat* in rituals are distinguished by their clothes (a garment similar to a sari with the head covered and a decoration on the forehead or between the eyebrows (*bindi*) usually worn by Indian women), their way of dancing, and a higher pitched tone of voice in songs. They might also have a title indicating a higher rank (like Lord), *raja* or *pacha*, these titles qualifying the Indian figures according to their religion, respectively Hindu and Muslim. *Kala* spirits in this case are mostly characteristic of a region in western Rakhine State and/or relationships and interactions with the *kala* population.

Another *kala nat* plays a central role at the end of the ceremony dedicated to the village's guardian spirit. It is like a ritual specialist (*punna*) of Indian origin who has to perform the ritual's final sequence, like those who were officiating at the Rakhine or Burmese courts (Leider 2005). This is the representation of the sacrifice of a goat, and the success of the ceremony depends on it.

Kala Spirit is not Indigenous

The figure of *kala* appears to be more present in rituals, testimony to a complex and plural society with an Indian influence and culture but with Rakhine traditions and history. However, in this domain this figure of *kala* is also seen and conceived as external, or in a way foreign to local society. This is indicated by the label itself (that is, *kala*), but especially by the fact, as a medium informed me, that when the guardian spirit of a village is "*kala*" (or Burmese), there is no post/palace dedicated to "Madjya", the brother of the guardian spirit of the village. Also, in this case, the medium and drum player do not have to sing songs in which there is a pair of sibling (brother/sister) spirits. This suggests that these *kala* spirits are not considered indigenous, but settlers or guests, a category of "other" based on a foreign origin.

POWER CENTRES AND PERIPHERIES

Analysing ritual incantations is complex. I have already done this as a way of drawing mental maps of Rakhine social space (de Mersan 2010, pp. 34–48), so I shall not go too deeply into the details here. Suffice it to say that they are primarily mental topographies that describe and exalt the land (*prañ*, as space and resources, soil and land — what in French is called *terroir*, that combines the concepts of place and culture) through the evocation of the characteristics of each spirit's domain. It is specifically through these details that one gains an understanding of what their land means to the Rakhine. Their words bring this inhabited, socialized space alive and describe its specificity. The domains of the *nat* and their trajectories mentioned during the rituals are a series of familiar places and landscapes that are more or less known to the audience who have travelled through them and sometimes experienced them — one could even go so far as to say possessing an incorporated knowledge through both their daily and extraordinary activities. Their words make sense to the audience, and they enlighten by describing a known environment.

I call these incantations mental maps of Rakhine social space, maps in the sense that they are based on Rakhine topography, and that their enunciation reflects more or less the Rakhine landscape, but does not correspond to the empirical, geographic reality of Rakhine State. The Rakhine country (*praññ*) which emerges in the course of ritual incantations does not correspond to the actual administrative frontiers of Rakhine State even though gateways, thresholds, towns, islands, et cetera, each with its guardian *nat*, are mentioned and thereby confirm the pertinent, territory-based, social units of Rakhine society, which are different scales of identification.

These incantations are more than that. As mentioned, territorial cults are the celebration of specific localities through everything that constitutes and characterizes them, every feature by which each locality would define itself — mostly by its land, but also its values, social organization, relationships, history, and so on.[18] Content thus depends on the place and the moment of enunciation. For example, in Mrauk U region, one of its most characteristic components is its former royal city status; this is expressed in various ways among which is the final sacrifice of a goat as a palace ritual. It appears also that the world of spirits is connected to the former kingdom of Arakan in a political sense. The configuration of *nat* domains is similar to the administrative divisions of the former kingdom. Their recitation also represents a territory as a politically controlled domain, in this case, by a Buddhist monarch, reflecting the network of relationships he deployed from his capital, his sphere of influence, or (at least) his nominal authority over local populations, conquered or not. Domains evoked in songs dedicated to spirits correspond more or less to the golden age of Arakan kingdom expansion in the seventeenth century. Although there are few traces of former territorial cults in Rakhine State and little evidence of the kind of rituals that were practised at the time of the former kingdom, it seems that the Rakhine king might have relied on the local cults, or might have founded rituals dedicated to spirits to strenghten his authority over relevant localities.[19] This connection to territorial cults is based on the principle that to control the spirits of the land is to control (*sim theim*) the inhabitants but also, in other words, those performing territorial cults are masters of the land.

The domain as portrayed in incantations during the ritual reveals a kind of network of relationships (seemingly organized into a hierarchy) which requires further investigation to be better qualified; but they suggest a network of relationships that constitutes the frontiers of group identity in a way similar to Burmese spirit cults (Brac de la Perrière 2002, pp. 33, 36–38; Brac de la Perrière 2008, pp. 42–44), in a process by which assigning an identity to others is a way of establishing one's self.

POLITICAL USE OF TERRITORIAL CULTS

Social practices such as territorial cults embody a narrative at another level of Rakhine society, one of specific localities (each of them encompassing Rakhine values) which tempers the inevitable and necessary reified discourse that the Rakhine have to produce in another context, when facing Burmese hegemony based on strong ethnic frontier groups (see Gravers 2007).

I had already been told about an attempt in the early 2000s by an emblematic figure of Rakhine nationalism to transform spirit cults in Mrauk U. This person considered that since spirit cults belong to the domain of "traditions", they should be patronized and promoted as such. He organized a meeting in the town to which he invited all those involved in the spirit cults so that he could find out exactly how the ritual is organized and celebrated, and subsequently prepare a similar ceremony, like a show, during a pagoda festival. He learned on this occasion about the invitation given to all these guest spirits: lords of the country, Burmese spirits, *kala* spirits and so on. Astonished if not angry, he then sponsored a ceremony but with only "Rakhine *nat* and no 'foreign *nat*'". Indeed he considered that the Burmese and *kala* presence in Rakhine State, was already excessive in daily life, like invaders, the Burmese being associated with the army and civil servants in key positions settled in Rakhine state on the one hand, and the *kala* associated with "waves" of illegal immigrants on the other. This was rather an exceptional situation, and was more an entertainment than a ritual, but it illustrates the possible manipulation or what can happen when the field of culture is employed as a form of political contestation and resistance against hegemony (de Mersan 2015).

To summarize, the *kala* figure tends to be ignored or to be minimized in narratives related to the most valued domains of practices, which reflect the general opinion towards those seen as *kala*. However, this figure still exists in practices considered marginal such as spirit cults so long as they are not seen to be worth investing with a political purpose. The figure of *kala* in spirit cults is seen at the margin of the country in terms of localization, as a neighbour, or, less often, as local groups (although not indigenous). In any case, it is viewed as a guest with whom interrelationships in daily life take place, as with the Burmese or Chin. Although these relationships were hierarchical and not valued, they were revealed in rituals. In other words, these cults indicate cultural (or ethnic) differenciation between groups (based more or less on their territorialization) not so much to oppose strong cultural frontiers as to underline relationships between them.

RITUALS SINCE 2012 — A CLEAR RUPTURE

Cults are more or less an immediate reflection of the sociopolitical context of the localities which celebrate them, and allow the observer to grasp their evolution. For instance, in 2008 mediums explained to me that some spirits that had been invited to the annual ceremony "failed to attend", as they were already "busy with a meeting in Singapore". Saying this is a way of underlining the fact that emigration from Rakhine State to Singapore was (and is still) an important factor in this place. Since then many villages have been depopulated by the departure of a significant social component of their population.

In the aftermath of the events of June 2012, I was interested to study the possible effects on cults dedicated to the spirits, and what ritual would have to say about the conflict. As rituals show, two different moments can be distinguished: the crisis was at its peak in 2012, and continued to be omnipresent but less extreme in 2013. The events of 2012 happened to coincide with the June–July period of the year, preceding the Buddhist Lent, when the inhabitants make spirit offerings. In Sittwe, the ceremony was shortened and performed in a single day because there was a curfew and it was dangerous to be out. However, despite the climate of violence and fear, hundreds of people attended as usual, making their offerings to the *nat*, begging its protection or demonstrating their gratitude towards it.

The main ceremony performed in Mrauk U as mentioned at the beginning of this article was unusual due to the large number and different categories of inhabitants who were involved among whom were those who are not usually involved, at least not publicly and even those who condemn these practices. The ceremony clearly identified the enemy from the Rakhine point of view: it pointed to the *kala*, the people from the West, and begged the assistance of the palace guardian spirit, one of the highest spirit authorities. Thus, all the social components of the town were gathered together to face the enemy in a ceremony quite distinct from the annual territorial cults.

Then in 2013, I observed two rituals in Rakhine State: one near Mrauk U, for the guardian spirit of a village, and the other in Sittwe, for the tutelary spirit of the town.

Nat Pwe near Mrauk U

The social and political situation in Rakhine State in relation to the conflict affected everything. The conflict was omnipresent in people's thoughts and daily conversations and in implicit or explicit actions in the course of the rituals. Nothing explicit in relation to the conflict was done during the ritual over the three-day ceremony near Mrauk U, but perhaps the most visible fact was that no spirit identified as *kala* was invited. Interestingly a new *nat* had been invited, which I had never seen in previous ceremonies. It was named '*doppa nat*'; it was physically handicapped because of a misdeed in a former life (he had eaten the food of a monk, I was told). In other words, it was a way of reminding people of the law of *kamma* and the consequences of mistreating Buddhism. Also, the new site, which had to be found for the palace of the spirit, was well located: it was within sight of the monastery to the north so it could then pray to the Buddha, but also, since it was situated on the top of a hillock, it could see any enemies that might come from the side where the villages had mostly Muslim inhabitants and with whom there had been violent incidents a few months earlier.

The final sequence ("the sacrifice of the goat") was carried out as usual with the *kala nat*. However, when later questioned about the identity of this *nat*, the drummer answered that it was a servant of the guardian spirit of the village, employed for this more menial task. In other words, the rank of the *nat* had been diminished, inverted even, but this *nat* remains inherently linked with Rakhine kingship.

Finally the structure of the ceremony was not significantly altered except that some spirit guests became undesirable or were downgraded, as relationships with the *kala* in daily life were all broken. However the demand for protection from a now clearly identified enemy appeared to have taken on greater significance. It is important to note that this village organizing the ceremony with a population of less than one thousand has fifty inhabitants working in Malaysia. At that time there were migrants workers from Myanmar, who were victims of attacks in Malaysia in retaliation for what had happened to Muslims in Myanmar. People in the village were thus very worried. Pleas for protection were repeated many times.

And in Sittwe

As usual, in addition to the Rakhine, the inhabitants attending the *pwe* in Sittwe included Hindus and Marma (see note 8), which confirms their common ritual language. However, they were aware of the need to conform to the ritual norm in this moment of high tensions, and aware that they should appear to be close to the dominant group through common cultural practices (that is, Rakhine).[20]

Rituals function as mirrors of the political and social situation. In observing how they were possibly affected by the 2012 conflict, we also learned that these rituals express inter-relationships. Further protection was expected during the crisis and subsequent to it, indicating that a climate of fear and insecurity prevailed.

CONCLUSION

In this chapter we have seen how the denomination of *kala* is a local category of others within Rakhine society. The word *kala* has always carried the idea of exteriority, or outsider *par nature*, as it indicates a foreigner or external origin. In the past, it did not necessarily mean that those named as such, those of a different origin (and consequently with different religious practices, language and so on) who were recognized or considered foreigners, did not participate in the life of the city, or were not considered social components of society. Ritual specialists at the Rakhine court would illustrate this. Foreign origin was not incompatible with participation in local life.

This became problematic when groups had to identify through territoriality. In contemporary Myanmar, participation in the life of the nation through citizenship is based on ethnicity, which implies recognition of "autochthony" or "indigenousness", but also ethnicity based on the idea of a community of religion, language and territory.

The Rakhine consider themselves the masters, owners of the land and they see *kala* as guests. This is expressed through the implicit recognition that those performing territorial cults are masters of the land (that is, of their inhabitants). This is not problematic so long as other groups do not claim any rights or control over the land.

Returning to our earlier question: what do rituals or territorial cults have to say about the social and political situation? Firstly they express the link the Rakhine have to their territory. As such they express narratives and embody values on a scale of belonging at the level of localities different from the State/ethnic one. They also reflect political and social situations. In a normal context they reflect the daily interactions and interrelationships between the Rakhine and other groups in Rakhine State whether Burmese, Chin or Muslims. Those groups enjoy several positions in the local ritual system although cults express a conception of them as not being indigenous. In other words, territorial cults can be analysed as the ritual expression of social relationships based on territory. In this case, the analysis of ritual indicates a process of differentiation among groups, in terms of interaction. It appears that groups are incorporated into a domain so as to be better differentiated and thus find a place for themselves.

At the same time, they belong to a domain of practices which, till now and even after, was not invested with a political purpose. This tempers a more socially dominant and controlled narrative which does not celebrate them and is silent about them. However, although there has been no political use of rituals dedicated to spirits by the Rakhine elite after the events of 2012, today's cult situation indicates a clear break with the past between communities. And we do not know how long this situation will last.

Notes

1. As a token of my respect and friendship, this article is dedicated to the memory of the late Bagyi Shwe Maung Thar, who had a clear understanding of spirit cults as a very valuable source of information on Rakhine culture in its broadest sense. Thanks to him, ritual specialists agreed to share part of their knowledge with me. I would also like to express my gratitude to them and my thanks also to Bénédicte Brac de la Perrière, Jacques Leider and Chris Fisher for reading and commenting on this chapter.
2. The word "Rakhine" is an ethnonym and can be used as an adjective. The use of the term Arakan versus Rakhine at times provokes heated discussions among the Arakanese. Although the word "Rakhine" is closer to the Arakanese pronunciation when they refer to themselves and their country, it was imposed by the former junta which in 1991 changed names including that of the country and certain regions and population groups in order to, as it was claimed, break with British colonial heritage. "Arakan" became "Yakhine", according to the Burmese pronunciation of the word. Finally, it is not so much the term than the Romanization/Anglicization of their ethnonym based on their own pronunciation, which is "Rakhine", that has been adopted in Myanmar and internationally, and which competes with or is as legitimate — maybe — as the term "Arakan". In this article Arakan is used to refer to the former kingdom and to the period prior to the official change. Note that the main political party created in 2014 is known in English as the *Arakan National Party*.
3. In those cases, use of the word Rohingya (or more precisely "Rohangya" at that time, according to the Rakhine pronunciation) was influenced by the media. Furthermore, until recently most Muslims would not have used the term when referring to themselves.
4. Hindus are seen today as a specific ethnic group/race. They are less numerous than the Muslims, and when there are mixed marriages between Hindus and Buddhists, the children are Hindu or/and Buddhist. It means there is no need to convert religion.
5. That is why, although problematic, I still use the word. In doing so, there is no intention to insult or to belittle any group.
6. Published texts on Arakan are mostly restricted to Rakhine authors in Myanmar. Among foreign scholars, one may however note P. Gutman's thesis on ancient

Arakan (1976) and works on linguistics (Bernot 1958, 1965; Okell 1995). Since the 1990s, new research has been undertaken in history (see among others Jacques Leider 2004, 2008; Michael Charney 1999, 2002; Stephan Van Galen 2008), art (see Catherine Raymond 1998) and anthropology (see Alexandra de Mersan 2005, 2012, 2015; Celine Coderey 2011, 2012). Works have also been published by Japanese researchers, but these are mostly in Japanese (except Okamoto 2010).

7. As well as language and subsequently religion. On the adoption by the Burmese of Western notions such as racial classification and territorial definition throughout the nineteenth century, see Candier (2010, pp. 90–92) and Gravers (2007, pp. 19–22).
8. When Burma was under monarchic rule, the king's subjects identified themselves in relation to either a professional group or by their feudal obligations towards the ruler. This system seems to have progressively collapsed after the fall of the Arakan monarchy. There have also been many Rakhine who escaped to the other side of the present-day border and settled there when the Burmese conquered the region in 1785 (they are known as Marma or Marama gree). Some *kala* also joined this exodus. More information can be found in the monographs of the anthropologist Lucien Bernot (1967) who spent one and a half years among the Marma in the Chittagong Hill Tracts in the late 1950s.
9. Although the term Rohingya is ancient (referenced by Buchanan in 1798) — its use at least predates the colonial period — there are no traces of it in colonial literature until the late 1940s. That is why my hypothesis is that the term was used to define one specific social group and not all *kala* in Arakan. The term "Rohingya" might have survived among those families deported to Ava. The re-emergence of the term in Burma in the 1930s is concomitant with the rise of Burmese anti-British nationalism and/or the mapping of a frontier when Burma was separated from British India in 1937. On Rohingya, see Leider (2015).

The Buchanan reference was only discovered recently (fifteen years ago). This explains why the Rakhine claim that the word was invented by Mujaheed, or Muslims fighting for their own state distinct from the Arakan (i.e. Buddhist) State in 1948. Despite arguments over the term, there can be no dispute that most of the *kala* came during the colonial period. Recognition as an ethnic group of Myanmar means implicitly that it is indigenous — that is before British colonization. They are thus seen as migrants from that time and consequently not considered indigenous. That is the main reason why asking the Rakhine to recognize the presence of an ethnic group named Rohingya which identifies most Muslims in Arakan has provoked such an angry reaction among them.
10. What is less well known (or less emphasized) is that many Burmese also settled there.
11. Things are more complex in reports and censuses as categories and criteria used to establish such population categorization evolved from one census to another.
12. One of Arakan's iconic figures is the monk U Ottama, famous all over Myanmar for having fought against the British during the nationalist period; see Schober

(2011, pp. 103-05). Celebration and homage dedicated to the monk which have always occurred in Arakan have increased since 2012.
13. For a similar approach, see articles by Sadan (2007, p. 38) and Dean (2007, p. 127) in Gravers (2007).
14. As it is the case in southern Thailand between Muslims and Buddhists, see Horstmann (2011).
15. In the 1990s, the Burmese junta decided to promote Mrauk U as a tourist destination. As such, houses, which had been built on the ruins of the ancient palace, for example, had to be removed. If the owners were Muslim, they had to move out of the town. It was also said that Muslims had to leave some nearby villages to live in a place near the Bangladeshi border.
16. Both have a shrine in the village, the two of them being side by side. Madjya is usually honoured during the annual ceremony.
17. There is also no doubt that more than a hundred years of colonization, which delimited and categorized this field of practices as superstition, had influence on the local elite's approach to and conception of it. Data is therefore scarce. However, some Rakhine have recorded and written of spirit cults as traditions.
18. These localities are encompassed within Buddhist cosmology. It would also be interesting to study territorial cults in places near the current frontier between Myanmar and Bangladesh like Maungdaw or Buthidaung.
19. For relationships between former kingship and spirits cults in Burma proper see, amongst others, works of Brac de la Perrière (1989, 1998) and Lehman (2003). The listing of songs connected to royal domains and kingship is also found in other parts of Southeast Asia, like in Cambodia, Chandler (1976) and Mikaelian (2007). Also the practice of reciting a list of places associated with spirits is widespread in insular Southeast Asia, see Fox (1997).
20. Progress also differed here because the Burmese authorities have taken control of it over the past decade, gradually transforming the guardian spirit from a tutelary one linked to the land into a guardian spirit of Buddhism. In short there is a process of Burmanization underway here through Buddhism.

References

Bernot, Denise. "Rapports phonétiques entre le dialecte marma et le birman" [Phonetic similarities and differences between Marma dialect and Burmese Language]. *Bulletin de la société de linguistique de Paris* 53, fasc 1 (1958): 273-94.

———. "The Vowel Systems of Arakanese and Tavoyan". *Lingua* (1965): 942-53.

Bernot, Lucien. *Les paysans arakanais du Pakistan Oriental: l'histoire, le monde végétal et l'organisation sociale des réfugiés Marma (Mog)* [The Arakanese Peasants of Eastern Pakistan: The History, their World of Vegetable Ressources and the Social Organization of Marma Refugees (Mog)]. Paris, La Haye: Editions Mouton & Co., Ecole Pratique des Hautes Etudes, 1967.

Buchanan, Francis M.D. "A Comparative Vocabulary of Some of the Languages Spoken in the Burma Empire". *Asiatic Researches* 5 (1798): 219-40.

Brac de la Perrière, Bénédicte. *Les rituels de Possession en Birmanie: du Culte d'état aux Cérémonies Privées* [Possession Rituals in Burma: From State Cult to Private Ceremony]. Paris: Editions Recherches sur les Civilisations, 1989.

———. "Le Cycle des Fêtes de *naq* en Birmanie Centrale: une Circumambulation de l'espace Birman" [The *naq* Festivals Cycle of Central Burma: A Circumambulation of Burmese Space]. In *Etudes birmanes en hommage à Denise Bernot* [Burmese Studies in Homage to Denise Bernot], edited by Pierre Pichard and François Robinne. Paris: École française d'Extrême-Orient, 1998, pp. 289–331.

———. "Sibling Relationships in the *Nat* stories of the Burmese Cult to the 'Thirty-seven'". *Moussons* 5 (2002): 31–48.

———."De l'élaboration de l'identité birmane comme hégémonie à travers le culte birman des Trente-sept Seigneurs" [The Development of Burmese Identity as Hegemony across the Burmese Cult of Thirty-Seven Lords]. *Aséanie* 22 (2008): 95–119.

Candier, Aurore."Convergences conceptuelles en Birmanie: La Transition du xixe Siècle" [Conceptual Convergences in Burma: the 19th Century Period of Transition], *Moussons* 16 (2010): 81–101.

Chandler, David P. "Maps for the Ancestors: Sacralized Topography and Echoes of Angkor in Two Cambodians Texts". *Journal of the Siam Society* 64, no. 2 (1976): 170–87.

Charney, Michael W. *Where Jambudipa and Islamdom Converged: Religious Change and the Emergence of Buddhist Communalism in Early Modern Arakan (Fifteenth to Nineteenth Centuries)*. Doctoral dissertation, University of Michigan: 1999.

———. "Beyond State-centered Histories in Western Burma: Missionizing Monks and Intra-regional Migrants in the Arakan Littoral, c. 1784–1860". In *The Maritime Frontier of Burma. Exploring Political, Cultural and Commercial Interaction in the Indian Ocean World, 1200–1800*, edited by Jos Gommans and Jacques Leider. Leiden: KITLV Press, 2002, pp. 213–24.

Coderey, Céline. *Les maîtres du "reste": la quête de l'équilibre dans les conceptions et les pratiques thérapeutiques en Arakan (Birmanie)* [Masters of the 'Remainder': the Search for Balance in the Therapeutic Conceptions and Practices in Arakan (Burma)], Marseille: Université de Provence, 2011.

———. "The *weikza*'s role in Arakanese healing practices". *Journal of Burma Studies* 16, no. 2 (2012): 181–211.

de Mersan, Alexandra."*Espace Rituel et Construction de la Localité. Contribution à l'étude Ethnographique d'une Population de la Birmanie Contemporaine: les Arakanais*" [Ritual Space and the Making of a Locality. Contribution to the Ethnography of the Arakanese Population of Contemporary Burma]. Doctoral Dissertation, Ecole des Hautes Etudes en Sciences Socials, 2005.

———."A New Palace for Mra Swan Dewi. Changes in Spirit Cults in Arakan (Rakhine) State". *Asian Ethnology* 68, no. 2 (2009): 307–32.

———."La Construction Rituelle du Territoire à Travers la Tradition Orale. Étude d'une Incantation aux Esprits d'Arakan (Birmanie)" [Ritual Territory Building through the Oral Tradition: Study of an Ode to the Spirits of Arakan (Burma)]. *Aséanie* 26 (2010): 31–55.

——. "The 'Land of the Great Image' and the Test of Time. The Making of a Buddha Image in Arakan (Burma/Myanmar)". In *The Spirit of Things: Materiality in the Age of Religious Diversity in Southeast Asia*, edited by Julius Bautista. Cornell: Southeast Asia Program Publications, 2012, pp. 95-110.

——. "The 2010 Election and the Making of a Parliamentary Representative". In *Metamorphosis: Studies in Social and Political Change in Myanmar*, edited by Renaud Egreteau and François Robinne. Bangkok/Singapore: Research Institute on Contemporary Southeast Asia (IRASEC)/National University of Singapore (NUS) Press, 2015, pp. 43-68.

Dean, Karin. "Mapping the Kachin political landscape: constructing, contesting and crossing borders". In *Exploring Ethnic Diversity in Burma*, edited by Mikael Gravers. Copenhagen: Nordic Institute of Asian Studies (NIAS) Press, 2007, pp. 123-48.

D'Hubert, Thibaut, and Leider, Jacques. "Traders and Poets at the Mrauk U Court. Commerce and Cultural Links in Seventeenth-Century Arakan". In *Pelagic Passageways: The Northern Bay of Bengal before Colonialism*, edited by Rila Mukherjee. Delhi: Primus Books, 2011, pp. 77-111.

Fox, James, ed. *The Poetic Power of Place. Comparative Perspectives on Austronesian Ideas of Locality*. Canberra: Australian National University, 1997.

Gravers, Mikael, ed. *Exploring Ethnic Diversity in Burma*. Copenhagen: Nordic Institute of Asian Studies (NIAS) Press, 2007.

Gutman, Pamela Christine. "Ancient Arakan with Special Reference to its Cultural History between the 5th and 11th Centuries". Doctoral dissertation, Australian University, 1976.

Horstmann, Alexander. "Living Together: The Transformation of Multi-Religious Coexistence in Southern Thailand". *Journal of Southeast Asian Studies* 42, no. 3 (2011): 487-510.

Houghton, Bernard M.R.A.S., "The Arakanese Dialect of the Burman Language", *Journal of the Asiatic Society of Bengal* (1897): 453-61.

Houtman, Gustaaf. *Mental Culture in Burmese Crisis Politics. Aung San Suu Kyi and the National League for Democracy*. Tokyo: Institute for the Study of Languages and Cultures of Asia and Africa, 1999.

Leach, Edmund. "The Frontiers of 'Burma'". *Comparative Studies in Society and History* 3, no. 1 (1960): 49-68.

Lehman, Frederic K. "The Relevance of the Founders' Cult for Understanding the Political Systems of the Peoples of Northern Southeast Asia and Its Chinese Borderlands". In *Founders' Cults in Southeast Asia: Ancestors, Polity, and Identity*, Monograph 52, edited by Nicola Tannenbaum and Cornelia Ann Kammerer. New Heaven: Yale University Southeast Asia Studies, 2003, pp. 15-39.

Leider, Jacques. "These Buddhist Kings with Muslim Names... A Discussion of Muslim Influence in the Mrauk-U Period". In *Etudes Birmanes en Hommage à Denise Bernot* [Burmese Studies in Homage to Denise Bernot], edited by Pierre Pichard and François Robinne. Paris: Ecole Française d'Extrême-Orient, Etudes thématiques 9, 1998, pp. 189-215.

——. *Le Royaume d'Arakan, Birmanie. Son Histoire Politique entre le Début du XVè et la fin du XVIIè Siècle* [The Kingdom of Arakan, Burma. Its Political History between the Fifteen and the Beginning of the End of the Seventeenth Century]. Paris: École française d'Extrême-Orient, 2004.

——. "Specialists for Ritual, Magic, and Devotion: The Court Brahmins (*Punna*) of the Konbaung Kings (1752-1885)". *Journal of Burma Studies* 10 (2005-2006): 159-202.

——. "Forging Buddhist Credentials as a Tool of Legitimacy and Ethnic Identity". *Journal of the Economic and Social History of the Orient* 51 (2008): 409-59.

——. "Competing Identities and the Hybridized History of the Rohingyas". In *Metamorphosis: Studies in Social and Political Change in Myanmar*, edited by Renaud Egretau and François Robinne. Bangkok/Singapore: Research Institute on Contemporary Southeast Asia (IRASEC)/National University of Singapore (NUS) Press, 2015, pp. 151-78.

Mikaelian, Grégory. "Notes sur la Première Cartographie Provinciale Cambodgienne (c.1897)" [Notes on the First Mapping of a Cambodian Province 1897]. *Péninsule* 54, no. 1 (2007): 99-136.

Okamato, Ikuko. "The Movement of Rural Labour. A Case Study Based on Rakhine State". In *Ruling Myanmar, From Cyclone Nargis to National Elections*, edited by Nick Cheesman, Monique Skidmore and Trevor Wilson. Singapore: Institute of Southeast Asian Studies, 2010: 168-93.

Okell, John. "Three Burmese Dialects". In *Papers in Southeast Asian Linguistics No. 13: Studies in Burmese Languages*, edited by David Bradley. Pacific Linguistics, A-83, 1995: 1-138.

Raymond, Catherine. "Wathundayé, divinité de la Terre en Birmanie et en Arakan" [Wathundaye, Earth-Goddess in Burma and in Arakan]. In *Etudes Birmanes en Hommage à Denise Bernot* [Burmese Studies in Homage to Denise Bernot], edited by Pierre Pichard and François Robinne. Paris: Ecole Française d'Extrême-Orient, Etudes thématiques 9, 1998: 113-27.

Robinne, François. "Jeux d'échelle et Enjeux: Dynamiques Identitaires des Cérémonies Processionnelles en Birmanie Bouddhique" [Scale Games and Issues: Identity Dynamics of Processional Ceremonies in Buddhist Burma]. *Aséanie* 22 (2008): 121-50.

——. "To Be Burmese is Not (Only) Being Buddhist". In *Metamorphosis: Studies in Social and Political Change in Myanmar*, edited by Renaud Egreteau and François Robinne. Bangkok/Singapore: Research Institute on Contemporary Southeast Asia (IRASEC)/National University of Singapore (NUS) Press, 2015, pp. 346-67.

Rozenberg, Guillaume. "Etre birman, c'est être bouddhiste... » [To be Burmese is to be Buddhist...]. In *Birmanie Contemporaine* [Contemporary Burma], edited by Gabriel Defert. Bangkok/Paris: Research Institute on Contemporary Southeast Asia (IRASEC)/Les Indes savantes, 2008, pp. 29-52.

Sadan, Mandy. "Decolonizing Kachin: Ethnic Diversity and the Making of an Ethnic Category". In *Exploring Ethnic Diversity in Burma*, edited by Mikael Gravers. Copenhagen: Nordic Institute of Asian Studies (NIAS) Press, 2007, pp. 34-76.

Schlemmer, Grégoire. "Rituals, Territories and Powers in the Sino-Indian Margins". *Moussons* 19 (2012): 19-31.

Schober, Juliane. *Modern Buddhist Conjunctures in Myanmar. Cultural Narratives, Colonial Legacies, and Civil Society*. Honolulu: University of Hawaii Press, 2011.

Spearman, Horace, *The British Burma Gazetteer*, Volume 2. Rangoon: The Government Press, 1879.

Temple, Richard C. *The Thirty-Seven Nats: A Phase of Spirit-Worship Prevailing in Burma*. London: W. Griggs, 1906.

Tinker, Hugh. "Indians in Southeast Asia: Imperial Auxiliaries". In *South Asians overseas: Migration and Ethnicity*, edited by Colin Clarke, Ceri Peach and Steven Vertovec. Cambridge/New York: Cambridge University Press, 1990, pp. 39–56.

van Galen, Stephan. "The Rise and Decline of the Mrauk U kingdom (Burma) from the fifteenth to the seventeenth century AD". Doctoral dissertation, Leiden: Universiteit Leiden, 2008.

Yegar, Moshe. *Between Integration and Secession — The Muslim Communities of the Southern Philippines, Southern Thailand, and Western Burma/Myanmar*. Lanham: Lexington Books, 2002.

6

Rohingya Territoriality in Myanmar and Bangladesh: Humanitarian Crisis and National Disordering

Anders Bjornberg

An estimated two million Muslim Rohingya live in the region surrounding the 200-kilometre long border between Bangladesh and Myanmar. The history of the population in reference to this border remains a contentious issue, as in both countries they represent a political challenge to, in Liisa Malkki's influential phrasing, "the national order of things" (Malkki 1995, p. 495). The large-scale denial of the Rohingya's claims to territory or belonging in either country betrays the uneasy fit between nation, state, and the interstate order. Both countries adhere to what Amena Mohsin has aptly described as the French, "state-centred and assimilationist" model of nationhood (Mohsin 1997, p. 2). Such a drive towards forging culturally homogenous nations in turn forces claims made by minorities into a particular political idiom: as "new nations" requiring a state of their own. However, in both Bangladesh and Myanmar, the Rohingya have been excluded even from the assimilation process, effectively being cast out of both nations and states.

Myanmar's stateless Rohingya minority is estimated to number approximately two million, hundreds of thousands of whom have fled to neighbouring Bangladesh. Bangladesh has been wary of accepting these immigrants, arguing first that they contribute to an extant situation of overpopulation and resource scarcity, and that they do not fit within the nationalist project of Islamic Bengaliness. In the last few years these tensions have reached a breaking point, leading to outbreaks of ethnically-based violence in Bangladesh and Myanmar between Muslim Rohingya and

Buddhist Rakhine. As ethnic and communal homogeneity and territorial integrity have served as the ideal but impossible core of contemporary nationalisms in Myanmar and Bangladesh, these conflicts resonate beyond their immediate contexts.

This chapter argues that the Rohingya (as well as the Rakhine, the majority population in Rakhine State, of whom a significant number are currently living in Bangladesh) have been configured in changing ways through state-making projects over time. They have been enlisted in various projects of regional development in multiple capacities: in the case of the Rohingya, as labourers and surplus population, while the Rakhine were relocated as settlers and landowners. This has been at every step a relational process — while the state has made them, they have also made the state(s). The chapter will advance two main lines of argument: first, it will illustrate a few ways in which the Rohingya unsettle the national projects of Myanmar and Bangladesh. It will then argue that the United Nations High Commissioner for Refugees (UNHCR) intervention in Bangladesh has constituted a scale of power that does not neatly encompass the reproduction of the Bangladeshi state.

The region under discussion, southeastern Bangladesh and Rakhine State in Myanmar, is highly marginal. The border between Myanmar and Bangladesh is dwarfed in political discussion by Bangladesh's border with India. As highlighted by Willem van Schendel, this border also constitutes a scholarly border between South and Southeast Asia, and often escapes the notice of area studies scholars who tend to stick to their region (van Schendel 2002, p. 656). This scholarly divide has in many ways overly reified the Bangladesh-Myanmar border, where the border itself is nebulous. The border is not demarcated and formally closed, though evidence suggests that informally the border is a major channel for weapons, drugs, and other goods, the traffic of which is illegal, dangerous, and highly profitable (van Schendel 2006, p. 7). All of which is to indicate that the region and its inhabitants largely inhabit an informal and volatile space, attributes which have in some ways "rubbed off" on its denizens and those who move through it, especially the Rohingya.

Geographically, Rakhine State and Bengal share many attributes that allowed them to form far more cohesive a territorial unit than Rakhine State and Myanmar. Rakhine state itself is made up of a mixture of densely forested hills and valleys in the north and deltaic jungle in the south. Together, these two terrains allowed for the coexistence of hunter-gatherers, fishermen, and shifting cultivation in the hills alongside rice farming near the coast, a geographical symbiosis similar to that found in Bengal. The

Rakhine region is separated from the rest of what is now Myanmar by the Yoma mountain range. These mountains provided a formidable obstacle to trade between Arakan and the Burmese kingdom for centuries, as passages across this treacherous range were closed by political conflict as quickly as they were opened (van Galen 2008, p. 16). As such, trade and cultural exchange between Arakan and Bengal was far more robust than Arakan's easterly trade with Burma.

This historical mobility threatens the coherence of the modern states of Myanmar and Bangladesh. In both countries, while the Rohingya have not constituted a substantial military threat, they do pose an ideological and symbolic one. The Rohingya represent a history that the national states of Myanmar and Bangladesh seek to obliterate. Their existence calls to mind historical mobilities and cultural exchange that undermine contemporary constructions of nationalism.

UNSETTLING THE NATIONAL PROJECTS OF BANGLADESH AND MYANMAR

Historical sociological theorizations of the state, vis-à-vis Philip Abrams, Derek Sayer, and Philip Corrigan, have sought to integrate functional accounts of the capitalist state as managing political and economic inequality with understandings of the social processes by which authority is produced and maintained. These accounts place state formation at the important juncture between cultural and political economic forms of domination. The state's hegemony as the sole authorized repository of political authority relies on the production of a discursive divide between state and society, whereby the state was presented as unitary, abstract, removed from political discourse, and intervening according to higher principles of social order and justice (Abrams 1988; Corrigan 1994; Gupta 1995; Mitchell 1999). According to Corrigan, Ramsay and Sayer:

> The State within capitalist production, regulates and orchestrates — in short, organizes — in such a way that the defining material characteristics of capitalist production relations (individualisation, formal equality, and a host of social forms) are made to appear the only way those social activities could be conducted and arranged (Corrigan et al. 1980, p. 15).

Philip Abrams' *Notes on the Difficulty of Studying the State* describes the state as an "ideological thing", which cannot be reduced to any constitutive institutions, "the 'idea' of which has a significant political reality" as "a rather powerful agent... in terms of which subjection is legitimated" (Abrams 1988, p. 68). Abrams' formulation proved incredibly influential for a whole generation of scholars interested in the state. The "difficulty", then, of studying the state lies in honouring while resisting the reification that defines the state. The state exists as a principle of moral order, hegemonic to the point of rendering itself invisible, operating through and within culture. Corrigan and Sayer drew upon Abrams to understand how the state produces the effect of its non-existence through moral regulation: "a project of normalising, rendering natural, taken for granted, in a word 'obvious', what are in fact ontological and epistemological premises of a particular and historical form of social order" (Corrigan and Sayer 1985, p. 4).

In providing language and an analytic frame for this evasive yet defining aspect of modern political life, Abrams helps us think about the ways in which the state has infiltrated and shaped everyday life. By his formulation these interventions extend beyond those that we associate with the disciplinary and bio-political tendrils of the state — policing, tax collection, bureaucratic population controls — to include a broad range of interventions including the micro-practices of subject formation, which can take both direct and indirect forms.

The hybrid form of the national state became the dominant mode of political organization in the middle of the twentieth century. In anti-colonial struggles, the nation became the vehicle for anti-colonial expressions — "freeing the nation" involved "seizing the state". The path from colonial rule to national liberation entailed reclaiming the colonial state and achieving the ideal of national state sovereignty. With decolonization, the break-up of imperial powers, and the parcelling off of colonies into (nominally) independent nation states following the Second World War, the nation state was widely adopted as the primary unit of political organization and membership. Nations were posited as cultural and historical entities, territorial communities of affinity which were imagined to span back to a pre-modern time before colonization. As Chatterjee argues, anti-colonial movements relied strongly on the nation as a strategy of drawing together opposition, overcoming group boundaries and differences to concentrate on the shared imperative of breaking ties with their colonial oppressors (Chatterjee 1993). However, nationalism certainly has shown itself to be a divisive factor in post-colonial state formation. Pandey has argued that national communities are necessarily formed through sets of exclusions (Pandey 1999, p. 608). Some are relatively fixed, as in Bangladesh, Bengali cultural identity has remained relatively constant as a marker of nationalism. But other sets of exclusions are more dynamic and shifting, like the interplay between Islamism and secularism within the realm of politics. Even within national communities the boundaries of what constitutes the "true" nation are always shifting and being redefined, and oftentimes the minorities produced through these exclusions in turn trouble the coherence of the boundaries themselves.

In Myanmar, post-colonial state-making has been organized around the construction of being ethnically Burman and religiously Buddhist. Myanmar's ruling regime has pursued this project by means of the eradication of difference and the suppression of minority uprisings. The most prominent threats to the regime has been the long-standing Communist insurgency dating from Myanmar's independence and interlinked rebellions by ethnic minorities such as most prominently the Kachin, Karen/Kayin, Shan, and Mon groups, all of which have launched large-scale insurgencies. After Ne Win's Revolutionary Council seized power in 1962, his regime increased control over the economy, instituted strict censorship measures, and redoubled campaigns to crush the Burmese Communist Party's armed insurgency in the Pegu Hills, setting a precedent for the next few decades (South 2008).

Myanmar's struggles with ethnicity have in many ways driven its post-colonial political history: giving purpose to military expansion, social engineering, and driving the production of a national community. The state is in actuality a patchwork quilt of ethnicities, formerly independent kingdoms rendered into a single state only relatively recently under colonial administration. As scholars of nationalism remind us, around the world modern political order has found form and meaning in the shape of the national state, wherein the authority to influence relations of production and exchange within a particular bounded economic space is legitimized through ongoing attempts to produce a single community of affinity and belonging (Anderson 1991; Goswami 2004).

In Myanmar, this formulation has been complicated by the rich and omnipresent prehistory of the nation, according to which a unified Burmese nation or state borders on nonsensical. Prior to its establishment as an administrative entity by the East India Company in 1886, the contemporary geo-body of Myanmar had no historical precedent. Before the British conquest of the region through a series of wars starting in 1825 and their subsequent administrative consolidation, finalized in 1886, these kingdoms co-existed for centuries, not in their current form, and not without periodic conflict, but as discrete political entities. As such its current borders can be seen to have emerged out of a drive for colonial extraction. Ethnic polities were brought into an uneasy balance, using "divide and rule" policies of racial hierarchization to sow the seeds of inter-ethnic animosity. This process intensified the core-periphery exploitation. This long history has deeply informed contemporary ethnic politics in Myanmar, where the state eagerly seeks to retire these ethnic allegiances to a pre-modern past and unify the country under the banner of a Buddhist nationalist unity.

The advent of Burmese nationalism is commonly described as emerging in response to the brutalities of British colonial rule. Under the yoke of an increasingly restrictive foreign rule that sought to fragment society and group identities, Burma's colonial subjects came together for the first time, unified in anti-colonial sentiment through shared Buddhist faith (A. Turner 2011). Less commonly discussed are the subsequent reformations of nationalism following the obsolescence of its original form. In Myanmar, demands for independence and democracy came to fruition only to be subverted and betrayed by decades of restrictive military rule. How has nationalism adapted to fit changing contexts of political economy in Myanmar? This question has been further complicated by the ambivalence so many feel towards the notion of a unified modern Myanmar, as secessionist movements continue to rage at the margins of the country (Gravers 2007; Smith 1999). Does a singular conception of nationalism as a community of affinity still hold true in a country where a large proportion of the population challenges the state's legitimacy? One way to work through this impasse is by considering nationalism as an ongoing project, wherein state ideology plays an important — but not decisive — role in (re)defining an ever-morphing popularly imagined notion of a national project.

Through the political history of Myanmar, we can see the development and intensification of an exclusionist Buddhist national project, starting with U Nu's early positioning of Buddhist nationalism as the heart of autocratic Burmese governance. In the late 1970s, Ne Win's restructuring of citizenship laws to categorically exclude the Rohingya closely followed the unification of insurgent groups threatening the state into the National Democratic Front as well as a global economic crisis that brought Burmese economic growth to a crawl. The late 1980s and early 1990s, following another economic crisis, saw a massive wave of Rohingya expulsions as the State Law and Order Restoration Council (SLORC) took power and sought to refigure the national project to minimize ethnic politics and draw citizens together as the people of "Myanmar" (Charney 2009, p. 171). In a recent analysis, Yhome points out how the Burmese national project has been constructed as under the threat of domination at the hands of foreign and non-Buddhist elements (Yhome 2014, p. 57). The Rohingya fill both criteria, and their vilification has provided a common ground to draw citizens together under the aegis of the state's efforts to persecute them.

In light of these ongoing efforts to produce an ethnically-inclusive national identity drawing coherence from shared Buddhist heritage, the persecution of the Rohingya, a Muslim group stubbornly refusing assimilation or resettlement, starts to make sense. At this point, it is clear that the threat the Rohingya pose in Myanmar is almost purely symbolic, rather than military. The Rohingya stick out like a sore thumb as a non-national group which has resisted assimilation, threatening the very coherence of the Burmese nation state. Putting aside the separatist sentiments expressed by a group of Rohingya who lobbied for the 1947 Partition of South Asia to include a homeland for the Rakhine, the persecution of the Rohingya in Myanmar is remarkable for the near-absence of resistance the Rohingya are able to raise against the campaign of "slow genocide" being levied against them. Their rumoured social depravity — abuse of women, plural marriage, illicit trades in drugs and other contraband — must be understood as part of this project of racialized persecution and left aside.

The Rohingya have mainly been the passive objects of these increasingly severe discriminatory policies. Unlike these other minorities, they have mounted only a few scattered movements calling for the autonomy of Rakhine State, nothing approaching the widespread resistance of the Kachin or Karen/Kayin insurgencies. Further, compared to other minority groups in Myanmar, the mechanisms by which the Rohingya have been repressed have gone beyond disciplining them into loyal subjects towards eliminating them from the body politic entirely.

The persecution of the Rohingya has steadily intensified through increasing amounts of violence at the hands of Myanmar's successive restrictive military regimes, focused on making conditions in Myanmar as unliveable as possible for the Rohingya. Though radical factions among them continue to organize and advocate for the separation of Rakhine State, the western-most state of Myanmar in which the Rohingya are based, Rohingya separatist movements do not pose as distinct a threat to national order as the more violent or successful movements such as the Karen National Union (KNU).

This discrimination has been escalated at a few contentious points — most notably with the revocation of their citizenship rights in 1982 under Ne Win's Operation Dragon King. This law created a three-tier system of citizenship, giving colour-coded identity cards to the members of three main groups: full, granted to indigenous Burmese; second, resident citizens, a category which included pre-1948 immigrants who had properly applied for citizenship in 1948; and third, naturalized citizens, those who had not applied for citizenship in 1948 but who qualified for the status. Qualification was determined by ethnic identity, and the list of those accepted groups excluded the Rohingya, as well as two other Muslim groups from China and Malaysia respectively (Ahmed 2001). This policy effectively stripped the Rohingya of their citizenship rights and gave way to a new era of intensified discrimination against them. In 1988, the ruling State Law and Order Restoration Council started to build new military cantonments in regions of Rakhine State where the Rohingya were the majority. At the time, 20,000 new troops were stationed in the region. These cantonments, as well as settlements in the surrounding area where Buddhists from other parts of the country were brought in to inhabit, were built through the extraction of Rohingya labour.

In 2010, the Irish Centre for Human Rights found that the Rohingya in North Rakhine State are being disproportionately forced to labour in a variety of ways in service of the military, police, and local government, enlisted unpredictably at a moment's notice and for lengths of time that significantly hinder their ability to secure livelihoods (Irish Centre for Human Rights 2010). These tasks include forced portering: men and boys are forced into carrying supplies and equipment for the military and are taken from their homes, families and communities for months at a time. The Rohingya are additionally forced to undertake road and building construction and maintenance, as well as forced agricultural labour in development schemes to produce rice, sunflowers, rubber and shrimp, among other products. Together, the ever-present threat of being taken from home and family for hard labour to benefit the military at threat of beatings, death or retribution against family members constitutes the most significant motivation to flee the country.

The escalation of forced labour and persecution in the late 1980s and early 1990s increased a steady flow of irregular migrants into a torrent of mass exodus of Rohingya to Bangladesh. Though looking for a more hospitable social and political environment in Bangladesh, they faced a different, but in many ways equivalent, set of exclusions.

After its inception in 1971, Bangladesh's efforts to form a coherent national project and a viable state have taken a circuitous path. Severing its neo-colonial relationship to Pakistan, of which it had previously been a non-contiguous and unequal part, the newly independent Bangladesh was forged through a liberation war that contained two humanitarian crises. The first was a genocide at the hands of the Pakistanis which targeted intellectuals and prominent political figures thought to total 1.7 million dead throughout Bangladesh. The second was a massive exodus of refugees fleeing the violence which displaced an estimated ten million refugees into temporary camps in India (Mohaiemen 2011, p. 42). Founded in accordance with secular Bengali cultural values but still a fertile political climate for Islamic rhetoric, the oscillation between "Bengaliness" and Islamism as the dominant mode of political discourse has since animated the major political conflicts in Bangladesh (van Schendel 2009, pp. 201-09).

In Bangladesh, the Rohingya have been cast into a contested position within the Bangladeshi national project, as they are located at the conjuncture of the documented historical tensions over pluralist identity, inclusive democracy and indigeneity (Feldman 2003, p. 111; Kabeer 1991, p. 38; Mohsin 1997, p. 3; van Schendel 2009, p. 211). Initially, the Rohingya found shelter in the twenty camps that were established by the government of Bangladesh. However, in the face of the 1992-93 mass exodus, the UNHCR intervened to bolster Bangladesh's efforts to support the influx of Rohingya from Myanmar (Kiragu et al. 2011, p. 1). As neither Bangladesh nor Myanmar is a signatory to the 1951 United Nations Convention on the Status of Refugees, until 1993, Rohingya refugees had all been integrated into Bangladesh without the international supports set up to mediate refugee crises (Cheung 2012, p. 52).

In Bangladesh, historical narratives continue to drive contemporary political debate. The major political upheavals of the twentieth century, which progressively constituted Bangladesh, are remarkable in the centrality of contestations of history. The tension between Bengali cultural identity and a historical narrative of Bangladeshi independence has contributed to the production of a particularly restrictive form of nationalism. Scholars have elaborated how the cultural dominance of Bengaliness has been co-constituted with state policies of exclusion against minorities. Mohsin has elaborated how a narrow and exclusive form of Bangladeshi nationalism has excluded the Chittagong Hill Tracts from the national imagination, leading to the contemporary political and economic exclusion of indigenous populations (Mohsin 1997, p. 3). Bal has shown how national exclusions drive processes of ethnicization (Bal 2007, p. 441) and Feldman has highlighted how Partition normalized displacement as it remakes the complicated and heterogeneous reality of sociocultural diversity to better resemble an official imagination of Bangladeshi national space (Feldman 2003, p. 118).

Willem van Schendel situates these displacements and erosions of minority rights in the Chittagong Hill Tracts within a long history of state formation in the region extending from colonial times whereby colonial domination was replaced by nationalist developmentalism (van Schendel 1992). And as we can see, social marginalization has gone hand-in-hand with economic exploitation. Minorities have been both directly and indirectly exploited for land, labour, and resources through the formal and informal erosion of legal and social protections. Many have shown how land grabbing in the Chittagong Hill Tracts fulfils both economic and social goals. Shapan Adnan has argued that the undocumented Rohingya get placed into a position of political and economic clientelism, where they must continuously secure their social positions by proving their value as docile, surplus labour (Adnan 2014, p. 8). In Bangladesh, the state facilitates the marginalization of minority populations, consolidating a culturally, politically, and socially dominant Bengali majority against a disorganized "outside" category, a heterogeneous group of misfits. I contend that this notion of "outside" is spatialized as well: members of the Bengali majority can make durable claims to territorial rootedness, while in comparison minorities are constructed as transient and misplaced.

The history of the Rohingya, as nested within a long history of robust interconnections and interactions between what is now Rakhine state and the southeastern area of Bangladesh, is of ongoing contention. Also questionable is their origin as a people which has been differently emphasized at different points of time. Recent historical work has begun to excavate the pre-national history of this region, recovering narratives of autonomy and regional power struggles of the Arakan kingdom. Such narratives reveal contemporary political entities in their full contingency, allowing scholars to reclaim the political conjunctures which sought to sever, and now conceal, these historical patterns.

Owing to its eclipse by the Burmese kingdom, politically as well as discursively, the history of the Arakan kingdom has remained largely obscure, rarely studied for its own sake. The eventual conquest of Arakan tends to over-determine its study, as contemporary boundaries are extrapolated back through history. Only in the last few decades has Arakan come under closer examination by a new generation of scholars. Jacques Leider is perhaps the most prominent historian of the "golden age" of the Arakan kingdom, whose territory included varying amounts of southeastern Bengal for centuries at a time.

Prior to its conquest by the Burmese in 1784, Arakan had existed as an independent kingdom for millennia. After intermittently expanding into Bengal at moments of strength, Leider describes the period from roughly 1570–1630 as the "age of warrior kings", when Arakan was able to conquer and hold the region of Bengal stretching all the way up to Chittagong and even occasionally Dhaka (Leider 2002a, p. 65). King Man Phalaung, as part of an alliance with Tripura, was able to conquer Chittagong "not as the result of a single invasion but the gradual outcome of the convergence of political circumstances" (Leider 2002b, p. 138). Chittagong was at that point a very important port, and a huge source of revenue. This facilitated intensified trade connections between Arakan and Bengal. Leider's work challenges earlier accounts of Arakan expansion that held that Arakan's incursions into Bengal were only to flee from slave raids. In contrast, he argues Arakan was a substantial regional power which ruled areas of Bengal for an extended period. He also posits that the fall of Chittagong in 1666 was the beginning of the downfall of the Arakan state as an autonomous entity. Its power in the region steadily waned over the next century until it was annexed by Burma in 1784.

One important episode in the history of Arakan relations with Bengal is the oft-discussed but probably apocryphal exile of King Naramithla (Leider 2002b). By some accounts Arakan was taken by the Burmese in 1406 and King Naramithla was exiled to Bengal, where a sultan of Bengal, Jalal Ud-Din, sheltered him and helped him gain the military strength to retake Arakan in 1428. Though evidence in Arakan suggests this is likely just a legend, and no historical evidence has been found in Bengal, this story functions to denote a long-standing debt owed from Arakan to Bengal for this support.

Popular narratives have emerged which seek to neutralize and delegitimize the implications of this long history. Such accounts target popular memory, history's unstable cousin (Jalal 2013). These new narratives bear analysis, as they reveal the sites where the state's attempts to render the Rohingya invisible have fallen short or failed to penetrate fully. Efforts to destabilize Rohingya identity vis-à-vis their historical origins have in many ways hit their mark, as contemporary identity politics of the Rohingya have been rendered unstable and decentralized (de Chickera 2012).

The Rohingya's opponents, chiefly the Burmese state which revoked their citizenship rights in 1982, as well as members of the Rakhine ethnic majority of Rakhine state claim that they are a manufactured and false ethnic group, holding that the very term "Rohingya" was first used only in the 1970s (Rezwan 2012). Those subscribing to this view consider the Rohingya a group of ne'er-do-wells and vagrants seeking to mobilize international sympathy for undeserved monetary gain. Many Rakhine claim that "Rohingya" is derived from the Rakhine word for "homeless", and that they do not deserve the attention they receive from humanitarian and non-profit organizations. Those from this perspective insist on referring to them as "Bengali aliens", emphasizing their foreign origin and non-belonging. Another story holds that the Rohingya are descended from the survivors of a shipwreck in AD 788, when an Arab ship was stranded on an island off of the coast of Myanmar (Aye Chan 2005). Rescued and brought back to health, these individuals supposedly constituted the first members of the Rohingya. This narrative, though admitting a long history of Rohingya settlement in the region, bolsters the idea that the Rohingya are an alien race within Myanmar.

Other narratives trace the exclusion of the Rohingya back to just before Partition. These accounts hold that the Rohingya were brought from Bangladesh into Myanmar to fill a labour shortage. Thousands of Rohingya were transported and resettled in northern Rakhine State, soon constituting 90 per cent of the population in that area. When the end of British rule became imminent, a group of activists made a push for a separate Muslim Arakan State (Charney 2009). This particular tale justifies the discriminatory measures against the Rohingya at the hands of the Burmese state, and leads many to refer to them as "illegal Bengali migrants". Neither of these two narratives — the Rohingya as impoverished vagrants or their relocation as a colonial project — is an outright falsification and can be supported with historical evidence. However, both do not tell the whole story of their racial formation.

THE UNHCR'S INTERVENTION IN BANGLADESH: A SCALE OF POWER THAT DOES NOT NEATLY ENCOMPASS THE REPRODUCTION OF THE BANGLADESHI STATE

Recent reports documenting the intensifying persecution of the Rohingya in Myanmar have made their plight increasingly impossible to ignore, even for those most dedicated to keeping their heads in the sand. Early discussions of Myanmar's liberalization sidestepped the poor human rights situation of the Rohingya. However, now even Aung San Suu Kyi is being brought to account for the Burmese Government's escalating efforts to snuff out the Rohingya minority in Myanmar. The Burmese Government colludes with local actors to render Myanmar increasingly uninhabitable for the Rohingya. Policies like the denial of citizenship rights, exclusion from the national census, forced labour, sexual slavery, a two-child policy and restricted access to medical care show an attempt to eliminate the ethnic minority from the Burmese body politic entirely. The state also encourages and supports ethnic hatred against the Rohingya: in January 2014, Fortify

Rights published documentation of the Burmese Government's policies of inciting and enabling ethnic hatred, exposing the official policies of standing by while entire Rohingya settlements and villages were burned to the ground (Fortify Rights 2014). After communal riots in the Rohingya settlements in Yin They near Mrauk U in October 2012 which killed seventy and caused the displacement of 200,000 Rohingya families, the only ones to be persecuted were two Rohingya, for allegedly inciting these aggressions.

At this point, it is no longer possible to avoid describing the situation in Myanmar as anything other than a "slow-burning genocide", in Dr Maung Zarni's words (Maung Zarni and Cowley 2014, p. 681). Unsurprisingly, many Rohingya have relocated to Bangladesh to escape this systematic and heartless persecution. Though an exact number of the current number of undocumented Rohingya is virtually impossible to surmise, the number most commonly posited is between 200,000 and 500,000, most of whom are thought to reside in the Chittagong District in and around Cox's Bazar. Chris Lewa, of the Arakan Project, estimates that 100,000 Rohingya crossed into Bangladesh since the intensification of the violence against the Rohingya in 2012 (McDowell 2014).

Through the 1990s and early 2000s, Bangladesh sought to stem the flow of Rohingya by maintaining an implicit policy of enforced inhospitability. Violating the widely-accepted policy of non-refoulement, by which migrants' claims that repatriation would place them in mortal danger must be logged and evaluated, Bangladesh arrested untold numbers of fleeing Rohingya crossing in improvised boats, turning them over to the Burmese *NaSaKa* border force or simply pushing them back to sea. During this time the Rohingya were aptly described as being caught "between a crocodile and a snake": Myanmar was the crocodile, trying to swallow the Rohingya alive, while Bangladesh was the snake, constricting and suffocating them. Both countries used the language of "invaders", contending that the Rohingya belonged elsewhere — effectively revealing that they truly belonged nowhere.

At this point it is quite clear that this policy was a failure. Criminalized and denied legal protection, the Rohingya have been especially vulnerable to the exploitations visited upon Bangladesh's ultra-poor. The Rohingya are thought to have undermined the local labour market in and around Cox's Bazar. The flood of underemployed and desperate Rohingya in the area has driven down wages for local labourers, cutting the going rates for day labour in construction and rickshaw-pulling by half or more.

Effectively, the Bangladeshi Government's policy of minimizing pull factors has driven growing racism against the Rohingya in Bangladesh, and has served to proliferate notions that the Rohingya are morally corrupt and the epicentre of a laundry list of transgressions including fundamentalist terrorism, the smuggling of drugs and guns, plural marriage, even the recent wave of abductions. While some undocumented Rohingya have been able to achieve de facto integration and been accepted into communities which have supported and sheltered them, this delicate balance has been made increasingly precarious through growing antagonism against them.

The UNHCR, the United Nations agency which deals with refugee crises around the world, has been managing two camps for the Rohingya in southeastern Bangladesh since 1991, sheltering almost 30,000 Rohingya. The protection they provide to these refugees is administered in negotiation with the government of Bangladesh, whose long-standing policy of passive inhospitality has placed limitations on the scope of the UNHCR's operations in the region. The UNHCR's funding comes entirely from international sources, and the size and scope of its operations come up for annual review and reauthorization at the hands of the government of Bangladesh's Ministry of Disaster Management and Relief. In effect, this is an annual tug-of-war, where the UNHCR's goals of documentation and assistance to all Rohingya residing in Bangladesh clash with the goals of the Bangladeshi Government to minimize the pull factors attracting Rohingya to cross over the border into Bangladesh, of which, they consider UNHCR assistance one of the main factors. For regular operations, local staff in Cox's Bazar coordinate with the neighbouring government-run office of the Rohingya Refugee Resettlement Commission.

Currently, 29,000 Rohingya are thought to be officially residing in Bangladesh in camps established by the UNHCR. The estimates for the undocumented population in the surrounding areas range from 200,000–400,000. Assistance for the Rohingya living in the two camps from the UNHCR is predicated upon the UNHCR's negotiations with Bangladesh and Myanmar to continue to allow the provision of aid. As such, at the insistence of the Bangladeshi Government, the camps' were subjected to two major repatriation efforts in 1992–93 and 1997–98. In both camps, conditions of life are poor and access to resources is tenuous, marked by sexual abuse, poor health conditions and inability to access adequate nutrition (Kibreab 2003; Pittaway 2008).

Less is known about the undocumented Rohingya in Bangladesh. Each of the two official camps is ringed by an unofficial camp, where Rohingya hoping to someday obtain documentation and receive UNHCR services have established residence. Without education, basic security protections or economic opportunities for the refugees living in these camps for decades, these places have gained a reputation for criminal activity, thought to be regional hubs for the illicit cross-border drug smuggling which traverses the area (van Schendel 2006). On 3 August 2012, Bangladesh formally banned three non-governmental organizations (NGOs) which were working with these populations, forcing them to discontinue these services and abandoning these camps to decay into further lawlessness and squalor (*New York Times* 2012). Research among these undocumented communities has highlighted their resilience in the face of their feelings of loss and insecurity (Farzana 2011, p. 231).

Caught between two assimilationist national state spaces but unwilling or unable to assimilate into either, how and where the Rohingya navigate habitation in this borderland space are questions with important political implications. For the Rohingya in Bangladesh, the UNHCR intervention has had ambivalent results. While the 29,000 Rohingya living in the two camps have been reasonably protected from the violence and discrimination they faced in Myanmar, the intervention of the UNHCR shifted the scale of the problem from national to international, which in turn has made social integration for those who did not receive official protection more tenuous in a few key ways.

To make sense of the implications of this intervention, I draw upon what Ferguson and Gupta have termed the "spatialization of the state", to examine how spatial metaphors allow us to better understand this crisis (Ferguson and Gupta 2009, p. 982). They describe two key concepts: verticality refers to the "central and pervasive idea of the state as an institution somehow 'above' civil society" (ibid.), a privileged position from whence power emits and acts upon its subjects, and encompassment refers to the notion that society consists of an ever-widening set of spheres, starting from the family, which is contained by the community, contained by the locality, contained by the region, and the region in turn is contained within the nation state. These two metaphors evoke a topographic effect, whereby the state's power intensively permeates the entirety of its bounded territory from on high.

In seeking to locate the ramifications of the growing importance of the transnational upon this imaginary, they argue that transnational governmentality presents the need for new spatial metaphors. They write:

> (The transnational apparatus of governmentality) does not replace the older system of nation states but overlays and coexists with it. In this optic, it might make sense to think of the new organisations that have sprung up in recent years not as challengers pressing up against the state from below but as horizontal contemporaries of the organs of the state — sometimes rivals; sometimes servants; sometimes watchdogs; sometimes

parasites; but in every case operating on the same level, and in the same global space (Ferguson and Gupta 2009, p. 994).

In Bangladesh, the UNHCR has a protective mission of sheltering and providing resources to the two camps Bangladesh established and handed over to them in 1991. Besides assuring their survival, the UNHCR must also take pains to present its efforts as neutral, purely humanitarian and devoid of political context, while other UN agencies pursue political redress through other channels. In Bangladesh this project is especially fragile, as neither Myanmar nor Bangladesh is signatory to the international conventions which establish the UNHCR's jurisdiction in refugee crises: the UNHCR is allowed to operate only as the Bangladeshi Government will allow them continued access. In this light Simon Turner's observations on the UNHCR's imperative to render the space of a camp "a community of innocent, ahistorical, apolitical victims in need of help" seem quite apt (S. Turner 2005, p. 332).

Determining how the protective intervention of the UNHCR has "overlaid" onto this conflict reveals the discomforts between these two sets of practices of power: on the one hand, the intervention has complemented Bangladesh's state-making practices by validating and legitimizing the political exclusion of the Rohingya, marking their presence in Bangladesh as an aberration from the national order requiring extra-state action. On the other hand, the limited scale of this operation and the UNHCR's increasingly intensive expectations of the role of the Bangladeshi Government challenge the state at the highest level of power within its territory — in turn challenging its ability to reproduce the effects of verticality and encompassment.

The other effect of the UNHCR's intervention has been to bring a new political vocabulary to the situation. The intervention validated the discursive frames of "refugee" and "stateless", terms that as Liisa Malkki has observed, can have the effect of typologizing and abstracting groups from "much larger constellations of socio-political and cultural processes and practices" (Malkki 1995, p. 496). The applicability of these terms notwithstanding, deploying such language has had the discursive effect of displacing the problem of Rohingya resettlement to an international scale, transferring responsibility for its resolution to the United Nations. This only went to affirm the inefficacy of the national scale for sorting out this complicated modern problem and mark the Rohingya as "out of place", which has endangered the ability of Rohingya to "blend in" or to negotiate their places in the majority Bengali communities outside the camps. The assistance given to the Rohingya also fomented resentment among poor Bengalis in their communities, endangering their chances of finding support and social inclusion through their own negotiations within a given territory.

Such essentialization and decontextualization of the Rohingya as refugees was evident in the media's coverage of the wave of violence between the Rakhine majority and the Rohingya in the town of Maungdaw in Rakhine State in June of 2014. After the widely reported rape and murder of a young Rakhine woman at the hands of three Rohingya men, waves of retaliatory ethnic violence shook Rakhine State. In Rakhine's capital, Sittwe, homes, property and mosques were sent up in flames and an estimated 100,000 Rohingya were left homeless and displaced. This caused what was estimated to be the largest mass relocation since 1992–93 for the Bangladeshi border, where they were met and repelled by a large military presence. In the months that followed, thousands of Rohingya seeking shelter in Bangladesh were intercepted, denied the right to claim asylum and repatriated to Myanmar (Bjornberg 2012, p. 3).

Reactions to this migration in Bangladesh generally dealt with short-term solutions for the immediate crisis until the UNHCR was able to sort things out and repatriate them to Myanmar or another country. Whether denouncing the Bangladeshi Government for squandering precious resources by providing refuge to the Rohingya or pointing to international human rights law to assert the necessity of providing such support, extending rights of permanent refuge to the Rohingya was a foregone possibility, as the problem was being worked out at the "proper" scale — that is, the international.

In 2012, Senior Protection Officer Samuel Cheung, previously posted to the UNHCR's Bangladesh programme, published a provocative dissension in the *Journal of Refugee Studies* which highlighted a key distinction among Rohingya refugees who had migrated to Bangladesh: those who were granted official recognition as refugees, and those who have been otherwise able to achieve, in his phrase, "de facto social integration" independent of the UNHCR (Cheung 2012, p. 66). The first category consists of those Rohingya who came and received documentation during the 1991–92 wave of immigration. Far less is known about this second category of Rohingya in Bangladesh: estimated to number around 200,000, they have been able to achieve (varying, to be certain) integration into communities through their own negotiations with their neighbours. Cheung writes that these de facto integrated refugees often "have the capacity to carve out their own protection space and achieve a level of de facto integration, even in the face of punitive immigration enforcement measures and sometimes beyond what international actors or the formal refugee framework can offer" (ibid.). Whether they have achieved this through convincing their neighbours to accept their presence by concealing their origins, the fact remains that they have established localized claims to territory which short-circuit those of the state or international order. The tenacity of these claims has yet to be seen, and these claims are certainly weaker, oftentimes enabling abuse and exploitation at the hands of those with more secure citizenship status.

The Rohingya's illicit habitation within Bangladesh, in a phrase borrowed from Liza Schuster, "renders visible the contingent character of states" (Schuster 2009, p. 288). Their presence undermines the Bangladeshi state's claims of encompassment. The undocumented Rohingya posit a different sort of territoriality, based on subsistence, occupation, and social negotiation. They experience the borderlands as a space where state control is uneven and contingent. Though without recourse to greater legal bodies in situations where their status is being exploited, these de facto claims can be more durable than those dependent on state or international assurance. By remaining illegible to the Bangladeshi state and the UNHCR, the de facto integrated Rohingya are able to avoid periodic repatriation campaigns.

CONCLUSION

To conclude, I would like to offer some observations on how the precarious social and political status of the Rohingya in Bangladesh can help us think productively about what is being unsettled and how. Their historical and contemporary displacement speaks to how border spaces are constantly being made and remade at multiple scales which can work at counter-purpose. Undocumented Rohingya's claims to territory unsettle not only national narratives but also undermine the UNHCR's claims to a transnational guarantee of human rights, suggesting that the project of "fixing" borders is always more accurately a set of projects being undertaken simultaneously at multiple scales. A border-making project planned from the seat of national power can have almost no similiarities to one implemented by borderland dwellers within their own communities. These disparate projects are often affiliated, rather than aligned, through loose ideological orientation. They seek to draw continuity by appeals to shared concepts like security, development, identity, humanity, but in practice these pronouncements occupy separate registers, often oblique, incomprehensible or falling prey to misinterpretation. For the Rohingya, this clash of imperatives has created a situation wherein eluding the influence of these actors becomes the most effective strategy for securing livelihood. Faced with a modern political framework organized by states and nations, the Rohingya instead opt for a "none of the above" solution akin to that described in Scott's *The Art of Not Being Governed* (2009), expanding the evasion of institutional authority to include INGOs like the UNHCR alongside states.

In practice, this approach has produced a volatile social situation, an uneasy peace that can quickly and unpredictably ignite into armed conflict. This was shown on the night of 29 September 2012, when well-coordinated attacks on Buddhist temples began in Ramu and quickly spread along the border down to Teknaf. In these attacks over a dozen Buddhist temples were set afire in the dead of night, provoked by a doctored Facebook post defaming the Koran and attributed to a Barua (Buddhist Bengali) youth. These attacks targeted both Barua and Rakhine communities. While the government of Bangladesh rushed to reconstruct many of the destroyed temples, to date no one has been prosecuted for the attacks. The flimsiness of this justification suggests that deeper resentments and tensions were brought into play here, and that the persecution of Muslims in Myanmar is straining relations between Muslims and Buddhists throughout the region.

Spilling outside the traditional national state-centric categories of scholarly analysis, there is a need to understand the Rohingya organically and on their own terms. The political analyses which help us understand the peculiar condition of statelessness into which the Rohingya have been cast has drawn needed international attention to their plight, but has revealed little about the actual content of Rohingya life. In this regard there is a need for more ethnographic accounts such as the recent work by Kazi Fahmida Farzana (2011, in this volume) whose work provides a glimpse into the Rohingya's own notions of homeland, security, and resistance. Also relevant is the 2010 study organized by Imtiaz Ahmed examining the conditions of uprooting, passage and settlement as social processes (Ahmed 2010). The Rohingya's own cultural assemblages are especially important as the efficacy of their input into policy discussions is contingent on a better understanding of their political and cultural structures. By privileging the negotiations of social inclusion in their complexity and foregrounding the heretofore invisible de facto integrated Rohingya, perhaps a new regional, as opposed to national or transnational history can be brought into being.

References

Abrams, Philip. "Notes on the Difficulty of Studying the State". *Journal of Historical Sociology* 1, no. 1 (1988): 58–89.

Adnan, Shapan. "Rethinking Food Sovereignty in a Limiting Context: Refugees From

Myanmar in Bangladesh Without Land and Citizenship". In *Food Sovereignty: A Critical Dialogue*, 14–15 September 2015. New Haven, Connectticut. New Haven: Programme in Agrarian Studies, Yale University, July 2013.

Ahmed, Imtiaz. "Bangladesh-Myanmar Relations and the Stateless Rohingyas". In *Library*, 2001 <http://www.burmalibrary.org> (accessed 18 August 2012).

———. *The Plight of the Stateless Rohingyas: Responses of the State, Society and the International Community*. Dhaka: University Press Limited, 2010.

Anderson, Benedict. *Imagined Communities: Reflections on the Origin and Spread of Nationalism*. New York: Verso, 1991.

Aye Chan. "The Development of A Muslim Enclave in Arakan (Rakhine) State". *SOAS Bulletin of Burma Research* 3, no. 2 (2005): 396–420.

Bal, Ellen. "Becoming the Garos of Bangladesh: Policies of Exclusion and the Ethnicisation of a 'Tribal' Minority". *Journal of South Asian Studies* 30, no. 3 (2007): 439–55.

Bjornberg, Anders. "Displaced Rohingya at the Margins: An Historical Context of the Current Crisis". *South Asia Journal* 6 (2012): 3–12.

Charney, Michael. *A History of Modern Burma*. New York: Cambridge University Press, 2009.

Chatterjee, Partha. *The Nation and its Fragments: Colonial and Postcolonial Histories*. Princeton: Princeton University Press, 1993.

Cheung, Samuel. "Migration Control and the Solutions Impasse in South and Southeast Asia: Implications from the Rohingya Experience". *Journal of Refugee Studies* 25, no. 1 (2012): 50–70.

Corrigan, Philip. "State Formation". In *Everyday Forms of State Formation: Revolution and the Negotiation of Rule in Modern Mexico*, edited by Gilbert M. Joseph and Daniel Nugent. Durham: Duke University Press, 1994.

———, and Derek Sayer. *The Great Arch: English State Formation as Cultural Revolution*. New York: Blackwell, 1985.

———, Harvie Ramsay and Derek Sayer. "The State as a Relation of Production". In *Capitalism, State Formation and Marxist Theory*, edited by Philip Corrigan. New York: Quartet Books, 1980.

de Chickera, Amal. "Stateless in Burma: Rohingya Word Wars". In *openDemocracy*, 12 October 2012 <https://www.opendemocracy.net/5050/amal-de-chickera/stateless-in-burma-rohingya-word-wars> (accessed 15 September 2013).

Farzana, Kazi Farmida. "Music and Artistic Artefacts: Symbols of Rohingya Identity and Everyday Resistance in Borderlands". *Austrian Journal of South-East Asian Studies* 4, no. 2 (2011): 215–36.

Feldman, Shelley. "Bengali State and Nation Making: Partition and Displacement Revisited". *International Social Science Journal* 55, no. 175 (2003): 111–21.

Ferguson, James and Akhil Gupta. "Spatialising States: Toward an Ethnography of Neoliberal Governmentality". *American Ethnologist* 29, no. 4 (2009): 981–1002.

Fortify Rights. "Policies of Persecution: Ending Abusive State Policies Against Rohingya Muslims in Myanmar". Thailand: Fortify Rights, 2014.

Goswami, Manu. *Producing India: From Colonial Economy to National Space*. Chicago: University of Chicago Press, 2004.
Gravers, Mikael. "Introduction: Ethnicity against the State — State against Ethnic Diversity?" In *Exploring Ethnic Diversity in Burma*, edited by Mikael Gravers. Copenhagen: Netherlands Institute for Advanced Study (NIAS), 2007.
Gupta, Akhil. "Blurred Boundaries: The Discourse of Corruption, the Culture of Politics, and the Imagined State". *American Ethnologist* 22, no. 2 (1995): 375–402.
Irish Centre for Human Rights. "Crimes against Humanity in Western Burma: The Situation of the Rohingyas", 2010 <http://www.nuigalway.ie/media/intranet/Crimes-Against-Humanit-in-Western-Burma.pdf> (accessed 29 April 2012).
Jalal, Ayesha. *The Pity of Partition: Manto's Life, Times, and Work Across the India-Pakistan Divide*. Princeton: Princeton University Press, 2013.
Kabeer, Naila. "The Quest for National Identity: Women, Islam and the State in Bangladesh". *Feminist Review* 37 (1991): 38–58.
Kibreab, Gaim. "Displacement, Host Governments' Policies, and Constraints on the Construction of Sustainable Livelihoods". *International Social Science Journal* 55, no. 175 (2003): 57–67.
Kiragu, Esther, Angela Li Rosi, and Tim Morris. "States of Denial: A Review of UNHCR's Response to the Protracted Situation of Stateless Rohingya Refugees in Bangladesh". Geneva: United Nations High Commissioner for Refugees Policy Development and Evaluation Service (PDES), December 2011.
Leider, Jacques. "Arakan's Ascent during the Mrauk U period". In *Recalling Local Pasts: Autonomous History in Southeast Asia*, edited by Sunait Chutintaranond and Chris J. Baker. Chiang Mai: Silkworm Books, 2002*a*: 53–87.
———. "On Arakanese Territorial Expansion: Origins, Context, Means and Practice". In *The Maritime Frontier of Burma: Exploring Political, Cultural and Commercial Interaction in the Indian Ocean World, 1200–1800*, edited by Jos J.L. Gommans and Jacques Leider. Amsterdam: Koninklijke Nederlandse Akademie van Wetenschappen, 2002*b*: 127–50.
Malkki, Liisa. "Refugees and Exile: From 'Refugee Studies' to the National Order of Things". *Annual Review of Anthropology* 24 (1995): 495–523.
Maung Zarni and Alice Cowley. "The Slow-Burning Genocide of Myanmar's Rohingya". *Pacific Rim Law & Policy Journal* 23, no. 3 (2014): 681–752.
McDowell, Robin. "Number of Rohingya Fleeing Burma Tops 100,000". In *The Irrawaddy Journal*, 27 October 2014 <http://www.irrawaddy.org/burma/number-rohingya-fleeing-burma-tops-100000.html> (accessed 2 November 2014).
Mitchell, Timothy. "State, Society and the State Effect". In *State/Culture: State Formation after the Cultural Turn*, edited by George Steinmetz. Ithaca: Cornell University Press, 1999, pp. 76–98.
Mohaiemen, Naeem. "Flying Blind: Waiting for a Real Reckoning on 1971". *Economic and Political Weekly* xlvi, 3 September 2011, pp. 40–52.
Mohsin, Amena. *The Politics of Nationalism: The Case of the Chittagong Hill Tracts*. Dhaka: University Press Limited, 1997.

New York Times. "Bangladesh: Refugee Aid Discouraged", 2 August 2012.
Pandey, Gyanendra. "Can a Muslim Be an Indian?" *Comparative Studies in Society and History* 41, no. 4 (1999): 608–29.
Pittaway, Ellen. "The Rohingya Refugees in Bangladesh: A Failure of the International Protection Regime". In *Protracted Displacement in Asia: No Place to Call Home*, edited by Howard Adelman. Burlington: Ashgate Publishing Company, 2008, pp. 1–29.
Rezwan. "Bangladesh: Citizenship Rights for Bangladesh's Rohingya?" In *Global Voices*, 7 August 2012 <http://globalvoicesonline.org> (accessed 21 August 2012).
Schuster, Liza. "Kindness to Strangers". *History Workshop Journal* 68 (2009): 287–92.
Scott, James C. *The Art of Not Being Governed: An Anarchist History of Upland Southeast Asia*. New Haven: Yale University Press, 2009.
Smith, Martin. *Burma: Insurgency and the Politics of Ethnicity*. London: Zed Books, 1999.
South, Ashley. *Ethnic Politics in Burma: States of Conflict*. London: Routledge, 2008.
Turner, Alicia. "Narratives of Nation, Questions of Community: Examining Burmese Sources without the Lens of Nation". *Journal of Burma Studies* 15, no. 2 (2011): 263–82.
Turner, Simon. "Suspended Spaces — Contesting Sovereignties in a Refugee Camp". In *Sovereign Bodies: Citizens, Migrants, and States in the Postcolonial World*, edited by Thomas Blom Hansen and Finn Stepputat. Princeton: Princeton University Press, 2005, pp. 312–33.
van Galen, Stephan. "Arakan and Bengal: The Rise and Decline of the Mrauk U kingdom (Burma) from the Fifteenth to the Seventeeth Century AD". Doctoral dissertation, Leiden University, 2008.
van Schendel, Willem. "Invention of the 'Jummas': State Formation and Ethnicity in Southeastern Bangladesh". *Modern Asian Studies* 26, no. 1 (1992): 95–128.
──. "Geographies of Knowing, Geographies of Ignorance: Jumping Scale in Southeast Asia". *Environment and Planning D: Society and Space* 20, no. 6 (2002): 647–68.
──. "Guns and Gas in Southeast Asia: Transnational Flows in the Burma-Bangladesh Borderland". In *Kyoto Review of Southeast Asia* 7, March 2006 <http://kyotoreview.org/issue-7/guns-and-gas-in-southeast-asia-transnational-flows-in-the-burma-bangladesh-borderland/> (accessed 22 March 2012).
──. *A History of Bangladesh*. New York: Cambridge University Press, 2009.
Yhome, Khriezo. "Mapping the Meaning of Burman Nationalism". *Himalayan and Central Asian Studies* 18, no. 1-2 (2014): 52–63.

Section III

Social Organization and Border Economies

7

The Culture and Landscape of the Humanitarian Economy among the Karen (Kayin) in the Borderland of Southeast Myanmar and Northwest Thailand[1]

ALEXANDER HORSTMANN

This chapter provides a concise map of faith-based and secular humanitarian assistance to the Karen in the Thai-Burmese borderland to show the emergence and development of a humanitarian economy for Karen villagers in southeast Myanmar, and in the nine refugee camps in northwest Thailand. I understand humanitarianism to be a culture of humanitarian aid, compassion and relief, but prefer a broader definition that includes agency which encompasses a range of services — from emergency healthcare to advocacy work, such as training for documentation of human rights violations. I suggest that decades of civil war and repression in southeast Myanmar have created a particular landscape of humanitarianism in the borderlands of southeast Myanmar and northwest Thailand that is characterized by the dense presence of local and international humanitarian organizations. The chapter advances the thesis that humanitarianism takes over state functions in the social services as the economy, health and education sector in southeast Myanmar have largely collapsed (South 2012; Decha Tangseefa 2006). Humanitarianism thus contributes in a crucial way to the consolidation of social support networks of Karen villagers and a parallel state or self-governance of the Karen in the context of open state terror and hostility.

Outlining this specific culture of humanitarianism as it developed in the Thai-Burmese borderland, I find the theory of landscape useful.

Describing landscape, cultural geographers were either interested in the materiality of landscape or in the politics of representation and power. I am interested in the relationship between the two: landscape is the way in which specific actors shape a region or area with their practices and the way that a region is imagined and represented. I thus concur with Janet C. Sturgeon's claim that landscapes are more than just physical topography and land cover, but sites for manoeuvre and struggle (Sturgeon 2005, p. 3ff). Humanitarian work, in its informal and underground nature (as in southeast Myanmar), or formal and engineered (as in the camps in northwest Thailand) can be seen as what Sturgeon calls "landscape plasticity", that is a contribution to negotiated landscapes. In this sense, landscapes are being constantly remodelled and the presence of humanitarian organizations and city-like camps contribute to shaping the materiality of the borderland (Agier 2002).

In Karen State, for example, Buddhism competes with Christianity to shape the landscape: charismatic monks construct temples, pagodas and ordination halls on every mountain to make merit, while Christians build churches and erect huge crosses to mark and symbolize the inroads made by Christianity into the area (Gravers 2007; Hayami 2004). Christian landscapes are also reproduced in the refugee camps, where Christian missionary networks have been instrumental in building Christian humanitarian spaces and refugee camps have become centres for proselytizing among vulnerable refugees (Horstmann 2011).

People in southeast Myanmar are slowly recovering from trauma. The area may be described as a landscape of fear (see Grundy-Warr and Chin in this volume) where people were living in anxiety and the air was thick with dread. The *Tatmadaw* (Burmese Army) was leading warfare targeting the villagers in an attempt to cut out the support base of the insurgents; soldiers tortured and killed indiscriminately. The rest of the chapter describes the humanitarian agencies and their work as a transformative project in which humanitarians are trying to transform a landscape of horror and despair into a space of recovery and hope.

HUMANITARIAN AGENCIES AND LANDSCAPE TRANSFORMATION

The culture of humanitarian assistance enabled Karen and Karenni people to establish a niche and the financial and material support to run a whole underground system of alternative, mobile healthcare, education and social support networks. It really began to shape the borderland and its people in the early 1980s. The military assault of the Burmese Army drove the Karen National Liberation Army (KNLA) over the border and its scorched earth assault produced massive refugee flows within southeast Myanmar and across the border to Thailand. Humanitarian assistance became firmly established after the installation of the Thailand Burma Border Consortium that replaced the antecedent consortium of Christian orientation.

The Karen, Mon and Shan people, with the help of Western missionary networks that quickly identified the situation as a humanitarian crisis and moved from the Thai-Cambodian and Thai-Laotian border to the Thai-Burmese border in the early 1980s, established the first shelters. Unlike the Khmer and Hmong refugees, or the Vietnamese boat people, the Karen refugees had a very high degree of cohesion and organization. The villagers who moved across the border were mostly able to keep their communities intact. Organized Christians in the Baptist, Catholic and Seventh-Day Adventist churches worked smoothly with Western churches, brought their pastors and community leaders with them and immediately built churches in the emerging refugee camps. The school system reproduced strong patriotic and Christian values and the Christian Bible school provided everyday worship service and church choirs. Buddhist refugees in contrast often resented the Christian presence in the camps and tended to settle in migrant villages where they became tenant farmers of Karen peasants with Thai citizenship.

Humanitarianism quickly changed the face of the border town of Mae Sot. Once a sleepy market in the interstitial spaces of the Thai-Burmese border, the entrepreneurial segment of Mae Sot benefited tremendously from the emerging markets across the border. The quick establishment of international humanitarian agencies and non-governmental organizations (NGOs) in Mae Sot also shaped the town and substantially contributed to its expansion. Humanitarian workers worked and slept in the offices around the town and accessed the camps from there in their luxury cars. One could meet this group of expatriates with their laptops and smartphones in the cafés and restaurants catering to them. The nine shelters housed no less than 150,000 people at a time. The refugee camps thus became part of the humanitarian landscape, a form of dwelling that resembles urban informal settlements — bidonvilles — with their own cultural geography, architecture, markets, infrastructure, social services, schools, facilities, and resettlement programmes.

Looking at the emergence and installation of a specific humanitarian and advocacy sector, I am interested in resource mobilization and symbolic communication. My understanding is that this situation has produced a certain culture of suffering and subsequent help that binds certain people and organizations together in a specific place and geography. The humanitarian sector, financed by the international community, has been running for decades and has produced a specific humanitarian culture in the border landscape.

The situation has changed lately, as the growing openness of Myanmar has created more breathing space for a local civil society in eastern Myanmar, but remains framed using the discourse of healing the wounds. It is these atrocities committed by the Burmese Army that have motivated different types of organizations to mitigate the suffering endured by villagers. The humanitarian economy thus contrasts with the advocacy economy — development organizations that provide services and with the more activist NGOs carrying out more political work organizing villagers to document human rights violations and claim their rights.

In a context where international organizations are severely limited in movement and activities by a repressive political environment, grassroots organizations seem to fill a crucial vacuum as mediators between social support networks of Karen villagers and international humanitarian organizations, organized as The Border Consortium (TBC).[2] Looking closer at the dynamics of humanitarianism from the grassroots level in the Thai-Burmese borderland, I became aware that humanitarianism is fairly politicized and somewhat spiritual. Much activism on the Thai border was closely associated with Karen nationalism and the Karen National Union (KNU) in particular, although the new organizations emancipated themselves and quickly developed their own agenda. Much of humanitarian assistance was also spiritual, and local-global alliances of Christianity play a particularly conspicuous role in many initiatives. Now, after decades of political oppression, civil society in eastern Myanmar is picking up and interesting new initiatives and civil society networks are emerging. Again, many initiatives in eastern Myanmar are related to the idea that the Karen are a chosen race and a nation. Some of the new initiatives focus on the revitalization of Karen culture and literature. Humanitarianism from the ground is thus tied not only to expanding rights regimes, but also to the consciousness of Karen national identity and Karen culture (Horstmann 2015). It is also possible and realistic that the impact of some organizations is minimal and that the organizations are struggling increasingly for their own survival by justifying their existence vis-à-vis international sponsors.

This leads us to the impact of humanitarianism from the ground and the question of how the presence of so many — indeed hundreds — of very different initiatives on the border, are perceived and connected, or not connected, and the provocative question of whether some organizations actually impose themselves on the Karen villagers. Another crucial question is the relationship of the organizations to the state and non-state ethnic armed movements. Political environments crucially condition humanitarian organizations and many organizations on the Thai border moved under the radar of the state and crossed the border illegally. At the same time, the same organizations have operated under the protection and in the shadow of non-state armed movements and can be seen as the "humanitarian arm" of that movement. The current rapprochement of many organizations, such as the Back Pack Health Worker Team — an NGO specializing in emergency healthcare, with the Burmese Government illustrates the dilemmas of cooperation and non-cooperation, and the compromises that organizations have to make if they decide to legalize or make their engagement in society an official part of their formal work. On the other hand, the non-state "enemy" spaces that humanitarian organizations carve out may endanger villagers who are identified as working with the enemy. The current peace process may not only empower new civil society networks or facilitate ownership, but may also lead to a takeover of human rights advocacy by more powerful organizations, quickly marginalizing subaltern groups within that population (Horstmann 2012, p. 257). This points to the dilemma that arises when vulnerable people depend on alliances with more powerful educated and professional organizations that are able to connect to the international community and to speak for them.

The Karen conflict has been spiritually charged and associated in the international media with persecuted Christians, more so than with Buddhists, despite the fact that Mon/Karen Theravada Buddhism is the dominant culture and religion among the Karen. Southeast Myanmar and the Thai-Burmese border zones provide a very interesting case study for the power workings of religion, as northwest Thailand has become a hub of Christian outreach, and faith-based humanitarianism delivers the structure for the mobilization of people and the circulation of money. In the next section, I make a theoretical contribution by focusing on humanitarian assistance as reconstruction after civil war and utopian thinking in the form of ethno-nationalisms and religious utopias, driving development in Karen State. This utopian thinking comprises patriotic, ethno-nationalistic ideas about the reconstruction and future of Karen State, neo-Buddhist ideas about liberation from suffering and Christian ideas about progress and development, and recently fascist ideas about the ethnic cleansing of Muslims.

Against my earlier position that Karen nationalism and the KNU in particular have developed in tandem with Christianity (Baptist, Seventh-Day Adventist) (Horstmann 2011, p. 522), my more recent research with secular organizations has convinced me that a broad nationalist feeling exists among human rights NGO activists. This sentiment, which defends Karen cultural rights, has been very visible in the recent Karen Unity meetings in eastern Myanmar, where many different political and cultural organizations and factions came together to symbolize Karen unity. Moreover, Karen Buddhism has developed staunchly nationalist positions, whereby the competition for power, resources and influence have crossed and blurred religious boundaries. The KNU is not a Christian organization any more, and the competition between the KNU and the Democratic Karen Benevolent Army (DKBA) is not a competition between Christianity and Buddhism as it was before. I believe that it is necessary and valuable to analyse the interplay of secular and religious dynamics because a focus on either alone would be reductive and because the human rights activism of some NGOs can be explicitly evangelical as in the case of the Rangers, or become, in Oscar Salemink's words, "a quasi-religion". Many secular human rights NGOs working on the Thai border are sponsored by churches and many of their personnel are young educated Christians. Moreover, many churches that are engaged in humanitarian assistance have also built a wide-reaching ecumenical alliance of missionary societies and local missionaries who double as teachers, medical doctors and development workers.

Take the example of Adventist Development and Relief Agency (ADRA) Myanmar. While ADRA separates humanitarian assistance from development and religion, it is an openly Christian evangelical organization that follows the tenet of Christ caring for the poor. ADRA benefits greatly from the local embeddedness of the Seventh-Day Adventist movement throughout southeast Myanmar. The area has been a missionary focal point of the Seventh-Day Adventist Church for at least one hundred years, established by way of proselytizing an extensive web of local schools and clinics in the area. ADRA Myanmar acquires funds from international donors (Caritas, Johanniter, International Red Cross, governments, etc.) for diverse projects on health, livelihoods, water supply, and education and, more recently, on political training. ADRA remains one of the few international NGOs which only employs locals for managing day-to-day operations in the project sites and is thus a sought-after partner for organizations that are unable to carry out their projects *in situ*.[3]

THE HISTORY OF HUMANITARIAN ENGAGEMENT ON THE THAI-BURMESE BORDER

While the humanitarian economy and advocacy sector is now firmly entrenched in the Thai-Burmese border-scape, a map of humanitarianism reveals a complex picture in which humanitarian agencies of very different types operate side by side. The humanitarian landscape has been divided by the border and has developed differently on both sides of the border, creating a specific spatial order of humanitarianism in southeast Myanmar and northwest Thailand.

Humanitarian and missionary work in eastern Myanmar has been, for a variety of reasons, notoriously difficult. The most important hurdle remains the surveillance and repression by the military regime, which regards NGOs as potential allies of the insurgents and civil society as a political force. The territory in eastern Myanmar is a highly contested one and many military factions share pockets of the same area and are eager to impose themselves and exercise control. While the Border Guard Force receives salaries from the *Tatmadaw* (the Burmese Army), the KNU units still tax the populations under their control. Every humanitarian project has to be negotiated with local militia and their bosses. The area is highly militarized and full of military checkpoints. Nobody knows how many landmines are still active or being planted so much so that villagers sometimes step on their own mines. These factors limit the movement and operation of the NGOs that either work close to the Thai border or close to Hpa-an or Dawai.

The military assault on the Karen civil population in the early 1980s worsened rapidly when it was no longer possible for the villagers to return to their homes in the rainy season and the KNLA had to retreat to the border area. International organizations responded to this humanitarian crisis by mounting a comprehensive effort to provide shelter and food to no less than 140,000 people in nine refugee camps. A border consortium (the Thailand Burma Border Consortium, TBBC) emerged, succeeding in sheltering and feeding all the families in the camps. This is a feat that they have managed for over thirty years now. A Christian consortium in the beginning, it eventually transformed into a secular institution and incorporated numerous organizations, both secular and faith-based. Taking into account the long time frame, young people in the camp may have lived in the camp throughout their lives and have had little or no contact with Myanmar.

This new geopolitical situation framed the next few decades and placed international humanitarian organizations in a huge dilemma. The

Border Consortium received the mandate from the Thai Government to provide relief in the emerging camps, but international organizations were generally barred from crossing the border to help desperate people caught in the forests and hills. Yet, while many displaced people from the immediate border area moved to the Thai border, many more remained inside Myanmar, suffering from food crises, taxes, military assaults, human rights violations, relocations and forced labour. These people could only be reached by local organizations that came from the Karen organizations themselves. Unlike other ethnic minorities, the Karen had a large number of organizations under the umbrella of the nationalist movement and many of them were Christian.

The first wave of displaced migrants was mostly Christian Sgaw Karen. Whole communities were largely able to move across the border intact.[4] The refugees reconstructed their villages in the zones of the camp, kept the names of the villages and used largely the same materials to build their houses. The church was the community centre in the camp and Mae La refugee camp had fifty-four churches, Bible schools and Christian community centres. The pioneer Christian consortium identified in the beginning with persecuted fellow Christians and made a strategic choice to collaborate closely with the internal refugee camp committees to distribute rations as fairly and effectively as possible. The "refugee warriors" working with the KNU emerged as a "natural partner" for the Border Consortium and many international organizations in the consortium that were eager to gain access to the families. While the alliance and identification with the KNU and KNU-proxies was strong in the beginning (to the benefit of the families in the shelters), the relationship of the consortium and the Karen refugee administration gradually became more democratic and transparent (McConnachie 2012; South 2012). By far, the best space to provide rations, trainings, workshops, and so on, was the controlled space of the refugee camp in which social welfare services were also provided, especially education and healthcare. In addition to basic relief, the people in the camps also organized themselves in networks and community based organizations, covering many domains. However, while the Border Consortium, the international organizations and community organizations did an admirable job, many families resented the controlled space and the depressing livelihood conditions in the camps and eventually left to self-settle in migrant enclaves in the countryside of the Thai hills if they could find a place with a Thai Karen patron (Prasert Rangkla 2012).

In addition, later waves of refugees were more scattered and much less organized and belonged to different ethnic groups, spoke distinct languages and observed different religions. The majority of this group practised Buddhism and Animism, and a minority practised Islam. As a consequence, the camps became much more diverse, with considerable tension and competition developing among the different segments of the refugee population, and between the old and new residents. There were multiple reasons for the tension. The new residents were not Christian and often felt discriminated against and excluded from decisions taken by the camp administration. In response, the consortium reformed the administration, introduced more democratic and transparent decision-making and also included Buddhists in the refugee committees (TBBC 2010). Of course, neither the consortium nor the committees distributed aid partially, but it can be said that the KNU benefited in the first phase of humanitarian assistance. Without that assistance, the reconstruction of the nationalist movement on the Thai border and its humanitarian engagement inside Myanmar would not have been possible. However, humanitarian assistance in Karen state was largely limited to the KNLA-controlled areas. Later, when the United Nations Commissioner for Refugees (UNHCR) and the European Commission (EC) were allowed to establish their presence on the Thai border, the pressure for accountability increased and the consortium made great efforts to document the role of the various refugee populations and integrate them into community organizing in all aspects of camp life.[5]

In previous publications, I argued that the camps became centres for proselytizing. That, of course, does not mean that all incoming refugees became Christians. Far from that, Sandra Dudley has described how Animist Karenni villagers persisted in observing major rituals under difficult conditions in the camps and how these rituals and the traditional ways of weaving were central to safeguarding cultural identities (Dudley 2010). Some of the Animist groups felt that they had to propagate their Animism as a religion and ritual system in order to claim rights and create a niche in camp society. However, it is true that the camp elite mobilized resources to evangelize the newcomers and that young people were exposed to Christianity in the orphanages and schools. It is no secret that Karen pastors and personnel of the Kawthoolei Karen Baptist Churches actively aimed to bring "the lost" to Jesus Christ. People convert to Christianity in the local Karen churches every week. I was able to join a Baptist ceremony in Mae Ra Ma Luang, one of the northern refugee camps, in which some 500 Karen were baptized in a single day. This ceremony was seen as a major success for Christ and was presided over by Robert Htwe, chairperson of the Karen Refugee Committee (KRC). The "soft" evangelization in the camps belongs to the utopian thinking of the Christian churches to build a heavenly kingdom in the camps. It is also part and parcel of transforming the space of the camps from spaces of despair into spaces of hope.

HUMANITARIANISM OPERATING ON THE THAI BORDER

The Thai border has provided refuge and sanctuary for rights-orientated as well as service-oriented groups, secular as well as religious projects for decades. Karen Burmese nationals have operated in a dense network, organizing mobile schools, alternative schoolbooks, health services, human rights documentation, advocacy work and constant reports about the situation and condition of Karen villagers inside Myanmar (Horstmann 2012, p. 10). Local community based groups have become professional NGOs that recruited from the educated spectrum of Karen migrants (McConnachie 2012).

The Free Burma Rangers is a humanitarian relief organization and is openly evangelistic. Like the Back Pack Health Worker Team, the Free Burma Rangers is an offshoot of the KNU and is led by the missionary-militaristic Eubank family. This family understands the conflict as a sacred one in which good fights evil. So does the American church-based organization, Partners that collaborates closely with the Rangers. All these organizations operate independently (that is, they are not part of The Border Consortium). The Free Burma Rangers and the Back Packers are based in Thailand, but operate in the KNU-controlled areas across the border as well as many other marginal border areas inside Myanmar. They have to operate illegally as they would never be given a permit to do so by the Burmese Government and are perceived as enemies by the Burmese Army. While both the Rangers and Back Packers specialize in emergency healthcare, they pursue slightly different agendas. The Rangers use military training and are armed for protection. Both make use of the protection of KNLA troops. While the Free Burma Rangers are political, the Back Packers are not interested in propaganda and present themselves as professional nurses. The Free Burma Rangers also introduced the Good Life Club and hope to encourage villagers by playing games and providing worship services, while the Back Packers have no religious agenda. Humanitarian organizations on the Thai border that proselytize are the exception. Most organizations have political programmes and specialize in human rights. In a recent paper, I wrote about two local secular organizations that also came from KNU networks, but now work completely independently: Burma Issues and the Karen Human Rights Group (KHRG) (Horstmann 2012, pp. 273–77). Burma Issues and the KHRG work independently from each other, but share the same aims: they train villagers in the documentation of human rights violations to make *Tatmadaw* personnel accountable for their crimes and train people to claim their rights and empower them to negotiate with the Burmese authorities. Their work also includes advocacy work and public relations to defend the villagers' livelihoods (see KHRG 2013, 2014).

Interestingly, all these organizations depend heavily on volunteers and staff in Karen State to do anything meaningful. These networks in Karen State were probably crucial for the survival and training of displaced villagers in Karen State for decades. Again, one cannot say that any of these organizations privileged Christians, but it is safe to say that most find it much easier to work in Christian communities, as many of the new middle class in the NGOs are also Christian who find church networks very helpful for organizing their meetings, even if they try to mobilize villagers to conduct humanitarian or human rights work. Faith-based organizations are inherently different and diverse in character and fund-raising. The Jesuit Refugee Service, for example, works with the International Rescue Service on many projects in the Border Consortium. The Christian NGOs, ADRA Thailand of the Seventh-Day Adventist and ZOA International Relief used to also support a number of educational projects in the camps. All projects are coordinated with the Karen organizations, the internal Karen refugee committees in the refugee camps and the consortium. The Back Packers, the Free Burma Rangers, Burma Issues, Burma partnership and KHRG are not members of the consortium. All these organizations have their own funding, which consists of a mix of donations from churches, and government development agencies from the international Western community that were looking for local organizations to implement their projects.

The Back Packers and Free Burma Rangers have developed into very substantial humanitarian agencies that provide badly needed healthcare not only in Karen State, but also in many other areas. The Back Packers operate not fewer than eighty walking teams in all ethnic minority areas. These teams literally walk with medicine and money through the rainforest and rivers to isolated communities. The Free Burma Rangers also document human rights violations and campaign actively in churches in Chiang Mai and in the west. They finance themselves through donations and are doing well — unlike Burma Issues, which focuses on advocacy and rights training and whose budget is dwindling as donors shift their priorities to education, health and the environment in Myanmar.

Young Karen migrants who volunteer for Free Burma Rangers are drawn to its spirituality and political nature. In my project on refugees and Christianity, I have followed the life histories and refugee careers of young men who at different times of their life in exile have joined the journeys of the Free Burma Rangers whose teams regularly travel to the conflict areas. These young men saw it as their obligation to serve God and their communities and were quickly entangled in political projects. One of these young men is now working in the project *Save the Kids* that is run by an Australian Pentecostal church. This project is entirely financed through donations from Australia and provides free teaching in a fixed school organized by the church near the Thai border. While the boarding school is actually organized for orphans, most of the children come from poor parents. The school proselytizes among poor children, and integrates devotion and gospel into its teaching. The parents do not mind as long as the school provides education, food and board.

HUMANITARIANISM OPERATING IN SOUTHEAST MYANMAR

The situation inside Myanmar in the heart of Karen State looks entirely different. Thanks to the recent partial political opening of Myanmar, the Border Consortium has been invited to open an office in Yangon and to operate from Myanmar as camp closure and repatriation become imminent. This would have been unthinkable even in 2010 before the ceasefire talks began. The NGOs on the Thai border were filled with Karen educated activists and students and hence politicized. However, political organizations were unable to survive censorship, surveillance and arrest in Myanmar. Karen indigenous intellectuals like pastors or grassroots activists who were associated with the KNU or even provided shelter were sentenced to long jail terms.

Organizations that survived the ordeal and constantly provided assistance under extremely difficult circumstances were church-based. Political organization and missionary work were both outlawed and the churches had to keep a low profile. Only recently has partial democratization enabled the mushrooming of many different civil society organizations in Hpa-an that have one common feature: they are all Karen. Many of the new organizations have now taken up projects of community mobilizing and political issues such as land confiscation and legal assistance. Many organizations concentrate on pressing problems of community organizing without calling attention to the name of the organization. Different associations working in education, health and development and cultural rights are members of the Karen Affairs Committee in which there is an interesting generational change taking place: young activists, female and male, have transcended the boundaries of potentially antagonistic political Karen organizations. Much of the new engagement is inspired by faith, even though religion is not in the foreground of humanitarian work. A significant European Union funded project entitled *Good Governance and Civil Education* centres on mobilizing the community to strengthen their organizational abilities to move forward in all sectors of development. A major relief project for displaced villagers in Dawai (southeast Myanmar) is coordinated both by Christian churches (Baptist and Anglican) and by a Buddhist charismatic monk and his Buddhist foundation in Hpa-an.

While many of the relief and development projects are coordinated and funded by Protestant churches in coordination with international NGOs (for example, the Norwegian Refugee Council), Catholic and Protestant churches in southeast Myanmar operate their own missionary societies. Local missionaries are completely integrated into the local communities in which they are embedded. As local missionaries do not want to be a burden on the community since they have to share resources and food with the villagers, they contribute to education, basic healthcare and gardening. The missionaries are basically local volunteer teachers who operate on very modest allowances and who are extremely committed to their mission. These missionaries and other project field staff regularly travel to remote villages by motorbike, by boat and on foot.

Relief and development in Karen State are always geared towards the vague idea of the self-determination of the Karen people. The Karen Affairs Committee has been highly involved in the organization of the recent Karen Unity seminars, where hundreds of people from different Karen organizations and political factions came together under the ideological umbrella of Karen nationalism. While some observers have emphasized the key role of American Christian missionaries for the emergence and development of Karen nationalism, ethno-nationalist thinking is very pronounced in the Buddhist Sangha, the DKBA, and in the NGO/civil society scene as well (see Gravers 2007).

In a lengthy conversation with me, the very charismatic Tauggalay monk in Hpa-an pointed out that the KNU is losing out in the ceasefire negotiations to the Burmese Government and that the Burmans (he used the ethnic term "Bamar") are not to be trusted. Civil society organizations and political parties in Karen State are highly patriotic and word their discourse in terms of Karen blood, Karen suffering in the hands of the

Burman/Bamar and the early history of the Karen people. Karen monasteries and churches keep alive spoken Karen and Karen literacy in a country where the Karen language is not taught in primary schools. Sometimes Karen children are punished by their parents for conversing in Burmese at home as Burmese is seen as the language of the oppressor and a threat to the Karen language. Karen traditions, popular religion and festivals are kept alive in the communities. For example, the very popular Don dance has changed from a symbol of social cohesion and village solidarity to a symbol of the Karen nation. Competitions in reciting Karen poetry and verse, Karen literacy, Don dance and Karen national drilling skills are held regularly outside of the government framework in locations near the Thai border. There is no doubt that much of Karen humanitarianism is highly defensive. This defensive position is structural, ideological and practical. It is practical as all humanitarian projects are heavily limited by political constraints.

Thammanya used to be a Buddhist pilgrimage centre in Karen State (not only for the Karen) which was named after U Thammanya, who is a Buddhist saint and ethnic patron who represents the fifth future Buddha (*Maitreya*) who appears from heaven and liberates the Karen from suffering and brings prosperity. This hugely popular monk was embalmed after his death, but his corpse was mysteriously stolen from the monastery. In his lifetime, U Thammanya's hilltop monastery was seen as a Karen spiritual centre of resistance to the military regime in Yangon. The centre of the DKBA is a monastery under the leadership of U Thammanya's student and successor, U Thuzana. U Thuzana is not only a monk practising in the forest monk tradition, but also a development monk, a military leader and a staunch nationalist. For a long time, the KNU leadership has been Christian. The insurgency has long been seen as Christian, although this might not be accurate. The ethnic character of Karen humanitarianism has partly estranged the Burmese democratic movement from the Karen one and the Karen have rarely worked with the more progressive and better-educated Burmese NGOs and professionals than in the centre of the country. The organizations in the Karen Affairs Committee are recruited from the Karen ethnic pool and are thus very inward-looking.

Due to the huge hurdles in collaborating with Christian organizations abroad, Christian churches in Karen State have not benefited from international church networks and donations in the way that Karen churches in Thailand — which are supported by missionaries and funding — have been. Christian Karen were perhaps more cosmopolitan and had contacts with the Western world and more opportunity to travel abroad than, for example, Buddhists. Ethno-nationalist thinking in Karen State was fuelled by resettlement from the refugee camps to the West where resettled communities have donated to churches and the KNU. Thus, the Karen are influenced by symbols in globalizing flows and also feed these flows with symbols of ethnic dress, discourse and funding. Christian churches have organized a yearly seminar in Chiang Mai, northern Thailand, on "Reading the Bible through Karen Eyes". Ethno-nationalism has recently been revived in ugly contexts. The monkhood in Karen State has generously supported U Wiratu's hatred campaign against Muslims in Karen State. Mosques have been attacked as a result, and Muslim businesses have been boycotted. Massacres of Muslims by Buddhists have so far been avoided, but there is strong support for the Buddhist non-marriage law and the anti-Muslim campaign, inspired by the abbot U Wirathu in Mandalay, and local mosques have been attacked. It seems that militant ultra-nationalist and anti-Muslim Buddhist movements elsewhere in Myanmar as well as in Sri Lanka have influenced the Karen monkhood. The 969 movement, which spreads hatred among lay people through horror stories of the domestic abuse suffered by Buddhist women at the hands of Muslim men, is a highly organized political campaign to gain legitimacy for the military and to create a scapegoat in the political landscape by inciting people's envy of the relative success of Muslim entrepreneurs in the city. The campaign is launched by elements of the right-wing military to instigate hatred and instability and to create a demand for the military. It seems fairly successful as anti-Muslim and anti-Indian sentiments about pushing the Muslim "other" away from Buddhist land are rampant in Karen State.

Theravada Buddhism and millenarian utopian thinking can also be seen as a modus to instal a new normative order to bring law, security and stability into a world that is characterized by cultural chaos (e.g. Gravers 2007). As shown above, some monks create small empires in which they propagate development by benefiting from government funds, probably drug laundering and donations from Thai business people. Christians talk about God's kingdom on earth while the Buddhist monkhood also wants to defend land demarcations in which Buddhist order and rules are prevalent. Christian volunteer-missionaries convert villagers and instal small chapels in the conflict zone. Humanitarianism thus comes in very different forms and constellations. Local organizations work together or vie with international faith-based NGOs and foreign missionary networks. Pentecostalism is quickly establishing itself in Karen State, building on existing structures of the Assembly of God. Pentecostalism focuses much less on social work or humanitarian assistance and more on worship and proselytizing, to the dismay of the declining Baptist churches and the Buddhist Sangha that denounces Pentecostal churches as a threat to the Buddhist Sangha. International faith-based organizations like World Vision now have come in as powerful partners, but again are still highly limited in their mobility and scope. Both secular and faith-based organizations rely heavily on existing social support networks of villagers, which may be Buddhist or Christian. Without those networks that allow organizations to work effectively with the community, too many hurdles obstruct efficient humanitarian assistance and entire organizations that criticize the constraints imposed by the government find themselves confined or sanctioned or even more constrained. Others conform to the government's regulations.

Until recently, all humanitarian assistance in Karen state was faith-based, and Christian and faith-based local organizations occupied a niche and were able to help effectively, with very modest means. The faith-based local organizations however, are unable to shoulder the new challenges of a more open Myanmar, with new problems of relocation and land confiscation and resource exploitation. Local faith-based organizations are going into new domains of rights claiming and political rights training which they have difficulty handling. Local secular organizations that were influenced by the Burmese democratic student movement on the Thai border are superbly equipped and have substantial experience, but seem to face a serious decline of international funding for capacity-building and advocacy work. Karen organizations mushrooming in civil society are now better integrated into mainstream Burmese civil society networks and social movements and young community leaders are able to overcome at least partly ethno-nationalist self-limitations.

As such, we have a structure of parallel humanitarianism with both secular and faith-based community organizations and international NGOs working with social support networks in the rural areas. The employees in these organizations are sometimes identical, as they tend to move from one organization to another. The culture of humanitarianism developed completely differently in Thailand and in Myanmar because of the political environment and the advocacy work of organizations working on the Thai border. While humanitarianism in southeast Myanmar has been faith-based, the position of the churches in humanitarian assistance and development is diminishing, although faith-based networks are still active in relief. The reason is that the new issues of advocacy work, human rights training and more political issues of land and environmental conflict cannot be satisfactorily tackled by Christian churches or Buddhist monasteries, although some church leaders and some monks are getting involved. The spatial aspect also remains important as community organizations on the Thai border still cross to work in ceasefire areas, while organizations working from Hpa-an are much more limited and have to undertake long journeys to access remote villages.

Community organizations in Thailand, on the other hand, do not have a wide enough reach into Myanmar and are still uncomfortable working in areas controlled by the Burmese Government. Funding constraints may push the politicized organizations on the Thai border to compromise and to move offices to Myanmar's capitals. Faith-based organizations in eastern Myanmar urgently need international exposure, training and international partners to move ahead in the difficult political transition. Christian and Buddhist actors are crucial in southeastern Myanmar and still provide the frame and infrastructure in which humanitarian and human rights organizations may work, but advocacy organizations are becoming more important in the near future. The next step will be cautious collaboration of NGOs with the Myanmar Government and this collaboration will attract funding from the international community and has the potential to marginalize humanitarian assistance and human rights work being done in non-state spaces.

CONCLUSION

This chapter has explored the formation and dynamic development of a humanitarian sector and how this sector has been instrumental in helping people go on with their lives and gather new hope. It is in this space that social services were provided to displaced Karen, where resistance to the repression of the state could be enacted and where a parallel form of governance and economy could be established that enabled the Karen to plan for a future. I have argued elsewhere that humanitarianism allowed for the creation of corridors and *routes de passages* for re-entry into the dangerous area of southeast Myanmar (Horstmann 2014, pp. 2–3), although the ceasefire has changed the conditions by greatly facilitating border crossing. State-led development and business investors embarking on great industrial and infra-structural mega-projects seem to present a new challenge for Karen villagers who face eviction or relocation. New modes of territorialization are introduced by the Karen militia that gain power through the ceasefire. The immediate border area in southeast Myanmar becomes a zone where Thai currency is used. The future of the refugee camps is highly uncertain and its eventual closure will mean that a great humanitarian landscape in northwestern Thailand will disappear. While the peace process opens up new spaces for local civil society to take root in southeastern Myanmar among the Karen, the Shan and the Mon, Karen and Karenni villagers in southeast Myanmar are still incredibly poor and many are forced to seek work in Thailand.

This chapter has started an ethnographic study of the humanitarian sector, which contrasts starkly with the capitalist sector, and the flow of migrant labour into the migrant enclaves of Mae Sot (cf. Oh in this volume).[6] Many Karen families have been resettled from the refugee camps to other countries by the UNHCR and formed diasporic communities in the United States, Australia, Canada, Norway, Sweden, and Denmark. Humanitarianism in different shapes will continue to mark the landscape in southeast Myanmar for some time to come and many Karen have used this sector extensively to contribute to a better future for people in Myanmar.

Coming back to the production of landscapes, one can say that humanitarianism provided the means for "landscape plasticity" in which the Karen were able to counter the production of landscapes of armed rule and terror. The humanitarian economy provided alternative education and health services in a time when neither was available. Of all the ethnic minority areas, the humanitarian economy, the specific humanitarian milieu and culture and humanitarian network on the Thai-Burmese border was the most extensive. Regarding the transformation of Myanmar's marginal areas, one can say that the partnership that has evolved between humanitarian aid and the Karen is somewhat unique, and it has resulted in a fantastic project of reconsolidating Karen society in exile. Other more marginal ethnic groups did not have the chance and did not benefit from aid as much as the Karen did. The success of the Karen community in transforming the border landscape is due to the very high degree of internal coherence and networking of the first generation of displaced in the refugee camps, combined with their ability to connect to international faith-based organizations, international church networks and to keep traditional communities largely intact. It is difficult to say what the future holds, as the remittances from living abroad are becoming more important for a new start for many Karen in southeast Myanmar.

Notes

1. The chapter incorporates recent observations from my project funded by the Thailand Research Fund entitled *Humanitarianism from Below* community-based organizations of the Karen and the role of the international community. Fieldwork for the project was done in conjunction with the project group Streams

of Knowledge along the Thai-Burmese Border Zones: Multiple Dimensions of People, Capital and Culture, coordinated by Decha Tangseefa (Bangkok). All data collected are my own and based on observations gained from ethnographic fieldwork. I would like to thank Sirijit Sunanta, Decha Tangseefa and Su-Ann Oh for their warm and friendly support and for inspiring this article. Note that I use the designation of Karen and Karenni, which I prefer to the official designation Kayin and Kayah.
2. The Border Consortium, the former Thailand Burma Border Consortium (TBBC), consists of voluntary humanitarian organizations that oversee and manage humanitarian assistance and rations to the camp and support Karen voluntary groups working with the Karen on all aspects of livelihood in the camps. See the excellent report of the consortium's experiences and moving engagement in TBBC (2010). I would like to thank the board of The Border Consortium for answering to all of my questions relating to their wonderful work.
3. I would like to express my gratitude to the staff of ADRA who generously accepted me as a guest researcher and opened many doors for me in eastern Myanmar that would otherwise have been closed to me.
4. The majority of the Christian Karen are Skaw (also spelt as Sgaw), in relation to the Pwo Karen who are mostly Buddhist and also belong to indigenous groups and religions.
5. The excellent reports and surveys on conflict, displacement and poverty are available for download on TBBC's website http://theborderconsortium.org/.
6. See the excellent article by Su-Ann Oh in this volume.

References

Agier, Michel. "Between War and City: Towards an urban anthropology of refugee camps". *Ethnography* 3, no. 3 (2002): 317–43.
Decha Tangseefa. "Taking Flight in Condemned Grounds. Forcibly Displaced Karen and the Thai-Burmese in-Between Spaces". *Alternatives* 31 (2006): 405–29.
Dudley, Sandra. *Materialising Exile: Material Culture and Embodied Experience Among Karenni Refugees in Thailand*. Oxford: Berghahn, 2010.
Gravers, Mikael, ed. "Conversion and Identity: Religion and the Formation of Karen Ethnic Identity in Burma". In *Exploring Ethnic Diversity in Burma*. Copenhagen: Nordic Institute of Asian Studies (NIAS) Press, 2007, pp. 227–58.
Hayami Yoko. *Between Hills and Plains: Power and Practice in Socio-Religious Dynamics among Karen*. Kyoto: Kyoto University Press, 2004.
Horstmann, Alexander. "Ethical Dilemmas and Identifications of Faith-based Humanitarian Organisations in the Karen Refugee Crisis". *Journal of Refugee Studies* 24, no. 3 (2011): 513–32.
———. "Mediating the Suffering of Karen Refugees and the Representation of Their Rights". *Sangkomsat Chiang Mai Journal of Social Sciences* 24, no. 1-2/2555 (2012): 243–84.
———. "Stretching the Border. Confinement, Mobility and the Refugee Public among

Karen Refugees in Thailand and Burma". *Journal of Borderlands Studies*, no. 1 (2014): 47–61.

———. "Uneasy Pairs: Revitalization of Karen Ethno-Nationalism and Civil Society across the Thai-Burmese Border". *Journal of Maritime and Territorial Studies* 2, no. 2 (2015): 33–52.

Karen Human Rights Group (KHRG). "Losing Ground. Land Conflicts and Collective Action in Eastern Myanmar". Mae Sot: KHRG, 2013.

———. "Truce or Transition? Trends in Human Rights Abuse and Local Response in Southeast Myanmar since the 2012 Ceasefire". Mae Sot: KHRG, 2014.

McConnachie, Kirsten. "Rethinking the 'Refugee Warrior': The Karen National Union and Refugee Protection on the Thai–Burma Border". *Journal of Human Rights Practice* 4, no. 1 (2012): 30–56.

Prasert Rangkla. "Karen Refugees' Self-Settlement: Refuge in Local Administration and Contingent Relations". *Sangkomsat Chiang Mai Journal of Social Sciences* 24, no. 1-2/2555 (2012): 159–95.

South, Ashley. "The Politics of Protection in Burma". *Critical Asian Studies* 44, no. 2 (2012): 175–204.

Sturgeon, Janet C. *Border Landscapes. The Politics of Akha Land Use in China and Thailand*. Seattle and London: University of Washington Press, 2005.

The Thailand Burma Border Consortium (TBBC). "Nine Thousand Nights. Refugees from Burma: A People's Scrapbook". Bangkok: Thailand Burma Border Consortium, 2010.

8

Navigating Learning, Employment and Economies in the Mae Sot-Myawaddy Borderland[1]

Su-Ann Oh

The Mae Sot-Myawaddy borderland is teeming with peoples of varying ethnicities, social classes and qualifications working and studying in a myriad of organizations. The diversity of motivations, trajectories and institutions is at once overwhelming and fascinating. This chapter attempts to make sense of this complexity by focusing on the learning and employment adventures of Miriam, a young Burmese woman living in Mae Sot.[2] Although Miriam does not embody an ideal-type, nor does her story represent the experiences of the diverse individuals living on this border, her narrative provides a fascinating account of and the way in which wider structures — both material and intangible — shape an individual life.

Essentially, this chapter asserts that the lives of Burmese migrants in the Mae Sot–Myawaddy border area are largely affected by two economies — the neoliberal and the humanitarian (see Horstmann, this volume) — operating under and outside the jurisdiction of the central Thai and Burmese states, and local (formal and informal) authorities on both sides of the border. While I am aware of other economies operating in this region — the war economy for example, I focus on these two economies because there are a range of learning and employment institutions that make up and support them. The neoliberal market economy as applied to this region brings to mind border trade, garment factories and special economic zones. This is where Miriam's story begins. As we follow her journey into and out of a garment factory and then into various community and non-governmental organizations that make up the humanitarian economy, we discover the workings of these two economies.

By linking individual pathways and institutions to employment in distinct sectors, this chapter identifies the ideologies, beliefs and customs being reproduced and that form the socio-cultural base of the humanitarian industry in this borderland. It also shows that educational institutions are not uniform across the board: some provide training in the skills and attitudes suitable for joining the capitalist underclass in Thailand, others provide training in competencies for employment in community based and non-governmental organizations in the humanitarian sector. While the latter is a step up from precarious factory work, its dependence on donors subjects it to funding fads and donors' whims.

This chapter fills a gap in the scholarship on this region, which has tended to focus on the work and lives of Burmese migrants employed in the neoliberal economy or the beneficiaries of the humanitarian economy (Lang 2002; Decha Tangseefa 2006; Hull 2009; Lanjouw et al. 2000), keeping the two separate and discrete. Instead, I argue that in order to more fully understand this borderland, it is necessary to consider the schooling, training and employment of Burmese migrants as a whole and their links with these distinct economies, regardless of their geographical location (town/refugee camp) or administrative category (migrant/refugee).

The chapter concludes by drawing our attention to the nature of this borderland as an evolving space that is continually shaped by its denizens in the face of state and local authority. This is significant in the following ways. First, Burmese nationals have carved out a humanitarian space that serves their needs. Second, this humanitarian space is distinctive as it combines local and international skills, beliefs and customs, thus distinguishing it from humanitarianism in the North. Finally, this distinctive sector has created employment which validates the cultural capital that Burmese nationals already possess, skills and competencies that are often unrecognized and underrated by the Thai Government and employers.

THE NEOLIBERAL AND HUMANITARIAN ECONOMIES IN THE MAE SOT–MYAWADDY BORDERLAND

Mae Sot, a town in the northwest of Thailand, borders Myanmar; its Burmese counterpart is Myawaddy. With a bustling and mobile population of migrants, refugees and Thai citizens, it is estimated that a third (100,000 to 200,000) of the town's population is from Myanmar (Lee 2008). This border area thrives on (legal and illicit) trade between the two countries, a substantial export factory industry on the Thai side and a small but significant humanitarian sector that serves the needs of Burmese nationals on both sides of the border.

Precariousness pervades the lives of Burmese nationals living in this borderland. On the Burmese side of the border, decades of armed conflict, Burmese state neglect, dubious development endeavours and displacement have created a landscape of danger, competing multiple authorities, shifting alliances, fear, anxiety and mistrust (Grundy-Warr and Chin, this volume), suffering (Decha Tangseefa, this volume) and humanitarian need (Lang 2002). On the Thai side, insecurity in employment (Arnold and Pickles 2011; Hewison and Tularak 2013), livelihoods, place of residence and legal status plague Burmese nationals.

In attempting to cope with this, Burmese nationals practise individual acts of charity, engage in a range of intimate relationships (Lyttleton 2014, pp. 129–38), and participate in organized humanitarian action, among other activities. The latter takes place through local community-based organizations (CBOs), non-governmental organizations (NGOs), trade unions, committees, medical clinics, human rights advocacy organizations, cross-border aid and learning institutions. There are networks of Karen organizations that may or may not be affiliated with the Karen National Union (KNU), dissident Burmese political organizations, migrant organizations, faith-based organizations and Thai NGOs with distinct political, ethnic and religious affiliations. These organizations seek to improve human welfare in the material, moral and symbolic sense while operating within a distinct set of cultural norms, values, and practices, which are, to a certain extent, influenced by principles espoused by international aid organizations and/or networks of faith-based organizations. Horstmann (this volume) does an excellent job of identifying and chronicling the emergence and development of this humanitarian economy, and explicating its philosophical, ethno-nationalist and spiritual bases.

By "economy", I refer to the production, distribution and consumption of material and immaterial things, such as goods, "labour, services, knowledge and myth, names and charms, and so on" (Carrier 2012, p. 4). In economic sociology, the critical point to understanding "economies" is that economic life and economic actions are "embedded in concrete, ongoing systems of social relations" (Granovetter 1985, p. 487). By social relations, I mean the wider political, social, cultural and cognitive web in which everyday lives are conducted (e.g. Zukin and DiMaggio 1990; Zelizer 1988; Nee and Ingram 1998).

Through Miriam's narrative, we observe the intersection of economic interests and social relations in the two economies. The market realm of the neoliberal capitalist economy is often conceived of as abstract and impersonal. Here, people are motivated by the desire to accumulate profit and by competitive or instrumental goals. In reality, economies are composed of two realms that are dialectically related (Gudeman 2012) — the market and the "community" in which social relationships, values, and imagined solidarities between individuals play a real and vital role. In real life, individuals and even corporations mix the two dimensions of the economy in their practices and depend on community relations and resources to achieve success.

In the neoliberal capitalist economy in Mae Sot, scholars have studied the working and living conditions of migrant workers in the global supply chain (Arnold and Hewison 2007; Arnold and Pickles 2011; Pearson and Kusakabe 2012; Nobpaon Rabibhadana and Hayami 2013), and the forms of protest and resistance they have undertaken (Arnold 2013; Campbell 2013). However, less work has been done on the intersection of market and social relations within these factories in relation to those who hold power. For example, do factory managers and owners always behave in accordance with market principles when running and managing factories? How do social class, ethnic, religious and other social relations affect their everyday work decisions?

Another gap in the literature is the ways in which the neoliberal market economy and humanitarian economy intersect. One notable example is Stephen Campbell's (2012) work on how ethnic and class solidarity in factories is affected by migrant workers' access to humanitarian aid. Equally, this chapter shows how various learning institutions and employment opportunities are connected to the two economies identified.

This leads us to an examination of the humanitarian economy. By "humanitarian", I mean the improvement of human welfare — a fairly broad definition. I believe that we can define this phenomenon as an economy and not just an industry because of three features. First, what is produced and distributed in this economy is a combination of social services (e.g. education, healthcare) and goods (e.g. Bibles) that are aimed at improving human welfare, particularly of people who have little or no access to other resources. Second, the principles of distribution are based not on market supply and demand but on a certain culture of support ("serving the community") and suffering, in (ethno)-nationalist politics and belonging, faith-based tenets and notions of democracy, liberation, human rights and aid. Third, the distribution of resources is carried according to need rather than the possession of resources for exchange. In the refugee camps, until recently, rations were provided for all since the 1980s with special provisions made for the vulnerable (defined as widows and orphans). Textbooks, rations and other resources have made their way to the eastern border of Myanmar, to be distributed to those living in internally displaced persons (IDP) camps, isolated villages and political organizations such as the KNU.

The panoply of institutions in the humanitarian economy — economic institutions characterized by "the mobilization of resources for collective action" (Granovetter 1992, p. 6) — seek to improve human welfare in the material, moral and symbolic sense while operating within a distinct set of cultural norms, values, and practices, which are, to a certain extent, influenced by principles espoused by international aid organizations. This is the set of social relations in which the humanitarian economy is embedded.

MIGRANTS, CULTURAL CAPITAL AND REPRODUCTION

The cultural reproduction of this set of norms, values and practices in learning institutions and workplaces forms the topic of this chapter. Studies on migration and cultural reproduction have tended to examine how migrants acquire the cultural capital of the host society. This — how Burmese migrants acquire cultural capital to navigate Thai society in Mae Sot — in itself would be interesting but is not the focus of this chapter. Rather, it examines Burmese nationals' endeavours in acquiring cultural capital to obtain and succeed in employment in the humanitarian sector in this borderland.

This sector is particularly interesting for two reasons. First, it is in fact one of the few sectors where Burmese migrants are able to gain access to skilled employment, career advancement and higher social status, and, importantly, where their cultural capital is valued. Second, it is based on an amalgamation of local (read Burmese, Karen and other ethnic groups from Myanmar) understandings of need, service, culture, power and suffering, and international (or rather Northern) tenets of humanitarianism. In a very real sense, this humanitarian sector and the civil society involved in its activities have emerged from the geographic, political, economic, social and cultural specificities of this borderland.

Undoubtedly, Burmese nationals in Mae Sot bring their own set of cultural capital in the form of language, attitudes, outlook, skills and national certificates of educational attainment. However, this exists in hierarchical structures of economic, cultural, social and symbolic capital. In the Thai economy, the employment avenues open to Burmese nationals without legal migrant status or recognized Thai credentials are severely limited. For example, to obtain a job as a cashier at a local supermarket, applicants are required to possess Thai school Grade 6 qualifications at the very least. Thus, the main types of employment available to Burmese nationals in this geographical region are: non- or semi-skilled work (factory work, waitressing, domestic work, construction, seasonal farming, sex work, service jobs in restaurants, hotels, launderettes and other menial labour jobs), trading and business. Combined with the restrictions on mobility, Burmese migrants' opportunities for employment and advancement are acutely constrained.

Many end up working in the factories that dominate Mae Sot's economy. In Tak Province where Mae Sot is located, the official number of workers in apparel factories was more than 30,000 in 2006 (Pearson and Kusakabe 2012, p. 49). In 2011, about 400 factories (the majority of which were registered) — textile, garment, agro-industries, food and others — operated in Mae Sot (Lyttleton 2014, p. 123).

In the humanitarian sector, the possession of national (Burmese) cultural capital gets one's foot in the door, but it is not enough to guarantee a good wage and career advancement. This is where acquiring new forms of cultural capital becomes vital. This may take place in various social spheres but the most obvious and common route is through schooling and work-based learning. Studies on cultural reproduction on this border have tended to focus on the reproduction of ethnic and political culture in schools in the nearby refugee camps (Dudley 2006; Oh 2012; Rajah 2002) as a means of building and sustaining ethno-nationalism or on learning, institutions or policy per se (Lee 2014; Oh and van der Stouwe 2008; Purkey 2010; Johnson 2013). What is missing is an examination of the linkages between the various types of schools and the employment available in this borderland. This chapter thus fills a gap in the scholarship on this region by looking specifically at the types of cultural capital Burmese migrants are acquiring in order to move one step up the employment ladder.

Moreover, I am cognisant of the fact that socialization is inflected by class inequalities and local material contexts (Bourdieu and Passeron 1990). This brings nuance to the literature on schooling in this region which has tended to study schools based on the administrative categories that have been applied to them — migrant and refugee — rather than as part of wider social structures. This chapter maintains that it is necessary to consider the schooling, training and employment of Burmese migrants as a whole and to foreground these learning encounters in the political economy and stratified sociocultural structures of this region.

We begin with Miriam's narrative of learning and employment in Mae Sot. Recognizing that the narrative as a form of data has its methodological limitations (memory lapses, the view of one person only, the positionality of the interlocutor and so on), this chapter approaches it as "the unique expression of experiences that are inscribed in, produced within, and productive of a larger context" (Giordano 2008, p. 590).[3] Thus, the learning and employment experiences recounted by Miriam act as a portal to some of the institutions and social practices of this region.

MIRIAM'S EMPLOYMENT AND LEARNING TRAJECTORY

Miriam, a thirty-year-old Muslim woman from Taungoo in Myanmar, lives in Mae Sot. She obtained her degree in agriculture in Myanmar, but was unable to find a job in her hometown.[4] In 2006, at age twenty-three, she travelled to Mae Sot to join her mother as a worker in a garment factory. Her mother, Mya, had worked there for about a decade and had been able to send only small amounts of money to Miriam and her sister, Fara, in Myanmar. Mya hoped that with Miriam there to pool rent and other expenses, they would be able to save more money.

Miriam imagined having her own desk and earning a decent income in the factory. Her rosy vision of factory work and Thailand was shattered when she arrived at the garment factory. She was appalled by the security measures and working conditions. She exclaimed in the interview, "Oh my God! It was like a prison!" She worked twelve-hour days with two breaks and was only allowed out once a month. The conditions were cramped and back-breaking; the pay was a pittance.

After twenty-eight days in the factory, she borrowed 3,000 baht (US$83) from her fellow workers and, through her aunt (who lives in Taungoo), was able to contact a Burmese political organization based in Mae Sot. Two members of this community-based organization came in a truck to take her from the factory and they subsequently installed her in the office of the organization. Here, she was given her own room and provided with training on human rights, democracy and management skills. She was also able to acquire office and computer skills and a network of friends and contacts from this milieu. Her mother provided her with some "pocket money"; her food and lodging were provided for by the organization.

After six months, Miriam became frustrated with the lack of progression in skills training and prospects in this organization. Through discussions with non-Burman/non-Bamar colleagues, she came to believe that the way forward was to learn English. She believed that if she could speak English, she would be able to obtain employment that paid a decent wage.

She planned to enrol in an advanced English language programme in one of the camps. However, on receiving the application form (written in English), she realized that she was not able to apply because she could not understand the form. She decided to move to the camp where this programme is based so that she would have somewhere to live for free (free rations and shelter) and would face no danger of arrest and/or deportation. She believed that she would be able to find a low-paid job in camp and that she would have more time to study and learn English since people have "nothing to do in camp".

While working at the political organization, she made friends who had registered for resettlement with the UNHCR (United Nations High Commission for Refugees) and were obliged to live in camp. These friends encouraged her to move in with them. Her mind made up, Miriam went up to the camp in the KNU (Karen National Union) truck with 300 baht borrowed from one of her friends with which she paid the driver. She lived in camp with these two friends who were eventually resettled in 2008. On arriving, she thought to herself, "I have bamboo house, very cute bamboo house!" After two or three months in camp, she obtained a job in a Muslim school where she taught Grade 3 and 4 students. The following year, she worked as a teacher in a vocational training programme.

Miriam was able to learn English on her own and after two years in camp, she applied for the English programme, took the entrance examinations and was accepted. The programme lasted a year, where the students were taught English by two foreigners. Through the programme, she obtained an internship at an international NGO which developed into a full-time job. When the contract ended, she moved on to a full-time job at another international NGO. She is now a board member of the first NGO.

FACTORY, CBO AND NGO EMPLOYMENT

It is interesting to note the similarities and differences in the work conditions and remuneration of employment in factories and community-based organizations (CBOs). As Miriam described, staff members are provided food and lodging in both cases. Factory workers are often housed within the factory compound and a certain amount of money is deducted from their wages to cover accommodation and food. Many factory workers prefer to do their own shopping and cooking, despite the time and logistical difficulties involved (Pearson and Kusakabe 2012, p. 92).

The staff members of CBOs live on office premises. In Miriam's case, she, together with another young woman in the organization, cooked the meals for all staff members. The cost of food and lodging was paid for by the CBO. Most staff members, especially those at the lowest rung of the hierarchy, do not receive remuneration. In fact, Miriam's mother supported her during that time by providing her with "pocket money" of a few hundred Thai baht.

Factory workers work twelve-hour days, are paid 70–150 baht a day and have two days off per month. Due to deductions made by the employers for items such as registration fees, work permit fees, an "immigration fee", mistakes, absences and so on (Pearson and Kusakabe 2012, pp. 94–95), factory workers actually earn very little. This is evidenced by Miriam's mother, Mya, who was unable to support Miriam and her sister financially in Myanmar during the decade that she was employed in a garment factory in Mae Sot. In fact, her reason for persuading Miriam to join her in the garment factory was to pool expenses and therefore augment her ability to save.

In fact, garment factory workers often find themselves unable to save or in debt (Pearson and Kusakabe 2012, pp. 96–97). It appears that monetarily, factory workers and CBO staff face similar circumstances in that there is little or even negative net monetary gain from their labours.

Given the lack of monetary benefit from CBO work, what benefits are there in CBO work over factory work? In the interviews with Miriam, these were revealed to be increased but limited physical mobility, access to social networks and the social capital therein, on-the-job learning and skills training, objects for learning and transport (computers, books, motorcycles) and shorter working hours. Crucially, membership in a CBO provides a staff member access to other employment opportunities, particularly in NGOs.

However, these benefits were tempered by the limited potential for upward mobility and career advancement within the organization, particularly since Miriam is not Burman/Bamar. In addition, although Miriam's foray into the world of political activism in Mae Sot was facilitated by her aunt in Myanmar, her continued membership of this circle was dependent on her successful performance as a political activist and her adherence to the social rules therein. Through contact with dissidents, exiles, organization members and other associated individuals, training programmes, meetings and work-based learning, she acquired the necessary skills, ideological knowledge and cultural practice to be fluent in the discourse, politics and practice of human rights, democracy and nationalism as observed in this setting. Miriam refashioned herself to fit into this world and to present herself as one of them, although she did not fully take on these values. In fact, she laughed when she recounted the types of training that she could have continued receiving from the organization, such as repetitive video sessions about human rights and democracy.

Miriam's experience in an NGO revealed that the pay structure is different from that in a factory or in a CBO: employees are paid a higher monthly wage. Nevertheless, as in CBOs, employees have to be able to perform certain skills and beliefs that satisfy Northern donors.

Although this process of socialization takes place in this borderland through a variety of institutions, this chapter confines itself to an examination of the schooling, training and on-the-job learning that Burmese migrants undertake in Mae Sot. In doing so, the ideological foundations and social practices of the CBO and NGO sectors are revealed.

SCHOOLING AND TRAINING IN MAE SOT

The various communities from Myanmar on this border, their organization and their interaction with local and international aid organizations have spawned a plethora of learning (and other) institutions which serve a variety of functions. I posit that this schooling has several inter-related functions.

First, the (re)production of ethno-nationalist notions of Karen (and other ethnic) statehood is combined with certain values and norms that equip young people with the skills and attitudes to take up employment in the CBO sector or NGO sector. Second, at the lower levels of schooling, young people are provided with adequate skills and competencies to join the capitalist underclass in Thailand.

Mae Sot and its surroundings have an unusually large number of migrant schools (seventy-four) (referred to as learning centres by the Thai Ministry of Education) in total (VSO 2013, p. 24) compared to other border towns Ranong (VSO 2013, p. 24), the Three Pagodas Pass (Pearson and Kusakabe 2012, p.130) and even Bangkok (VSO 2013, p. 24). In 2008, it was estimated that there were 15,855 students and 981 teachers in the then eighty-eight migrant schools (OEC 2008, p. 17). These schools are run by a variety of faith-based and secular organizations and individuals, using distinct curricula — the Burmese curriculum, the Karen one developed in the refugee camps, and others from various other countries.

When combined with the thirty-two schools in Mae La refugee camp (ZOA 2010, p. 54), which is just outside Mae Sot, there are more than a hundred schools for non-Thais. This number does not include the schools in Myawaddy across the border.[5]

The Karen community has its further education programmes in the refugee camps, in Mae Sot and across the border, a network of schools affiliated with various Christian groups, particularly the Seventh-Day Adventist Church, providing education for various leadership positions and imbued with ethno-nationalist sentiments (Dudley 2006; Oh 2012; Rajah 2002). There is a myriad of further learning schools and countless training programmes in camps and in town, as well as three post-secondary programmes that prioritize English language and community development skills.[6]

These three post-secondary programmes — English Immersion Programme (EIP), Wide Horizons (WH) and Minmahaw — focus on teaching English and community development skills. Another training programme, Youth Connect, links skills to employment.[7] Each of these institutions possesses its own network of institutions and contacts. EIP is located in one of the refugee camps and is supported by World Education, an NGO with headquarters in the United States. It was started by two American teachers in response to requests from the Karen Education Department (KED). The aim of the school was, as its name suggests, to produce students who are fluent in English through total immersion in the language and to ensure that the ethos of "serving the community" was inculcated into the curriculum.

Wide Horizons is modelled along the lines of EIP but is based in town. It is also a World Education project, and is funded under a USAID project. On its Facebook page, it describes itself as "A 2-year leadership development program dedicated to building the capacity of young adults from Burma to work effectively in civil society organizations (Wide Horizons Facebook page)".[8]

Minmahaw is a school for migrants with a post-secondary programme that aims to

> improve student's [sic] English, awareness of Burmese issues and general knowledge. English classes will focus on grammar, form, vocabulary and skills work, which includes speaking, reading, listening and writing. Mathematics, Chemistry, Physics and Social Studies are taught to expose the students to the wider world, democratic ideals, develop their functional numeracy, increase their social awareness and develop their critical thinking. There are also Art and computer skills classes on a regular basis. The teaching materials used were created specifically for students on the border and in refugee camps. The materials are relevant for their situation as well as incorporating modern teaching methodology which provides interactive lessons and fosters critical thinking (Minmahaw website).[9]

Most importantly for employment purposes, these institutions have adopted the model of internship that was spearheaded by EIP in its attempt to incorporate the ethos of "serving the community". The programmes take place over two years. In the first year, students attend courses and in the second, they undertake internships in local and international organizations based in Mae Sot. Ostensibly, the internship aims are to foster the idea of contribution to the community and to facilitate work-based learning. This promotes the acquisition of skills, values and cultural practices necessary for working successfully in CBOs and NGOs. These internships also pave the way to jobs in CBOs and (local and international) NGOs while providing cheap skilled labour to these organisations. Through the internships, young people also become inserted into the network of individuals and organizations in this sector, through which information about opportunities and other forms of knowledge circulate.

Some respondents in my study found it necessary to enrol in secondary schools in Mae Sot before they felt ready to attend the further learning schools. David attended 9th Standard in a migrant school even though he had completed secondary schooling in Myanmar and is in possession of a Psychology degree; Miriam went to camp to learn English before applying to study at EIP.

There is a strong link between high schools in the refugee camps, town and the further education programmes. Students in the high schools are taught the political context and the cultural references of this geographical, social and political space, knowledge that Fara only became aware of when she enrolled in EIP directly from Myanmar.

> I studied community development but the teacher just talked about the refugee camp. Every student is very familiar with that subject. But I was very unhappy. I didn't have this knowledge. So I stayed quiet (interview with Fara 2012).[10]

Although an understanding of the local context is an advantage for students who enrol in the high schools and further education programmes, it does not compensate for the difficulties migrant students in Mae Sot face in gaining access to secondary schooling. There are at least six high schools in the surrounding camps and five in town, all of which are accessible to migrants — those who come directly from Myanmar and those who study in the migrant areas. The places in these schools are sought after because of the higher quality of teaching and the content taught. University learning by distance education is also offered by the Australian Catholic University (see Purkey 2010).

Each set of institutions possesses its own network of institutions and contacts, paving the way for graduates to obtain jobs in CBOs, international NGOs, and/or scholarships to universities in Thailand or other countries. Like many of my young adult respondents, Miriam had graduated with a Bachelor's degree in Myanmar but this certificate did not open the doors to employment in the NGO sector. However, I believe that her higher levels of education provided her with an edge in identifying the necessary skills training, to gain access to the courses of study and then to acquire these skills in order to obtain jobs in the humanitarian industry.

However, this is not the case for everyone. Despite the large number of higher level schools, migrant primary schools provide very few opportunities for children to obtain further education and employment opportunities beyond unskilled or low-skilled work. First, many of the migrant primary schools are, in reality, crèches organized by the Burmese migrant community to care for the children of Burmese migrants who work in other parts of the country. These migrant parents do not have family in Mae Sot or Myawaddy and are thus reliant on these "boarding schools" to care for their children. In other words, the care of these children is outsourced by migrant parents so that they can move to places where low-skilled jobs are available in the Thai economy.

Second, to a large extent, these migrant "boarding schools" provide few opportunities for children to move beyond factory work and the like. First, limited skills training and knowledge are provided by the schools. Second, the schools do not provide certificates that are recognized by Thai employers, although there are steps being taken to have the learning accredited by the Thai Ministry of Education. Third, unless these schools have strong connections to other organizations and employers, they do not provide access to social networks that will aid their graduates in obtaining well-paid jobs that do not require a Thai certificate. Fourth, the education, often based on the one in Myanmar, promotes unquestioning acceptance of facts, ideology and practice. For decades the aim in Myanmar was to socialize young people to accept the status quo of military rule; in Thailand, the goal is to socialize students to accept the status quo of factory work. Thus, in contrast to the higher level schools, these migrant primary schools provide very few opportunities for children to move beyond unskilled or low-skilled work. I posit that these schools are part of the process of social reproduction by which young Burmese nationals become integrated into the Thai economy, eventually replacing their parents in the factories, fisheries and farms of Thailand.

In fact, it appears that very few migrant children in Mae Sot go on to secondary school. The number of students enrolled in the schools providing middle and high school education is estimated to be between 2,500 and 3,000.[11] These figures include students in the primary cycle as these schools also provide primary schooling. We can deduce that the number of students enrolled in the high school grades is much lower than 3,000. Compared to the estimated total of 15,855 students in and around Mae Sot, less than a fifth of students go on to the higher levels of schooling. This could be because the students 1) who finish primary school do not go on to middle school, 2) enrol in Thai schools, 3) enrol in schools in Myawaddy or 4) enrol in schools elsewhere in Thailand or Myanmar.

The likely answer is that many leave school after completing the primary cycle. Haikin (2009, p. 20) reported an 84 per cent and 87 per cent dropout rate for students in migrant and Thai schools respectively. A small number of migrant children attend Thai schools (133 schools in total) in Tak Province (MOE 2009 as cited in Haikin 2009, p. 10) and some families also send their children to schools in Myawaddy (VSO 2013, p. 24). Nevertheless, the vast majority of migrant children are enrolled in migrant schools in Mae Sot rather than in the Thai schools or in Myawaddy (VSO 2013, p. 24).

CULTURAL REPRODUCTION FOR BORDER WORK

As discussed in the previous section, certain learning institutions provide training in the forms of knowledge, values and attitudes required by these two separate sectors. The garment factory industry does not require highly-skilled individuals. The sewing trade has undergone "Macdonaldization" where the entire sewing process has been cut up and stripped down into low-skill components that may be performed by someone with minimal training in sewing. Workers are required to possess basic competence in using a sewing machine (for which they are given training on-site) and in reading and writing. Even basic competence in Thai is not required. Instead, what is valued are attitudes towards and fortitude in working long hours in confined spaces for low pay.

This contrasts strongly with the cultural capital valued in the humanitarian sector. The ideological foundation that Miriam had to acquire and perform in the CBO has already been described in a previous section. She goes further by describing the different skills and practices that she had to acquire and to embody in order to obtain paid employment. The skill that is highly valued and sought after in this sphere is fluency in the English language.

> I wanted to learn English, get work, find a job. The office people spoke English and when I went to training sessions, the trainers were foreigners with interpreters (I wanted to be an interpreter). And I didn't know how to speak. Some participants could speak English. When I was in Myanmar, I was interested in learning English — I would look at signposts in English and Burmese and read them, with bad pronunciation (laughs).
>
> My first goal was to learn English, I really liked to watch English movies. If I could speak English, I could get a job (interview with Miriam 2013, paraphrased).[12]

However, the English programme that Miriam enrolled in did not just teach English. It emphasized "critical thinking" as well as community development skills.

> In Thailand they focus on critical thinking a lot. In Myanmar, they learn by heart everything. In Thailand, they ask questions in many different ways, have to think of answers in different ways. The first month was difficult because I didn't have thinking skills at all.
>
> In [the English programme] they learnt project management, public speaking, how to talk in a nice way, teaching skills. They had a two-week internship in a school. There was lesson planning. They also had interpreting (interview with Miriam 2013).[13]

This sentiment was echoed by another respondent, SM.

> Migrant schools are different. Teacher wants us to think critically. I didn't know about that before. In Myanmar, students study by heart. I listen, I copy, I memorize (interview with SM 2012).[14]

"Critical thinking" is an approach to learning that has gained ground in international education circles and aid organizations. Although it was originally conceived as a mode of interpretation and evaluation to guide beliefs and actions in the 1940s, it has become associated with questioning conventional wisdom, knowledge and values, and certain forms of pedagogy. The teaching of critical thinking has now taken on many forms. Wide-ranging in its methods, it has been used extensively in learning institutions and teacher training in the refugee camps and in some of the migrant schools. As SM's quote reveals, it is frequently associated with a freer, more engaging style, and with migrant and foreign learning institutions and foreigners, as opposed to the rote-learning and drilling techniques favoured by Burmese teachers and schools. Implicit in the comments made about critical thinking is the higher value accorded to its epistemological and pedagogical underpinnings. Miriam clearly values this way of thinking (and interacting) more than what she experienced in school in Myanmar.

Besides critical thinking skills, Miriam acquired the competence necessary for contributing to community development as defined in this area — managing projects, conducting surveys, needs assessments and evaluations, writing proposals and reports. Moreover, a large part of the programme inculcated the values embedded within the notion of "contributing to the community" through involvement in camp-based activities, CBOs, political organizations and NGOs.[15] These are the competencies and values that permeate the official discourse of CBOs and NGOs in this borderland.

School and training were merely the starting point in transforming Miriam into an NGO worker. Miriam acquired knowledge and skills in different settings (school, work, training, social situations) in this border area. As part of the programme's community development component, she had to work as an intern for an organization (either a CBO or an NGO) for a fixed period of time. This meant that she was placed on a certain career trajectory and was groomed while on the job. Miriam learnt how to behave in a culturally appropriate manner with foreigners at a personal and "professional" level. For example, she learnt how to "fake confidence" when speaking with donors and how to speak to them as equals. She learnt how to present herself as a responsible employee and how to marshal her thoughts and communicate them in English in a professional context.[16] Although Miriam had already mastered the body of knowledge required to do her job successfully, she needed to learn how to project a certain image of professionalism that fit foreign (mostly Western and middle class) donors' idea of an NGO employee — articulate, outgoing, confident and competent — who could be trusted to manage the money they donated.

The network of institutions described in this chapter provides migrants like Miriam the opportunity to move out of low-skilled employment in the factories into more empowering and better paid ones in the humanitarian industry. Nevertheless, these jobs are also precarious. If the NGOs pull out, the Burmese migrants employed by them will be thrust back into the Thai economy where 3D (dirty, dangerous and difficult) jobs are often their most feasible option and/or they must find other ways of supporting themselves. This is already happening as NGO funding for camp rations falls and donor funds are diverted to Myanmar. As another respondent who works with an NGO explained, if the NGO she works in leaves town, she will most likely start a business or, as a last resort, teach in a Thai school.[17] Ultimately, Miriam and her colleagues are dependent on a certain cultural and knowledge production system (Freeman 2000) that is not indigenous or sustainable without a steady supply of funding from donors.

CONCLUSION

Scholars have framed this border region in a variety of ways: as a space that is intimately connected to the industrial development of the Thai capitalist economy, or as Arnold and Pickles' (2011) put it, a "geography of production", and/or as a space of fear, suffering (Grundy-Warr and Chin, this volume), and humanitarian need (Lang 2002). This chapter conceptualizes this border as consisting of multiple economies that emerged from a landscape of armed conflict and political repression on the Burmese side of the border and neoliberal policies on the Thai side. In doing so, it has attempted to "place people's economic activities, their thoughts and beliefs about those activities and the social institutions implicated in those activities, all within the context of the social and cultural world of the people being studied" (Carrier 2012, p. 4).

This allows us to view the institutions and activities of local and international organizations working on improving the welfare of those in this border region as a whole which interacts with the local (and international) environment within the political constraints of the region. By linking individual pathways and institutions to economies, this chapter attempts to bring a more simplified and holistic approach to understanding this borderland and the multifarious endeavours and enterprises that have sprung up in it.

This was demonstrated by the identification of learning institutions (both formal and informal) that, by design, play a role in the cultural production of distinct forms of knowledge (dissident, ethnicized politics, humanitarian, Occidentalist, international development, service to the community) and performance that are valued and valuable in the humanitarian industry. Other learning institutions, by default, provide competencies that prepare people to become fodder for the supply chain of capitalist production in Thailand. Moreover, the description and analysis of the learning institutions and workplaces have revealed the ideological foundations of the humanitarian economy. This is not to say that all the organizations in this sector are homogenous. Although they exhibit some commonalities (service to the community for example), they are heterogenous in their espousal of principles and degree of politicization.

This leads us to the final point: humanitarianism in this borderland is grounded in local configurations of social relations and cultural norms, distinctly political, and linked to international forms of humanitarianism (see Pacitto and Fiddian-Qasmiyeh 2013). This form of humanitarianism is the result of the endeavours of Burmese nationals, whose organizational and institutional efforts shape the landscape in material and symbolic ways. Significantly, in doing so, they have created their own mechanisms for validating their own cultural capital while assimilating that of the international NGOs that operate in the area. This goes some way towards opposing the dominance of state-defined and validated cultural capital and speaks to the creativity and resourcefulness of these borderlanders.

Notes

1. I would like to thank Nicolas Lainez, Itty Abraham, Yoko Hayami, Wu Keping, Jennifer Jones and Alexander Horstmann for their insightful comments and suggestions on previous drafts of this chapter. I am also grateful to my respondents for their time. My heartfelt thanks go to Veena Nair for her excellent editing skills.
2. All names used are pseudonyms.
3. This chapter focuses on Miriam's narrative while drawing on the narratives of twenty-one other individuals living in Mae Sot and Myawaddy.
4. Three interviews lasting between one and three hours were conducted between 13 September 2013 and 4 April 2014. Interviewed by Su-Ann Oh via Skype in Singapore, respondent in Mae Sot, Tak Province, Thailand.
5. I am currently trying to ascertain this number.
6. Some examples of further learning programmes are the Further Studies Program and the Leadership and Management Training College in Mae La camp. The English Immersion Programme (EIP), Wide Horizons and Minmahaw School only take twenty-four students per school year.
7. The Youth Connect Foundation is a social enterprise.
8. See https://www.facebook.com/widehorizonsmaesot (accessed 14 October 2014).
9. See http://www.mae-sot.org/minmahaw/index.php (accessed 14 October 2014).
10. Interview with Fara. Interviewed by Jennifer Jones, Mae Sot, Tak Province, Thailand, 28 December 2012.
11. The Child Development Centre run by Mae Tao Clinic (http://maetaoclinic.org/child-protection/cdc-school/) has 1,000 students in primary middle and high school and is the second biggest migrant school. Hsa Thoo Lei has about 800 students (http://maesot.pbworks.com/w/page/11365104/Hsa%20Thoo%20Lei%20Learning%20Centre), BHSOH 308 (http://www.helfwithoutfrontiers.org/project/bhsoh), New Blood 450 (http://roomtogrowfoundation.org/new-blood-school-and-boarding-house/) and Kway Ke Baw 417 students (Room to Grow Foundation records).

12. Interview with Miriam. Interviewed by Su-Ann Oh via Skype in Singapore, respondent in Mae Sot, Tak Province, Thailand, 13 September 2013.
13. Ibid.
14. Interview with SM. Interviewed by Jennifer Jones, Mae Sot, Tak Province, Thailand, 29 December 2012.
15. Interview with former teacher at the English programme Miriam attended. Interviewed by Su-Ann Oh via Skype in Singapore, respondent in Mae Sot, Tak Province, Thailand, 23 October 2013.
16. Interview with Miriam's supervisor at the organization where she was an intern. Interviewed by Su-Ann Oh via Skype in Singapore, respondent in Mae Sot, Tak Province, Thailand, 23 October 2013.
17. Interview with Say Wah. Interviewed by Su-Ann Oh via Skype in Singapore, respondent in Mae Sot, Tak Province, Thailand, 13 September 2013.

References

Arnold, Dennis. *Flexible Labor in the Thai-Burma Border Economy*. Bangkok: Office of Human Rights Studies and Social Development, Mahidol University, 2007.

———. "Burmese Social Movements in Exile: Labour, Migration and Democracy." In *Social Activism in Southeast Asia*, edited by Michele Ford. London: Routledge, 2013, pp. 89–103.

——— and Kevin Hewison. "Exploitation in Global Supply Chains: Burmese Workers in Mae Sot, Thailand". In *Migrant Workers: A Socio-Legal Debate*, edited by D. Sujatha. Hyderabad: Amicus Books of the Icfai University Press, 2007, pp. 198–230.

——— and John Pickles. "Global Work, Surplus Labor, and the Precarious Economies of the Border". *Antipode* 43, no. 5 (2011): 1598–624.

Bourdieu, Pierre and Jean-Claude Passeron. *Reproduction in Education, Society and Culture, 2nd Edition*. Thousand Oaks: Sage Publications, 1990.

Campbell, Stephen. "Cross-ethnic Labour Solidarities among Myanmar Workers in Thailand". *Sojourn: Journal of Social Issues in Southeast Asia* 27, no. 2 (2012): 260–84.

———. "Solidarity Formations Under Flexibilisation: Workplace Struggles of Precarious Migrants in Thailand". *Global Labour Journal* 4, no. 2 (2013): 134–51.

Carrier, James, G. "Introduction". In *A Handbook of Economic Anthropology, Second Edition*, edited by James G. Carrier. Cheltenham: Edward Elgar, 2012, pp. 1–12.

Decha Tangseefa. "Taking Flight in Condemned Grounds: Forcibly Displaced Karens and the Thai-Burmese In-between Spaces". *Alternatives: Global, Local, Political* 31, no. 4 (2006): 405–29.

Dudley, Sandra. "Re-shaping Karenni-ness in Exile: Education, Nationalism and Being in the Wider World". In *Exploring Ethnicity in Burma*, edited by Mikael Gravers. Copenhagen: Nordic Institute for Asian Studies (NIAS) Press, 2006, pp. 77–106.

Freeman, Carla. *High Tech and High Heels in the Global Economy: Women, Work and Pink Collar Identities in the Caribbean*. Durham: Duke University Press, 2000.

Giordano, Cristiana. "Practices of Translation and the Making of Migrant Subjectivities in Contemporary Italy". *American Ethnologist* 35, no. 4 (2008): 588–606.
Granovetter, Mark. "Economic Action and Social Structure: The Problem of Embeddedness." *American Journal of Sociology* 91 (1985): 481–510.
———. "Economic Institutions as Social Constructions: A Framework for Analysis." *Acta Sociologica* 35 (1992): 3–11.
Gudeman, Stephen. "Community and Economy: Economy's Base". In *A Handbook of Economic Anthropology, Second Edition*, edited by James G. Carrier. Cheltenham: Edward Elgar, 2012, pp. 94–108.
Haikin, Marina. *Survey of Inclusion*. Bangkok: Voluntary Service Overseas Thailand, 2009.
Hewison, Kevin, and Woradul Tularak. "Thailand and Precarious Work: An Assessment". *American Behavioural Scientist* 57, no. 4 (2013): 444–67.
Hull, Stephen. "The 'Everyday Politics' of IDP Protection in Karen State". *Journal of Current Southeast Asian Affairs* 28, no. 2 (2009): 7–21.
Johnson, Kim. "Education for Children Along the Thailand-Burma Border: Governance and Governmentality in a Global Policyscape Context". In *Refugee, Immigrations and Education in the Global South: Lives in Motion*, edited by Lesley Bartlett and Ameena Ghaffar-Kucher. New York: Routledge, 2013, pp. 149–65.
Lang, Hazel J. *Fear and Sanctuary: Burmese Refugees in Thailand*. Ithaca: Cornell University Southeast Asian Programme, 2002.
Lanjouw, Steven, Graham Mortimer and Vicky Bamforth. "Internal Displacement in Burma". *Disasters* 24, no. 3 (2000): 228–39.
Lee, Sang Kook. "State in a State: Administration and Governance in a Thailand–Burma Border Town". *Asian Journal of Social Science* 36, no. 2 (2008): 187–233.
———. "Migrant Schools on the Thailand-Burma Border". *Asia Pacific Journal of Education* 34, no. 1 (2014): 125–38.
Lyttleton, Chris. *Intimate Economies of Development: Mobility, Sexuality and Health in Asia*. Abingdon: Routledge, 2014.
Nee, Victor, and Paul Ingram. "Embeddedness and Beyond: Institutions, Exchange, and Social Structure." In *The New Institutionalism in Sociology*, edited by Mary C. Brinton and Victor Nee. New York: Russell Sage Foundation, 1998, pp. 19–45.
Nobpaon Rabibhadana, and Yoko Hayami. "Seeking Haven and Seeking Jobs: Migrant Workers' Networks in Two Thai Locales". *Southeast Asian Studies* 2, no. 2 (2013): 243–83.
Office of the Education Council (OEC). *Educational Provision for Stateless and Cross National Migrant Children in Thailand Bangkok*. Bangkok: Office of the Education Council, 2008.
Oh, Su-Ann. "Identity and Inclusion Education in Refugee Camps in Thailand". In *Refugee and Immigrant Students: Achieving Equity in Education*, edited by Florence E. McCarthy and Margaret Heather Vickers. Charlotte: Information Age, 2012, pp. 65–88.

―― and Marc van der Stouwe. "Education, Diversity, and Inclusion in Burmese Refugee Camps in Thailand". *Comparative Education Review* 52, no. 4 (2008): 589–618.

Pacitto, Julia and Elena Fiddian-Qasmiyeh. "Writing the 'Other' into Humanitarian Discourse: Framing Theory and Practice in South-South Responses to Forced Displacement". *New Issues In Refugee Research Paper* no. 257. Geneva: Office of the United Nations High Commissioner for Refugees, 2013.

Pearson, Ruth and Kyoko Kusakabe. *Thailand's Hidden Workforce: Burmese Migrant Women Factory Workers.* London: Zed books, 2012.

Purkey, Mary. "Paths to a Future for Youth in Protracted Refugee Situations: A View from the Thai-Burmese Border". *Refuge* 27, no. 2 (2010): 97–102.

Rajah, Ananda. "A 'Nation of Intent' in Burma: Karen Ethno-nationalism, Nationalism and Narrations of Nation". *The Pacific Review* 15, no. 4 (2002): 517–37.

Voluntary Service Overseas (VSO). "In School, in Society: Early Childhood Development in Migrant Communities in Thailand". Bangkok: VSO Thailand/Myanmar, 2013.

Zelizer, Viviana. "Beyond the Polemics of the Market: Establishing a Theoretical and Empirical Agenda". *Sociological Forum* 3 (1988): 614–34.

ZOA. *Education Survey 2010.* Mae Sot: ZOA, 2010.

Zukin, Sharon and Paul DiMaggio, eds. *Structures of Capital: The Social Organization of the Economy.* Cambridge: Cambridge University Press, 1990.

Section IV

Mobile Practices and Moving Borders

9

The Spatiality and Borderless-ness of Contentious Politics: Kachin Mobilities as Capability[1]

Karin Dean

INTRODUCTION: CONTENTIOUS POLITICS AND RELEVANCE OF SPATIALITY

While a wider spatial turn in social sciences is datable to the 1980s, transforming many areas of social and economic scholarship, the research on social movements and contentious politics has until recently remained largely aspatial, focusing on identity, grievances, political opportunities and resources (Martin and Miller 2003; Tilly 2000). It is most explicit in Myanmar where the complex decades-long ethnic-based armed struggle for autonomy has been coined ubiquitously as an "ethnic issue", "ethnic problem" or "ethnic politics" by both the national and international community, including politicians, media, representatives of various groups and organizations, and also by academics. While the geo-body of Myanmar is known to be fiercely contested by a plethora of stakeholders since its establishment in 1948, with all projects and struggles by all contestants concerned with the spatial and institutional organization of political rule, "ethnic" foregrounds and thus exaggerates the role of ethnicity and ethnic markers, and fully eliminates the "spatial" as the point of contention. However, territorial autonomy — seen as involving local authority over ethnic homelands and natural resources, with the rights to farm, engage peacefully in community life, speak the mother tongue, or enjoy a clean environment — lies at the heart of the ongoing peace negotiations between the Kachin Independence Organization (KIO) and the government. It is the only accepted political solution for lasting peace, thus making the "spatial" fully relevant.

Thus the lens of contentious place-bound politics, of an intricate assemblage of places and persons connected through shared ideas and networked arrangements as "…engaged in a complex set of political mobilisations at one point in time," provides a perspective in this chapter that enables the incorporation of more subtleties and shades than the analysis of politics, ethnicity or territory and borders alone (Allen and Cochrane 2007, p. 1171).

The problematic issue is that contention in politics — a phenomenon of organized social resistance to hegemonic norms — is used to refer to social movements, rebellions, protests and various other activism described as "non-formal" or non-state (see Tilly 2000; McAdam et al. 2001; Martin and Miller 2003). This chapter follows the critique by Leitner et al. (2008, p. 157) who find the definitions in sociology overly state-centric and interest-oriented, and instead view contentious politics as referring to "…concerted, counter-hegemonic, social and political action, in which differently positioned participants come together to challenge dominant systems of authority, in order to promote and enact alternative imaginaries." It is in this view that the ongoing widespread Kachin political mobilization that has constructed alliances across space, scales and positionalities, between various groups, organizations and civilians is framed in this chapter as Kachin contentious politics. Leitner et al. (2008, p. 160) argue that the way that space has mattered to the mobilization, practices and trajectories of contentious politics has most often been represented as a politics of scale, while they show that there are "other spatialities not readily reducible to scale". These include socio-spatial connectivities through trans-local networks, mobility across space, and the building of social relations in place. It is on the latter that the chapter will focus, showing, furthermore, that the mobilities within the communities around and beyond the Kachin Hills — that today have become a part of northern Myanmar — involving the basic process of moving bodies and ideas, and thus extending imagination, present a continuity with the "past". It shows that there is continuity in the "mobilities as a geographical fact" (Cresswell 2011, p. 551), arguing that only their forms, dispositions and obviously, speed, but also organizing logics, have transformed over time, while the twenty-first century has added the suffix "technical" to the social networks that continue to shape and define Kachin communities. Attesting to this is the nuance that the entire region, defined by its ecosystem seen as moulding much of the way of life in the hilly areas, has in retrospect been constructed through past mobilities and social networks. This chapter will use the past to analyse change by showing how between the Kachin Hills and Yunnan, mobilities and networks have always helped to define and shape the way of living, relying on the author's interviews with elderly Kachin and on other ethnographies on the region (e.g. interview with Maran Tu Ring 2012;[2] Chang 2004, 2009). The chapter will then present mobilities as a trans-local process, linking multiple localities within the same social space and across (territorial) places — but more importantly, also across time — via the movement of people, ideas and feelings, furnishing the socio-spatial collective productions that Sassen (2006) calls capabilities.

KACHIN MOBILITIES AS CONTINUITY

Mobility (of people, of ideas, of things) has been foregrounded "as a geographical fact that lies at the centre of constellations of power, the creation of identities and the microgeographies of everyday life" (Cresswell 2011, p. 551). Mobilities are multiple, while various forms of geographical mobility have long been linked to self-improvement and as paths towards better life or success. The increasing realization of the historic and contemporary importance of movement on individuals and society has been coined, constructed and imagined as "the new mobilities paradigm", commonly associated with sociology, with contributions from anthropology, cultural studies, geography, migration studies, science and technology studies, tourism and transport studies (Sheller and Urry 2006, p. 207). Mobilities as these are understood through the "new mobilities paradigm", range from global to everyday, from the physical movement of the body to movement enhanced by technologies (such as cars, trains, planes), to movement of images and information in media and virtual space (Sheller and Urry 2006). It is even about immobile infrastructures through which the flows of people, goods and ideas are often arranged. In this, mobilities have been constructed as something relentlessly new, hyper, or urban (Sheller and Urry 2006; Cresswell 2010) — with the coining of new paradigms suggesting a break from an earlier understanding. The association of mobilities with the new and modern, with technology and novelty, relegating the past as more fixed, is one of the caveats of recent mobility research, warns Cresswell (2010, pp. 168–69) in his article on the politics of mobility, the most downloaded article in *Environment and Planning D: Society and Space* during a one-year period.

Mobilities indeed are not new and movements have been the focus of the study of many disciplines — but as opposed to earlier studies of movements concerning just tourism, or migration or transportation, what is new is the way the system is examined as a whole, holistically, by the authors ascribing to the "new mobilities paradigm". This whole includes the movements of bodies both as everyday practice, migration and travel, the movement in air, by sea, by roads or via virtual space, where the infrastructure, organizational methods, and transfer and expression of ideas, policies or cultural transfers are also included in the discussion. It is a step towards seeing the whole regardless of borders that need to be crossed that would categorize actions into cross- or transborder, inter- or transnational. It is for the latter reason that mobilities are used in this chapter as a mechanism for avoiding the trap of categories that owe their construction to the borders regardless of the fact that these have become meaningless in contemporary virtual networks.

The chapter takes a step further and views mobilities not only across space but also across time. It argues that mobilities have been one of the continuities at the foothills of the southern Himalayas in what today are known as northern Myanmar and southwest China. The earlier movements of people have been directly related to ecological conditions, seen as functionally moulding the dominant cultural practices and social systems constituting extensive social networks across space that channelled people and goods. Until about the middle of the nineteenth century, the inhabitants of the present Sino-Myanmar borderlands at higher elevations lived in the mountains practising slash-and-burn agriculture (growing dry rice, legumes and cotton, raising livestock, hunting and gathering forest products), and traded or bartered with others both from the hills and lowlands. This organization of life, particularly the perpetual search for arable land, dictated extensive mobilities as plots of land were cultivated for a certain number of years until drained of nutrients and abandoned for new uncultivated lands for farming. Economics including the shifting form of agriculture, hunting and gathering forest products, but also the exchange of goods with lowland communities, and wider trade, were the driving forces of life, involving strategic and frequent mobility.

People, things and ideas move in certain ways, or as Cresswell (2010, p. 24) says, mobility is channelled, moving along routes and conduits. The distinctive channels — the conduits — for moving people, things and ideas in the Kachin Hills have been social and economic networks such as the unique kinship system and trade routes that in the past were interrelated. Trade routes and economic factors have been identified as important movers for social change (Lehman 1997). Economics as a driving force in life have shaped the kinship-related trade routes, driving strategic and frequent mobility. Strategic networks were created through marriage that was closely mixed up with trade — women were "given out" as pledges of economic cooperation (Leach 1965, p. 66). Thus, as trade was vigorous in the vast hill tracts, so was marriage that maintained old kinship networks and established new ones, ultimately evolving into the present spatiality of lineage and network patterns that connect the Kachin across their different dialects or languages.[3] Furthermore, the entire vast and vaguely defined mountainous area has in retrospect been defined not in terms of geopolitical or juridical markers but by the type of activity that went on there — and that was trade and commerce directly feeding into long-distance and *longue durée* mobilities, connecting places into a web of social space long before the concepts such as flows and networks were employed in social sciences.

The Kachin today is an umbrella term for the people whose forefathers from the loosely connected tribes across space have evolved into a nation, today self-styled as a federation of six tribes in Myanmar, China and India, or "all kinds of Kachin combined"; or being the "same family but living in different countries" (interviews[4] with Lasham Htoi Ra 2000[5] and Lamung Seng Du 2000[6]). The Kachin self-definition as an association of six tribes in three countries (Myanmar, China and India) relies on connections and networks that cross ethnic boundaries between the six tribes and the territorial ones between three countries. From the "pre-Kachin period" when the term "Kachin" was initially used by outsiders and as a category and/or in reference to the Jinghpaw only, the Kachin have evolved from a sundry of loosely affiliated tribes, linguistic groups, assemblies of lineages and kinship lines into a self-defined nation.[7] References to mobility and freedom of movement are today an inherent part of Kachin self-definition and their presentation of the past, allowing us to conceptualize the fluidity and motion of social life across time and space. The establishment of states, China, Burma and India, meant that (Kachin) historical movements and networks spanning the Himalayan foothills, automatically and normatively became cross-border and transnational. With the border officially established only in 1961, the "organizing logics" of these mobilities, slowly but gradually started to "jump track" (Sassen 2006, pp. 10–17). Past trade and social contacts were transforming alongside the changing border economies, while also including, or melting into the networks catering to the armed resistance against newly established Burma by the KIO, created for that purpose in 1961. The establishment of nominally fixed spatial entities such as the state was thus followed by enduring place-based politics, centring on the territorial Kachin State, the location and centre of the traditional Kachin homelands (the Triangle area), where also the largest numbers of the tribes, increasingly conceived as the Kachin, lived. The Union of Burma had been envisaged, according to the 1947 constitution, as a Federal Union with wide autonomy granted to the ethnic states — the reason stated by the contemporary ethnic-based political resistance as the condition for their predecessors to join the Union. The People's Republic of China was established in 1949, with the Sino-Myanmar boundary, earlier just partially defined and imposed on China from the British power position, finalized only after difficult negotiations between China and Burma in 1960.

Reconstructions, analyses and ethnographies of twentieth-century long-distance trade and caravan routes at China's margins and present Yunnan-Thailand-Myanmar borderlands, and the networks and cross-border movements of the various small-scale entrepreneurs (soldiers, miners, merchants, migrants) have become a pre-eminent subject of contemporary academic interest (see Walker 1999, on contemporary connections across the entangled spaces of Laos, Thailand, Yunnan and Myanmar; Chang 2004, on the Yunnanese jade trade between Burma and Thailand; Hill 1998, on the Yunnanese Chinese trade into non-Chinese areas; Tagliacozzo and Chang 2011, on the networks and regional connectivity of Chinese merchants over a wide time span; Ma and Ma on Yunnanese mule caravans in this volume). However, the spatialities of the plethora of tribal peoples, other than the Yunnanese Chinese, and other types of mobilities, particularly those of knowledge and information, have not been a popular research subject (great exceptions are Davis 2003; Chang 2009; Sturgeon 2005). The contemporary ethnographies extend back in time not much more than a generation, relying on the narratives or biographies of the informants.

Attempts at opening up the centrality of mobilities in the lives of a lot of people, focusing on the movement and exchange of ideas, knowledge, feelings and sentiment — importantly, alongside trade — can be found in Chang's (2009) vivid ethnographies conducted with contemporary agents but spanning at least fifty years of the recent past. Although her main respondent (also quoted below) is a migrant Yunnanese, born in Myanmar's Shan State, many caravan trade routes extended also to the Kachin areas and had similar functions.

> It was a distinctive lifestyle in Yunnan and its neighboring countries for many centuries ... On the one hand, the existence of the trade satisfied the consumption demands of the people residing in a large part of the mountainous region; on the other hand, it resulted in webs of connections between different communities. An interesting point in Zhang dage's story has to do with the exchange of news about kith and

kin residing far away. Because of their historical mobility, the Yunnanese have relatives and friends located in different places. Caravans conveyed not only goods but also information. In one conversation, Zhang dage told me that in the days before electronic communication, the movement of caravans provided people with connections to the outside world. Oral messages were a common form of correspondence, but in case of urgent and important matters, the message sender would prepare a written note tied with a piece of dry chili to indicate its seriousness and hand it to a muleteer for delivery. This kind of "express mail" was especially resorted to by the militias (Chang 2009, p. 558).

Similar to Chang (2009), who writes about the Chinese traders, Davis (2003, p. 177) who writes on the revival of what she calls "premodern flows" of the pan-Tai transborder Buddhist network that for centuries channelled "…information, technology, and culture back and forth between rural villages over difficult mountain terrain" (in Yunnan-Thai-Burmese borderlands), argues for seeing a clear link between past and present networks. She even goes so far as to say that the network played an important role in fostering ethnic-religious identities: "This horizontal temple network once spanned the many fiercely independent local Tai states. … [T]he weak warp of a multicentered, consensus-based political system was held together by a horizontal woof of mobile intellectual" (Davis 2003, p. 178).

Mobile Kachin were described by two older men in Kachin State capital Myitkyina during my ethnographic fieldwork in 2012. One was involved in the trucking trade in the 1960s, the other was Maran Tu Ring, a grandson of a village chief (or *duwa* in Jinghpaw), who described life before the fighting started in 1962. In the 1960s people travelled either on foot or by bicycle. Typically, visitors in Tu Ring's childhood village stayed for three to four months, the reason being a failure in trade or business and the consequent need to regain losses before returning home by working in the village or nearby areas and thus needing accommodation (interview with Maran Tu Ring 2012[8]). The social system shared across the region established responsibility for the village chief or the kin to help and provide accommodation. This is explicit in Tu Ring's narration, where he explains that it was the *duwa*'s responsibility to provide accommodation to strangers and "feed them". The social system worked so that people usually stayed with their relatives, but if they had no place they were guaranteed boarding at the *duwa*'s house. *Duwas* taxed villagers, and a large part of this was used for food, with the tax constituting "a little" rice and hunted game (deer, wild boar; traditionally the *duwa* got one thigh).

Tu Ring said that 5 to 6 kilogrammes of rice were cooked at his household every day by young relatives who also stayed at his place, many to pursue their studies. Before 1962, "doors were open" — everybody could take a rest, go to the kitchen, make food for themselves. Tu Ring: "Just go to the kitchen, look for rice, just take it". The position of the bamboo cup conveyed the message: the bottom of the cup placed towards the visitor forbade him/her to take rice and the open end facing the visitor permitted him/her to take rice from the bamboo. Tu Ring: "The *duwa* would say: Oh, we're relatives. Just stay here. Don't worry about food. How many days do you want to stay? No problem!... So many relatives stayed in grandpa's compound" (interview with Maran Tu Ring 2012). Letters were given to caravans to pass on.

This biographic-narrative text illustrates explicitly what is generally common knowledge about Kachin society of the late twentieth century — the commonplace mobility of its individuals for reasons such as petty trade, opportunism and seasonal work, besides the more conventional social imperatives for mobilities such as kinship. While the traditional Kachin villages where the chief had an obligation to provide shelter to travellers have almost disappeared, people today, as in the past, can move around and find accommodation at relatives' places that the kinship system provides for aplenty. If the visitor can afford it, food is brought along. This system is particularly helpful for securing secondary education — children across the rural mountainous areas who are sent to larger centres to attend schools always stay with relatives.

Although the establishment of states and boundaries — spatializing and socializing the Kachin into China, Burma and India — and state services, such as education, slowly and gradually rerouted and transformed the historic mobilities of the tribal peoples into those that are more fixed in place, the process of movements of bodies and knowledge as a mode does not differ much from the pre-border period. Importantly, the border has not significantly stopped Kachin mobilities: a survey conducted amongst fifty-three Kachin respondents in Myanmar (Yangon and Myitkyina 2000–2001) shows that an overwhelming number of them have met the "Kachin in China", almost half have been to China, while over one-third have relatives in China. In the immediate borderlands, the economic development of China on the one hand, and the KIO armed resistance on the other, have created a whole new set of dynamics that sped and intensified mobilities, now cross-border and political-economic in their constitution, reconfiguring mobilities as a political and economic opportunity for the Kachin, the Chinese and many others.

The extent of contemporary cross-border networks is well illustrated by a Chinese Jingpo author who has titled one chapter of her Kunming-published book on Jingpo women "Cross-Boundary Marriage" (Jin 1995, pp. 38–41) — regardless of the fact that the Chinese Government usually discourages cross-boundary comparisons of its transnational ethnic groups. This implies that contemporary Chinese Jingpo cannot be characterized without their cross-border contacts, activities, networks and visits. According to the author, almost all Jingpo villages and "quite a number of Jingpo families" have blood ties and relationship by marriage with Myanmar's Keqin (Kachin) nationality (ibid.). In a style influenced by Chinese patriotic embellishments, the author writes that "...women living separately on both sides of the national boundary have woven a solid bond through their own marriages which closely links compatriots living separately in the two countries and have erected a bridge of friendship with love for the peace and tranquillity of the two peoples" (Jin 1995, pp. 40–41). The cross-boundary marriage pattern has changed directions due to China's economic development and higher living standards, and the inroads China has made into Myanmar in business, trade and overall influence, with more Kachin girls today China-bound. Regardless of the direction, cross-boundary marriages, dwelling on the rules of kinship, increase the number of relatives, social visits and contacts.

KACHIN CONTENTIOUS SPATIAL POLITICS

Generally in contentious politics, a multitude of mobile participants is involved in a diversity of spatialities such as scale, place, networks, socio-spatial positionality and mobility, always and simultaneously at work and made use of (Leitner at al. 2008). Kachin participants range from ethnic and religious elites to people with guns to people with money to individuals with education and/or privileged access to tools, resources and information, and most recently, to technology. These actors perform, practise, relate, mobilize and find meanings to their endeavours and each other in space that connects them to each other and to many further actors and processes, making spatiality not just a background but a shaping force of the practitioners' aspirations and strategies in contentious politics. The question is how to conceptualize these diversified mobilities that engage people in new ways — as nodes of communication — in theoretical analysis.

Present Kachin ethnic mobilization in response to the Myanmar Army's attacks on the people and places in Kachin State constitutes a concerted social movement heavily implicated in both the space of places and the space of flows. The Kachin Independence Organization (KIO) protects its territorial sovereignty while demanding autonomy for the entire Kachin State in a federalist structure, while the actual fighting and war cause tens of thousands of people to flee their native places and build temporary shelters at internally displaced persons (IDP) camps both in territories controlled by the government and the KIO — with the latter spatiality, furthermore, having different implications on their access to aid.[9] It is simultaneously imbricated in the space of flows involving Kachin social networks across space and borders mobilized for moral, medical and material support. All this has wider implications as Kachin solidarity and unity in the conflict is expressed and reconstructed through this concerted effort, consolidating the Kachin as the political subject.

For the Kachin as a political subject, the KIO is neither non-state, rebel or insurgent, nor marginalized or subaltern — a position where it has been deployed in most of the discourses created by national and international community, politicians and media. Also in academia such entities are an arrangement that realist approaches would prefer to pass up, "…with their existence undertheorised and their achievements under-reported" assuming that these will ultimately be defeated and incorporated into existing states (McConnell 2009, p. 344). KIO's empirical sovereignty derives power and legitimacy from its de facto control and administration of territories (enclaves) at the Sino-Myanmar border, an intensely spatial issue. Its sovereignty is bolstered further by recognition (diplomatic relations with China and the Myanmar Government) and from legitimacy earned by its sustenance of infrastructure, including provision of power from its hydroelectric stations, fostering an economic boom and urbanization at the Sino-Myanmar border (Laiza and Mai Ja Yang), and from its nationalist agendas on the preservation of Kachin languages and culture. The maintenance of KIO autonomous territory, borders and its military capabilities have enabled the KIO in the military-run state to articulate its political demands, clearly delineated in the nineteen-point proposal submitted to the National Convention in 2007 where the constitution was drafted. The proposal, which the military government refused to discuss, elaborated on the devolution of legislative power to the states, including the selection of state chief ministers by the states themselves and devolving power to the state legislative assembly to oversee management of land, natural resources, communications, health, education and many other issues. The fighting provoked in 2011 by the Myanmar Armed Forces by encroaching on KIO territory and leading to protracted armed clashes, but particularly the KIA's (Kachin Independence Army's) military skills and the KIO's adherence to its political demands of autonomy as a part of the place-bound contentious politics taking place mostly in Kachin and Shan states near local villages and towns close to or at KIO territory, has gained the KIO/KIA an unprecedented legitimacy within the Kachin population in Myanmar and amongst the Kachin globally. Importantly, the latter is embedded in the space of flows and new forms of power, constituted in networks. There is a widespread trend of NGO-ization of the Kachin counter-hegemonic resistance activities, evidenced in the number of exile- or border-based grassroots groups, various NGOs and advocacy groups, linked by mobile individuals, particularly in the Kachin-run relief missions, but also working with other issues such as environment, drug addiction and rural empowerment. This has far-reaching implications for Myanmar's politics and the Kachin community, thus a close examination of the mechanisms of this new level of mobilities will follow.

TAKING MOBILITIES TO A NEW LEVEL: NETWORKS AND ASSEMBLAGES OF POWER

Featherstone (2008, p. 31, emphasis added) notes that the foregrounding in analysis *"the relations that make up place-based politics* opens up more generous possibilities of the agency of place-based political activity" — it can be seen as "shaping political ideas which stretch beyond place". Relations usually concern an extensive set of (inter)connections and reference points across scales brought into contact by different kinds of networks. In the case of Myanmar, the KIO is the only political resistance group engaged in armed struggle refusing a ceasefire without political dialogue on the grounds that it already had this during 1994–2011. As the initiator of an ethnic coalition to get the Myanmar Government to discuss federalism, this affects the politics in the entire state and beyond. It affects China, impatient to have stability at its borders, while the UN wants a solution to the armed clashes affecting 100,000 civilians (IDPs). The following will show how mobilities have been taken to a qualitatively new level in contemporary Kachin society — to that of ideas and sentiment whirling alongside Kachin social and socio-technical networks beyond and between places. The theatre of war is only one type of (local) place, although essential, in the assemblage of scales and spatialities.

Kachin mobilities started to involve a wider span as the socio-technical networks capitalizing on communication technology became the order of the day. Today while Thailand remains an important place for various Burmese exile-based resistance activities, including the Kachin, the physical location of key actors matters much less. The space of places where performed practices and imaginations by the various Kachin contestants centring on territorial place such as Kachin State, or on Kachin "rights" to their traditional homeland, vary from the Kachin State capital Myitkyina and other Kachin communities both in the territories controlled by the government and the KIO to the Jingpo communities and KIO informal representations in China (in Dehong autonomous prefecture and Kunming) to the offices and homes of the diverse grassroots groups and individuals from Thailand and Malaysia to the United Kingdom, United States and Australia, to name a few. The latter is well exemplified in an open letter sent in 2012 by twenty-three Kachin groups across the globe to the then Member of the Myanmar Parliament, Aung San Suu Kyi, inviting her to visit refugee camps at the Sino-Myanmar border to observe first-hand the suffering of Kachin civilians as a result of Myanmar Armed Forces (MAF) attacks and government oppression. The contact persons for additional information in this letter had phone numbers prefixed by U.S., Thai and British country codes. At the heart of Kachin social life and contentious politics is thus mobility — of people with ideas and information. Implicated in this is the ever greater speed ranging from transport — since motor vehicles became the means of mass transport and air travel became increasingly affordable — to the revolution in technology as the modes for moving. The latter, commonly implied as the developments in a narrow field of highly sophisticated industries leading to the convergence of transportation and communication technology, has rendered people as more stationary nodes of communication, if viewed comparatively.

Empirical practice within and across scale, place, networks, socio-spatial positionality, mobility, and the co-implication of all (Leitner et al. 2008, p. 158) is conceptualized in this chapter through the notion of assemblage. McFarlane (2009, p. 566) proposes the use of the concept "translocal assemblage" to conceptualize space and power in contentious politics (i.e. social movements), pointing out that this "focuses attention more on the 'how' questions rather than the 'why' questions." Similarly, Allen and Cochrane (2007, p. 1162) have used the concept of an assemblage as "a more flexible spatial vocabulary" that better captures fluid sets of regional political relationships and power-plays in a time when the networked arrangements disrupt traditional and hierarchical forms of regulation and coordination.

While the brunt of fighting is borne by Kachin communities physically close to the battlegrounds and by the KIA fighters (and their families), there is a transgressing of scales, accounting to the relations between place-based political activity and the "geographies of connection" (Featherstone 2008, p. 30), as the consequent shockwave and emotions caused by burnt homes and uncertainty at refugee camps are felt by the Kachin not in direct contact with the war. Davis (2003, p. 177) explicitly described how the travel of knowledge and ideas in the Yunnan borderland region has switched from "palm leaves" to "floppy disks, videos, and CDs". However, after only a decade since her article was published, floppy discs and CDs have become obsolete and have been replaced by even faster and more capacious online formal and social media available for immediate and worldwide distribution, shaping ever contentious politics and creating new assemblages of power via nodes of communication and "socially decisive" networks (Castells 2009, p. 25).

The numerous Kachin NGOs and activist groups in Myanmar and other neighbouring countries regard their job to report, raise funds and help the IDPs in every possible way, channelling funds, aid workers, educators and reporters to the IDP camps at the border. However, an even larger audience feels and is impacted by the fighting and suffering by the way images accompanying news reports are made available via various online media. The latter efficiently spread along the news and advocacy group websites, well-known Burmese exile-based media outlets that, alongside other news, provide coverage of the war in Kachin State reporting on major battles and quoting KIO officials; on-site journalistic reports by occasional foreign correspondents, and press releases or reports by international or regional humanitarian groups. For those who are not online all the time, such news and information are collected by certain active individuals, performing voluntarily as nodes of communication, who convert these into PDF files and forward the selected collections of news two to three times a week, or more often, to mailing lists that may consist of over 800 people, especially inside Myanmar (interview with Lahpai Zau Bung 2011).[10] At the same time, more informal social media such as individual blogs, Facebook, Youtube, online Skype conferences have become not only an important source of information about the situation on fighting and refugees in Kachin State, but also a platform for sharing views, feelings and emotions. The above-mentioned forms of media have as their intrinsic characteristics built-in capabilities for almost instant feedback in the shape of exchanging views and feelings through commentaries and Facebook "likes".

In a survey of Kachin youth in Chiang Mai in December 2011, where respondents were asked to name four online sources they use most frequently for news and information on the happenings in Kachin State, the top source was Kachinnews.com, run by the Chiang Mai-based Kachin News Group

(KNG). With daily news production undertaken by six staff members at the main office in Chiang Mai, Thailand, and branch offices in New Delhi, the Sino-Myanmar border and Kachin State's capital Myitkyina, and more than ten "inside stringers", as reported by its website Kachinnews.com, the KNG falls under media that produces content professionally for consumption and is supported and sustained by commercial media businesses or public organizations.

However, the second source most cited by the Kachin respondents for online news in 2011 was a blog called Jinghpawkasa, while the well-known professional Burmese exile-based media, The Irrawaddy and Mizzima, with equal numbers of readers, followed closely behind. Four other blogs were listed. The phenomenon of Jinghpawkasa, run by a single person based in Kuala Lumpur, Malaysia, as the second most popular online source amongst the Kachin respondents on the war and other issues in Kachin State is significant for two reasons. First, it shows how the convergence of information and communication technology has changed the speed and organization of the way in which ideas and information move. From sealed letters travelling across local spaces, information today has come to traverse space in a second, and thus able to criss-cross the globe. The reason cited for the evolution of the Malaysia-based blog — initially established as an apolitical forum for the Malaysian Kachin community in 2009 — as a new site for news on the war at the Sino-Myanmar border was that there was no "proper knowledge about the situation" (interview with Tangbau Naw Seng 2012).[11] Tangbau Naw Seng who had friends and classmates within the KIO central committee officers, wanted the Kachin community to have "a proper knowledge about the situation", and thus started to post news after the fighting broke out. Initially he had to "hunt" for news — for example, if no reports had arrived during the day, he started to call people at the KIO territory ("my entire salary went on the communication") (interview with Tangbau Naw Seng 2012). After having established a reputation as an independent and critical reporter, with accurate and timely news and a large number of supporters and subscribers, collecting news and images became much easier. "When fighting starts they sms that the fighting has started, and later I call them up" (interview with Tangbau Naw Seng 2012). On the week of the interview (16–24 October 2012), the number of views ranged between 5,700–10,600 per day, on separate days.

Second, the phenomenon such as Jinghpawkasa is significant because it establishes an informal mediascape where content is generated by users by employing a unique architecture that makes it interactive and creates new social spaces. The possibility of hyperlinking to other blogs and websites and the comments section for readers results in the spread of information in a rapid "viral" form, making blogs the sites to be taken seriously as spaces for exchange and meaning-making (see Lobato et al. 2011 on user-generated media, and Tang 2009 on blogs). Tang (2009), talking about the Internet's role in the outcomes of the general elections in Malaysia and Singapore, emphasizes the hyperlinked environment of blogs that enables information, announcements, videos, audio files and pictures to be disseminated at an amazing speed, while importantly, providing space for different speech norms. These norms contrast with those that exist in real life, or even in professional online media, in that people have the freedom to appear more vocal, hyper-critical, emotional and definitely less diffident. The norm of according the political leaders a degree of respect due to their office is rendered meaningless (ibid.). "In the cold flicker of the computer monitor involving a text based discourse, a person is stripped from the aura and prestige of his or her office and is judged solely by the quality of his or her ideas" (Tang 2009, p. 22). There is definitely less fear of control or punishment over the feelings, views and perspectives expressed due to the possibility of remaining anonymous. It is suggested that these Internet norms have spillover effects into the offline world.

Even more aggravating speech norms, emotions and Kachin ethnic nationalist feelings are aroused by short Youtube video clips of the actual fighting, shooting, visuals of blood and occasional lifeless bodies, the Kachin soldiers fighting, drilling or praying before the battle, their sophisticated weaponry, civilians moving with their belongings, refugee camp ramshackle huts, IDP women with babies, the wounded being treated in the KIO hospital with faces twisted in pain, and many more powerful scenes. From the creation and distribution of information, such news, images and recipient commentaries transform and merge into the networked production of information (see Aday and Livingston 2008, p. 102, on transnational advocacy networks, that is, epistemic communities, changing press dynamics). Such sources have become authoritative provider-producers of information in the ongoing political and military crisis, while technology enables instant passing and positing of images and videos which embody a powerful tool.

The kind of networking that has evolved through the emergence of online options enabling quick responses such as Facebook or Youtube "likes", instant sharing and commentaries that due to their split-second speed come out more outspoken, vigorous and ardent, has led to a new, qualitatively different kind of association. In the span of ten years, knowledge and information have switched from handwritten or printed letters, CD-ROMs or disks being physically distributed to the instantaneous Internet with limitless space and a global span, compressing time and space. It is obvious that online connections enhance the interaction between people over distance, offering extra occasions to communicate. There is instant reach of quantitatively larger groups of recipients of the information, expressed feelings, views and perspectives, while these can be disseminated without censorship, permission of gatekeepers, or norms of public utterance. In Myanmar, or for the Kachin, the issue is not about carving out virtual space for free expression but about community mobilization behind the KIO in the ongoing military conflict. This has assembled and mobilized the Kachin in unprecedented ways — and "…unlike network, assemblage does more than emphasise a set of connections between sites in that it draws attention to history, labour, materiality and performance" (McFarlane 2009, p. 566). Looking at the present Kachin networks as an assemblage invokes mobilities in the construction of knowledge of living environments near and far, of each other and of sense-making of Myanmar politics from the perspective of Kachin interests.

> Start from this situation, this crisis, all of the Kachin people from around the world [are] getting more connected with each other. We have never done before like this…. We have never meet before in outside but we have already know a lot, with lots of people. And we just try to communicate with each other, and we just try to share the information. Sometimes we make lots of online conferences. Even though we have never seen each other. In the beginning of the crisis we usually make the online conference in once a week. People from inside, sometimes, people from Laiza, they join, really in the headquarters, they join, with us. People from Yangon, Philippines, Belgium, Rumania, American, or Japan, England, Malaysia, Thailand, everyone comes to join….
>
> Skype, we use Skype, and then we call…. There are [Kachin – K.D.] people from all around the world. We just come together and we share and then we [are] just … discussing about the situation and analysing…. This very very work. We are more closing together, by these … facilities, you know, online Internet.
>
> The KIA even does not have the official website, the very professional official website but the news is very spreading. Whatever they say, or something — it's just spreading around by the user… In my Facebook every time I check the update news, I share and share it again. This very very work, effective. Even news you can get, update news … what happens in Myitkyina, right now fighting frontline, we can get the news (Interview with Lahpai Zau Bung 2011).

Statements that the Kachin are more united than ever, that "this war has changed the Kachin" are indicative of strong mobilization within the Kachin communities far beyond the space of local "rebel territories". Supporting that such mobilization has occurred are the common statements within the Kachin communities everywhere that aside from the KIO fighting the MAF out of the territory under its control, the "number two enemy" of the Myanmar Government is the peaceful, religion-based Kachin Baptist Convention (KBC) with offices and branches situated predominantly in the government-controlled territory, and the "number three enemy" is the Kachin people. The space of flows connects the Kachin within and beyond Kachin State to substantive diasporas with proficiency, networks and money. An oft-repeated statement that epitomizes the situation is that "this is not a war between Burmese government and the KIO, it's a war between Burma and the Kachin" (interview with Lahpai Zau Bung 2011). It is not a mere network that has evolved between the Kachin communities from the Sino-Myanmar border to Yangon, to Thailand, Malaysia, Japan, the United States and United Kingdom, and so on — it is a set of connections that involves history, certain ways of life and other qualities originating and still emanating from the so-called Kachin heartland in the contemporary Kachin State or which are revoked by the earlier and contemporary nationalists. Most importantly, it involves labour put into the invoking, sustaining and nurturing of such connections.

At the heart of this are mobilities — that have been turned into capabilities, or "collective productions whose development entails time, making, competition, and conflicts" (Sassen 2006, p. 7). Mobilities of people, ideas and knowledge have since the nebulous past shaped the most important processes in the hilly region, including the ones that have led the different tribes to become self-defined as the Kachin. Integral to mobilities is networking — that earlier was conducted along distinct clan and kinship lines, and that is being transformed since ideas started to move virtually across the space between places. The ideas and knowledge, moving faster than people, are establishing spaces of flows, with certain more socially active individuals performing as nodes (for example, Lahpai forwarding news to his list of 800 people) or centres (such as Jinghpawkasa website) generating new content. But the spaces of flows assembling the Kachin physical and virtual communities, with ever new content, rely on the labour, materiality and performance, that is capabilities, necessary for their evolvement and endurance. In fact, the notion of hypermobility is used to describe the instantaneous circulation of digitalized material with a global span. Sassen (2006, p. 344) however, reminds us that digital content is produced by people, and is thus "deeply inflected by the cultures, the material practices, and the imaginaries that take place outside electronic space". She continues (ibid.): "The digital is embedded in the larger societal, cultural, subjective, economic, and imaginary structurations of lived experience and the systems within which we exist and operate." It is the Kachin who push the buttons, and this act coalesces into experience, knowledge, awareness, sentiment, perspective, skill and capabilities.

CONCLUSION

Mobilities are dynamic spatial practices, and in the Kachin Hills these have been part of defining activities that have performed as a continuous source of fuel and thus inseparable from the ways that the Kachin sustain and adapt themselves to ever-changing social, political and economic conditions. This chapter has shown that the mobilities in the Kachin Hills and in what today is the contested geo-body of Myanmar have provided economic, cultural, social and political opportunities across geographical and virtual spaces. Presently, Kachin State is the site of fierce contestation over territorial control between the state that for fifty years has been inseparable from its powerful military, and the place-based KIO with extensive support from and conferred legitimacy by the Kachin diaspora — in Myitkyina, Yangon, Shan State, China, Thailand, India, Japan, indeed everywhere the Kachin can be found. This chapter has shown the mechanism of Kachin political mobilization, at its peak since the start of the fighting in 2011, emphasizing the relevance and role of the idea that is deeply embedded in mobilities and that is common in the Kachin Hills — that is, a set of connections. And it is via mobilities that Kachin places have been connected across territorial and virtual space and time.

This chapter argues that from the trade and caravan routes, the trails criss-crossing the mountains, the paved roads and infrastructure, to the web of booming virtual connections via cable, wireless and satellite, Kachin mobilities have undergone a remarkable transformation in their adaptation to the "postmodernity" of the day. Mobilities both in form and ways have changed alongside greater, larger-than-life conditions, thus adapting to new "organising logics" (Sassen 2006, p. 10). While the extension of contemporary mobilities between places is fashioned by various developments such as the ongoing construction of paved roads and the enforcement of border regulation, uncontrollable dynamics, or the geographies of power and displacements caused by war, the use of technology has remarkably changed its routes, logic of circulation, span, conduits and forms, and thus, possibilities. Mobilities do not only link multiple localities within the same social space and across territorial places but also across time, developed here conceptually as capability. Thus, looking at mobilities as a competence that has been produced collectively over time, for different purposes at different times such as economic opportunities, social relationships, rebellion, political mobilization, establishes interconnectivity over time, places and space simultaneously, and challenges us to take a new approach towards borders and nation states. It theoretically frees the scrutiny from rigid and clumsy categorizations such as international, trans-border or cross-border by employing mobilities at the centre for understanding the current sociopolitical processes by looking at these as capabilities. It also provides an alternative to the centring of borders and its created special categories that more often than not delegate certain practices as subversive, subaltern or at least problematic (to the state), leading to the discursive construction of subaltern political agency and rigid presentation as the "Other" (Featherstone 2008, p. 7). The state and much academic literature engaged in discussions of borders and state territoriality, migration, transnationalism, and so on, have remained captives of the nation state. This has rendered the Kachin subaltern in the political stage in Myanmar, in addition to their existing marginalized position in social, economic and cultural terms as an ethnic minority in the country. Because of such a position, such subaltern voices, engaging with the world through various alternative and non-formal (social) media, are normatively designated radical, biased and not overly "trustworthy".

The focus on capabilities within the camp that would nominally be rendered marginalized (or subaltern by some), demonstrates more variables to the social world embroiled in various and constantly changing power configurations. It also enables us to see the changing nodes and socially shaping assemblages as constituting both the hegemonic and the subaltern within the Kachin themselves. For the technology is not accessible everywhere — nor by everybody — and although its use is spreading fast in Myanmar, it has not reached every corner of Kachin State. In the meantime, proximity to China provides mobile connections at its borders for those with mobile phones and laptops. However, the Kachin rely on mobilities via both the human and virtual modes. In each case, the understanding of movements of people, ideas and knowledge as practices embedded in space and as a part of complex assemblages of social relations, and the translation of struggles and solidarities within the agency into capabilities makes a more nuanced way of grasping the social world.

Notes

1. The ethnographic fieldwork and research leading to this article was provided with funding by the European Union Seventh Framework Programme FP7-SSH-2012-2 under grant agreement n°320221, the Estonian Science Foundation grant ETF8618 and the Estonian government research grant IUT3-2.
2. See endnote 8.
3. The Kachin kinship system derives from the Kachin marriage alliance system known as *mayu-dama* (wife-giver/wife-taker), according to which males are allowed to take brides from certain lineages and not from others. Knowing each other's lineage is thus crucial for the way individuals relate to each other — as a brother/sister (or mother/father depending on one's age), or as somebody whom one may potentially marry. The clans have been widely considered the cornerstone of Kachin society — and these, furthermore, importantly, cut across the different tribes and the international boundaries.
4. Names of all interviewees have been changed in order to protect their identities. The names used in reference to fieldwork interviewees reflect only the nationality and gender, and the Kachin surnames do not correspond to their real family/clan affiliation.
5. Interview in Mai Ja Yang. Interviewed by Karin Dean, Mai Ja Yang, Kachin State, Myanmar, 16 January 2000.
6. Interview in Yingjiang. Interviewed by Karin Dean, Yingjiang, Dai-Jingpo Autonomous Prefecture, Yunnan, People's Republic of China, 15 November 2000.
7. It is generally agreed that the "Kachin" was embarked upon as a nationalist project by the Jinghpaw Baptist elites in Burma, designating Jinghpaw as the *lingua franca* and being responsible for the images of Jinghpaw dress as representing the Kachin nation (see Sadan 2007). In China, the Jinghpaw are known and transliterated as Jingpo. For discussions on the Kachin nationalist project (that has been relatively successful, particularly if compared to other nationalist movements since the establishment of Myanmar), and the politics of their ethnic boundary and identity constructions, see Dean (2007); Sadan (2007, 2013); Smith (1999); Gravers (2007). The Kachin also started arriving in Thailand in the 1960s, following the jade trade, while the family members of the KIO leaders established a village in Chiang Mai Province that has expanded and become a "Kachin space" in Thailand. Since mid-2000, there has been a vigorous campaign to recognize the 2,000 or so Kachin in Thailand as an official "hilltribe", while the visually attractive Kachin national dress has, for a decade, been included in Thai tourist brochures alongside those of other ethnic peoples in Thailand.
8. Interview in Myitkyina. Interviewed by Karin Dean, Kachin State, Myanmar, 16 September 2012.
9. For example, except for two occasions, the Myanmar Government has continuously denied access to UN-led aid teams to the refugee camps at the KIO-controlled areas, stating security concerns, since the conflict began in 2011.
10. Interview in Bangkok. Interviewed by Karin Dean, Bangkok, 18 December 2011.

11. Interview in Kuala Lumpur. Interviewed by Karin Dean, Kuala Lumpur, Malaysia, 16 October 2012.

References

Aday, Sean and Steven Livingston. "Taking the State Out of State-Media Relations Theory: How Transnational Advocacy Networks are Changing the Press-State Dynamic". *Media, War and Conflict* 1, no. 1 (2008): 99–107.

Allen, John and Allan Cochrane. "Beyond the Territorial Fix: Regional Assemblages, Politics and Power". *Regional Studies* 41, no. 9 (2007): 1161–75.

Castells, Manuel. *Communication Power*. Oxford, New York: Oxford University Press, 2009.

Chang, Wen-Chin. "Guanxi and Regulation in Networks: The Yunnanese Jade Trade between Burma and Thailand, 1962–88". *Journal of Southeast Asian Studies* 35, no. 3 (2004): 479–501.

———. "Venturing into 'Barbarous' Regions: Transborder Trade Among Migrant Yunnanese between Thailand and Burma, 1960s–1980s". *The Journal of Asian Studies* 68, no. 2 (2009): 543–72.

Cresswell, Tim. "Towards a Politics of Mobility". *Environment and Planning D: Society and Space* 28, no. 1 (2010): 17–31.

———. "Mobilities I: Catching up". *Progress in Human Geography* 35, no. 4 (2011): 550–67.

Davis, Sara. "Premodern Flows in Postmodern China: Globalisation and the Sipsongpanna Tais". *Modern China* 29, no. 2 (2003): 176–203.

Dean, Karin. "Mapping Kachin Political Landscape: Constructing, Contesting and Crossing Boundaries". In *Exploring Ethnic Diversity in Burma*, edited by Mikael Gravers. Copenhagen: Nordic Institute of Asian Studies (NIAS) Press, 2007, pp. 123–48.

Featherstone, David. *Resistance, Space and Political Identities: The Making of Counter-Global Networks*. Chichester: Wiley-Blackwell, 2008.

Gravers, Mikael, ed. *Exploring Ethnic Diversity in Burma*. Copenhagen: Nordic Institute of Asian Studies (NIAS) Press, 2007.

Hill, Ann Maxwell. *Merchants and Migrants: Ethnicity and Trade among Yunnanese Chinese in Southeast Asia*. New Haven: Yale University Southeast Asia Studies, 1998.

Jin, Liyan. "Leaf-Letters and Straw-Bridges". In *The Jingpos, Women's Culture Series: Nationalities in Yunnan*, compiled by Yunnan Publicity Centre for Foreign Countries. Kunming: Yunnan Education Publishing House, 1995, pp. 33–50.

Leach, Edmund Ronald. "The Frontiers of Burma". *Comparative Studies in Society and History* 3, no 1 (1965): 49–68.

Lehman, Frederic K. "Foreword". In *The Jingpo: Kachin of the Yunnan Plateau*, edited by Zhuseng Wang. Arizona State University: Program for Southeast Asian Studies, 1997, pp. xiii–xviii.

Leitner, Helga, Eric Sheppard, and Kristin M. Sziarto. "The Spatialities of Contentious Politics". *Transactions of the Institute of British Geographers* 33 (2008): 157–72.

Lobato, Ramon, Julian Thomas, and Dan Hunter. "Histories of User-Generated

Content: Between Formal and Informal Media Economies". *International Journal of Communication* 5 (2011): 899–914.

Martin, Deborah G. and Byron Miller. "Space and Contentious Politics". *Mobilization: An International Journal* 8, no. 2 (2003): 143–56.

McAdam, Doug, Sidney Tarrow and Charles Tilly. *Dynamics of Contention*. Cambridge: Cambridge University Press, 2001.

McConnell, Fiona "De facto, Displaced, Tacit: The Sovereign Articulations of the Tibetan Government-in-Exile". *Political Geography* 28 (2009): 343–52.

McFarlane, Colin "Translocal Assemblages: Space, Power and Social Movements". *Geoforum* 40 (2009): 561–67.

Sadan, Mandy. "Decolonising Kachin: Ethnic Diversity and the Making of an Ethnic Category". In *Exploring Ethnic Diversity in Burma*, edited by Mikael Gravers. Copenhagen: NIAS Press, 2007, pp. 34–76.

———. "Being and Becoming Kachin: Histories Beyond the State and the Borderworlds of Burma". *British Academy Postdoctoral Fellowship Monographs*. Oxford: Oxford University Press, 2013.

Sassen, Saskia. *Territory, Authority, Rights: From Medieval to Global Assemblages*. Princeton: Princeton University Press, 2006.

Sheller, Mimi and John Urry. "The New Mobilities Paradigm". *Environment and Planning A* 38, no. 2 (2006): 207–26.

Smith, Martin. *Burma: Insurgency and the Politics of Ethnicity*. London: Zed Books, 1999.

Sturgeon, Janet C. *The Politics of Akha Land Use in China and Thailand*. Washington: University of Washington Press, 2005.

Tagliacozzo, Eric and Wen-Chin Chang, eds. *Chinese Circulations: Capital, Commodities, and Networks in Southeast Asia*. Durham: Duke University Press, 2011.

Tang, Hang Wu. "The Networked Electorate: The Internet and the Quiet Democratic Revolution in Malaysia and Singapore". In *Journal of Information, Law and Technology* 2, 2009 < http://www2.warwick.ac.uk/fac/soc/law/elj/jilt/2009_2/tang> (accessed 4 November 2014).

Tilly, Charles. "Spaces of Contention". *Mobilization: An International Journal* 5, no. 5 (2000): 135–59.

Walker, Andrew. *The Legend of the Golden Boat: Regulation, Trade and Traders in the Borderlands of Laos, Thailand, Burma and China*. Richmond: Curzon Press, 1999.

10

The Mule Caravans as Cross-Border Networks: Local Bands and their Stretch on the Frontier between Yunnan and Burma

JIANXIONG MA AND CUNZHAO MA

INTRODUCTION

In southwestern China, a transportation system based on horse (mule) caravan routes had been the infrastructure for networks with Chinese central plains and southwestern Asian counties as well as Tibet and India for a very long time in history. This transportation system provided a multi-layered social and physical mechanism for political, social and economic exchanges and mobility, but it relied seriously on the human-animal relationship, especially on mules, rather than horses, even though it was well-known as the horse caravan, *ma bang* (马帮), in Chinese. Since the 1990s, studies on "the ancient roads of tea and horse" have become a hot topic in Yunnan, with the rapid development of tourism in northwest Yunnan, such as Lijiang and the Tibetan area in the north of Lijiang. However, the exchange of tea and horses was just a small part of the material exchange between different regions, and the topic of the tea and horse trade and Yunnan–Tibet should not overlook the discussion of transportation and the circulation of goods (Tagliacozzo and Chang 2011, pp. 37–61; Lee 2012). Before 1938 when the first modern highway, the famous Burma Road, was constructed between Yunnan and (then) Burma, the transportation system was greatly reliant on animal and human power to cross rugged mountains and rough rivers. We should understand that transportation based on animal power and caravan bands, historically, had been in existence for a very long time. However, because this was a very local system in terms of its internal organization and travelling style, as well as its skill and knowledge being important social and cultural resources, this knowledge was never well recorded in traditional Chinese scholarship.[1]

Most recent reports and research on caravans focus on the historical change of transportation routes, the post-house system and markets. Wang and Zhang's research was the first piece of academic work on these issues, and gives a general description and introduction about the horse (mule) caravan system in Yunnan (Wang and Zhang 1993, p. 5). Hu's subsequent research was more focused on the relationship between the caravan business and the changes of business relations in different areas, especially during the Sino-Japanese war in the 1930s and the 1940s. For questions about local caravan organization and local communities, Hu's discussion could not go beyond the previous research of Wang and Zhang (Hu 1999). After 2000, more scholars discussed issues of the ancient tea and horse roads (*chama gudao* 茶马古道) (Li 2001) but lacking are questions about historical change of individual experiences and communities' connections along the road. Moreover, they simplified the issue of transportation to the exchange road between tea and horse, and limited the route to that between Yunnan and Tibet. Giersch (2010) points out that, according to William Skinner, China was comprised of nine separate urban systems, each occupying a major region of a county, and each of them, as nine macro-regions, contained core and peripheral areas. Later James Lee (2012) argued that migration helped transform the southwest macro-region from small and autonomous enclaves into an integrated hierarchy of central and hinterlands. Nevertheless, Giersch (2010) argues that, long-distance travel and mining should be used as cases to challenge the limitation of the core-periphery or macro-regional approach to the southwest, especially how commercialization throughout eastern Eurasia influenced Chinese migration, along with merchant and state economic activity. Therefore, long-distance commerce claims a central role in this perspective. The authors want to point out that the local knowledge of caravan muleteers and the band networks and migrations could work together with local communities in a shared transportation and mobility network, to highlight that, not only Chinese migration and Chinese markets, but also native agency and transportation networking were integrated into a huge system, through which different people could work with each other but could also keep their internal integration in the border-crossing movement in history.

Based on our long-term fieldwork and data set of life history of muleteers in this research, the authors want to highlight a different perspective of caravan study. Considering that mule caravans were seasonally organized by ordinary muleteers on a part-time basis alongside their role as agriculturists, communal ties, such as kinship ties or migrants from the same village over a network spanning different places over a huge terrain, need to be given serious attention. Those communal ties would include the links of kinship ties, religious pilgrimages, shared profits among the nodes (places or stations, transportation routes and commercial centres), shared knowledge and cultural identities and so on. Thus, we will come to understand why the caravans' specific organizational features are bound up with local culture: the Hui caravan bands, the Bai caravan bands, the Tengyue caravans or the Tibetan caravan bands. Flowing over the social-cultural networks among caravan businessmen, who came from different places, were business partners sharing a common local but network-based system. This is the social feature of these mule caravans in this study and this system had seriously shaped the social landscape of the Yunnan-Burma frontier.

THE REARING AND TRAINING OF MULES

In the history of Yunnan and southwest China, horses were specific items that ordinary households were taxed on by the Ming and Qing governments so as to feed the army. Therefore, raising horses as a state-required policy was a core issue in local politics (Wang 1689). Another interesting case is how the Ming and Qing states used the exchange of tea with horses from Tibet to control Tibet to a certain degree. However, besides the taxation and the exchange of horses as military equipment, horses were rarely used as the animal of choice in long-distance transportation. The animals trained for transportation carriers were normally the mule and ox, rather than the horse.[2] The mule is classified under the animal genus of Equus, which includes horses, donkeys and mules, but a mule is the offspring of a female horse and a male donkey, a hybrid. The natives in Yunnan believe that mules are more patient, sure-footed, hardy and enjoy longer lives than horses, and they are considered less obstinate, faster, and more intelligent than donkeys. They are easier to train than horses and donkeys and have historically been used for transportation. In the tradition of animal husbandry in Yunnan and during the period of the Nanzhao Kingdom (738–937), the Lijiang Region in the northwest was famous for horse rearing, as can be seen from the Dehua Inscription of Nanzhao (Anonymous 2000, p. 3). In the era of the Dali Kingdom, the Southern Song imported war-horses from the Dali Kingdom (Yang 1998, pp. 188, 244). Besides horse rearing, Yunnan has a long history of donkey rearing as well and was famous for the Yunnan grey donkey species. "There was no donkey in Qian (Guizhou area), but they are numerous in Yunnan. People use it to carry goods to the markets, and those driving animals in daily life are almost always donkeys, which occupies seventy to eighty percent. The mules are used in long distance carrying only" (Tan 1990, p. 152). In the history of transportation in Yunnan, donkeys were mainly used for daily and short-distance carrying work, while mules were used in long-distance transportation. "People rear donkeys everywhere in Yunnan; this animal has long ears and its body, with its gray colored skin, is smaller than that of a horse. Normally people use it to carry goods to markets a short distance away. However, mules have very strong bodies and are used for long-distance transportation only, and they can also be found everywhere in Yunnan" (Zhou 2007, p. 50). According to provincial records from the 1920s and 1930s, more than 300,000 horses and 120,000 donkeys were reared during this time, mainly in the northwestern, middle and southern counties (ibid.).

After the 1950s, local governments, such as the government of Lijiang Prefecture, began to import donkeys from Shanxi Province and horses from Xinjiang because their bodies were bigger than the traditional Yunnan horses and grey donkeys. However, these efforts, aimed at improving the quality of the hybrid mule, did not change mule rearing methods at all. In China, the horses reared in Yunnan belong to the family of southwest horses, and the traditional Yunnan mules used in caravans were hybrids from female Yunnan horses and male Yunnan grey donkeys. According to our fieldwork records, these donkeys are still reared in great numbers in many counties such as Yongsheng, in Xiaolianshan (小凉山) region, the Jinsha River valley, and also Xianyun and Nanjian counties in western Yunnan (Yu 2001, p. 65). For many peasants, to rear one or two animals, like a horse and a mule, as livestock is a basic need for carrying on with everyday life. For the villagers, there is no significant difference in methods of rearing a horse or a mule, in terms of feeding, training and healing. Based on the skills and experiences learned from older generations; both the breeding mare and the male donkey must be three years of age to beget a mule. A veterinarian we interviewed explains that, because the mule holds two sets of chromosomes, both the male and female mules could experience estrus, but neither are fertile (interview with Mou Gang 2014).[3] Traditionally in Yunnan, people categorize the mule of a stallion and a female donkey as *luoyang* (骡驤), which is also a kind of mule, and based on this category, a male horse is called *juzima* (驹子马), and a female horse is called *kema* (骒马). Both the mule *luo* and the *luoyang* are infertile. However, according to my informants, the male mules must be spayed before they reach three years of age, otherwise the male mules will experience estrus and their temper could become unstable. They also like to skip and might kick people. In the same way, the female mule will also be in estrus. A male mule is called *luozi* (骡子), but a female mule is called *keluo* (骒骡). The estrus of mules is normally in a period from the first month to the seventh month of the lunar calendar each year. In the livestock market, the price of a female mule is normally higher than a male mule by about 20 per cent, because a female mule is easier to work with. For most families in northwestern Yunnan, the purpose of rearing a horse is to have mules. The gestation period of a horse lasts about 320 days, or eleven months, after which the mule is born. A horse lives for about fifteen to sixteen years while a mule normally lives about thirty years. However, a mule can be used for carrying things for about seventeen to eighteen years during its lifetime after which its carrying power will decline.

In the basins and their surrounding mountains in northwest Yunnan, especially in Lijiang, Heqing and Jianchuan areas, animal husbandry has been a long-term economic resource for the locals, and this region has had a very long history of being the most important mule rearing base in southwest China. Mules from this region are sold to places all over Yunnan. The local villagers in these areas are rich in the experience of mule rearing, mule training and mule veterinary knowledge. According to local informants, until ten years ago, the income from mule production had been their most important economic source, but it has been declining and replaced due to rapidly developing tourism and the changes to transportation and vehicles in recently years.

> Almost all families in our village and this township rear horses and mules. If you have a female horse which gives birth to a mule each year, your life will be just wonderful. The purpose of rearing a horse is to have a mule. When a mule grows up, and if you have an able-minded man in the family, you can use the mule to carry lumber from the surrounding mountains. In my family, we always kept a horse at home, so we could have a baby mule almost every year. Sometimes we bought a baby mule to rear, which guaranteed that we could sell an adult mule at the annual livestock fair at the Temple of Son of Heaven (天子庙会), which happens on the fifth day of the first month of the lunar calendar. We began to rear a baby mule in summer, and sell it at the coming livestock markets in winter once it approached three years of age, no matter that the mule was bought or was borne by our horses. However, to rear a mule is hard work. I got up at six o'clock in the morning to cut grass for them, to search for a good price at the market, to train them. Once it approaches one year

in age, it's time to wean it. Two to three months after the weaning, the training is started, until it is three years old (interview with veterinarian Dr He Shunyong and his wife 2014).[4]

CARAVANS IN YUNNAN

Before the 1940s at the Yunnan-Burma frontier, every year after the rainy season in fall, winter and spring in Yunnan, normally from late September to early June the following year, villagers in basins along the transportation routes in Yunnan, especially in basins in the Dali area in the west, Chuxiong area centrally and Yuxi, Tonghai and Jianshui areas in the south, would organize their caravans for long-distance trade after their harvest. In this sense, they were also a group of seasonal migrants from local communities in Yunnan. A normal caravan was organized with forty to fifty mules, called a "horse band", but this kind of caravan was organized by big business companies or powerful families. However, many villagers would also organize their own bands, but the size of their caravans was fewer than fifty mules. Small caravans would have about twenty to thirty mules, and would follow the big caravans on their journey, providing security. Those caravans were called "the rigging-up bands (拼帮)". Some families sent their mules to join big caravan bands because they were kin or friends. As a small part of a big caravan, they called these muleteers and their animals "the joined band (搭伙)". Usually, a muleteer could take good care of a maximum of four to five mules, considering the long distance and long-term travel.

There were many different styles used to take care of mules; some muleteers had the job of driving two or three mules, but also helped the bands to take care of up to three other mules. A muleteer took care of his own carrier-team in a caravan band, which meant he had four or five mules to take care of and this was called "a grasp" (*yiba* 一把). "A grasp" therefore was a basic working unit in a caravan. Sometimes, if a caravan was run by big families or business companies, professional muleteers were hired to manage their grasps. When on the move, some small bands tagged along on the road. These were called the "following caravans" (*gen bang* 跟帮). According to the oral history of muleteers collected in the Dali area, we learned that, a mule caravan was temporarily organized for bands travelling on the roads. Once a caravan was organized, a strong mule would be selected as the head mule (*touluo* 头骡), followed by the second head and the third head mules (*erluo* 二骡, *sanluo* 三骡). The head mule walked in front of the band, well ornamented and carried a big, loud-sounding, copper bell. The second and third head mules, walking behind the head mule, and were fastened with a circle of eight or sixteen small copper bells, were called the "disperse bells" (*sanling* 散铃).

The caravan custom was to carry bowls, chopsticks and cookers using soft bamboo strips. Each mule carried a hemp bag called "the forage bag" (*liaobei* 料背). Every time the caravan took a break or made camp in the evening, the muleteer would make sure that there was enough cut hay mixed with beans, called *kaishao* (开稍), in this bag to feed the mule. The food, beans and hay could be bought easily in the villages they passed by. Some individual tools used for shodding, bowls, and pans were packed as a small set and added to the pack each time. The caravan travelling to Burma, Kunming, Sichuan or Tibet, normally camped outside the towns and villages on the road, called Kai Liang. The purpose of camping outside the residential villages and towns was to herd mules on the grassland and water them from the pools or streams, allowing the tired animals to recover and have a good rest. At the camp, the caravans set fires, boiled water, cooked, and slept.

Camping on a gradual slope helped muleteers and mules to recover quickly from the tiring travel, but they also needed to protect themselves from wild animals. Here, traditional experience was crucial. They needed to put some *caoguo* (草果) or cardamon, which is a popular spice in Yunnan cooking, into the fire. The intense smoke would quickly spread over the mountain slope, and wild animals would be driven away by its pungent spicy odour. Using their rich camp experiences, the muleteers would collect some dry oak leaves to use as a carpet, then cover it with a palm mat, and two blankets. The fire pit would be arranged around the sleeping sites such that, protected by the pungent odour of cardamom and smoke, the sleeping sites would be warm, dry, and safe until the following morning. If there was rain, which was uncommon in the dry season of caravan travel, the muleteers could put four to five pack-frames together in a row, then set the wood-based pack-saddle over the frame, taking one side as their sleeping bed, while the other side of the pack-saddle, facing the air, was a space, covered by the palm carpets and rain capes and used to shield sleeping men and the bound goods on the pack-frame. It would have been a difficult situation, but it did not happen very often.

In the evening at the camp, mules were tethered to an iron stick driven into the ground, which was also used as a frame for cooking over the fire. Some muleteers took turns as guards overnight at the camp, however, as a fundamental principle for caravans, no muleteer was ever allowed to leave their band. All mules slept standing up. If any lay down, this meant that the situation was dire. The animal was either ill, or terribly tired and needing to be healed; this was treated seriously. If the caravan had passed towns or cities and needed to stay at a caravanserai, one or two muleteers would be sent ahead to contact the caravanserai. This was called "to knock at the inn" (*dadian* 打店). Big and professional caravans had specific people appointed to the duties of caravanserai manager and investigator. Small caravan bands normally attached themselves to big bands and powerful groups with strong political and economic backgrounds, so that the whole system could cooperate with caravans organized at other places within a large network, and cooperatively transport goods.

Once a mule caravan band was organized, one particular muleteer would take on the tasks of an accountant and logistics manager. The original meaning of the head of a caravan is known as the head of cooking (*guotou* 锅头). This term was derived from the same term used at the mines for the logistics manager, as the caravan logistics performed a crucial role in the history of the mining industry in Yunnan. In a caravan, a cooking team was the most basic logistics unit. A team cooking and eating together was therefore called a *guo* (锅), meaning a cooking pan. In a caravan, the drivers of fifty mules was the maximum number forming an eating team, which meant about ten muleteers would be organized into an accounting group in their everyday cooperation and food expenses. The accounting was done for one trip only, which began when caravans left home and ended just before the caravans reached home. The caravan accountant had particulars of their costs, which had to be divided for each mule, and was called the "eating account" (*chizhang* 吃账). If a caravan was running a collective transportation business, each time they returned, the accountant would calculate their profits as well as their eating account, make clear how much of a profit they had made, and how much bonus they would finally share. If a muleteer was hired to work for a mule owner, the boss had to pay him a salary.

A muleteer's work therefore was not an easy job. Some foreigners praised the muleteers for their health and strength, and their ability to tolerate danger and a harsh life in the wild, drive their animals across high mountains, endure very frequent food shortages and walk a very long way in varying weather, like iron men (Forbes 1987). In their travels, it was common for them to cross big rivers such as the Mekong, the Salween, and the Jinsha (the upper Yangtse River), situations that were extremely dangerous. All the packs of goods needed to be moved off and onto the mules' backs at river crossings. This was back-breaking work, which included moving these packs onto boats or bamboo rafts from the river banks many times a day, before moving the animals across the rivers. Another heavy job involved carrying packs across soft bridges woven in rattan and bamboo. As these bridges were narrow, the muleteers had to carry one pack at a time while attempting to balance themselves on the soft, woven net. Meanwhile the mules had to be driven across the river. This must have been the hardest work for them. On some of the more arduous roads, the muleteers also needed to carry the packs carefully, while slowly driving the mules.

In general, the transportation routes which linked the cities between Kunming (昆明), Dali (大理), Tengyue (腾越), Yongchang (永昌) and Lijiang (丽江), as the main trunk roads of southwest China, with Burma and Tibet, had been well maintained by the Ming and the Qing states as the official routes based on the transportation institutions like the nine gates and eighteen stations, which guaranteed the safe flow of travellers and the circulation of goods because routes like these were protected by the official military force. Therefore, the potential profits for the caravans became competitively low, but the possible profits sought by west Yunnan caravan businessmen frequently shifted to businesses with Burma, Sichuan and Tibet.

CARAVAN AS A FORM OF LOCAL POLITICS

The goods which could be transported by caravans were also conditional on the seasons of production. For instance cotton, special local agricultural products, Chinese medicinal herbs, minerals, and later opium, were all available in different seasons. Besides these combined caravans, some caravans worked for big business companies based on long-term cooperation and credits. This kind of cooperation also operated as a kind of customary law, so that the caravan muleteer communities worked with businessmen and the time of business coincided with the local agricultural cycle, and an annual cultural festival scheduled to facilitate networking and mobility. In this sense, the caravan travels could be regarded as a way of confirming the relationships within their networks as well. However, these networks and economic flows were greatly shaped and reshaped by political powers. In order to understand this kind of political networking and its dynamics based on the exchange of goods between Yunnan and Burma, some particular cases are presented.

The first example is the case of the *shihuang* mineral ($AS2S3$, Orpimentum Orpiment 石磺) produced in the Zhaozhou mountains. At least as late as in the Ming Dynasty, this *shihuang* mineral had been recorded as a main product exported to Burma, mainly used for medicines and dyes, but mostly used to protect houses from being eaten by termites.

Once washed in *shihuang* liquid, wooden houses would last longer since the mineral repels termites. Zhaozhou caravans moved *shihuang* to Burma to exchange it for cotton which they brought back, and so the cotton textile workshops developed. On their return journey, they also transported tea from the Gengma and Fengqing areas. This network shows the crucial business connections over the caravan network between Zhaozhou and Burma. Up to the 1910s, about 1,000 tonnes of *shihuang* were transported to Burma. The caravan businessmen bought it locally for thirty silver dollars per tonne, but sold it for up to 280 silver dollars at Mandalay. The mining tax from *shihuang* had been used to pay schooling fees at Zhaozhou since the Ming Dynasty, and the amount had been doubled twice. Between 1856 and 1872, these mines were controlled by the Hui Muslim (Panthay) rebel army, but after that, General Yang Yuke (杨玉科), who was the main military commander, suppressed Du Wenxiu (杜文秀), who led the Panthay rebellion. In this way, these rich mines were controlled by him. Yang Yuke established a *shihuang* mining company (石磺局) controlled by the Heqing Chamber of Commerce (鹤庆商会) which supported Yang in the wars with the Hui. After the property rights shifted to a Heqing businessmen's group, they quickly cooperated with the businessmen bands that came from Tengyue, which had a good marketing network in Burma, which led to some other big companies, like the *Hongshengxiang* (洪盛祥) run by the Dong family (董耀廷), to monopolize the *shihuang* business in Burma.

After the 1911 Revolution, General Zhao Zhongqi (赵钟奇), a Hui commander from Zhaozhou, became the key official at Tengyue. As a result, the *shihuang* mineral transports were also monopolized by caravans coming from Zhaozhou, the hometown of General Zhao Zhongqi. For trading *shihuang* and cotton alone, about 2,000 to 3,000 packs needed to be sent via the caravans per year, and 400 to 500 mules were required. Up to 1930, the *Hongshengxiang* had exported about 1,500 tonnes of *shihuang* to Burma and had earned more than 700,000 silver dollars. After 1895, the company imported 3,000 to 5,000 packs of cotton into Yunnan per year (Zhou 2007, p. 173; Yang 1996, p. 399). As the most powerful member of the gentry at Zhaozhou, General Zhao's brother was one of the most powerful local men in communal affairs and he himself was also one of the most powerful caravan bosses at Zhaozhou, until 1950, when he was killed by the new Communist government (Yang Jiajing 1996, p. 682; Yang Huairong 1991, p. 31). Through this, we see that caravan businessmen cooperated closely with state power and local politicians. Without their political connections, the caravan businessmen could not have passed through cities and counties easily.

In the same way, another case shows a more dramatic connection between caravan muleteers and high political figures, demonstrating that transportation was not a simple matter in local politics. Ma Caiting was a powerful businessman from Menghua (Weishan today), but he was given the franchise to transport opium from the Wa Mountains after 1935, when there were at least 700,000 *mu* (about 46,000 hectares) for opium poppy cultivation. The opium tax had become an official importation income since the 1870s to support the military forces in Yunnan, but it was multiplied later because the price of opium had increased. In 1935, the provincial government led by Long Yun banned opium poppy plantations in most areas, but still allowed the frontier region in the Wa Mountains to keep their opium poppy fields (Qin 1998, p. 25). Meanwhile, because many Wa tribes practised headhunting, the official military forces could not get into the Wa lands. The transportation of opium produced in this area became the most important resource in producing official and private profits, if businessmen were willing to share the benefits with the provincial government that was controlled by the warlord.

After the opium ban was ordered in 1935, the market value of opium doubled. The Yunnan government established the Bureau of Special Goods to transport opium, and allowed some of the big companies such as *Yongchangxiang* (永昌祥) and *Maoheng* (茂恒), representing economic supermen in west Yunnan, to share the benefits with the government (Qin 1998, p. 265). Meanwhile, the Hui businessmen also shared their transport profits with these big businessmen, because the whole Yunnan warlord system was supported by this local political and economic elite. Thus, the Long Yun government allowed Ma Caiting to control caravans to control this opium transport franchise (Ma 2007, p. 165). The caravans started from Menghua, Zhaozhou and Dali and therefore could share much more business or smuggling profits than others who were not attached to this political elite, but this network was rooted in the construction of a social hierarchy in a long historical context of social changes before and after the Hui rebellions led by Du Wenxiu and the rise of gentry powers in northwest Yunnan, rather than simply being an issue of transportation routes or animals.

From another point of view, we also found that because different social communities held different political resources, their caravans could go farther than those caravans coming from different communities who could not access certain political resources. It depended on who the political representatives of the local economic powers were. The connections could be manipulated by local elites to bring about cooperation with higher political authorities; this explains why there were so many different caravan businessmen's groups coming from different political-economic groups, such as the Heqing business band (鹤庆帮), the Tengyue business band (腾越帮), the Menghua business band (蒙化帮), the Xizhou business band (喜洲帮) and the Zhaozhou business band (赵州帮) in west Yunnan. Based on this structure, kinship, religious communal networks, same hometown relations and shared business secrets could therefore be shifted to a business credit web. It was the local political elite who introduced their family-run caravan into economic fields. Through their political network, a village in west Yunnan was able to extend its business connections and market credit to Bahmo or Lashio in Upper Burma.

CARAVAN AS A WAY TO SET UP SOCIAL BOUNDARIES

The organization of mule caravans had been a way to maintain and extend local communal benefit for social groups. The different groupings of caravan bands crossed ethnic or class boundaries before geographic and state boundaries were traversed, but this was based on a local community, common benefit band, like the local term "business bands", of different basins and their radiating ties toward different economic and political resources. Therefore, the regional political-economic elite bands were an important social agent in the forming of Yunnan as China's southeast frontier linked to Burma and Tibet. This social characteristic of the Yunnan-Burma frontier has not been well studied in academic fields. In general, ordinary agriculturalists worked on a part-time basis with their regional social elites as caravan muleteers to organize their political and economic bands. Then, the local caravan bands cooperated with local elites in business or political transport, such as the fall of the Qing Dynasty and the rise of local warlords and so on. This *modus operandi* was a key element in helping us to understand Yunnan-Burma cross-border transport. Local elites could extend their ties to Upper Burma as well as into local political affairs. Therefore, there was a mechanism of "double agency" in Yunnan society, and it worked as a network stretching dynamically in different directions. Based on this "double agency" mechanism in shaping local bands, ordinary muleteers shared some benefits with their local leading elite, but also set their boundaries to exclude anyone who wanted to share these resources with them.

However, a mule caravan was always a provisional organization. For each journey, its life began when it left home and ended on its return, once the cooking account was settled. In this situation, the caravan's core aim was to be integrated into a short journey to enhance its own security and to make a profit. Thus, the most crucial law for muleteers was an extremely strong integration and organizational principle. The muleteers could be very cooperative and competitive inside and out, so to enforce this law was to set boundaries in their everyday practices during their travel. There are many ways to achieve these purposes. The adoption of signals in a specific language was the most common way to set boundaries. Yao points out that the caravan language and number system functioned as a special way to exclude outsiders (Yao 2002, pp. 67–75). Among the Hui Muslim caravan muleteers, a traditional language of signals was shared with Hui communities only. This signal system could be regarded as a language because it could not be used separately, easily identifying outsiders. The signals were combined with words from Persian, Arabic and the local Han dialect and used for detecting other groups, sending special information to partners, and in their business negotiations when they had to discuss matters in front of strangers.

Besides signal systems, another way boundaries were set up was the establishment of travel rituals. Caravans coming from different communities practised different rituals and taboos. For the Hui caravans, coming upon a funeral was interpreted as a fortunate event, but eating half-cooked rice indicated misfortune. The most important everyday ritual for them was the choice of eating sites. Eating together was the principal ritual that was linked to their fortunes on the road. The eating sites, called "the double-dragon mouth (摆二龙口)", had to be selected carefully. At least twice a day, a site was set up so that the travellers could rest and cook lunch, and have dinner in the late afternoon. One or two muleteers took turns to cook, setting up the copper rice pot (*tuoluoguo* 铜锣锅) in the middle of the camp. All muleteers had to be seated in two rows. According to generational hierarchy and age, they had to find their place in the row, in descending order. The two heads represented the head of two dragons, facing the direction of their future travels, while the younger and junior muleteers made up the tails of the double-dragon, the two rows of seats. The rice pot could hold enough rice for a repast for twenty people. Its cover could be turned over and used as a pan to cook vegetables after the rice was cooked. Additionally, the water boiler, the big copper cooker, and its cover, had to be set up in between the two rows of muleteers, as a middle row for cookers. None of the muleteers could change their places, or those of the cooking pots, during the meal, but they could take the small covers and use them as vessels for rice and vegetables, until the meal was finished.

If meat was cooked, it had to be divided equally. Good table manners were a basic requirement as a muleteer, and if anyone violated the prohibition he was fined, the payment of which involved the purchase of a big cock and its preparation for the team. Special language signals, taboos, daily rituals and caravan manners were all practised on the journey to set up boundaries, and they helped to maintain group integration and safety, and guaranteed everyday management of orderliness, thereby reducing risks of external threats.

Meanwhile, other dangers and threats which could not be guarded against by good manners and taboos, posed real challenges. Two of the biggest difficulties for the caravans were robbers and disease. Therefore, the caravan muleteers had to try their best to help each other in order to save themselves. Malaria and some unknown diseases with the symptoms of shivering and chills were called "the shaking disease" (*dabaizi* 打摆子), or the "barbarian places shaking" (*yifang baize* 夷方摆子). In the minds of the Yunnanese, the shaking disease was caused by a special "mist" (*zhangqi* 瘴气), which appeared during certain seasons and at certain places. There are many descriptions of the types of terrible shaking-disease mists in Yunnan. For instance,

> on the rivers of the Mekong and the Salween, sometimes in phases, the water becomes deep red, changed from its ordinary deep green. If so, the mist appears over the water. Once this mist spreads nobody dares to cross the river. This mist grows in spring, and disappears in late autumn. During this period, grasses on the river banks could also cross each other, followed by rising mists over the grasses, called "heads crossing shaking mist". Especially in May and June, something appears from the Mekong, its color like the frost, lightening like fire, making a sound like the cutting of trees. If anyone is touched by this mist, he immediately dies. Someone says this is the mother of all shaking diseases' mists, called the river of forbidden water (Yunnan People's Publishing House 2007, p. 559).

Through these descriptions, we can imagine how afraid these people were of these diseases and how dangerous the big rivers like the Mekong and the Salween were for the muleteers at that time.

As colleagues, the muleteers cooperated in a temporary cooperative band on a common journey, but their home communities also maintained a tradition of cooperation in their home places. In the same way, they followed the principles of internal cohesion, following a law of equality in terms of risk and responsibility taking, thus relying on one another.

Discipline in the caravan defined the accounting method for equality in the sharing of food and logistics costs, and their daily eating ritual in the form of a "double dragon" became a confirmation of generational hierarchy and symbolized that everything went as smoothly as a dragon. However, as a moving community on a seemingly endless journey, life was risky. Who knew if one would be the next victim after having buried one's colleague? Thanks to their speedy and nimble adjustments, this "moving community" extended their home ties to faraway places whenever they could. In this way, there was a continual confirmation of "self" and "other" boundaries premised on death and survival. Therefore, boundaries set by languages, rituals and taboos helped to maintain extended and moving boundaries and protected them in their cross-border business.

CARAVANS AND CROSS-BORDER NETWORKING

The political and economic principles of caravan organization were based on the communal ties at muleteers' hometowns as well as local bands and their extended representatives. Based on what we discussed in the previous sections, another factor that defined their business success was the validity of their network. It was only if the caravan muleteers could transform their hometown's political and economic resources into new resources at the target places, could they find trustworthy partners so far away from their hometown. In this way, the muleteers had to find some ties at their destinations, be they marital kinships, friendships, hometown connections, and so on. They had to develop certain relationships in other places in order to travel there. This is a core issue for our understanding of the cross-boundary movement of Yunnan caravans in Burma as well. In this way, the place of their arrival was also the end of their network. At this point the caravans would shift hands and go to other local political and economic bands which would travel over a different terrain toward another world.

Here, migration becomes important. The caravan networks in cities in west Yunnan and Upper Burma partly overlapped with the networks of seasonal and permanent migration, due to different historical reasons. This also provided an intermarriage network enabling people to look for personal connections in cities and basins, or among different local bands. After the harvest in the autumn, at the beginning of the dry season, unlike caravan muleteers, some villagers who came from relatively poor villages in west and central Yunnan migrated to Burma to be cotton planters in the western plains of the Salween River in the Mubang area, after which the caravan would move the harvested cotton back to Yunnan in spring. Some men came to be miners in the mountain areas on the frontier; most of the skilled construction workers came from the Dali area; and some businessmen came to collect tea and different local products. These traditional seasonal migrants had been very active, especially in Gengma, Mubang, Menglian and almost all the Shan-Dai chieftain areas, and in the Wa lands from as early as the Ming Dynasty (1368–1644). Following the migrants, businessmen also came to these places and were followed by the caravans.

This history highlights again that caravans used to be part of local political and economic bands, and functioned with other organisms of the local community bound with different religious, economic, ethnic and political categories of social relations. In this way, a caravan represented a way of communal extension to another place, but the caravan was not the only method of communal extension on the Yunnan-Burma frontier (Ma 2007, p. 51). For instance, caravans from the Dali area were very active on the Burma borders precisely because they had very strong ties with these areas. One reason was that natives from the Dali area who had been construction craftsmen, such as skilful carpenters and stonemasons working in the Shan-Dai areas in a tradition of long seasonal migration, in Ming and early Qing times, "came from Dali and Jichuan areas, they acted like the Han, but were in fact the Yi (at Shunning prefecture). They sing their songs in their own language, but they also go to school, or work as craftsmen building houses and making tools, but their purpose in coming here is simply to make money" (Fan 2001, p. 168). This document helps us to understand how these connections were established in history and maintained by caravans as part of these regional networks.

On the frontier of Yunnan and Burma, in the 1930s and the 1940s, the county magistrate needed to manipulate local gangsters, to use gangs as a measure for social control and to share resources and opportunities with his groups. This style of social management on one hand limited the transportation condition, but it also provided different resources for different groups based on their political and economic backgrounds. The sharing of social resources with different groups was reliant on secret societies rather than on governmental institutions which highlighted that, as late as the time when the Qing Dynasty was transformed into the Republic, the local powerful families and political elites were the real rulers of local affairs. So, caravan bands and secret societies needed to share a network with each other to connect the local powers (Ma 2012, pp. 87–122). For example, connections to gangsters (who could provide protection in the places they controlled) were made known through the use of special binding ties for the mule packs.[5] This shows us that details about how local bands cooperated and connected with one another other through networks were crucial practices of inclusion and exclusion.

Besides the connection with the network of local gangs, another more traditional and extreme way of regional cooperation and exclusion was business kidnapping. This could be regarded as another traditional way to deal with resource distribution and to set up the lowest permission for caravan business. It could also be regarded as the customary law of mule caravan transportation. The tripartite relationship between muleteers, robbers and innkeepers shows the mutual inclusion and exclusion between different local bands through caravan transportation. In many instances, especially at ferry-points on the big rivers and transportation gates, the inns provided food for the muleteers and animals. This was the only logistical possibility. Small caravans must follow big ones, and the local communities could extend their networks into the distance so that the flow of goods and cultural exchange became possible, but all of these extensions and exchanges had to be based on the strong cohesion of local bands, which could protect their outbound travellers and strengthen their common benefit over a vast, cross-border network, but the whole process of this strengthening strategy also required them to set up boundaries to enable them to network. In this way, we could surmise that, even if the roles of robbers, innkeepers and muleteers were in continual flux on the routes, the common benefits to their community bases were clearly defined. The mechanism of communal extension and encounters, in a mobile environment, could be considered in the analysis of the circulation of goods and cultural exchanges on the frontier.

CONCLUSION

Local traditional livestock husbandry provided excellent species of mules which could transport heavy loads over long distances. Caravan skills were passed on by older generations. Local Yunnan muleteers shared their very rich knowledge and experience of geography, ethnic groups, language, transport vehicles and methods (Geertz 1983). All of these formed a valuable pool of local knowledge about caravans but were shared by educated intellectuals, especially Confucian students, based on local history. However, such knowledge and the methods shared were also limited to the communities that owned the caravan, due to it being linked with a measure of access to economic resources. Therefore, it was also exclusive and was regarded as a kind of cultural capital by its owners.

Within the local bands, the cases we discussed have also shown that, the cohesive caravans were based on the same community ties in these Zhaozhou cases. They may have shared the same religious beliefs, or the collective shield of a certain political power, or they could have worked for this power, or they were the equal sites of a big web of kinship or interdependent friends, all so that they could share the same benefits and take the same risks when facing the challenges of transportation uncertainties. Therefore, deep trust and partnership could also empower this collective cultural capital through their travels. In this way, the temporary cooking account group was the basic unit in one or two journeys, but, in general, they were from the same group as their reciprocal community. Besides, official and political powers protected their real opportunities for business. Yunnanese caravans flourished because the muleteers were protected and privileges were given by their political elites. Under the shield of local-band elites, the members of a local band could cross barriers of ethnic and religious communities, linking caravan bosses and muleteers into a more open cohesion which crossed classes, religion and ethnic identities under the framework of local-band hierarchy. But such advantages could also be destroyed when there was a change of the leading political powers, such as the replacement of warlords or business interest parties.

The transportation method, therefore, depended on the "stretchability" of the different levels of a home community. The general reciprocity of muleteers and local economic groups is based on a continuing and cohesive network or membership relationship at home. These networks could then be stretched to other places through methods such as intermarriage, religion, gangsters, or special product and marketing benefit ties. However, based on the local climate, ecological and geographic conditions, most of their mobility was based on seasonal cooperation. This seasonal separation also provided time for repair work, animal training and social relationship renewal procedures. This could be described as social and cultural capital accumulation seasons. The depth of social ties in a local-band community also guaranteed the depth of the collective confidence in the external, stretched ends of their journeys. Thus, the intensity of caravan networks is also due to the degree of social cohesion in their home communities. The quality of exclusion and inclusion should be two ends of a single path that defines the local limitation and cross-border ability of Yunnan mule caravans. In summary, local communities, through transportation routes, relied on the social agency of muleteers who extended their socioeconomic scope to faraway places across social and physical boundaries. In this system, a local community was bound to a trans-regional economic network through caravan activities from a micro-layer into a macro-layer between Yunnan and Burma. At the same time, rivalry and cooperation between local gangs were mutually developed in almost all dimensions of politics, cultural and economic connections. This highlights the importance of the caravan in the construction of local networks in this borderland.

Notes
1. This article is based on a database of caravan muleteer oral history built in west Yunnan from 2002 to 2004. This oral history project was supported by Mr Philip Chien Yip-bang, Yunnan Normal University, South China Research Centre of the Hong Kong University of Science and Technology. The authors presented a previous version of the chapter at the Conference of Mobility and Daily Life: Histories and Possibilities of "Backward" and "Progressive" Means of Transport International Symposium, at Shanghai Academy of Social Sciences on 5–7 January 2012. The authors acknowledge a grant supported by the UGC-AoE Project "The Historical Anthropology of Chinese Society", the RGC/GRF642112 and the SBI Grant (SBI14HS01) of the Hong Kong University of Science and Technology.
2. Interview with Lui Yuandong. Interviewed by Ma Jianxiong, in Kunming, Yunnan, China, 13 August 2010.
3. Interview in Maidi village. Interviewed by Ma Jianxiong, Yangbi county, Yunnan, China, 12 March 2014.
4. Interview in Qihe village. Interviewed by Ma Jianxiong, Yulong county, Yunnan, China, 12 March 2014.
5. The use of special pack ties as signals to show the caravan muleteers' gang identity also featured in the stories recounted by Jianxiong Ma's grandfathers about how they travelled in different places.

References

Anonymous (佚名). "Nanzhao Dehuabei (南诏德化碑)" [The Dehua Inscription of Nanzhao]. In *Dali Lidai Mingbei* (大理历代名碑) [The Historical Inscription in Dali], edited by Duan Jinlu and Zhang Xilu. Kunming: Yunnan Minzu Chubanshe, 2000.

"Appendix No. One". In *The New Compiled Yunnan Gazeteer, Volume 263*, edited by Zhou Zhongyue. Kunming: Yunnan People's Publishing House, 2007.

Fan, Pu (范溥), ed. "Yongzheng Shunningfu Zhi (雍正顺宁府志)" [The Yongzheng Gazetteer of Shunning Prefecture]. In *The Five Gazetteers of Shunning Prefecture Volume 9*, edited by the county government of Fengqing and Local Gazetteer Bureau. Hong Kong: Tianma Tushu Gongsi, 2001.

Forbes, Andrew D.W. "The Role of Hui Muslims in the Traditional Caravan Trade between Yunnan and Thailand". In *Asian Merchants and Businessman in the*

Indian Ocean and China Sea: 13–20 Centuries, French Journal Published under the Direction of Denys Lombard and Jean Aubin, Paris: School of Higher Studies in Social Sciences, 1987. Cited in Maung Maung Lay. "Study on Chinese Muslims in Burma: Emergence of the Panthay Community in Mandalay". *Southeast Asian Affairs* 129, no. 1 (2007): 50–55.

Geertz, Clifford. *Local Knowledge: Further Essays in Interpretive Anthropology*. New York: Basic Books, 1983.

Giersch, C. Patterson. "Copper, Caravan, and Empire: Long-Distance Commerce and the Transformation of Southwest China". *Minzuxue Pinlun* [Ethnological Review] 3 (2010): 211–32.

Hu, Yangquan (胡阳全). *Yunnan Mabang* (云南马帮) [Yunnan Horse Caravan]. Fuzhou: Fujiang Renmin Chubanshe, 1999.

Lee, James (李中清). *Zhongguo Xinan Bianjiang de Shehui Jingji* (中国西南边疆的社会经济: 1250–1850) [Social and Economic History of Southwest China: 1250–1850]. Beijing: Renmin Chubanshe, 2012.

Li, Xu (李旭). *Zangke* (藏客) [Guests in Tibet: The Caravan Career on the Ancient Road of Tea and Horse]. Kunming: Yunnan Renmin Chubanshe, 2001.

Ma, Cunzhao (马存兆). *Chama Gudao Shang Yuanqu de Lingsheng* (茶马古道上远去的铃声) [The Fading Away Bells on the Ancient Road of Tea and Horse: Oral History of Caravan Muleteers]. Kunming: Yunnan Daxue Chubanshe, 2007.

Ma, Jianxiong (马健雄). "'Bianfang Sanlao': Qingmo Minchu Nanduan Dianmian Bianjiangshang de Guojia Dailiren ('边防三老': 清末民初南段滇缅边疆上的国家代理人)" [Three Elders of Frontier Defence: State Agents and the Formation of Yunnan-Burma Frontier in Late Qing and Early Republic]. *Lishi Renleixue Xuekan Kan* [Journal of History and Anthropology] 10, no. 1 (2012): 87–122.

Qin, Heping (秦和平). *Yunnan Yapian Wenti yu Jinyan Yundong* (云南鸦片问题与禁烟运动) [The Opium Problem and the Banning Movements in Yunnan]. Chengdu: Sichuan Renmin Chubanshe, 1998.

Tagliacozzo, Eric and Wen-Chin Chang, eds. *Chinese Circulations: Capital, Commodities, and Networks in Southeast Asia*. Durham and London: Duke University Press, 2011.

Tan, Cui (檀萃). *Dianhai Yuhengzhi (Jiaozhu), Zhishou* (滇海虞衡志(校注), 志兽第七) [The Natural Gazetteer of Yunnan (1799), Volume 7, Animals]. Kunming: Yunnan Remin Chubanshe, 1990.

Wang, Mingda and Zhang Xilu (王明达, 张锡禄). *Mabang Wenhua* (马帮文化) [The Horse Caravan Culture]. Kunming: Yunnan Renmin Chubanshe, 1993.

Wang, Qingxian (王清贤 纂), ed. *Kangxi Wudingfu Zhi* (康熙武定府) [The Kangxi Gazetteer of Wuding Prefecture]. 1689.

Yang, Huairong (杨怀荣). "Hongshengxian Jianshi (洪盛祥简史)" [The Brief of Hongshengxiang Company]. In *Tengchong Zhengxie Wenshi Ziliao Xuanji* (腾冲政协文史资料选辑) [Local Literature and Historical Materials Selective Collection of Tengchong, Volume 3]. Tengchong: The People's Political Consultative Conference of Tengchong County, 1991.

Yang, Jiajing (杨嘉靖 编), ed. *Fengyi Zhi* (凤仪志) [The Gazeteer of Fengyi]. Kunming: Yunnan Daxue Chubanshe, 1996.

Yang, Zuo (杨佐). "Yunnan Maima Ji (云南买马记)" [The Records of Purchasing Horses in Yunnan]. In *Yunnan Shiliao Congkan* (云南史料丛刊) [Yunnan Historical Materials Collection, Volume 2], edited by Fang Guoyu (方国瑜 主编). Kunming: Yunnan Daxue Chubanshe. 1998: 188–244.

Yao, Jide (姚继德). "Yunnan Huizu Mabang de Zuzhi yu Fengbu (云南回族马帮的组织与分布)" [The Organisation and Distribution of the Hui People's Trade Caravans in Yunnan]. *Huizu Yanjiu* (回族研究) [Researches on the Hui] 46, no. 2 (2002): 67–75.

Yu, Qingyuan (余庆远). "Weixi Jianwen Ji (维西见闻记)" [Record about Weixi (1767)]. In *Yunnan Shiliao Congkan* (云南史料丛刊) [Yunnan Historical Materials Collection, Volume 12], edited by Fang Guoyu (方国瑜 主编). Kunming: Yunnan Daxue Chubanshe, 2001.

Zhou Zhongyue (周钟岳). "Juan Liushiwu zhi Wuchan Kao (卷六十五之物产考八)" [Items of Products, No. Eight]. In *Xinzuan Yunnan Tongzhi* (新纂云南通志) [The New Compiled Yunnan Gazetteer (1949), Volume 4]. Kunming: Yunnan Renmin Chubanshe, 2007.

Section V

Identity Construction and the Politics of Belonging

"I Want to Stay Forever in You"

Decha Tangseefa

WAR, MOTHER AND YOUTH[1]

From independence in 1948 to the 2010 historic general election, the voices of peoples in Burma/Myanmar were by and large imperceptible. During those sixty-two years, Burma/Myanmar did not figure much in world politics, compared to the chronicity of political crises therein. The first fourteen years saw it engaged in a chaotic form of democracy that ended when it became a hermit state after General Ne Win's *coup d'état* in 1962. Before the 2010 election, the world community turned its eyes to Burma/Myanmar only when there were mass killings: the 8/8/88 massacre and the Saffron Revolution from 18 to 26 September 2007. In other words, the international community did not by and large regard crises in Burma/Myanmar as international problems — until crisis struck the country again. In this light, the 2010 election was the dawn of metamorphosis both inside and along the country's border zones. However, the international community has been too optimistic about this metamorphosis.

Until May 2014, I had been reflecting upon Burma/Myanmar's future through its past. Even though the country's future looks promising, it is hard to ignore the reality that many people are still suffering: Muslims, the Kachin, and hundreds of thousands of people living in what the Thai state calls "temporary shelter areas" along the Thai-Burmese border.[2] This article is written to record the voices of some of the people living along the border — especially those of the young — without which they will be forgotten. In this introduction, I present a montage of events occurring from 2009 to 2010, before this seemingly promising period of political change.

CHILDREN AND A MOTHER'S MEMORY

Fighting broke out along the Thai-Burmese border zones one day after the historic election on 7 November 2010. For many of those attempting to flee to Thailand, weakened health caused by the displacement led to an early death. For others, it came upon them abruptly without much time for those left behind to prepare themselves emotionally.

Such fragility of life happened to a group of villagers attempting to flee to Thailand. They had been vigilant about the fighting between the State Peace and Development Council (SPDC) and a breakaway faction of the then Democratic Karen Buddhist Army (DKBA). Having decided to leave their village, they attempted to cross the Moei River, the state boundary on that part of the border, by boat. It was early November, the end of the rainy season and the beginning of winter for southeastern Burma/Myanmar. Hence, the river was high and in some areas the tide was perilous. The first ride went well. Unfortunately, the second did not. Too many passengers and too much panic. The boat could not carry them all and finally sank. Not everyone could swim or had the physical strength to do so. Some were too young to help themselves. A mother who could swim was able to save herself but not her two children. She had them with her, one on her shoulder and the other in her arms. However, she could not hold the two children while swimming and they drowned in the rapid tides of the river. She told our fieldworker that she could not forgive herself for this tragic loss. She decided to swim back to the village on the riverbank and went back to her place of origin where our fieldworkers eventually met her for an interview. If children symbolize a mother's hope and future, this mother lost hers during the displacement (interview with a displaced person 2011).[3]

A Young Person's Question

7 June 2009

Dear Nan,

I have some bad news to share with you.

Did you know that DKBA + SPDC try to conquer Brigade 7. The fighting broke out around many villages which are Kler Day, Kler La, Pa Nway Pu, Kwee Law Plo, Dae Lo La, Ler Per Her, Kray Ta and Mae La Hta. More than 3,400 people fled to Thailand to take refugee on Thai side few days ago. More and more people are coming each day.

We don't know how long the attacks will last and how many life will be in suffering. Indeed, there has been countless suffering over the last 60 years of civil war. Things are getting worse each year and I don't think we can win the war by arm struggle alone. But till now we don't find a peaceful solution for long existing problems. So, as a Thai what do you think about Karen People? Any ideas or suggestion to this problems [sic] so far?

Thank You,
Naw Paw Paw[4]

My former student wrote an email to my niece who was teaching and helping me as a research assistant in the Blae Koh "temporary shelter area". Between 2007 and 2011, when I was conducting research and teaching there, Naw Paw Paw was one of my best students. She later won a scholarship and was allowed to live outside the shelter area to further her studies through an online university in Australia. Although her academic achievement was exceptional (Decha Tangseefa 2010*b*, p. 3), her question in the email is more revealing: "So, as a Thai what do you think about Karen People? Any ideas or suggestion to this problems [sic] so far?"

It is these kinds of memories that exemplify human tragedy in Burma/Myanmar as well as along the border (see also Grundy-Warr and Chin's chapter in this volume). Within such a context of displacement, this article presents the voices of displaced young Karens residing in Blae Koh. It does so amidst the changing political landscape of Burma/Myanmar which has led the Thai state to plan the closure of all the shelter areas and repatriate people to their "homeland". This is a worrying proposition.[5]

EXCEPTION AND MIGRATION

This chapter is part of a research project that studies the intertwining relationship between identity, music, and socialization and ways in which they affect peoples' conceptions and experiences of "home", especially those of the young Karens in Blae Koh. Studying the notion of "home" is crucial because many of the peoples — forced to leave home by war and/or dictatorship — had been living in a string of security spaces. Hence, it is a study of a "people of exception" in a "space of exception".[6] Throughout the study, I was open to possibilities that "home" could become a signifier, a metaphor and/or a material condition that was embedded in these displaced peoples' quotidian lives in streams of consciousness and unconsciousness. The study focused on music as a vehicle of socialization by the old and as a means of cultural production of the young. Hence, framed another way, I was interested in studying the nexus between creativity and marginalization (cf. Diehl 2002) in a marginal zone.

The study is based on ethnographic research conducted between February 2008 and March 2010 in the then highest educational institute of all nine shelter areas — the Leadership and Management College (hereafter LMTC) whose name belies the reality of its curriculum. Started in 2006, the school has since begun offering basic college-level education. Its students have been recruited from all shelter areas. However, there were also some students who came from war zones inside Burma/Myanmar. In many ways, this was the "elite" college which prepared a new generation of "leaders" among the displaced ethnic Karens along the border, especially during its first few years before the 2010 election. The school itself was a space of exception within a space of exception. During the fieldwork period, the school housed about sixty students in its hostels where they lived a more regimented life than most other adolescents in the shelter areas. One could argue that among other docile bodies in the "caging" shelter areas, theirs were doubly docile bodies perpetuating the processes of cultural transmission of the displaced Karen communities.[7]

Located in the genre of migration studies, this study is part of the field of involuntary migration in "the world of people on the move" (Appadurai 1996, p. 21; cf. Steiner et al. 2013). The stance taken by this study is echoed in Zygmunt Bauman's words regarding "the global mobility regime" written at the end of the 1990s, "traveling for profit is encouraged; traveling for survival is condemned" (2002, p. 84). Even after more than a decade, the truth of this sentence has not lost its strength. Marginalized people who migrate the world over, so as to survive in another country, always encounter myriad obstacles that they have little protection from. These obstacles include the nation-state's laws and/or human-trafficking rings. Thus "obstacles" could be either state-sponsored or outlawed mechanisms. In the former case, it becomes ironic then that the very machine and functionaries that are supposed to protect humans have ended up harming these vulnerable migrants. Many of these migrants were forced to leave their homes, like the 3,400 odd people mentioned in Naw Paw Paw's email. Such displacement represents the experiences of so many involuntary migrants and confirms that the world usually does not pay attention to involuntary displacement. As a Thai, I consider her question too difficult for Thai society to grapple with.

We pay too little attention to the voices of those who are involuntarily displaced, including displaced youth. Since the official establishment of the "temporary shelter areas" in 1984, we have known so little about displaced youth and their voices. Youth music and songs, manifested both as normal performances and as ways of communicating with the outside world, are phenomena that should be paid attention to because music can "float" outside shelter areas. Locating this phenomenon within the literature of forced migration, we can ask, as did Adelaida Reyes:

> In the context of forced migration, which often inhibits speech and induces guardedness in migrants in the face of danger and as a result of trauma, would music as an activity more readily shared with others have particular advantages as point of entry to other areas of life? (Reyes 1999, p. xiv).

In the context of Blae Koh, the answer has been resoundingly positive, whether one attempts to understand personal quotidian life or an ethnic nationality's journey through war and violence.

EXCEPTION AND MUSIC

Since independence in 1948, countless lives have taken flight from condemned grounds inside Burma/Myanmar and have crossed the state boundary to Thailand. Many of these peoples have entered the shelter areas to be legally protected. Their flight and strategies for survival along the border have been precarious. Before the 2010 election, in the Burman-Karen war zones, for example, teams of Karen medics, teachers, and church workers were exemplary. These small groups of people resisted any attempts by the Burmese junta to strip their fellow Karens of their forms-of-life — be they farmer, teacher, soldier, midwife, animist, or Christian — and hence become "naked" lives, that is, becoming sheer facts of living.[8]

Once the displaced Karens arrived at or passed through Thailand's "doorways", their plight became more perceptible than when they were fleeing for safety inside Burma/Myanmar. Because perceptibility implies particular modes of inscription of lives by certain sovereign powers at their thresholds — be they intelligible language (for example, Aristotelian distinction of *logos* and *phone*) community, nation, state, empire, religion, among others — varieties of political subjects have been inscribed by various discourses and practices of each sovereign.[9] As for those displaced from Burma/Myanmar, they have been inscribed by the Thai state and manifold discursive practices, for example, "temporary shelter area".[10] The Karens' forms-of-life, however, are collectively perceived and flourish in the shelter area.[11] It is thus ironic that the very power that can strip them naked is the same power that enables them to strengthen their form-of-life as a Karen nation. They find themselves in a paradox of perceptibility.

It has been thirty years since the official establishment of the first "temporary shelter area". Blae Koh was established later — after some small shelter areas were ordered closed or relocated and gathered together for better risk management due to attacks by the Burmese Army and its allies. Sometime in the past, Blae Koh housed more than 50,000 registered residents.

At the Blae Koh "Temporary Shelter Area"

As I wrote in 2007, influenced by Michel Foucault, the "temporary shelter areas" are heterotopias (Foucault 1986; Decha Tangseefa 2007, p. 245). They are spaces of exception — especially regarding the dimension of time in space (Decha Tangseefa 2010*b*, p. 17). For the most part and before the 2010 election, peoples' lives inside were slower than peoples' lives outside. Confinement and limited contact with the world outside were two of the most important elements constituting this ethos. Generally, people outside were not allowed to enter the space; and people inside were not allowed to leave. Not until December 2005 were people in Blae Koh able to use mobile phones to contact the outside world.

The rhythms of quotidian life were, moreover, very predictable: youths walked to school; mothers opened their small grocery shops; big sisters carried little brothers on their backs after school and walked to the neighbour's house to chat; an uncle gazed out to a faraway land, his mind drifting. Day in and day out, these scenes did not seem to change. Yet, these people's future in the long run was very uncertain. Such routine and uncertainty are inextricably and tightly woven inside the confinement of bamboo and barbwire fences as well as the "fence" of the Thai state's security discourses. Most people lived their lives under such an ethos while the shadow of the past both nourished and haunted their present. After the 2010 election, some shelter residents sneaked back into Burma/Myanmar — that is, repatriating themselves. Lives inside have gradually been transforming, a bit more quickly and less predictably than before.

The path that I usually walked to enter Blae Koh took me to a playground under a big rain tree. I walked on a bridge, crossing a stream, enveloped by beautiful scenery, especially on the side of the stream where it curved and disappeared into a valley, and especially when a curtain of mist covered the valley and a mountain range which partitioned Burma/Myanmar behind it. I walked alongside bamboo-fenced houses and into a small alley, passing houses, small shops, a school and a church. December 2007 was the first time I was going back to this shelter area since my first round of fieldwork between 2000 and 2001 along the Thai-Burmese border. However, this time, what surprised me was that shortly after crossing the bridge, I heard music, alternating between guitar chords and singing voices. Whenever I walked past the church, I often heard the sounds of a piano or keyboard or sometimes the soft sounds of a violin. At times, I could not help but feel that I was walking into a realm where people used music to communicate their emotions. They were articulating what they were feeling, no matter what the "messages" in the lyrics or melodies were. This could range from today's happiness or yesterday's misery, loneliness of the present or warmth of the past, longing for loved ones far away, so far that they might never see one another again or pleas to God for his mercy. No matter what the "messages" were, what I heard was mostly very pleasing to the ear. Such pleasantness was at times contradictory to the scenes of people passing by: loaded with full baskets on their heads, a baby suckling at his mother's breast while she carried a full bucket of water and disappeared into the bamboo fences or a one-legged person attempting to "walk-on".

These images I saw and sounds I heard made me reflect upon an incongruence between the sufferings of the shelter residents, who had struggled to survive and whose lives had been "wounded", and the musical sounds that enveloped these scenes. Whether these scenes were perfect or not depended on how a person "read" the images. Or, were such pictures another kind of "congruence"? After continuously going back to conduct fieldwork in the shelter area since 2007, I came to realize that there was a more half-open-half-closed ethos in the shelter area. This was an ethos of two aspects: physicality and authority. Physically, such ethos relates to two dimensions: door and body.[12] The shelter's "door" that seemed to be closed was open and the "door" that seemed to be open was closed, not allowing unauthorized persons to pass through. Bodies that seemed unable to leave the shelter area could find a way to leave. Music could not only "sneak through" the fence, but musical subjects became, to follow the Indian traditions, *Gandharvas* who can "fly over" shelter areas' fences.[13] Music, thus, became an essential part of people's lives here, especially for the youth, both male and female.

At the LMTC
Students here tended to downplay their musical abilities, saying that they were not musicians in the way many people outside the shelter areas would normally define them.[14] However, one of my research assistants informed me of the very impressive musical abilities of some of the students at LMTC.[15] An excerpt from his fieldnotes reads:

> For me, LMTC has several students who are pretty good in music, such as Saw Tha Poe who can play continuous bass line, Saw Sun playing guitar

with dense rhythm and clear sound, different from other students playing mainly with force, and Saw Journey who can play rhythm guitar without the notes in almost all songs their friends request [sic] (from Krishna Monthathip's fieldnotes written on 29 November 2009).

I was interested in why LMTC's students would not admit to their musical abilities. Through the survey conducted, most students responded that they usually sang songs only a few times per day. However, having spent time at the LMTC for more than two years, week in and week out and often staying overnight for a few nights each time, I witnessed otherwise. Most students sang whenever they were free, many sang even when they cooked or chopped vegetables. When I stayed overnight in the college, my team and I were always woken up by students singing before dawn.

For hostel students, each would set out to do their school chores after waking up. Many of them sang when they walked. Everyone going for their daily meals in the kitchen had to walk past the guest house where we stayed. Hence, morning until night, we heard songs being sung, or the guitar being played. When they had free time, some students played sports while others got into groups to sing, play the guitar or practise with their band.

After spending time in the college, I came to realize the reasons for the students' underestimation of their musical talent. Music for them was an important part of their quotidian lives, unlike most people outside the shelter area, especially before the era of singing contests which have become globally pervasive. They identified themselves only as people with some interest in music. Most did not consider themselves singers or musicians unlike people around the world who spend the same amount of time playing music.

Of all the college's 134 students, seven had written at least one song. Some of them wrote gospel songs, others wrote national songs, while some others wrote love songs. A few had tried their hand at all three genres. Although only a few had written songs, one of them — Saw Tha Poe — had written more than thirty songs and had been attempting to get support to produce an album. Saw Beck (together with his friends) wrote forty-plus songs in the span of three years while staying in another shelter area before coming to study at this college. Some of his songs were responses to the horrendous news of killings inside Burma/Myanmar. A few students in this school set up a band called "Peace Stars" to sing all genres of songs in various languages, in Karen, Burmese, or English. These young people wanted to sing![16]

Why is music so pervasive in the "temporary shelter areas" where people are confined? During a class discussion one day, I asked my twelve students: "Do you think music is important to life in 'camps'? Why?" They unanimously answered yes to the first question. Without music, one said he "become sad, lonely". Another shared that he listened to music to "remember our country", which was affirmed by a fellow student who said that he missed his homeland. Another response from a student was that he listened to music because "I am not free" to which his classmate added that "I don't know how to get free". One student who was quiet for a while said that he listened to music because he missed friends in Burma/Myanmar and those who had left for "third countries". Yet, another said in a soft but somewhat grim voice that he listened to music because "I don't know what going to happen in future". The student sitting next to him said he listened because nothing else could console him. The last response was by a student who said that she did not know "how to stand by ourselves" without music.

I then asked, "How does music help you?" Some of them responded that it "depended on the words of music". Another uttered that it helped her "forget our thinking". Some students added that music helped them to "visualize mothers, lovers, country, family", that is, "about the past". A couple of them added that music "encourages us to care… to love".

In this regard, Naw Wah Wah's answer to my essay question — how does music relate to the tradition of cross-border Karens? — is illuminating. Her passage, in her homework, shows how music strengthened "caged life" in "camps":

> To cross border Karen area there are many refugee camp. When we live in refugee camp. We are not allowed leave. We have no freedom. We are confined and feel like Caged Life. Other people said that we have no hope. Sometime we sad and listening to music or produce the music to give us strengthing, faith, satification, and music can make strong emotion, and encourage us.
>
> When we live in camp we remember our homeland but we cannot do anything at that time we sing a song about our once we have our own place but now we far away. that is very disappointed about that but when we sing a song some word give us strong emotion, not to give up. We should try hard. To do the best thing when we live in refugee camp.
>
> Music also very important to cross border Karen. When we sing a song about national song that is remind a bout the past not to forget past history, to let the next Karen generation about the past. To maintain culture, traditional belief and music. We know that if we for get that we nation will be lost (Naw Wah Wah, August 2008).

For Naw Wah Wah, living in the shelter area saddened her and others. Life without freedom became an unbearable life, but music soothed and strengthened them. She also emphasized that music functioned as a reminder of the past, as she put it clearly, "When We sing a song about national song that is remind about the past not to forget past history... *We know that if we for get that we nation will be lost*" (my emphasis).

Technically speaking, Blae Koh is a "refugee camp", no matter what its official name is. Generally, a "refugee camp" means a special zone where cultural performances are aplenty. This is because peoples there have more free time as well as peculiar kinds of psychological and cultural needs. As Dwight Conquergood aptly states:

> Refugee camps are liminal zones where people displaced by trauma and crisis ... must try to regroup and salvage what is left of their lives. They are in passage ... not quite sure where they will end up or what their lives will become. Betwixt and between worlds, suspended between past and future, they fall back on the performance of their traditions as an empowering way of securing continuity and some semblance of stability. ... They are good reasons why in the crucible of refugee crisis, performative behaviors intensify (Conquergood 1988, p. 180).

DISCURSIVE FABRIC AND PERCEPTIBILITY

Why is music so powerful or consoling? One could argue that, for the displaced, to perform music is to participate in a moment when "sounds, images, and feelings fleetingly coalesce to create a place that feels like home" (Diehl 2002, p. 14; Bender and Winer 2001). This expression of the desire for home has a potential to become "a substitute for home" and to embody "the emotion attendant upon the image" (Seidel 1986, p. 11; quoted in Diehl 2002, p. 14). It is home-building and place-building through music. It is, to quote Steven Feld, an "acoustic knowing" that enables one to understand the nexus of "sound and felt balance in the sense and sensuality of emplacement, of making place" (Feld 1996, p. 87). Feld calls this kind of knowing acoustemology (ibid.). Answers from my three students — for an assignment: Give me one *Pwa K' Nyaw* (Karen) song that signifies who you are as a *Pwa K' Nyaw* and explain why — evinces this notion:

(1) I want to stay forever in you
V1. Oh, Kaw Thoo Lei that I love the most, is a wonderful place which
I was born.
Inherit that our ancestors left for us.
full with beautiful nature, everytime comfort my heart.
alot of treasure are in you give me advantage.

> V2. When the sun was rising on the mountain, you beauty was shining.
> Birds are singing with happiness.
> When the light has gonein the evening, every creatures are quiet
> Everything look beautiful in our Kaw Thoo Lei.
>
> Chorus. I always wish to see your beauty.
> To give me satisfaction.
> I will always remember you when I stay away from you.
> I want to stay forever in you.[17]
>
> (2) When we study at Mae Ra Moe River side,[18]
> We remember our Kaw Thoo Lei
> When we are in studying
> We miss Kaw Thoo Lei and our tear flow down
> (Beautiful of our Kaw Thoo Lei) ~ if we forget you
> Our righ han forget every things
> You are the place of our ancestors, the country of our grand parents.
> Oh! Beautiful Kaw Thoo Lei
> We always remember and miss you.

Three students chose these two songs to describe their identity of being *Pwa K' Nyaw*. The songs connected their identity as Karens with Kawthoolei, their homeland. Since they were staying in a "temporary shelter area", which was not Kawthoolei, this identity could only be confirmed through memory. Such identification by youths represents a larger scale reenactment of identity by all Karens who sing these songs. When the two songs are sung, strands of the past are reconnected with those of the present and the connections are tightened, strengthened and secured. At that moment, the songs allow the Karens to embrace one another and unite through some images that signify Kawthoolei. It is the intertwining of identity, space and memory. Within both songs, three discourses are interwoven: ancestors, nature and beauty. In the second song, a discourse of friendship is also added. All these discourses become tightly interwoven and reaffirm the desire to go "home".

In other words, Kawthoolei is a signifier of the space representing Karen ancestors. Its literal meaning is "a land free of all evils, famine, misery and strife". Kawthoolei does not have an exact territorial border although the Burmese junta designated the space called the "Karen State" across Thailand disregarding a reality that many Karens also reside in the Shan State as well as the Central Burma Basin, among others. When one sings these songs, the signified of *Karen-ness*, that many Karens wherever always perform and re-enact through those discourses, is reconfirmed. Such reconfirmation works through the signifier "Kawthoolei" as well as through memories about Kawthoolei. When this song is sung, this signifier takes them "home". This signifier is thus essential for both the singers and listeners. At that moment, "home" is being built again. "Home" that must not be forgotten, especially because he or she has been forcibly displaced: "... if we forget you, our righ han forget every things".

Songs like these evince music as a discursive fabric. Such fabrics result from an interweaving of many discourses — they are warp and weft woven as "fabrics" covering the displaced people's bodies, minds and souls so that they will not be "naked" or lonely. Most discourses, moreover, enable them to unwittingly maintain their forms-of-life. Such discourses are, for example: nation, home, homeland, religion, natural beauty of their homeland, mother, family and friendship. Lyrics thus become a fabric covering their hearts and souls which have been wounded from war and displacement. As the forcibly displaced caged in the "cages", that is, the "temporary shelter areas", that confine their bodies, communities and ethnic nationalities, lyrics become an inscription not only of their perspectives of the present, but also their ethnic nationalities' histories.

Nonetheless, since these songs could "float" to listeners who are illiterate in Karen languages — or to non-Karen peoples who had the opportunity to appreciate Karen music and songs within spaces where the Karens were performing — an important question ensues. What are the implications of communicating in the Karen languages?

In the "temporary shelter areas", some had left their homes voluntarily, others involuntarily. Until the 2010 election, although the shelter areas had officially been operating for twenty-six years, communicating their plight, especially those of involuntary migrants, to the outside world had by and large been limited due to their lack of ability to communicate in other languages such as English and Thai. Elsewhere, I wrote:

> "...when those few who can write in languages that have a larger audience, such as English, they easily become unintelligible because the writers do not have adequate proficiency in English, like my student's story, and hence can be easily dismissed" (Decha Tangseefa 2006, p. 409).

In the case of my former students, these youth had been educated at the tertiary level over three years. Until then, the college had been providing the longest tertiary liberal arts education to migrant youth along the Thai-Burmese in-between spaces.[19] Moreover, the college had both foreign and

Karen instructors who had at least Bachelor's degree education. This meant that, in many ways, these students had been educated better than other displaced youth along the border, at least until the end of my fieldwork. The fact that the English proficiency of Naw Paw Paw, who wrote the email at the beginning of this article, was most likely the best among the 134 students of arguably the most elitist liberal-arts school along the border, was ominous. "It hints at dark clouds of silence covering those tormented bodies that have taken flight … [from] … the condemned border zones" (ibid.). She could not be regarded

> as a representative of either her peers or the majority of the forcibly displaced Karens fleeing fighting both inside Burma/Myanmar and on Thai soil. Hence, we have disregarded an inexhaustible number of stories because the writings are seemingly unintelligible (ibid.).[20]

Until the 2010 election, the displaced Karens, by and large, had to rely on others to voice their sufferings, which in the long term could be detrimental rather than empowering as the politics of representation would be intensified. In this light, writing lyrics and composing melodies had become enunciative and melodic vehicles for making themselves perceptible and intelligible, though only to those who understood their languages or have attempted to get closer to them.

NOT TO FORGET…

Some LMTC students left their home inside Burma/Myanmar; others were born on Thai soil, either inside or outside a string of shelter areas along the border. Even if they were born on the Thai side, as descendants of (what the Thai state labels) "people fleeing fighting", they have not, by and large, developed a sense of belonging with Thai society. This is because they were born in "spaces of exception" called "temporary shelter areas". As for those who were born outside such spaces, the sociocultural fabrics surrounding them have woven their identities into that of marginal Karens. Worse still, they are cross-border, marginal Karens, a phenomenon which has made marginalization even more complicated. Furthermore, many of these students were forced to leave their homes; they were part of what I call a passive voice of displacement. Such displacement has constructed a double marginalization — they are involuntarily cross-border, marginal Karens.

One must not forget that they were young persons, many of whom had experienced war or violence because of dictatorship rule. A question thus arises: How does war affect the young (cf. Boyden and de Berry 2005)? What is the price that "society" must pay when wounds from wars cut deep into both the bodies and psyches of the old and the young? Putting the word society in quotation marks is intended to address the whole human community, not only one nation-state. It is thus not only Thailand's or Burma/Myanmar's burden to bear. Every time there is a war, not only is the past killed, the future is detrimentally damaged as well. This is especially so for the young, as they will have to live longer than the old with wounds left by war. While I am writing these lines, I am reminded not to be celebratory about Burma/Myanmar's future.

Before the 2010 historic election, the *Tatmadaw* and its allies were wiping out resistant armed forces. The scene of more than 3,000 people fleeing fighting to the Thai side, as described in Naw Paw Paw's email, is just one act of a theatre of armed conflict along the border. Even now fighting in the Kachin State and violence against Muslims persist. All these wars and violence have not only killed soldiers, civilian lives have also been sent back to the soil. Many people and youth have become displaced as a result.

Within such a context, what do the young think? What do the young — who are the today of tomorrow — feel when they have to flee from "home", from the ones they love and care about? How do they articulate their feelings for their loved ones, lovers, friends, fellow nationals, or their nations? This article highlights how critical it is not only to listen to young voices, but also to be cognisant that theirs are the voices of essential agency. They are not only socialized, but they are also socializing themselves as well as their societies at large through their stories and cultural production and performance.

Although my students had never theorized such a nexus between music and home building, they at least were aware of how music enabled them to be "home" when visualizing their homeland. Had they known that the then Karen National Union (KNU) president — P'doh Ba Thin Sein — had said "We are a family without a home," they would not have disagreed.[21] Nonetheless, they were trying their best to construct their home while living in a cage. They were well aware that as long as they still had to be there, in a "temporary shelter area" — even though many of the shelter members had been there since 1984 — the discursive fabric called music was one of the very few things at their disposal that could carry them through life in a "cage". With its enunciative and melodic power, music covered their naked hearts and souls whenever they missed their loved ones or loved places. Music soothed their hearts and became representative of their homes, every time they sang or wrote songs. The hearth of music as home dwelled in the composers, the singers, and the listeners. At that moment "the family" was once again reunited. The hearth — as a fireplace — in each song warmed their lonely hearts and souls. As imperceptible naked-lives, they were covering their own bodies by writing the discursive fabric of music.[22]

Through music, they were also soothing the hearts and souls of their fellow Karen youth and any adult Karens interested in listening to their songs. It did not matter how little the world knew of their nakedness because they could not yet write English songs to voice their plight. At the very least, the music they had composed could remind them that they still had a national ethnicity called *Pwa K' Nyaw*. As painful as it was to weave discursive fabric about the lost *Pwa K' Nyaw* in war, they had to.

How can we forget?

(Father went to farm and went with a dog.
Mother take out a basket and followed the father.
Their little daughter stay at home
Carry the water, cooked the rice and cleaned her youngest brother.)~

Parents came back from the farm.
Their daughter prepared the dinner for them.
Father washed hand to eat.
After he washed his hand, the SPDC soldiers came and he ran away.

A little daughter and her mother couldn't run to escape.
After that, the SPDC soldiers tied them and burnd their house
A little daughter were durned and a mother were rapped
by the soldiers until her died.

Chorus. A daughter were burned
His wife were rapped
(So How will a father stay alife in his future life) ~[23]

Notes

1. This article is from my study "Music of the Hearth: Young Karens' Place-making in a 'Temporary Shelter Area'" (Decha Tangseefa 2010*b*, 2013), which was part of an umbrella research project led by Prof Yos Santasombat and supported by the Thailand Research Fund (TRF). Apart from my deep gratitude to my teacher Yos, I am also grateful to my two reviewers: Ajarns Attajak Sattayanurak and Yukti Mukdawijitra. The study was impossible without my three wonderful research

assistants: Warapree Tangseefa, Prapaipit Olanwat, and Krishna Monthathip. Most importantly, I am indebted to my Karen informants and friends.

The term "Karen" was originally used by outsiders, and its derivation is uncertain (Marshall 1922, pp. 6–8; Marshall 1945, p. 2; Hayami and Darlington 2000, p. 137). The Karens were officially renamed by the ruling State Law and Order Restoration Council (SLORC) in 1989 as "Kayin", a name that, at least until the historic 2010 election, the Karen nationalist leaders had rejected "as strongly as they" did "the historic Burman term for their country, Myanmar" (Smith 1999, p. 37). Under the term Karen, there are three major groups: the Pwo, the Bwe, and the Sgaw (Marshall 1922, p. 1).

In Father Sangermano's document, one of the earliest descriptions (Silverstein 1980, p. 15) written in the last quarter of the eighteenth century, the Karens are called "Carian" (Sangermano 1966, p. 44). In Michael Symes' book written afterwards, the Karens are referred to as "Carayners" or "Carianers" (Symes 1800, p.: V.2: 108). Because the Karens are composed of more than twenty subgroups, the term *"Pga K'Nyaw"* which is how the *Sgaw* Karen call themselves cannot be claimed to refer to the Karen peoples as a whole (Marshall 1945, p. 2).

In this article, the Republic of the Union of Myanmar is called 'Burma/Myanmar' in order to acknowledge the official name, Myanmar, as well as to emphasize traces of the Burmese junta's attempt to Burmanize the whole social fabric of this land, which has also had a deep impact on both the peoples and spaces along the Thai-Burmese/Myanmar border.

The Karen National Union (KNU) is one of the major governing bodies of the Karens. Before the 2010 election, the KNU had been one of the last remaining armed resistance organizations and the longest-standing one in Burma/Myanmar. They had fought against the Burmese Government since the official announcement of, as they call it, their "revolution" on 31 January 1949.

The Democratic Karen Buddhist Army (DKBA) broke away from the KNU toward the end of 1994, before the fall of Manerplaw on 27 January 1995. However, not long before the election on 7 November 2010, parts of the DKBA returned to join the KNU. Recently, the DKBA was renamed the Democratic Karen Benevolent Army.

The State Peace and Development Council (SPDC) was the official name of the Burmese junta. The council had previously been the SLORC (State Law and Order Restoration Council) in 1997. It was officially dissolved when Senior General Than Shwe signed a decree on 30 March 2011. Burma/Myanmar's Armed Forces are called the *Tatmadaw*.

2. There are two reasons for using quotation marks for the term "temporary shelter area". First, the term temporary negates a reality that shelter areas along the Thai-Burmese border zones were officially established in 1984 and hence have been in existence for thirty years. An entire generation was born and raised during that time. Hence, the term temporary does not capture this reality, though one could understand that it is the Thai state's intention to emphasize the temporariness of

the residence of those staying in these spaces and on Thai soil. Second, peoples who have come to be involved with these shelter areas call them "camps". In 2001, while I was interviewing the Ministry of Interior's (MOI) personnel who supervised a shelter area, I unconsciously called the shelter "camps" and was corrected by MOI personnel almost every time I uttered the word "camps". Moreover, since Thailand is not a signatory of the 1951 Convention Relating to the Status of Refugees as well as the 1967 Protocol Relating to the Status of Refugees, the term "refugee" is not part of the official lexicon of the Thai state, which designated forcibly displaced peoples from Burma/Myanmar, as "people fleeing fighting". Nonetheless, although the term "refugee camp" is not officially used by the Thai state's apparatuses, it has been used by a variety of people who have come to be involved with these shelter areas (see more details in Decha Tangseefa 2007).

In this article, the shortened form Blae Koh, the name that Karen shelter-residents use, is preferred instead of the Blae Koh "temporary shelter area" unless it is necessary to use the term in an official capacity. This discursive practice is used to record names from the Karens' perspective, as a way of recording their memories so that they will not be easily forgotten.

3. Interview of a displaced person. Interviewed by two fieldworkers, Karen State, Burma/Myanmar, 5 May 2011.
4. For the Sgaw Karen, the female name is preceded by Naw and the male by Saw. A female teacher's name is preceded by Th'aramu and a male's by Th'ara.

All quotations in this article are cited verbatim. Except for changing my students' names, following ethnographic etiquette, I mostly retain the original ungrammatical and/or misspelled text for an important reason that will become clear below.

5. Repatriation, it may be, however. Since many people were born and have been raised in these shelter areas since their official establishment in 1984, the notion of repatriation as returning home for them could become problematic. Not to mention that many of them have never been to Burma/Myanmar, their so-called "homeland". For a very interesting study on repatriation, see Hammond (2004).

On the process of repatriation, a few crucial questions arise: to what extent have decision-makers listened to shelter residents' voices, involved them in such a process and ascertained that the process has been adequately transparent? The decision-makers must not forget that one of the most important principles of repatriation is voluntariness — so that when it takes place, it will not be a forced repatriation.

Since August 2013, I have been part of a research project commissioned by Thailand's National Human Rights Commission to conduct research in shelter areas in order to: a) study shelter residents' livelihoods; b) assess their needs if and when repatriation will take place. In other words, the study aims to contribute to concerned parties' attempts to ensure that whatever happens to these shelter residents, when all shelters are closed, it will be a durable solution.

6. My studies on the forcibly displaced Karens have been inspired by Kierkegaard (1983) and Benjamin (especially 1968). The conception of exception deployed has mainly been influenced by Agamben's work (especially 1998, 2000, 2005). Agamben's is a decisionist notion of exception, which, in turn, is influenced by Carl Schmitt (especially 1985). For my development of this conception for studying the displaced Karen, see Decha Tangseefa (2003, 2006, 2007 and 2010*a*).
7. Due to limited space, please see Decha Tangseefa (2010*b*) for more details of the disciplinary practices of the college. For the shelter area as a disciplinary space, see Decha Tangseefa (2007). Surely, the conception of docile bodies here is influenced by Foucault (1978).
8. For the concepts of form-of-life, naked life, as well as relations between sovereign power and human life, see Agamben (1998, 1999 and 2000) as well as Decha Tangseefa (2003, 2006, 2007 and 2010*a*).
9. Aristotle 1995, 1253*a*, pp. 7–18.

    See my discussion of the nexus between language and perceptibility, especially regarding the displaced Karens in Decha Tangseefa (2006). As for my direct treatment of the conception of perceptibility, see Decha Tangseefa (2003, 2007 and 2010*a*).
10. As a researcher attempting to make the displaced Karens' plight perceptible, I must be inscribed by the Thai sovereign power as well (Decha Tangseefa 2007).
11. Although being inscribed means that they could be abandoned whenever Thai sovereign power deems necessary. For instance, in June 2009, the KNU was fighting with the DKBA on the right side of the Moei state boundary, about sixty kilometres north of Blae Koh. The DKBA finally seized the KNU's 7th Brigade which was the latter's strongest base. Due to the fighting, more than 3,000 people fled to the Thai side, the same group that Naw Paw Paw reported in her email above. Quite a few informants in Blae Koh told me later that one afternoon during the fighting, there were no Thai authorities at all in Blae Koh. There had been rumours that the DKBA had declared that they would not stop their campaign until they burnt Blae Koh down because they deemed that this shelter area had been a very important hiding ground of the KNU's operatives. It meant that more than 50,000 of Blae Koh's residents were left to protect themselves. Given that Blae Koh (and most of the other eight shelter areas) are located in very remote areas, far away from communities where Thai citizens live, leaving them without protection was possible because it would not have affected the Thai communities closest to these areas.

    One could also argue that the Thai State would not have allowed any troops to cross the state boundary and attack Blae Koh. However, such an attack has happened before, for example, in 1997 (see Decha Tangseefa 2007). More importantly is how forms-of-life could become naked lives because a figure of sovereign power left them vulnerable to threats from another sovereign.
12. See the complex relations between door and body in Decha Tangseefa (2007). I was also inspired by Kafka's *Before the Law* (1984, pp. 213–15) and constructed

the Thai-Burmese border version of "Before the Law" with great help from Brian Richardson.
13. *Gandharva* is a name used for mythological beings in Hinduism and Buddhism. It is also a term for skilled singers in Indian classical music. For more details on musical subjects "flying over" the shelter fences, see Decha Tangseefa (2010*b*).
14. Results from survey questionnaires that our team collected corresponded with data from case studies and in-depth interviews. For more details, see Decha Tangseefa (2010*b*).
15. Krishna Monthathip had not only been a part of a band during his high school years, but had been playing the guitar and a few other instruments for more than ten years. Hence, he had developed a much keener sense of musical ability than I had. Moreover, because he was of similar age to the LMTC students, they treated him as a friend. During the fieldwork, Krishna and his friends spent a lot of time learning about each others' lives, comparing the lives of those living outside the shelter area with those living inside. These comparisons were later analysed as contextual knowledge of youth in this space by our team. This method of information gathering followed one of the most important methodologies of this research: anthropology of children and childhood. With this methodology, all youth involved with this study were part of the research team and not just "research assistants" in the strict sense of the term. This research method was not without its obstacles though (see more details in Decha Tangseefa 2010*b*, 2013).
16. Since my first journey into the displaced Karens' communities in 2000, I have gradually developed an admiration for how well Karen peoples sing and how pervasive music has been in their social fabric (cf. Marshall 1922; Renard et al. 1991). However, there are degrees of difference between Christian and Buddhist Karens. Music is intimately tied to Christian Karens' social lives because of their religious practices at least during the weekend, whereas for the Buddhists, music does not play such an instrumental role. Hence, for the LMTC's Christian Karen students, singing as they walked, cooked, cleaned, and rested, was, by and large, a part of their quotidian modes. See how religion plays roles in some students' musical journeys in Decha Tangseefa (2010*b*, 2013).
17. While I was teaching in the college for three years, the medium of my instruction was English. Since I am illiterate in Karen languages, I needed to rely on translators. All songs were translated by two groups of young people: from Karen languages to English and from Karen languages to Thai. In order to ensure that the translated versions were as close to the original as possible, my team designed a four-step procedure: a) we asked my students, whose English were the best, to both cross-check and group-edit the English version; b) we compared the English versions with those of the Thai; c) consulted with translators to settle differences in the translated versions; d) we quoted the final English version verbatim (even if it was ungrammatical).
18. Two students chose this song in response to this assignment. Both did not provide the song's title. However, each had some slightly different translations and line

arrangements. Here, I chose the student whose language was more intelligible. His reason for choosing this song was: "This song is about Pa kanyaw who live [in] a refugee camp. Kaw Thoo Lei is Pa kanyaw home land. One day, Pa kanyaw will be back in Kaw Thoo Lei state."
19. For my development of the conception of "in-between space" see Decha Tangseefa (2003, 2006, 2009).
20. In this quoted article, see also my philosophical argument that opens a theoretical space for these forcibly displaced peoples.
21. One morning in December 2000, I had breakfast with the President and he mentioned this statement during our conversation.
22. See Decha Tangseefa (2003, 2010a) for my construction of the concept of imperceptible naked-life as an apparatus of recognition, following Agamben and Rancière (1999, 2001).
23. Composed by Saw Beck in 2004, two years before he came to study at the LMTC.

References

Agamben, Giorgio. *Homo Sacer: Sovereign Power and Bare Life*. Translated by Daniel Heller-Roazen. Stanford: Stanford University Press, 1998.

——. "The Messiah and the Sovereign: The Problem of Law in Walter Benjamin". In *Potentialities: Collected Essays in Philosophy*, edited and translated by Daniel Heller-Roazen. Stanford: Stanford University Press, 1999, pp. 160–74.

——. *Means without Ends: Notes on Politics*. Translated by Vincenzo Binetti and Cesare Casarino. Minneapolis: University of Minnesota Press, 2000.

——. *State of Exception*. Translated by Kevin Attell. Chicago: University of Chicago Press, 2005.

Appadurai, Arjun. *Modernity at Large: Cultural Dimensions of Globalization*. Minneapolis: University of Minnesota Press, 1996.

Aristotle. *Politics (Book I and II)*. Translated with a Commentary by Travor J. Saunders. New York: Oxford University Press, 1995.

Bauman, Zygmunt. *Society Under Siege*. Cambridge: Polity, 2002.

Bender, Barbara and Margot Winer, eds. *Contested Landscapes: Movement, Exile and Place*. Oxford: BERG, 2001.

Benjamin, Walter. "Theses on the Philosophy of History". In *Illumination*, edited by Hannah Arendt. Translated by Harry Zohn. New York: Harcourt, Brace & World, Inc., 1968, pp. 253–64.

Boyden, Jo and Joanna de Berry. *Children and Youth on the Front Line: Ethnography, Armed Conflict and Displacement*. Oxford: Berghahn Books, 2005.

Conquergood, Dwight. "Health Theatre in a Hmong Refugee Camp: Performance, Communication, and Culture". *Journal of Performance Studies* 32, no. 3 (1988): 174–206.

Decha Tangseefa. "Imperceptible Naked-lives and Atrocities: Forcibly Displaced Peoples and the Thai-Burmese In-between Spaces". Doctoral dissertation, University of Hawaiʻi, 2003.

——. "Taking Flight in Condemned Grounds: Forcibly Displaced Karens and the Thai-Burmese In-between Spaces". *Alternatives: Global, Local, Political* 31, no. 4 (2006): 405–29.

——. "'Temporary Shelter Areas' and Paradox of Perceptibility: Imperceptible Naked-Karens in the Thai-Burmese Border Zones". In *Borderscapes: Hidden Geographies and Politics at Territory's Edge*, edited by Prem Kumar Rajaram and Carl Grundy-Warr. Minneapolis: University of Minnesota Press, 2007, pp. 231–62.

——. "Reading 'Bureaucrat Manuals', Writing Cultural Space: The Thai State's Cultural Discourses and the Thai-Malay In-between Spaces". In *Imagined Land?: The State and Southern Violence in Thailand*, edited by Chaiwat Satha-Anand. Tokyo: the Research Institute for Languages and Culture of Asia and Africa (ILCAA), Tokyo University of Foreign Studies, 2009, pp. 121–44.

——. "Imperceptible Naked-lives: Constructing a Theoretical Space to Account for Non-statist Subjectivities". In *Margins, Peripheries and Excluded Bodies: International Relations and States of Exception*, edited by Shampa Biswas and Sheila Nair. New York: Routledge, 2010a, pp. 116–39.

——. "Music of the Hearth: Young Karens' Place-making in a 'Temporary Shelter Area'". Mimeographed. Bangkok: Thailand Research Fund, 2010b (in Thai).

——. "Learning, Longing and Lying: Youths' Musical Voices in a 'Temporary Shelter Area' along the Thai-Burmese Border Zones". In *Greater Mekong Subregion Underneath an Economic Quadrangle*, Yos Santasombat et al. Chiang Mai: Biodiversity and Indigenous Knowledge Research Center for Sustainable Development (BIRD), 2013 (In Thai), pp. 399–480.

Diehl, Keila. *Echoes from Dharamsala: Music in the Life of a Tibetan Refugee Community*. Berkeley: University of California Press, 2002.

Feld, Steven. "Waterfalls of Song: An Acoustemology of Place Resounding in Bosavi, Papua New Guinea". In *Senses of Place*, edited by Steven Feld and Keith H. Basso. Santa Fe: School of American Research Press, 1996, pp. 91–135.

Foucault, Michel. *Discipline and Punish: The Birth of the Prison*. Translated by Alan Sheridan. New York: Pantheon Books, 1978.

Foucault, Michel. "Of Other Spaces". *Diacritics* 16, no. 1 (1986): 22–27.

Hammond, Laura C. *This Place Will Become Home: Refugee Repatriation to Ethiopia*. Ithaca: Cornell University Press, 2004.

Hayami Yoko, and Susan M. Darlington. "The Karen of Burma and Thailand". In *Endangered Peoples of Southeast and East Asia: Struggles to Survive and Thrive*, edited by Leslie E. Sponsel. Connecticut: Greenwood Press, 2000, pp. 137–55.

Kafka, Franz. *The Trial*. Translated by Willa and Edwin Muir, revised, and with additional material translated by E. M. Butler. New York: Schocken Books, 1984.

Kierkegaard, Søren. *Fear and Trembling: Repetition*. Edited and translated by Howard V. Hong and Edna H. Hong. Princeton: Princeton University Press, 1983.

Marshall, Harry Ignatius. *The Karen People of Burma: A Study in Anthropology and Ethnology*. Columbus: The Ohio State University, 1922.

——. *The Karens of Burma*. Burma Pamphlets No. 8. Published for the Burma Research Society. London: Longmans, Green & Co., Ltd., 1945.

Rancière, Jacques. *Disagreement: Politics and Philosophy*. Translated by Julie Rose. Minneapolis: University of Minnesota Press, 1999.

———. "Ten Theses on Politics". *Theory & Events* 5, no. 3 (2001).

Renard, Ronald D., Ruthjaporn Prachadetsuwat, and Soe Moe. *Some Notes on the Karen and Their Music*. Chiang Mai: Center for Arts and Culture, Payap University, 1991.

Reyes, Adelaida. *Songs of the Caged, Songs of the Free: Music and the Vietnamese Refugee Experience*. Philadelphia: Temple University Press, 1999.

Sangermano, Father. *A Description of the Burmese Empire*. 5th ed. Translated by William Tandy, D.D. London: Susil Gupta, 1966.

Schmitt, Carl. *Political Theology: Four Chapters on the Concept of Sovereignty*. Translated by George Schwab. Cambridge: Massachusetts Institute of Technology Press, 1985.

Seidel, Michael. *Exile and the Narrative Imagination*. New Haven and London: Yale University Press, 1986.

Silverstein, Josef. *Burmese Politics: The Dilemma of National Union*. New Brunswich: Rutgers University Press, 1980.

Smith, Martin. *Burma: Insurgency and the Politics of Ethnicity*. 2nd ed. London: Zed Books, 1999.

Steiner, Niklaus, Robert Mason, and Anna Hayes, eds. *Migration and Insecurity: Citizenship and Social Inclusion in a Transnational Era*. New York: Routledge, 2013.

Symes, Michael. *An Account of an Embassy to the Kingdom of Ava Vol. 2–3*. London: Wilson and Co., 1800.

12

Life along the Naf Border: Identity Politics of the Rohingya Refugees in Bangladesh

Kazi Fahmida Farzana

INTRODUCTION

The effects of the June 2012 communal violence had barely faded away, when the ethnic Rohingya minority people in northern Rakhine (previously Arakan) State found themselves face-to-face with new existential challenges that included food shortages, malnourishment, and health crises. Amid these challenges, the Myanmar Government quickly swooped in and expelled international aid agencies, whose role was to provide aid to the displaced Rohingya. The Rohingya continue to flee their country in droves, fearing continued persecution and threats to their lives. There are about two million Rohingya in Myanmar, approximately 800,000 of whom live in northern Rakhine State. An estimated 328,500 now live in Bangladesh, as documented and undocumented refugees. About half a million have migrated to other parts of the world. Substantial numbers remain, on either side of the Naf River, where they lead displaced lives and face an uncertain future.

Externally, Myanmar's political transformation appears successful, with a large number of communities having gone "home", as they say, but the future of the ethnic Rohingya minority remains uncertain. Central to their uncertainty is the question of the group's political identity and hence its belonging. The Myanmar Government considers them "Bengali", "illegal immigrants", and "never" having been a part of Myanmar's history. Hence, they ought to be excluded from Myanmar's national identity. Meanwhile, the Bangladeshi Government maintains that the Rohingya were not originally from Bangladesh. They were not officially known until 1977, when they first crossed the border from Myanmar in huge numbers because of political upheaval in their land of origin. Hence, the Bangladeshi Government notes, they are rightfully labelled "refugees" and ought to return.[1] Such political denials on both sides increase the complexity of the situation, and prolong the crisis by pushing the Rohingya back and forth across state boundaries. This makes the border an intriguing part of Rohingya identity.

This chapter has two objectives: firstly, it explores how the state created sociopolitical identities for the Rohingya people in the context of the historical development of Myanmar, and secondly, it examines how the Rohingya people define and construct their own identity given the politics of belonging they are enmeshed in within the context of the Naf border. While there is a growing body of literature on Myanmar's individual ethnic groups, such as the Karen/Kayin, Karenni/Kayah, Mon, Chin, Shan and Kachin, there have been comparatively few academic works specifically on the ethnic Rohingya minority group living along the Myanmar-Bangladesh border. The existing handful of studies dealing with the Rohingya refugees are by Bahar (2010), Berlie (2008), Habibullah (1995), Karim (2000), Rahman (2005), Razzaq and Haque (1995), Saltsman (2009), Wong (1996), Yegar (1981) and Yunus (1994). Although these are important pieces of research covering various aspects of the Rohingya population, none has addressed the issue of identity construction from the refugee group's perspective. This reflects how neglected this group has been even among scholars.

This chapter adopts an ethnographic approach in addressing the central questions posed earlier. It explores the social construction of identity formation among the refugee population by analysing textual clues found in Rohingya narratives and cultural life (specifically, in music and art). To do so, it first focuses on the historical settings in which political boundaries were created. Second, it discusses state-imposed boundaries that have been prescribed onto people, creating and separating identities. Third, it analyses refugees' narratives and their documentary records which they use to construct a distinct collectivity — "the Rohingya refugees, an exiled nation from Arakan" — and as informal resistance to their experiences and sufferings. The chapter concludes by arguing that, although these narratives were reproduced during the refugees' exiled life in Bangladesh, they provide clues to, and should be regarded as, a part of the Rohingya's construction of reality, and should therefore have a place in the discourse of constructions of the Rohingya problem in Myanmar. It is hoped that this cultural perspective will bring about a deeper understanding of "the Rohingya problem", and raise awareness of a group that has remained weak and systematically marginalized.

METHODOLOGY

The data for this chapter came from six months of ethnographic fieldwork conducted between 2009 and 2010 in southeastern Bangladesh, adjacent to Myanmar, as part of a large-scale research study on the Rohingya refugees' identity, perceptions and exiled life in the area. Data was drawn from my interviews with sixty-two respondents, half of whom were registered refugees from United Nations High Commissioner for Refugees (UNHCR) Nayapara camp, and the remaining were undocumented refugees living in the Cox's Bazar sub-district of Teknaf Upazila in Bangladesh. The bulk of my fieldwork involved interviewing the refugees about their life stories, individually and in small focus-group discussions. While conducting the research, I discovered that ethnographic observation opened the door to non-conventional aspects of refugee life, as contained in their drawings, songs and poems. In all, I collected thirty-two drawings and twenty-one songs from the refugees interviewed. This chapter will explain, using three of their drawings and two songs, how their artistic renderings illustrate their perspectives and deep longing for their homeland, their perceived identity, and their sense of belonging. These are invaluable primary documents.

In analysing the content of their songs and drawings, I have tried to hold true to the refugees' perspective, in terms of what they had to say about these texts, as well as from my understanding as a researcher, in explaining the texts. My purpose in using these artefacts was to bring out their voices, and the individuals behind those voices. I understood the music and drawings to be symbolic expressions of the refugees' identity and reflections of their stranded situations.

HISTORICAL CONSTRUCTION AND REPRESENTATION OF ROHINGYA ETHNIC MINORITY

Until recently, and in the Rohingya's distant and distinct memories, the Naf River, which today borders Myanmar and Bangladesh, was not originally conceptualized in their historical past as the "boundary" — or line separating two political jurisdictions — between two communities. The area's history is redolent with accounts of Rohingya having travelled back and forth over the centuries, across the river, which is now widely viewed as delineating a boundary. As Amartya Sen pointed out, "the geographical areas, now northern Arakan or Rakhine state, changed hands among neighbouring feudal rulers and boundaries were always elastic in the old pre-colonial days" (quoted in Maung Zarni 2013, p. 3).

Perhaps the geographic location of Rakhine State, separated from central Myanmar by the Mayu mountain range, is also an important factor that binds this group into a sociological unit. The region's pre-colonial historical background suggests that Arakan or Rakhine State was not always a part of Myanmar. In 1459, the Arakan kingdom conquered Bangladesh's Chittagong district and ruled until 1666, when the Mughals seized control. From the fifteenth to seventeenth centuries, the Mrauk U (the ancient name of Arakan) Kingdom had a good relationship with the Bengals of India, which explains the Bengali influence in Arakan. As Blackburn explained, during this time, "an attitude of tolerance prevailed, with Theravada and Mahayana Buddhism, together with Brahmanism, Hinduism, Animism and other beliefs flourished side by side" (Blackburn 2000, p. 14).

The Arakan issue traces its origin to 1784, when the Burman King Bodawpaya conquered and incorporated the Arakan region into the kingdom of Ava in central Burma. Following the Burmese invasion, continued disorder was reported, as the Arakanese started rebelling against Burmese oppression (Harvey 1967, p. 280). The relationship between the state of Arakan and the Burman king was marked by animosity and deep mistrust. As the British prepared to take over Myanmar in 1824, the Arakanese, who were oppressed by the Burman king, decided to extend their support to the British colonial masters.[2]

COLONIAL PERIOD

One important factor in Myanmar's colonial history was the British policy of "divide-and-rule", which sparked historic ethnic tensions between different communities during the colonial period. The British abolished the monarchy and introduced dual administration to Burma. In the 1920s, a limited form of parliamentary Home Rule was introduced in ministerial Burma by the British. In contrast, the ethnic, minority-based frontier areas became subject to positive discrimination. In the Karen and federal Shan states, traditional rulers were allowed to retain their titles and to continue to govern the areas under their control. That was how colonial history came to create the idea of ethnic boundaries and enforced territorial ownership.

Secondly, the British favoured individuals from different ethnic and religious groups, who were, consequently, able to reach the higher echelons of the colonial services (Smith 1999, p. 23). During this time, Arakanese, Karen, Shan and many other minority groups in the peripheral states collaborated with the British colonial powers against the Burmese state.[3] This antagonism was pivotal, and eventually resulted in distinct boundaries between the Arakanese and the Burman. This physical border was viewed by nationalist Burmese as an affront, and the antagonism remained in the background when state decisions were made, post-independence.

Thirdly, for administrative convenience, the British ruled Burma as a province of colonial India from 1886 to 1937, after which it was declared a separate, self-governing colony. This administrative rearrangement stimulated intra-regional labour flows, further prompting inward-migration to Burma until about 1937. These large-scale historic movements included millions of Chinese and Indians (Dupont 2001, p. 143). Indian workers were often the hired help on plantations, docks and municipal services (Brookes 2000, p. 161). Many of the Indian labourers stayed on in Burma after the departure of the British. The Burmese Government often claimed that the Rohingya first entered Burma during the colonial years. However, it does not differentiate between the Rohingya Muslim Arakanese who had settled in the area since the ninth century (Yegar 1972, p. 2), and those who settled much later, during the British era. The Burmese nationalists regarded the British as their arch-enemy, and hence those who collaborated with the British were also viewed as their enemies.

British colonization eventually created political and social conditions that gave rise to indigenous independence movements. However, the British exploited the minorities' aspirations for their own benefit, and abandoned them when it suited them. Although it was the British authorities that had encouraged nationalist campaigns among the minority groups, they did not take responsibility for them afterwards.[4] The artificial and arbitrary boundary lines drawn by the British colonial authority between India and Burma, separated and divided the minorities in the borderland.[5] As Edmund Leach observed, "Burma as represented on a modern political map is not a natural geographical or historical entity; it is a creation of the armed diplomacy and administrative convenience of late nineteenth-century British Imperialism" (Leach 1963, p. 125).

There are allegations that, at this stage, prior to 1947, several Muslim Rohingya leaders lobbied to incorporate Arakan to (East) Pakistan, rather than Burma, but this failed (Tinker 1957, p. 34). Subsequently, following Burma's independence in 1948, the situation in these peripheral states deteriorated, and conflict with the Burmese Government increased. With independence, the Burmese Government incorporated Rakhine State into the national territory, but failed to incorporate its diverse population. The Rohingya were treated as second-class citizens, and discriminated against due to their race, religion, and role in history. Therefore, it can be argued that the mapping of the new state started a battle for the Rohingya minority that has yet to be resolved. The evolving nature of borderlands' geography has played an important role in inducing, reshaping, and complicating the Rohingya identity in the borderland. Therefore, an understanding of the border's historical context is crucial. The impact of these major historical events connects with the current treatment of the Rohingya within Myanmar.

STATE IMPOSED BOUNDARIES IN SHAPING IDENTITY

To understand the Myanmar State's attitude in the post-independence era, we need to relate it to the modern conceptualization of the state, which represents "us" and creates "them". Hence, the "us" represents a homogenous population perceived to have a common culture, common history, common language, religion and so on. Those who fall outside of the mainstream population of the state are "them" or "others"; therefore, they often remain marginalized.[6] The failure of the Myanmar state to accommodate its diverse minorities, including the Rohingya population, is thus due to its built-in limitations. This has been reflected in state attitudes since its independence. In contrast with Aung San's (the leading architect of Burma's independence movement) liberal stance towards minorities, the post-independence leaders, such as U Nu of the Anti-Fascist Peoples Freedom League (AFPFL), argued that British policy, which had artificially created ethnic, cultural and territorial divisions, was to be replaced by national unity through the development and use of a common language, education system and a national culture. The minority leaders saw this nationalistic approach as a violation of promises Aung San had made, and a threat to their own cultural and ethnic distinctiveness.

State policy is such that the Burmans/Bamar dominate Burmese society, and minorities are relegated to the periphery. The Burmans/Bamar perceived the Rohingya as enemies, for having collaborated with the British and, therefore unsuitable for promoting a sense of national solidarity. Religion became a tool with which Burmese Government officials constructed notions of belonging. The Rohingya, being Muslim, were represented as "other" because they did not practise Buddhism, the dominant religion in the country. The Rohingya were deemed inferior "outsiders", justifying an exclusion from benefits that were reserved for "insiders".

This act of "other-ing" was very vividly expressed, from the very beginning of the country's independence, and written in its constitution.

The Constitution of September 1947 is explicitly discriminatory, with the different ethnic groups treated differently: the Shan, the Kachin, the Karen, the Karenni and the Chin were named "a constituent unit of the Union of Burma" and were awarded the voluntary right of secession after a ten-year trial period, whereas the Mon and the Arakanese ended up "without even a state of their own" (Smith, 1994, p. 24; The Constitution of the Union of Burma: Chapter X, Section 202).

Successive Myanmar authorities' citizenship policies were shaped to fit their own inclusion-exclusion strategy. Ethnic exclusion has been codified in law. For example, Army General Ne Win and his Burma Socialist Programme Party (BSPP) drastically changed the constitution and the Burma Citizenship Law (1982), making the Rohingya non-citizens, including the generations that had been born in the country. The Rohingya of Arakan were thus transformed into a stateless minority, and their community identity undermined. This imposed stateless identity had a radical impact on their lives, and labelled them as deviant.

The state's claim to boundary in the process of identity formation is reinforced through military installations. As part of nation-building policy, the Myanmar Government militarized its troubled border areas to secure the borderland zones (Callahan 2004, p. 103). The *Tatmadaw* has established several military bases close to Rohingya settlements.[7] This has effectively brought about the social separation of ethnic minorities. Moreover, it was not just about military presence; systematic coercion, surveillance and demand for forced labour also made a tremendous impact on the Rohingya's everyday lives. The community faced many restrictions, such as a two-child limit, were outlawed from marrying Buddhists, and faced restrictions on their movement.

That was how the state of Myanmar differentiated between social groups, separating the Rohingya as "others", and distorting people's understanding of history. The problem, therefore, is deeply embedded in the complex historical development of the country, as well as in government policies of exclusion and ethnicization that have shaped the boundaries of this minority (Farzana 2010, p. 106). As Charles Taylor argued in his *Politics of Recognition*:

> Our identity is partly shaped by recognition or its absence, often by the misrecognition of others, and so a person or group of people can suffer real damage, real distortion, if the people or society around them mirror back a confining or demeaning or contemptible picture of themselves (Taylor 1992, p. 225).

Clearly, the misrecognition of the Rohingya community by the Myanmar state was tuned to the needs and aspirations of the dominant community; and the Rohingya people being the subordinate group continued to be marginalized within the state of Myanmar. In the process of "us" and "other-ing" it is the viewpoint of the state authority which prevailed. It is the state which defined the Rohingya. But what do the Rohingya say about themselves? The following section looks at the Rohingya's understanding and construction of their identity and how they represent their community.

ROHINGYA REFUGEE IDENTITY POLITICS ALONG THE BORDERLINE

Lately, Rohingya identity has become highly political, producing a politics of identity in which the "other" organize themselves to "achieve the recognition that they believe is being unfairly withheld from them" (Cox 2002, p. 161). In other words, the excluded have not necessarily accepted their exclusion. Rohingya people living in exile construct their own community identity through collective memory. Refugees' memories of Rakhine State, and their present memories in exile in Bangladesh, have been expressed through their narratives and their cultural life using aesthetic expressions such as songs (*taranas*) and drawings.[8] These are produced by ordinary refugees as natural expressions of mind and self; therefore, these are highly significant in illustrating their sense of identity and belonging, and in expressing a different form of resistance, without direct confrontation or protest, against the discrimination they have experienced.

The Rohingya Construction of *Desh* (Homeland)

The use of visual art (drawings and paintings) is quite common among the Rohingya. Although, they do not intentionally use this or send them on to the authorities as coded messages, they use it to tell stories to their children and to explain why they are in exile, and to send messages to outsiders interested in their case.[9] However, whether it is verbal expression or visual expression, a concept that repeatedly appears is desh which refers to their "homeland". For example, in the drawing below (Figure 12.1), Kalaya Chan, forty-four years of age, a refugee of Nayapara camp, explicitly wrote "Arkan Desh" on his drawing.[10]

This artwork, as he described, has many dimensions. First, the word *desh* refers to the Arakan/Rakhine State of Myanmar. During interviews, the refugees often mentioned "*arar desh vagi diche*" highlighting that their

FIGURE 12.1
Drawing 1: Peaceful Rakhine State in the Distant Past

Source: Kalaya Chan, forty-four, a refugee from Nayapara camp, drawing used with his permission.

homeland was destroyed, and that is why they had to choose a life in exile. Here, *desh* not only means "birthplace", but also a connection with the land, with one's family, relatives, and society. They feel a strong attachment to their home which is not far away (just on the other side of the Naf River). The second dimension of this drawing is that it presents an idyllic peaceful pastoral scene showing how home is imagined. In the distant past, home is constructed as peaceful life, where people were mostly involved in agriculture, where life's blessings were portrayed through vast agricultural lands, freedom of work, and stability in life. The third dimension is that this constructed notion of homeland contrasts with the lived reality of life in Rakhine State: statelessness, loss of livelihoods and physical insecurity. Home in reality is not the same as it is imagined. They realize that home does not welcome them, and life in exile in refugee camps does not allow them to settle. This contrast motivates the Rohingya to hold on to their roots, their homeland and the need to fight for it.

Fighting for the Homeland

Struggle for a homeland is indicative of a claim of belonging and identity; and in the case of Rohingya refugees such a claim and identity are expressed through cultural channels such as songs. Songs or *taranas* are quite widespread among the Rohingya and they play an important role in the life of the displaced Rohingya community. They are produced and used by ordinary refugees from every strata of life — registered and unregistered, male and female, rickshaw pullers, day labourers, and even beggars. The major types of songs they sing are country songs, religious songs, and songs that represent their everyday life in camp. Among these, country songs are the most popular within the registered as well as unregistered refugees. For example, Ismail Hossain, a forty-year-old male refugee from Nayapara camp, composed the patriotic *tarana* below (Figure 12.2).

Ismail Hossain crossed the border into Bangladesh with his parents in 1991, when he was just nineteen years old. During his twenty-one-year exile in Bangladesh, he married a Rohingya woman, and fathered six children. In 2005, his father died of natural causes in the camp. His elderly mother currently lives with him and nine other siblings who live in huts next to his. He recalled his early years in Rakhine State, pointing to their lack of rights, and described being punished with hard labour for having supported Aung Sun Suu Kyi's party in the 1990 elections. He also spoke of the military's frequent raids, of children dying of hunger, and families being separated. It was for these reasons that his family, like many others, chose refugee life in Bangladesh (interview with Ismail Hossain 2009).[11]

When Ismail sang this song, some refugees spontaneously joined in the chorus, indicating the popularity of this song among ordinary camp

FIGURE 12.2
Rohingya Song 1

ARKANI ORIGINAL	ENGLISH TRANSLATION
Dukkho-shuker gaan	***Rhymes of Sorrow and Happiness***
Oo Rohingya vai shuinno ni	O fellow Rohingya lend me your ears
Inka kam koriba ni	Come to a mission O dear
Mog Bormar loi joddho kori	Let's fight with the Mogs of Burma
Shonar Arkan goriba ni	And let's build our golden Arakan

Source: Ismail Hossain, a registered refugee living in Nayapara camp.

dwelling refugees.[12] The message of this song is to save Rakhine State for the Rohingya. Although the lyrics have never been committed to paper, the Rohingya have memorized it, and the words and music flow easily from them. Refugees mentioned that they sing it all the time, lest they forget their sacrifices and sufferings (*julm, nirjaton*) as a community in Rakhine State.

This *tarana* urges fellow Rohingya to join in the mission to fight against the Rakhine (Mogs), and to rebuild their golden homeland. This song articulates, from their viewpoint, that something went very wrong in their history, and they have consequently lost their homes. In their hearts, they have a steely resolve to take responsibility and "do something" to save their homeland. Thus apparently this song is designed to recruit individuals for the resistance movement that was active in the border area during the 1990s.[13] According to Ismail, the Myanmar military and Bangladesh border security have crushed their ability to be involved in active resistance. Yet, the song persists and circulates among ordinary Rohingya. Such a song definitely reflects a resistance to dominance and oppression. This also indicates that ordinary individuals are aware of their powerless situation. In Ismail's words:

> We are like people without knees (*amra hattu chara manush*), we are not able to protest against anyone (*arare je jen gorigo goruk, kichu koi no paijjum, biyagin shojjo koron poribo*), so *tarana* or songs/poems are the only way to tell our sorrows and sufferings to another person. That's how we keep our memory alive (interview with Ismail Hossain 2009).

The expression, "we are like people without knees", refers to the powerlessness that has prevented them from saying or doing anything against those who have displaced them from their homes and made their lives miserable. Yet this could not make them voiceless or make them stop resisting, in their own way, against all these injustices. Perhaps for them, this *tarana* serves as a constant reminder of their past, making their pain even more poignant.

Other studies have looked at various forms of resistance and various types of hidden transcripts that are used by the powerless. In this regard, James Scott's book, *Weapons of the Weak*, looked at powerless people's everyday resistance where they use signs and symbols, and a vocabulary of exploitation (Scott 1985, p. 292). Thus, when Jobeda Begum, a sixty-year-old Rohingya beggar, from unregistered Leda camp described her life in Myanmar as "whatever they want to do on us will do, we are not supposed to say anything, everything has to be accepted" (interview with Jobeda Begum 2009), she is referring to their subordinate status in their homeland and expressing their frustration because of the oppression they suffer.[14] Simultaneously, it clearly expresses negation of the system of domination. Weitz (2001, p. 670) referred to these as "actions that not only reject subordination but do so by challenging the ideologies that support that subordination."

Another patriotic song (Figure 12.3) entitled *Free Arakan* is particularly expressive showing the need for the Rohingya to fight for their homeland. It was composed by Muhammad Mojid, forty-six, a Rohingya singer and *tarana* producer who lives in Nayapara camp.[15]

This song captures the acute problem in Buthidaung — the Mogs' (Buddhist Rakhine) and the military's persecution of the Rohingya Muslims. Therefore, the song calls on fellow Muslims to take an oath to fight against the oppressors. It also makes reference to Muslim religious establishments that had been demolished by the military, and replaced with military establishments and settlements. Such acts significantly hurt the Rohingya's religious sentiment, and they set about to produce these *taranas* as their way of spreading the message to other Rohingya. The *tarana* was sung with huge enthusiasm and passion, as demonstrated by hand movements and

FIGURE 12.3
Rohingya Song 2

ARKANI ORIGINAL	ENGLISH TRANSLATION
Azad Arakan	**Free Arakan**
O mosolman punnoni, ekkhan hota raibani	O Muslims shall we make a promise
Mog Bormar loi juddho gori, Arakan azad chaibani (II)	Fighting with Mogs of Burma We will make Arakan free
Oi Ooo...Buthidongor taiman boli jai military	Behold! The march of military in Buthidaung
Ekhan Mosjid vangi banche tarar ghor-bari (II)	Demolishing a mosque there they built their home
Mosolman punnoni, inkalab gori ba ni	O Muslims, Shall we make a revolution
Mog Burmar loi juddho gori, Arakan azad chaibani (II)	Shall we free Arakan Fighting with the Burmese Mogs.

Source: Muhammad Mojid, forty-six, a Rohingya singer and *tarana* producer from Nayapara camp.

facial gestures. Songs like this demonstrate how music has been used as an effective means to remember many things of the past. These are painful memories that they hide as they go about their everyday lives. However, they continue to carry these memories in their minds and sustain them by composing songs.

Other studies have looked at music as a medium for marginalized communities to keep their history alive, preserve their identity and display passive resistance. Diehl (2002) studied the nexus between creativity and marginalization among the Tibetan refugee community in northern India. His study shows how music is used to express exile Tibetan identity and people's understanding of their new circumstances. Joseph Brodsky's work (1992) shows poetry or songs as a form of resistance to reality. According to him, people who have experienced tragedy "do not really care about the means by which tragedy is expressed" (Brodsky 1992, p. 221). When they produce musical art (poems or songs), the artist's own experience of physical pain, hunger and other dissatisfactions are intensely reflected through their productions. To him these are "true art[s]" which is "always democratic" as no one can subjugate them (ibid.). Similarly, in the case of the Rohingya exile community at the Bangladesh-Myanmar borderland, their production of music is significant; not only because it reflects their experiences and preserves their identity but also because it expresses their way of adapting to new circumstances. These songs are cathartic, and may demonstrate an indirect form of resistance that does not directly confront the oppressors, but simply expresses their refusal to accept their condition. Such songs are memories they carry and cherish in their everyday life, binding them through a common experience, as part of a displaced community. In this way, songs become a clear reflection of their identity.

Similar to songs, a drawing (Figure 12.4) by Anser Ullah, thirty-seven years old, an unregistered refugee, reflects the perceptions and beliefs of the Rohingya in terms of how they are treated by the Buddhist state and Buddhist monks in Rakhine State. It depicts a state official speaking to a group of monks (indicated by their orange robes and bald heads); the crowd shows their excitement by raising their hands in support. Close by, other monks are portrayed with sticks in their hands, beating ordinary Rohingya villagers.

This artistic production shows the clash of identities between the Rohingya (a powerless community) and the Rakhine and Buddhist monks. This perception of powerlessness of the Rohingya probably came from their awareness of state-imposed statelessness and therefore being unwanted at home. Exclusion from official recognition has made them subject to various

FIGURE 12.4
Drawing 2: Life in Rakhine State

Source: Anser Ullah, thirty-seven, an unregistered refugee from Maungdaw village, northern Rakhine State, drawing used with his permission.

forms of discrimination and persecution. During the interview, Anser Ullah, the producer of this art, mentioned that before the military came to power (1962), relations between the Rohingya and the Rakhine were not as conflict-ridden as it is now. Now as the Buddhist government discriminates and persecutes Muslim Rohingya, they encourage the Buddhist monks and Rakhine community to enact violence against the Rohingya so as to gain the government's favour (interview with Anser Ullah 2009).[16] Reports also show that the Burmese Government reportedly worded their propaganda in terms such as "*Tatmadaw* and the people, cooperate and crush all those harming the union" (Goldston 1990, p. 7). Unfortunately, these public announcements only stirred up more unrest.

The government and the Rakhine may have their own reasons for their construction of the Rohingya as "outsiders" that may be rooted in the political economy, the struggle over land rights and scarce resources and so on. The treatment of the Rohingya by the government therefore apparently may look rational in the sense that exclusion of non-citizens is necessary for defining national identity. Indeed, the official accounts of Myanmar and some historical documents suggest that government operations in Rakhine were basically counter-insurgency operations to dismantle the Rohingya's social and political organizations (Taylor 2001, p. 156). For example, during Operation Nagamin, the government justified its actions by saying that the operation would be a nationwide initiative to confirm citizenship by checking their identification cards. The attempt therefore was an effort to register citizens and check their identity cards, and screen out foreigners prior to a national census. Moreover, the Ministry for Home and Religious Affairs declared on 16 November 1977, that Operation Nagamin was an attempt to take "actions against foreigners who have filtered into the country illegally" (Smith 1999, p. 237). However, the majority of works on the Burmese history of minority treatment upholds the view that the government's purposive exclusionary policy has led it to adopt discriminatory measures that resulted in forced migration or internal displacement.

On the other hand, the Rakhine people might have different reasons from the government for behaving this way towards the Rohingya. Being one of the indigenous communities in Rakhine State, they may also view the Rohingya crisis as an opportunity for them to return to a time in the early period of the Arakan Kingdom, when it was dominated by Buddhist Rakhine. Perhaps they feel that their view was supported by the government's exclusionary approach towards the Rohingya. Whatever the reasons for Rakhine Buddhists' collusion with the government in persecuting the Rohingya (and other Muslims), it appears that all these conflicts have contributed to strengthening Rohingya identity.

An artwork like this illustrates a reality that is imperfect, therefore suggesting that a better alternative should be sought. It also clearly demonstrates the agony and hatred of the oppressed against the oppressors (both the government and the Buddhist Rakhine). The sectarian violence in Rakhine State that has been occurring since mid-2012 also explains the culture of distrust that has developed between the communities over many decades, a situation that is unlikely to disappear anytime soon. The conflict led to a vast number of Rohingya fleeing for their lives (Beech 2013, p. 20). Moreover, the Rohingya are aware of the politics of labelling. That is why, during the government registration process in November 2012 which attempted to categorize the Rohingya as "Bengali", the Rohingya refused to register, thereby indicating their resistance towards state-imposed "definition and manipulations of ethnicity, and hence criteria of belonging" (Oh 2012, p. 2).

Exile and the Formation of Collective Identity

Realities on both sides of the Naf River show that, for the Rohingya, life along the border is complicated and difficult. Life in exile in these temporary shelter areas is secluded, heavily controlled and monitored. It reveals the imposition of restrictions by one, or a combination of many authorities, on a group of people living in a designated "exceptional space" (Agamben 2000, p. 40). Figure 12.5 (Drawing 3) depicts Rohingya exile life in squalid refugee camps in Bangladesh. This drawing portrays the refugees' perspective, and illustrates that their only hope — for a better life across the border — has been shattered by their experience in Bangladesh. To them, life as documented or undocumented refugees is merely one of identity but in reality, still subjects them to similar restrictions and persecution. Life in exile, in congested living spaces, harsh conditions and a torturous social reality, provides no better option (Wade 2014).

In their narratives, and in their minds, the Naf River represents a boundary that divides Myanmar from Bangladesh. This is significant,

FIGURE 12.5
Drawing 3: Life in Bangladesh — At the Nayapara Refugee Camp

Source: Boshir Ahmed, a young refugee from Nayapara camp, drawing used with his permission.

because it means that, in their minds, the river symbolizes the international border between the two countries. As Boshir Ahmed said, "We came to this side to save our lives." — that is, they crossed over to Bangladesh with hopes that life would be different (interview with Boshir Ahmed 2009).[17] Unfortunately, living in exile in Bangladesh, they are again treated as "lesser" human beings. The literature on human rights abounds with examples of such torture, humiliation and continued persecution, and their eventual repatriation to Myanmar. As Boshir said, "We came from Burma to save our life leaving behind everything we had; now here [in Bangladesh], we face the same *julm* (persecution) again. What a pathetic life we have." His art expresses his deep sadness and his perspective about refugee life: of the loss of identity and the right to belong to some place. Therefore, it can be argued that their current situation is the direct consequence of a state's policy decisions. Their new identity as refugees did not replace the old. They are considered outsiders in Bangladesh as well.

Their representations point to a particular geographical space in Rakhine State where the refugees had once maintained their physical presence. People often developed a strong sense of belonging to their homeland, even if their citizenship rights were non-existent. Memories of a past are not easily erased by many years in exile, perhaps because of the many restrictions placed on them by the host state. As refugees, they are constantly reminded of their statelessness, foreign origin, and separate identity. They see their current exile in Bangladesh refugee camps as a zone of marginalization that does not allow them to forget their "otherness". Instead it reinforces the formation of their collective identity. This is the Rohingya representation of their past and present. What people write, draw and compose is a selected representation based on their experience. Here it shows that Rohingya suffering has created a collective consciousness of identity, expressed through their cultural life as they pronounce their frustrations together, recall their memories, transmit them to the new generation, and bond themselves together.

The foregoing discussion iterates several points. Firstly, Rohingya refugee narratives (verbal and visual) highlight a contrasting paradigm of identity perception, social reality and history. As opposed to the official claim that the Rohingya are foreigners and settlers, Rohingya narratives and cultural expressions suggest that, in their view, they are native and indigenous to Rakhine State. These means of artistic expression express their awareness and sense of belonging as to where they feel they really belong. They recognize Rakhine State as their ancestral homeland, from where they were forcefully displaced. Their rootedness in the land is so deep that, in their minds, their long absence from the land cannot delete their memories. Long residences, historical memories of place-building, rootedness to the land, are all part and parcel of developing a strong sense of place, a strong sense of belonging.

Secondly, these expressions also reflect their existence in statelessness. Hanna Arendt defined statelessness thus: "left their homeland they remained homeless, once they had left their state they became stateless, and once they had been deprived of their human rights they were rightless" (Arendt 1966, p. 267). Burmese society's ascription of "otherness" has impacted the Rohingya psyche, bringing to the surface their feelings of inadequacy and inferiority — a painful reminder of how sad their lives have become. Living in exile in Bangladesh, they have not found any respite. They are still subject to many of the same restrictions and abuses. Within this harsh and confined social context, their unhappy social memories of the past persist, refusing to fade. In their day-by-day experiences, negotiations, and manoeuvres in the refugee camps, they are constantly reminded of their "foreign" identity, their statelessness, and the temporariness of refugee life. Their struggles and anguish in Bangladesh may also be seen as an outcome of their original stateless situation. Thus, camp life is simply a miniature reproduction, reflecting the harsh realities from their distant past, as they continue to maintain their self-identity as Rohingya from Rakhine State.

Thirdly, lyrics of their songs and drawings are "live" stories of the Rohingya's social experiences and struggles, telling of their agony and hatred against those who have made their lives miserable and expressing their sorrows and frustrations as well as their resentment towards their home state, its military, and the local Rakhine. They resent the restrictions that have been placed on them in exile, and the many similar types of torture they have had to endure as they continue to challenge their oppressors. Thus, they resist, not only their socioeconomic and political conditions, but also the identity that has been imposed on them by officials and society, rendering them subjects without protection at the periphery of the law. As Joseph Brodsky noted, "Art is a form of resistance to the imperfection of reality, as well as an attempt to create an alternative reality, an alternative that one hopes will possess the hallmarks of a conceivable, if not an achievable, perfection" (Brodsky 1992, p. 221).

Fourthly, the Rohingya perspective clearly denies the state's version of them as non-citizens. As individuals, they are aware of overt discrimination. Their cultural life illustrates a non-confrontational resistance against such discrimination and calls for reform.

Finally, these are voices of the oppressed, and that makes it very significant. What it tries to achieve is some social equality, so that they may gain "a sense of social worth". Through cultural expression, they remind themselves, and the world, of who they are.

CONCLUSION

This chapter has looked at the three ways in which Rohingya identity has been constructed: first, through pre-colonial and colonial constructions and the formation of borders; second, the politics of belonging which was defined by the state in the process of developing Myanmar as a nation; and finally, through an ethnographic survey of the Rohingya refugees' cultural artefacts.

Historical evidence shows that border politics during the pre-colonial and colonial periods was fluid and people claimed belonging to either side of the Naf River. However, identity and claims of belonging became disputed during post-independence Myanmar. The Myanmar state's attempt to construct the Rohingya as outsiders has drawn on two things. First, the state's policy of unified nationalization and citizenship maintains its claim on land but denies the Rohingya living on it citizenship. Second, the Myanmar Government uses identity and cultural markers to distinguish the Rohingya from the rest of the populace. This, in combination with policies of exclusion, expulsion and persecution, has caused countless Rohingya to be displaced and/or to migrate. It has also resulted in an intense contestation over identity politics.

Living in exile in Bangladesh, the Rohingya cannot but be aware of the importance of the politics of identity. This is evidenced by the findings reported in this study. The ethnographic survey of the refugees' cultural artefacts such as drawings and songs confirm that Rohingya refugees strongly maintain the claim that northern Rakhine State is their homeland (*desh*). Second, persecution (by the Burman, Rakhine and Bangladeshi), powerlessness, particularly in the case of camp refugees, reinforces a sense of identity and solidarity. Third, identity markers such as Islam, language and so on have been emphasized so as to claim a separate identity. These are used to resist state-imposed notions of identity and belonging. The Rohingya cultural artefacts that are presented in this chapter, therefore, are part of the wider politics of belonging that is being played out by the state, the Rakhine population and the Rohingya themselves. The Rohingya are using all the tools available to them to claim their belonging to Rakhine State and hence to Myanmar.

These narratives/silenced histories demand political legitimacy, recognition, and respect. The Rohingya construction of reality suggests change and demands rights to their existence as a community, their claims to various forms of belonging, and could serve to deny officially imposed marginalized identities. As Myanmar continues to move forward, along with its "roadmap to democracy", this could open up prospects for more political developments, and offer a different approach — of tolerance in the face of diversity—and confidence-building among societies, through inter-dialogue and cooperation.

Notes

1. The first major Rohingya crisis recorded in history was in 1977 and 1978, when the military's "Dragon King Operation" forced over 200,000 Rohingya into Bangladesh (Mattern 1978, p. 31). By 1979, the majority had been returned to Myanmar under a repatriation agreement, but many were pushed back into Bangladesh by a military operation named *Pyi Thaya* [Prosperous Country] in the early 1990s. The current refugees in Bangladesh's refugee camps were those who had entered the country in the 1990s, during what is regarded as the second phase of cross-border migration.
2. The British imperial power colonized Burma for sixty-two years (1824–86), during which the British used Arakan as a buffer zone to invade mainland Burma. The first Anglo-Burmese War (March 1824–February 1826) occurred within the cross-border setting.
3. The British criteria in recruiting for its colonial armed forces further added fuel to border demarcations. For example, the Karen/Kayin formed the core of the British military forces in Burma. Although they formed less than 10 per cent of the total population, they were the largest group in the army, comprising 40 per cent of the Burmese Army. The British military force also deployed Karen/Kayin armed groups to suppress Burmese resistance to British rule (Moscotti 1977, p. 177). It undoubtedly created a conflict between the Burmese and the Karen/Kayin.
4. For example, the British in Malaya brought the Chinese and Indians to the peninsula. Upon their departure, the British ensured that both groups were constitutionally accepted into the system. However, they did not do so for the Rohingya in Myanmar.
5. The borders where the Karen/Kayin live were arbitrarily demarcated, so that their territory is now divided between Thailand and Myanmar.
6. When society constructs others it not only defines them as different, but also as minor (undeserving) and, at the same time, constructs the "us" as superior to the rest.
7. The Myanmar Government's military operation in northern Arakan began in 1962 with militarization and various operations in that area.

8. Songs and poems are quite popular among the displaced Rohingya community. These are commonly known as *tarana* in their language.
9. Because they fear that it would be more damaging and dangerous for them. However, they hope that the authority will notice and realize it one day.
10. All Rohingya names in this paper are pseudonyms. Interview in Teknaf. Interviewed by Kazi Fahmida Farzana, Cox's Bazar, Bangladesh, 19 January 2014.
11. Interview in Teknaf. Interviewed by Kazi Fahmida Farzana, Cox's Bazar, Bangladesh, 14 July 2009.
12. I could not verify if this song is also popular among unregistered refugees, but displaced unregistered refugees shared many country songs expressing their love and longing for their "homeland".
13. Allegedly, there were some active Rohingya resistance movements in the Bangladesh-Myanmar border. However, the Myanmar Government's military operations in Arakan that started from 1962 with militarization and various military operations in the area crushed all the movements. In 1997, the Bangladeshi Government also banned all forms of resistance movements within the Chittagong Hill Tracts area, and minority groups' fighters surrendered their weapons to the then government (Adnan 2005, p. 131). The Bangladeshi Government then militarized that area, and extended their activities to the northeastern part of the Bangladesh-Myanmar border area to disperse any possible Rohingya insurgency.
14. Interview in Teknaf. Interviewed by Kazi Fahmida Farzana, Cox's Bazar, Bangladesh, 12 June 2009.
15. Ibid., 15 December 2010.
16. Ibid., 4 November 2009.
17. Ibid., 28 July 2009.

References

Adnan, Shapan. "Ethnicity and Identity in South Asia: Managing the Divide". In *Engaging South Asia: Challenges and Opportunities*, edited by Hernaikh Singh and Jayan Jose Thomas. Singapore: Marshall Cavendish Academic, 2005, pp. 129–66.

Agamben, Giorgio. *Means without End: Notes on Politics*. Minneapolis: University of Minnesota Press, 2000.

Arendt, Hannah. *The Origin of Totalitarianism*. London: Harvest Book, 1966 [1958].

Bahar, Abid. *Burma's Missing Dots: The Emerging Face of Genocide*. Chicago: Xlibris Corporation, 2010.

Beech, Hannah. "The Face of Buddhist Terror". *Time* 182, no. 1 (1 July 2013): 14–21.

Berlie, Jean A. *The Burmanisation of Myanmar's Muslims*. Bangkok: White Lotus Press, 2008.

Blackburn, Terence R. *The British Humiliation of Burma*. Bangkok: Orchid Press, 2000.

Brodsky, Joseph. "Poetry as a Form of Resistance to Reality". *Publications of the Modern Language Association of America* 107, no. 2 (1992): 220–25.

Brookes, Stephen. *Through the Jungle of Death: A Boy's Escape from Wartime Burma*. London: John Murray Publishers Ltd., 2000.

Callahan, Mary P. "Making Myanmars: Language, Territory, and Belonging in Post-Socialist Burma". In *Boundaries and Belonging: States and Societies in the Struggle to Shape Identities and Local Practices*, edited by Joel S. Migdal. United Kingdom: Cambridge, 2004, pp. 99–120.

Cox, Kevin R. *Political Geography: Territory, State, and Society*. Oxford: Blackwell Publishers Ltd, 2002.

Diehl, Keila. *Echoes from Dharamsala: Music in the Life of a Tibetan Refugee Community*. Berkeley: University of California Press, 2002.

Dupont, Alan. *East Asia Imperilled: Transnational Challenges to Security*. Cambridge: Cambridge University Press, 2001.

Farzana, Kazi F. "Identity Formation and Policies of Exclusion and the Ethnicisation of 'Minorities' in Burma: A Comparative Study of Burmese Policies Towards the Rohingya, Karens and Shans". In *Ethnic Relations: Issues and Challenges*, edited by Maya Khemlani David, James McLellan, Ngeow Yeok Meng, Lean Mei Li, and Wendy Yee Mei Tien. Kuala Lumpur: Strategic Information and Research Development Centre, 2010, pp. 87–108.

Goldston, James. *Human Rights in Burma*. United States of America: Human Rights Watch, 1990.

Government of Myanmar. *The Constitution of the Union of Burma*: Chapter X, Section 202. Myanmar, 1948.

Habibullah, Muhammad. *Rohingya Jatir Itihas* [History of the Rohingyas]. Dhaka: Bangladesh Co-Operative Book Society Ltd., 1995.

Harvey, Godfrey E. *History of Burma: From the Earliest Times to 10 March 1824, the Beginning of the English Conquest*. London: Frank Cass and Co. Ltd., 1967.

Karim, Abdul. *The Rohingyas: A Short Account of their History and Culture*. Chittagong: Arakan Historical Society, 2000.

Leach, Edmund R. *The Political Future of Burma*. Geneva: Droz, 1963.

Mattern, William. "Burma's Brand of Apartheid". *Far Eastern Economic Review*, 14 July 1978, pp. 30–32.

Maung Zarni. *Analysis of the Report of Myanmar's Official Rohingya Ethnic Cleansing Inquiry Commission* (unpublished paper), 2013.

Moscotti, Albert. *Burma's Constitution and Elections of 1974*. Singapore: Institute of Southeast Asian Studies (ISEAS), 1977.

Oh, Su-Ann. "Rohingya or Bengali? Revisiting the Politics of Labelling". *ISEAS Perspective* no. 19 (December 2012).

Rahman, Abdur. *Rohingya Shamassa: Bangladesher Dristibhangi* [Rohingya Problems: Attitude of Bangladesh]. Dhaka: Islamic Foundation Press, 2005.

Razzaq, Abdul and Mahfuzul Haque. *A Tale of Refugees: Rohingyas in Bangladesh*. Dhaka: The Centre for Human Rights, 1995.

Saltsman, Adam. "Contested Rights: Subjugation and Struggle among Burmese Forced Migrants in Exile". Master's thesis, Boston College, 2009.

Scott, James. *Weapons of the Weak: Everyday Forms of Peasant Resistance*. New Haven: Yale University Press, 1985.

Smith, Martin. *Ethnic Groups in Burma: Development, Democracy and Human Rights*. London: Anti-Slavery International, 1994.
———. *Burma: Insurgency and the Politics of Ethnicity*. London: Zed Books Ltd., 1999.
Taylor, Charles. *Multiculturalism and 'the Politics of Recognition': An Essay*. Princeton: Princeton University Press, 1992.
Taylor, Robert. *Burma: Political Economy Under Military Rule*. New York: Palgrave Macmillan, 2001.
Tinker, Hugh. *The Union of Burma: A Study of the First Year of Independence*. London: Oxford University Press, 1957.
Wade, Francis. "Burma's Rohingya are Now Being Forced to Live in Squalid Ghettos Watched by Guards". In *Time*, 4 February 2014 <http://time.com/3982/rohingya-ghettos-of-burma/> (accessed 15 October 2014).
Weitz, Rose. "Women and Their Hair: Seeking Power Through Resistance and Accommodation". *Gender & Society* 15, no. 5 (2001): 667–86.
Wong, Elaine Siew Yin. *Comparative Political Geography of Ethnic Minorities Across Borders: The Muslim Minorities in Arakan and Pattani*. Bachelor of Arts (Hons) thesis, National University of Singapore, 1996.
Yegar, Moshe. *The Muslims of Burma: A Study of Minority Groups*. Jerusalem: Hebrew University Press, 1981 [1972].
Yunus, Mohammed. *A History of Arakan: Past and Present*. Riyadh: World Assembly of Muslim Youth (WAMY), 1994.

13

Home of the Housekeeper: Will Shan Migrants Return after a Decade of Migration?

Amporn Jirattikorn

Over the past two decades, economic hardship and political conflict have driven Burmese migrants, refugees and political dissidents across the border from Myanmar into Thailand at an unprecedented scale. According to estimates, the number of Burmese migrant workers in Thailand may have reached about three million whereas the number of Burmese asylum seekers registered with the United Nations High Commissioner for Refugees (UNHCR) approximates 15,000.[1] While the past decades saw a massive flow of Burmese nationals coming across the border into Thailand, in recent years a counter-current has emerged with the return movement of Burmese exiles to Myanmar. This is due to a series of political and economic reforms in Myanmar which began to take place in 2011. A new civilian government has loosened internet restrictions, freed political prisoners and pursued economic reforms to attract more foreign investors. As part of the reforms, in August 2011, Myanmar's president Thein Sein called on all exiles to return. According to government rhetoric, Burmese exiles' departure to escape persecution by the military resulted in a massive drain that deprived Myanmar of some of its best minds.

As a result, over the past two years, a growing number of Burmese political exiles have returned to their home country. Returnees state the reason for return as "we want to contribute to the country" (Rose 2012; Horn 2012). Cheery Zahau, in her talk about returnees at the Burma Update Conference 2013 at the Australian National University, states that, in the past two years, three types of returnees may be identified: those in armed resistance groups, activists, and immigrants who see opportunities in Myanmar. She notes that all three groups go back because they want to contribute to the country's development (Cheery Zahau 2013).

While an aspect of Burmese exiles returning home has been celebrated in the press as part of the reforms, the question of whether Burmese labour migrants have contemplated return has been largely ignored. In May 2012, the international press (BBC 2012; Whiteman 2012) wrote about Aung San Suu Kyi's visit to Burmese migrants at Mahachai in Thailand, a hub for processing and canning seafood which employs tens of thousands of Burmese workers. The articles pointed out that Aung San Suu Kyi's visit had given hope to migrants' dream of going home. The literature on return migration talks about changes in the economic balance between the place of origin and the place of destination as one of the main reasons which affects migrants' decision to return (Plaza and Henry 2006, p. 3). While it remains to be seen if Myanmar's economy will improve to the point where migrants decide to return, their contemplation of return demands attention.

This chapter has two objectives. Firstly, it explores the thoughts about "return" in the minds of Burmese migrants by taking the case of Shan migrants living and working in the city of Chiang Mai, Thailand. Secondly, it examines the individual's social, economic and cultural conditions that shape the different ways migrants ascribe to the notion of home and return. The chapter brings together the context of current positive changes in Myanmar as a result of political and economic reforms since 2011 and perspectives of return in migration studies. It attempts to understand how return has been addressed by Shan migrants who spent most of their adult life working and living in Thailand. The intention is to understand the driving force behind the choices migrants make, either to stay or to leave, as well as to introduce the concept of the cultural politics of belonging, as an approach to understanding current changes in Myanmar from the perspective of the migrant population.

In what follows, I introduce the Shan migrant community in Chiang Mai, Thailand. I then present my data and discuss my analysis of how return has been addressed by Shan migrants. Data presented in this chapter is based on my informal interviews with around twenty Shan migrants. Although I tried to ensure diversity amongst the respondents as far as possible in terms of gender, length of stay, province of origin and occupation in Chiang Mai, most of the informants are female migrants working as housekeepers in the area around the city of Chiang Mai.

THE SHAN MIGRANT COMMUNITY IN CHIANG MAI, THAILAND

The Shan is the largest of the seven main ethnic minority groups in Myanmar. Shan State is located in the east central part of Myanmar and shares borders with China to the north and Thailand in the east and south. The Shan people are ethnically related to the Thai with whom they share a similar language, the Shan language being a member of the Tai family of languages. Here I use the term "Shan" — an English word borrowed from Burmese — to refer to this group of people. Their self-designation is, however, "Tai" while the Thai call them "Thai Yai" (Greater Thai) and the Burman/Bamar call them "Shan". The Shan territory makes up approximately a quarter of Myanmar's land mass and the Shan comprise 10 per cent of the country's population, or about four to five million.

The Shan migrant community in Chiang Mai provides an interesting case to examine the many ways in which the notion of homeland and ethnic identity can be imagined. After 1996, when the Burmese Government introduced a forced relocation policy in many areas of Shan State in order to break up alleged links or support for armed opposition groups, northern Thailand began to experience massive migratory flows of Shan ethnic nationals from Myanmar. These new migrants did not arrive in one day, but over the past two decades they have come to make up one-sixth of the total population of Chiang Mai, or around 200,000 in this city of about 1.2 million.

Not only does the influx of Shan migrant workers into the city create an interesting relationship between recent migrants and the Chiang Mai inhabitants who employ migrant workers as cheap labour, it also brings the new arrivals into close contact with an existing group of Shan in the city. There is a pre-existing Shan community in Chiang Mai whose members had settled there before the recent wave of Shan ethnic nationals from Myanmar beginning around the 1990s. Due to the geographical proximity between Shan State and northern Thailand, the Shan have long traded in and migrated for work to this region. For many decades, migrants drifted across the border easily both as individuals attracted by the possibility of employment for wages, and as families moving for trade. These people have come to form a group of long-term resident Shan living in Chiang Mai whom I call an "ethnic community". Prior to the 1990s, Shan migrants came in small numbers and could find work and assimilate easily into an existing ethnic Shan community. However, as a result of the forced relocation policy and the deterioration of the Burmese economy, the 1990s saw a major shift in the pattern of Shan migration. The new arrivals came in much larger numbers. They work in low-paying jobs which involve everything from construction work, agricultural farming and serving as housemaids to food vendors and selling various goods in the markets. The new arrivals form a group of Shan migrants who differ from long-term residents. I call these new arrivals the "migrant community".

In a broader context, as Thailand shares a 2,401-kilometre stretch of border with Myanmar, Shan migration is in fact part and parcel of the large-scale migration of a wide range of ethnic groups from Myanmar into Thailand which has been happening in the past decade. This has in turn created migrant towns in several provinces of Thailand which border Myanmar, such as Ranong and Tak. While such provinces host migrants and refugees mostly from Mon, Karen/Kayin or Burman/Bamar ethnic groups, Chiang Mai has become home to a large population of Shan migrants due to three reasons in particular: its provincial border with Shan State in Myanmar, the similarity in language between the northern Thai dialect and Shan language, and Chiang Mai's status as a metropolitan centre in the north where there is a great deal of demand for cheap labour.

The city of Chiang Mai itself provides an interesting setting for Shan migration. Migration to Thailand is not always a one-step movement. Some migrants move first to the border towns in Chiang Mai, Chiang Rai or Mae Hong Son provinces, then migrate to the city of Chiang Mai where there are more jobs available. The moment migrants enter the city of Chiang Mai, they enter a liminal space that is both foreign and familiar. Shan migration to the villages in the border towns in northern Thailand is often a migration to existing Shan communities, where many Shan migrants find work as hired labourers in village farms (see Eberhardt 2008; Tannenbaum 2007), and everyday interaction can be limited to contact between migrants and local Shan households. The city of Chiang Mai offers a different, ambiguous space where the Shan encounter friends, relatives, and a prevalence of the Shan language while at the same time facing an urban environment which creates low-paying jobs in which migrants are treated as "alien" and exploited only for their cheap labour.

The aspect of familiar and foreign may also be applied to the relationship between migrants and the host community. Due to some claims of kin relationship between the Shan and the Thai dating from the distant past, and the linguistic similarity between the Shan and the Thai, the Shan tend to think of the Thais as their ethnic kin or cousins. More particularly, the perceived closeness between the Shan and northern Thais in terms of dialect, skin colour, physical features as well as geographical similarities between the Shan State and northern Thailand can lead Shan migrants to associate Chiang Mai as proximate in many ways.

However, the situation is more complex than simply that of "ethnic kin" migrating to the land of "brotherhood". Anxious and fearful of the perceived threat of an influx of Shan migrants into the city, northern Thais can never think of this new source of cheap labour as their "brothers and sisters" (Amporn Jirattikorn 2012, p. 336). These contexts provide an interesting setting in which to examine the experience of transnational lives that figure in the process of identity construction and to what extent this experience affects the choice of return.

WILL SHAN MIGRANTS RETURN AFTER A DECADE OF MIGRATION?

Studies about return migrants have been explored in many ways. It is understood that a return is to be expected in any long-distance movement. Migration studies view return as part and parcel of the migration project and posit that return will occur once the migrant's objectives are met in destination countries (Cassarino 2004, pp. 255–56).

Bovenkerk (1974) notes the distance to place of origin and length of stay as variables for choice of return. He states that "the shorter the distance of emigration, the higher the incidence of return migration; the longer the emigrants stay away the less chance they will return" (Bovenkerk 1974, p. 17). Changes in the economic balance between the place of origin and the place of destination also directly affect the volume of return migration. In the case of Shan migrants, the distance to place of origin should be a favourable factor for the decision to return, as migrants could drift across the border easily if they decided to return. The length of stay, therefore, should be considered a significant factor for the choice of return for Shan migrants.

In addition, Sills (2000) notes that there are more variations that define return migration. This includes labour migrants who have returned to live in the country of origin as a result of successfully earning enough money, individuals who have returned to retire in their native land, individuals who have returned to their country of origin in order to take advantage of improved social, economic or political conditions, and migrants who failed to obtain work and returned shortly after arriving in the destination country (Plaza and Henry 2006, p. 3, citing Sills 2000). Taking these categories into consideration, we may assume that Shan migrants' decision to return is most likely affected by successfully earning enough money as well as the improvement of social, economic or political conditions in Myanmar. While this is the question I would like to pursue, the volume of the return movement of Shan migrants to Myanmar has yet to occur to the point where we can call it a "return movement". This chapter will, therefore, explore aspects of return from migrants' perceptions of return, and factors which might influence the decision to return, be it nostalgia, patriotism, financial success, marriage or other factors.

On the other hand, studies about transnational migration raise new questions for return migration. Scholars of transnationalism argue that migrants have no sense of distance because they experience several places at the same time. Transnationalism is the process by which immigrants "forge and sustain multi-stranded social relations that link together their societies of origin and settlement" (Basch et al. 1994, p. 7). Transmigrants take actions, make decisions, and develop subjectivities and identities embedded in networks of relationships that connect them simultaneously to two or more nation states (Basch et al. 1994, p. 7). The question raised by transnational scholars is then: what is the significance of return when migrants can experience "home" and "away" simultaneously? Furthermore, where is home for migrants?

Within the context of Burmese migrant workers in Thailand, Nobpaon Rabibhadana and Hayami (2013, pp. 243–83) discuss the ways in which locality plays an important role in shaping and conditioning migrants' perceptions of home. Choosing two locales in Thailand for comparison — the border town of Mae Sot and the interior town of Samut Sakorn — they explore how Burmese migrants living in two different locales differ in terms of working and living conditions, cultural adaptation, and modes of connecting with the homeland. Their findings indicate that in the case of the interior town of Samut Sakorn, migrants tend to send their children back to Myanmar for education and remittances are sent regularly for their children's school fees and living expenses. In the border town of Mae Sot, however, most of the Burmese migrants tend to raise their children in Mae Sot because they cannot afford to send regular remittances to their parents to look after their children. Nobpaon Rabibhadana and Hayami maintain that while mutual dependence of childcare and remittance migrants sent home for their children's education are significant to maintaining cultural and social ties with the homeland, physical proximity to the homeland such as in the border town of Mae Sot does not indicate the strength of migrants' ties to it.

Nobpaon Rabibhadana and Hayami (2013, pp. 243–83) base their argument on different power structures that are at play in these two different locales, which in turn shape different modes of connection with the homeland in Myanmar. This study is informed by such a line of analysis in trying to understand how the intersections of different social, material and political conditions shape the different ways people ascribe to the notion of home and return. In the case of Shan migrants living in northern Thailand, however, we also need to take into account the cultural identity of belonging. As stated, the number of Shan migrants living in Chiang Mai is estimated to be around 150,000 or one-sixth of the total population of Chiang Mai (Amporn Jirattikorn 2011, pp. 29–30). Once in Chiang Mai, Shan migrants encounter friends, relatives, and a prevalence of the Shan language. My research seeks to understand not only what factors may influence the decision to return but also how the notion of home is influenced by the environment in which these Shan migrants live.

The next section will examine Shan migrants living and working in the city of Chiang Mai to look at different ways in which migrants ascribe to the notion of home and return.

THE "MYTH OF RETURN": TO LEAVE OR TO STAY

Nu who is thirty years old and married with no children, replied to my question about home by saying that she does not miss home because she does not know where home is.[2] She was born in the rural area of Shan State, Myanmar. When she was about fifteen years old, her whole family was forced to relocate to town as a result of the forced relocation policy carried out by the Burmese military government from 1996–98. After wandering around in a jungle for a year, the family decided to cross the border into Thailand. After spending about a year in Fang district working as a waged labourer on a lychee farm, Nu came to see the lights of the city in Chiang Mai when she was eighteen years old. She worked as a nanny for a year, after which she landed a job as a housekeeper in an office in downtown Chiang Mai. She has been working as a housekeeper in this office for around ten years.

As her working hours are between 8:00 a.m. and 4:00 p.m., she finds herself with extra time to engage in side-line jobs. Two years ago, she started a small coffee-stall business in front of her office where she sold coffee after work. She spends extra hours at home and in the office making handicraft. She has also invested in a salad stall at the Sunday walking street where she does everything from preparing ingredients to cooking and selling. When asked about her future plans, she said her dream was to have a house of her own. She also wants to save enough money to set up her own restaurant. Nu replied to my question about "home" by saying that she thinks she has three "homes" but she does not belong to any of them. For her, Shan State is home in the past where she cannot return. Thailand is a present home where she has no rights to stay because she does not have citizenship. As for the future, she hopes only to be able to stay in Chiang Mai and one day be able to own a house. However, she realizes that this is only a dream from which she has to remind herself to wake up.

It is believed that no matter how settled, migrants still dream of returning to their homeland eventually (Teo 2011, p. 806). While return is seen as an important part of the migration ethos, Nu's account reveals that for some migrants, return is neither a choice nor a desire. She wants to go "home" — the home in the past where she grew up — only to fulfil nostalgic desires about childhood. As the whole family left Myanmar by force, they cut off their ties with their homeland emotionally and economically. After spending more than ten years in Thailand, she still has not acquired any form of Thai citizenship. Therefore, the present "home" for her is where she works as a housekeeper, taking care of someone else's house. Nu's story is similar to those of thousands of Shan migrants working and living in Chiang Mai where home is no longer in the past nor in the present. She exemplifies how, among many migrants, the notion of home is always ambiguous, imperfect, and unsettled.

Nu's story presents a picture of migrants who do not even consider the possibility of return, for they have no more ties with the homeland. Five female migrants working as housekeepers at Chiang Mai University also share similar experiences. All of them migrated to seek work in Thailand and have been there between ten and fifteen years. Most of them are around twenty-five to thirty-five years old, which means they have spent most of their adult lives working and living in Thailand. They were married when they were around twenty years old, having met their husbands, who are also Shan migrant workers, while working in Thailand. They all have one or two children. Their statuses for living and working in Thailand vary as some of them have managed to acquire some sort of "highlander card",[3] while others have only "working permits" which allow them to stay for one year but are renewable.

Given these many similarities, it might not be surprising that their responses to my question of return were also similar. While the thought of return might have crossed their minds, they were quick to point out their two main concerns. One was that they would return when there were jobs available for them at home. They commented that even though the reforms look bright from the other side of the border, the benefit of reforms had yet to reach remote areas such as Shan State. While they responded to my question about the improvement of Myanmar's economy by simply saying that they would "wait and see", the other concern which is foremost on their minds is their children's welfare. Nang Lang[4] who is twenty-seven years old and a mother revealed:

> Now my daughter is only six years old. She likes going to school in Chiang Mai very much. She does not speak Shan but she can understand it, because my husband and I speak Shan to each other. Even though I miss home and want to go back, we will have to stay here because I am concerned about my daughter's future. We want her to have a better education. Besides, my child is already familiar with life here.

Muay[5] who is twenty-nine years old and working as a housekeeper at my department, says:

> By the time we could go back because we would have saved enough money to start a small shop at home, our children would not want to go back anymore. Over there is not their home, they grew up here. They don't even speak the language, it would be difficult for them. So I think we will stay here no matter what.

When asked if she had any legal status that allowed her to stay and work in Thailand, she stated that she only had a working permit which had to be renewed every year. However, her husband managed to acquire a "highlander card" which reflects his status as a person who was born or has lived on Thai soil, but has yet to obtain Thai citizenship. Although she herself has no right to stay, with her husband's highlander card, he can register their children as Thai. While the issue of citizenship in Thailand is a lot more complex and is beyond the scope of this chapter, this issue will be raised later to consider the lack of citizenship as a factor for migrants' decision to return. What is suggested here, however, is that for many migrants, their children are the most important factor affecting their decision to stay. Shan migrants were concerned that their children, after having grown up in an urban Thai environment and receiving Thai education, would be unable to adjust to life in Shan State, Myanmar. They also see no future for their children receiving education in Myanmar as they see no value in Burmese education. These five female housekeepers whom I spoke to had no doubts about their decision to stay despite their lack of citizenship.

I have stated two reasons for migrants' decision to stay: one was having no ties left with their homeland, the other was their concern about their children's welfare. The third and fourth reasons, which we may consider together, are the desire to return after successfully earning enough money, and the improvement of social, economic or political conditions in Myanmar. So far, I have met a few Shan migrants who had returned to Myanmar in the last few years. Sai Na,[6] for example, returned from Singapore after working as a chef in a small Mexican restaurant for four years. In 2010, he started his small Mexican food stall in Yangon. A year later, he bought a mini-van using four years of savings in order to expand his business to food delivery, which at that time was a new thing in Myanmar. When asked for the reasons of his return, he said:

> If I go back to my country, I want to return a success. I did not earn a lot of money working in Singapore but it was just enough to start a small business. Only in the past two to three years when the economy has picked up did I start to see the opportunities. Rangoon has also developed so much. I thought I can use the skills I learned from working in Singapore at home. So why not come back? With the help of my British friend, we invested in this restaurant. My friend also used his network of foreign friends living in Rangoon to get us more customers. Our restaurant is located in the trendy part of Rangoon where there are a lot of university students living. They also want to try out our food.

Sai Na concludes that "If you want to ride the wave, you need to do it fast before the competition gets started".

I also met Sai Long,[7] a Shan migrant who, after ten years of working in Thailand, has returned to work as a manager in a restaurant at Naypyitaw, the new capital city of Myanmar. He exemplifies the decision migrants make to return as a result of the improvement of social, economic or political conditions at home. He states that since the construction of Naypyitaw was completed, and the new government started to open up the country to foreign investment, there have been many Thai business people coming to Naypyitaw to seek business opportunities. Working there, he could make use of his Thai language skills to cater to the needs of Thai customers. As the restaurant is located in the food centre in the central part of Naypyitaw, it attracts Thai customers. He said that the owner of the restaurant was happy to have him because he could deal with Thai customers who are quite picky when it comes to food. When asked about how he felt about returning home, he states that: "Thailand is fun but here is home. I am happy to return to live close to my parents and my relatives".

Besides these two individuals, at Tachilek, a border town with Mae Sai in the north of Thailand, I met two Shan couples who had returned recently. One couple — the husband used to work for an international non-governmental organization (NGO) based in Chiang Mai while his wife worked as a housekeeper — returned two years ago to open an Internet shop in Tachilek. The other couple — the wife had worked as a shop assistant at the night bazaar in Chiang Mai and the husband as a painter — returned to Tachilek two years ago to set up a shop that sells paint for construction. They say that their business is going well because Tachilek is growing fast as a result of the economic development in Myanmar and China.

In considering these returnees' success, we may assume that the reasons migrants have for return come from two main factors: having successfully earned enough money, and the improvement of social, economic or political conditions in Myanmar. Obviously, the internal (having enough savings) and external (improvement of conditions in Myanmar) factors contribute to migrants' decision to return. However, we have to understand these returns in light of a variety of other factors as well. These include individual capital, migrant experiences and skills as well as the destination of return. From these individuals' stories, we may discern two further important points. Firstly, migrants who have successfully returned are those who have "capital", be it financial, social (network, kinship or relatives or friends), or cultural (language skills, knowledge in their chosen career). Secondly, return is not always a return to one's hometown. More often than not, migrants choose to return to a big city where there are more job opportunities.

The last segment of this chapter will address the acquisition of citizenship in the host country. Of the twenty Shan migrants working in Chiang Mai interviewed, only four of them have acquired a "highlander card" which indicates that the card holder may later apply for Thai citizenship. One of these four is the story of Nan Inn,[8] a Shan man who moved to Thailand as a novice monk when he was thirteen years old. When he turned twenty, he was ordained as a monk. During his stay in Thailand, he managed to acquire a "highlander card" by getting his relative to bribe the village headman. He has now left the monkhood in order to find work as a layman.

When asked if he ever contemplated going home as he now has a card which could one day be turned into Thai citizenship, his response was:

> I want to keep my choice of return open. I come from Mong Yong, where right now there are a lot of opportunities for jobs because Mong Yong is on the border with China. I am sending money back home every month, so that my parents can invest in their rubber plantation. I take my parents to Thailand every time they need a medical check-up or treatment. I can go home if I want. I can stay here as well if I want too. I can't say whether or not I would return permanently one day. I want to keep my choices open for now.

In the case of this former monk, citizenship has enabled him to keep his choice of return open. We can also see from his reflection some hidden factors that influence choice of return. This includes the "transnational social fields" (Basch et al. 1994) that allow migrants to simultaneously maintain membership in both home and host countries. Transnational scholars have emphasized the process by which migrants, through their daily life activities and social, economic and political relations, create social fields that cross national boundaries (Basch et al. 1994). As for the Shan, the recent flows of Shan ethnic nationals from Myanmar seeking work in northern Thailand began more than two decades ago. For the past two decades, I would argue, Shan migrants have "forged and sustained multi-stranded social relations that link together their societies of origin and settlement" (Basch et al. 1994, p. 7). This former monk exemplifies how Shan migrants have created a life that is both here and there, located in the present circumstances of Chiang Mai, Thailand as well as in Shan State, Myanmar. They can call home (in Myanmar) and connect to home at the same time (while being in Thailand). Arguably, "home" and "away" are situated simultaneously, because migrants have telephones, access to a satellite or can send remittances. Hence, they can keep their choice of return open.

However, while the lack of citizenship has significant impact on a migrant's life, it may not necessarily reflect the layered nuances of a migrant's cultural identity. Migration is not a one-time affair. As Gardner (1995, p. vii) states, as we move, "so too do our personal and social boundaries shift; in this sense, migration involves a constant process of reinvention and self-redefinition". When I asked Shan migrants where they see themselves belonging, the answers I received reflect ambiguity in their minds. They often said that they are Shan; they speak Shan; they live alongside Shan friends and relatives; they go to Shan festivals celebrated in the city of Chiang Mai. Culturally, they identify themselves as Shan. However, when asked if they contemplated going home as the situation at home was improving, their answer was that they could not possibly return because they have been away for too long. They were not "familiar" with life there any more.

It should be noted that most of the migrants who made this statement are those who had left home more than ten years ago. Most of them moved to Thailand when they were between ten and fifteen years old. With regard to citizenship, most do not have any form of Thai citizenship; they live and work here as illegal migrants with an "alien working permit".

These contradictory feelings of belonging — on the one hand, identifying themselves culturally as Shan, and on the other, lacking cultural ties with the homeland in Shan State, Myanmar — are not new. Arguably, it is a common feature shared among many migrant populations such as second generation Vietnamese migrants in the United States or overseas Chinese in Canada. As Teo (2011) argues, hybridized forms of cultural identification have become the norm for migrants whose homes are no longer tied to one place. What makes Shan migrants different from Vietnamese Americans or Chinese Canadians is that those who say that they cannot return because they do not feel a sense of cultural belonging, are, at the same time, those who have no rights to stay in the host country. For many Shan migrants whose stories I have described, even though they are Burmese, they have not lived much of their adult lives in Myanmar. As for Thailand, it is where they work, and where their friends and family are. Many of them have children who have not known a life beyond Thailand. Some may desire to stay, yet they have no rights to do so due to their lack of citizenship. Others may want to return, yet Myanmar no longer feels like home. While I do not want to assume that the majority of Shan migrants fit into this category, the record shows that the recent wave of Shan ethnic nationals from Myanmar began in 1996 after the Burmese Government introduced a forced relocation policy in many areas of Shan State (Shan Human Rights Foundation, SHRF 2003). Beginning in the 1990s, Chiang Mai began to experience a large-scale migration of the Shan whose adult lives have been spent living and working in Thailand. With the Shan population constantly crossing the border, these questions remain: Where and how will the desire to return be resolved? Will the heart ever settle?

CONCLUSION

This chapter has examined the circumstances of particular individual migrants in order to understand the complexity of the ways in which migrants construct, remember, and lay claim to the "homeland". It has attempted to show that there are in fact various factors which contribute to the motivation for return among many Shan migrants: changes in the social or political conditions in the homeland; marriage while in the destination country; having children in the new country of residence and the need to socialize them in the host country; the number of family members who have migrated; the acquisition of citizenship in the host country; length of stay in the host country; and the age at the time of migration. While these factors illustrate how different social, economic and political conditions shape the different ways migrants think about return, it is also important for those who do return to have two other things: capital (be it economic, social, or cultural capital) and a place to go, which is not necessarily always back to the motherland.

In reading Shan migrants' narratives of home, we come to see that the notion of home is fluid, ambiguous and unsettled. The stories of these individual migrants illustrate a constant process of displacement and emplacement, losing home and making new homes (Friedman 2007, p. 264). In trying to answer the question of what home actually is, my concern here is, however, different from those transnational scholars who ask: what is the significance of return when migrants can experience "home" and "away" simultaneously. Transnational scholars (see Basch et al. 1994; Portes et al. 1999; Smith 2003) maintain that once migrants cross the borders, we can no longer take the "nation state" as a primary unit of analysis. As Teo (2011, pp. 816–17) has metaphorically argued, the moon that shines in both the homeland and the foreign land is the same moon; hence an imaginary connection is drawn between the two when the migrant gazes at the moon. It may be true that we can no longer assume that the Shan in Thailand are divided from those in Myanmar by state frontiers, as many of them continue to travel back and forth across the border of the two nation states, maintaining trans-border connection through networks of families and friends and some, if not many, holding two national identification cards. But while theories of transnationalism often imply that migrants are no longer rooted, mentally or physically, in any geographical place, the reality of these Shan migrants is hardly ideal like those of Chinese "flexible" citizens migrating to Canada or the United States. For Shan migrants, remaining "transnational" forever is an unlikely option. At the same time, becoming a "diaspora" like the Vietnamese Americans or the Indian immigrants in Britain, is hardly a choice.

The mass migration that happened two decades ago as a result of Myanmar's oppressive military regime has not only had an impact on the lives of Shan migrants today living and working in Thailand. The Shan are only exemplified as "migrants" whereas the Karen/Kayin, the Karenni/Kayah or the Rohingya who have similar experiences may fall into the category of "refugees". The Shan are twice rejected; first by their own nation state which forced them to leave and second by their host nation state which denies their legal belonging so as to exploit their labour. The case of the Shan migrants is only an example that urges us to think beyond the scholarship of border and transnational studies to the reality of those who are victims of the nation state. It remains to be seen what will happen to this generation of Shan migrants who have been living and working in Thailand for more than a decade, who have neither the right to stay nor the option to return.

Notes

1. The UNHCR estimated that there are nearly 82,000 registered refugees and some 13,000 asylum seekers in Thailand (as of June 2013). Most refugees are ethnic minorities from Myanmar, mainly Karen/Kayin and Karenni/Kayah, who live in nine official camps in four provinces along the Thai-Burmese border. There were 1,111,541 Burmese migrant workers who registered for work permits with the Ministry of Labour in Thailand (as of 2013) (UNHCR 2013). However, government organizations and NGOs working on Burmese migrant worker issues in Thailand estimated that the real figure is far higher.
2. Interview in Chiang Mai. Interviewed by Amporn Jirattikorn, Chiang Mai, Thailand, 21 October 2013.
3. Thai citizenship is based on the principle of *ius soli* (literally, law of the soil), which means a person has to be born in the territory of a country. In considering the legal status of ethnic minorities, the state takes into consideration their birthplace or their date of entry into the kingdom, their parents' status and birthplace, and other supporting documents and witnesses. The laws and regulations stipulate that only the hill people who are considered "original" people, can apply to their district chief for registration of their citizenship in a household registration document. This group includes people born in Thailand during the period 10 April 1913 to 13 December 1972, the period during which the first Nationality Act was enforced (Mukdawan Sakboon 2011, pp. 205–43). While the statelessness of ethnic minorities in Thailand is a complicated issue and an effective system is needed in order to solve the problem of legal status, over the past decades, many Burmese migrants in the north of Thailand have managed to acquire highlander cards through illegal means.
4. Interview in Chiang Mai. Interviewed by Amporn Jirattikorn, Chiang Mai, Thailand, 10 October 2013.
5. Ibid., 8 October 2013.
6. Interview in Yangon. Interviewed by Amporn Jirattikorn, Yangon, Myanmar, 15 May 2013.
7. Interview in Naypyitaw. Interviewed by Amporn Jirattikorn, Naypyitaw, Myanmar, 13 May 2013.
8. Interview in Chiang Mai. Interviewed by Amporn Jirattikorn, Chiang Mai, Thailand, 12 February 2013.

References

Amporn Jirattikorn. "Shan Virtual Insurgency and the Spectatorship of the Nation". *Journal of Southeast Asian Studies* 42, no. 1 (2011): 17–38.

——. "Aberrant Modernity: The Construction of Nationhood among Shan Prisoners in Thailand". *Asian Studies Review* 36, no. 3 (2012): 327–43.

Basch, Linda, Nina Glick Schiller, and Cristina Szanton-Blanc. *Nation Unbound: Transnational Projects, Postcolonial Predicaments and Deterritorialised Nation States*. New York: Gordon and Breach, 1994.

BBC. "Aung San Suu Kyi Visits Burmese Migrants in Thailand", 30 May 2012 <http://www.bbc.co.uk/news/world-asia-18260160> (accessed 3 November 2013).

Bovenkerk, Frank. *The Sociology of Return Migration: A Bibliographic Essay*. The Hague: Martinus Nijoff, 1974.

Cassarino, Jean-Pierre. "Theorising Return Migration: The Conceptual Approach to Return Migrants Revisited". *International Journal on Multicultural Societies* 6, no. 2 (2004): 253–79.

Cheery Zahau. "The Return of Burma's Diaspora and Its Role in Social, Economic and Political Reform". *Myanmar/Burma Update Conference 2013*. 15–16 March 2013. Australia National University (ANU), Canberra: ANU, 2013 <http://asiapacific.anu.edu.au/news-events/podcasts/2013-myanmarburma-update-resistance-reengagement#.UoEFNJW_xUQ> (accessed 3 November 2013).

Eberhardt, Nancy. "Stepping into the Same River Twice? Re-studies of a Shan Community in Northern Thailand". *Annual Meeting of the Association for Asian Studies*. Atlanta: Conference Publication, 2008.

Friedman, Susan Stanford. "Migrations, Diasporas, and Borders". In *Introduction to Scholarship in Modern Languages and Literatures*, edited by David Nicholls. New York: Modern Language Association (MLA), 2007, pp. 260–93.

Gardner, Katy. *Global Migrants, Local Lives: Travel and Transformation in Rural Bangladesh*. Oxford: Clarendon Press, 1995.

Horn, Robert. "Going Home: Exiles Venture Back to Build a 'New Burma'". In *Time*, 10 February 2012 <http://world.time.com/2012/02/10/going-home-exiles-venture-back-to-build-a-new-burma/> (accessed 3 November 2013).

Mukdawan Sakboon. "The Border Within: The Akha at the Frontiers of National Integration". In *Transcending State Boundaries: Contesting Development, Social Suffering and Negotiation*, edited by Chayan Vaddhanaphuti and Amporn Jirattikorn. Chiang Mai: The Regional Centre for Social Science and Sustainable Development (RCSD), Chiang Mai University 2011, pp. 205–43.

Nobpaon Rabibhadana and Yoko Hayami. "Seeking Haven and Seeking Jobs: Migrant Workers' Networks in Two Thai Locales". *Southeast Asian Studies* 2, no. 2 (2013): 243–83.

Plaza, Dwaine and Frances Henry. "An Overview of Return Migration to the English-Speaking Caribbean". In *Returning to the Source: The Final Stage of the Caribbean Migration Circuit*, edited by Dwaine E. Plaza and Frances Henry. Jamaica: University of the West Indies Press, 2006, pp. 1–29.

Portes, Alejandro, Luis E. Guarnizo, and Patricia Landolt. "The Study of Transnationalism: Pitfalls and Promise of an Emergent Research Field". *Ethnic and Racial Studies* 22, no. 2 (1999): 217–37.

Rose, James. "As Burma Reforms, Exiles Dream of Home". In *Le Monde Diplomatique*, April 2012 <http://mondediplo.com/blogs/as-burma-reforms-exiles-dream-of-home> (accessed 3 November 2013).

Shan Human Rights Foundation (SHRF). "Charting the Exodus from Shan State: Patterns of Refugee Flows into Northern Chiang Mai Province of Thailand, 1997–2002". Chiang Mai: SHRF, 2003.

Sills, Stephen. *Return Migration*. Unpublished article, 2000.
Smith, Michael. "Transnationalism and Citizenship". In *Approaching Transnationalism: Studies on Transnational Societies, Multicultural Contacts, and Imagining of Home*, edited by Brenda S.A. Yeoh, Michael W. Charney and Tong Chee Kiong. Massachusetts: Kluwer Academic, 2003, pp. 15–38.
Tannenbaum, Nicola. "Being Shan on the Thai Side of the Border: Continuities and Transformation in Shan Culture and Identity in Mae Hong Son, Thailand". *International Conference on Shan Buddhism and Culture*. 8–9 December 2007, London: School of Oriental and African Studies (SOAS), 2007.
Teo, Sin Yin. "'The Moon Back Home is Brighter'?: Return Migration and the Cultural Politics of Belonging". *Journal of Ethnic and Migration Studies* 37, no. 5 (2011): 805–20.
United Nations High Commissioner for Refugees (UNHCR). "Refugees in Thailand", June 2013 <https://www.unhcr.or.th/refugee/thailand> (accessed 3 November 2013).
Whiteman, Hilary. "Suu Kyi Addresses Burmese migrants on Historic Thai Trip". In *CNN*, 30 May 2012 <http://edition.cnn.com/2012/05/29/world/asia/suu-kyi-thailand-migrants/index.html> (accessed 3 November 2013).

14

Moving On: Spaces of Uncertain Freedom and Engagement in the Kayah–Mae Hong Son Borderland

CARL GRUNDY-WARR AND CHIN WEI JUN

INTRODUCTION

Geopolitically induced forced migration created a legacy of chronic human insecurity, internal displacement, and cross-border exile for tens of thousands of Karenni people for over two decades. Under military rule the country was relatively isolated, except for exploitative resource economy investments by China, Thailand and other Asian neighbours. As Myanmar now goes through fundamental political economic reform processes, many profound changes are affecting the political and human landscape of ethnic border zones.

We focus on Karenni displaced persons, particularly cross-border refugee populations, who face dilemmas such as whether or not to return to lands many of them were coerced into leaving, and which even in relative peacetime have precarious human security. Simultaneously, Myanmar's contested borderlands are experiencing relative absence of armed conflict for the first time in decades, and they are being opened to inward investment, intensified resource exploitation and a complex array of new emerging relations with actors and agencies operating inside Myanmar.

Political and economic changes in the borderlands bring in forms of land and resource dispossession, exclusion/inclusion, and inequality in terms of ownership, access and property rights. We argue that agencies concerned with developmental change and human security need to seriously take into account legacies of past (and current) geopolitical conflicts whilst taking a critical look at the nature and purposes underlying political economic change. Understanding the cumulative legacy of past conflicts is vital to any current examination of the changing political economic landscape. Equally necessary is the analysis of Myanmar becoming a legitimized space for global investment, which generates many projects, but also carries dilemmas of highly differentiated economic benefits that do not necessarily alleviate poverty in former conflict zones.

The chapter focuses primarily upon key transformations in the lives of ordinary Karenni refugees living in Mae Hong Son, Thailand, and reflects upon the major transformations affecting the Kayah (Myanmar) — Mae Hong Son (Thailand) borderland, particularly in relation to issues of human and livelihood security for residents and returnees.[1] It maps lives across the border through ethnographic and everyday geographies relating to past and current contexts.

Previously, the geopolitics of national reconsolidation generated ceasefires between the military junta and various armed ethnic groups in the borderlands, whilst conflict continued with non-ceasefire groups, such as the Karenni National Progressive Party (KNPP). However, a new era of national reconciliation has opened up. How such political processes play out in border areas and with different groups has an intricate geography. Grounded knowledge of the complex political landscape is critically important to the future of ordinary people living in the borderlands, especially for many refugees contemplating whether to return or not. We suggest that this can only come through historically informed methodologies that are sensitive to the ways in which the border landscapes were violently rearranged during periods of low intensity warfare and militarized security, which create extremely intensive forms of brutality and displacement for numerous localized populations.

Finally, the chapter examines the quandary of rapid political economic change in Myanmar for Karenni people currently living in the Thai borderlands of Mae Hong Son province.[2] Do current ceasefires provide a basis for sustainable human security for ethnic populations in the borderlands? Are long-term refugees willing to return home? Do younger Karenni refugees want to return to their homelands? Is "moving on" really about moving back?

FREEDOM'S POSSIBILITIES

Development is indeed a momentous engagement with freedom's possibilities (Sen 1999, p. 298).

According to Amartya Sen, true development is entwined "with the process of enhancing individual freedoms and the social commitment to bring that about" (Sen 1999, p. 298). If we consider the "freedoms" that individual refugees, internally displaced persons (IDPs), and long-suffering borderland populations along the various troubled border regions of Myanmar, we could quickly draw the conclusion that there is not much in terms of "development" in Sen's sense of the term since Burma became independent in 1948. Indeed, for long periods of time, especially during spells of counter-insurgency operations affecting most ethnic groups and border zones (Smith 1999, pp. 258–62) the majority of people were trapped in landscapes of fear (Lang 2002, pp. 1–2). Rather than development, military conflict and insurgency have been highly destructive for the lives of most of the people living within contested ethnic borderlands, producing a political culture and identity based on fear, mistrust and suspicion of the Burmese military. Ordinary people had restricted freedoms — affected by warfare and few choices to speak of, except critical decisions to flee or not flee, to hide or not, or to relocate to militarily secured areas where restrictions on daily life and military demands for resources or labour meant that people were de facto enslaved populations (Grundy-Warr and Wong 2002, p. 112; Grundy-Warr 2004, p. 230). Violence, loss and bloodshed are deeply etched into the palimpsest political landscape of the borderlands, and this conflict legacy should be at the forefront of any consideration of political economic change in the context of ceasefires or more lasting peaceful conditions in the current decade.

Political, economic and human security issues are inevitably intertwined, so we should be cautious of prescribing only narrow ideas about primarily economic development in human landscapes that have been affected by many years of military, civil and ethnic violence. Recent political, economic, and legal reforms in Myanmar are opening up new, albeit uncertain, possibilities and potential "freedoms" within an evolving political architecture at national level that is no longer totally dominated by the military, with spaces for engagement for different political and ethnic parties, civil society and non-governmental organizations (NGOs), and the so-called "national reconciliation" processes (Cheesman et al. 2012, pp. 3–15). Within the borderlands, there are many socioeconomic and political changes underway, and the dominant themes are no longer ones of insurgency and counter-insurgency, or of militarized "not peace, not war" (Grundy-Warr and Dean 2011, pp. 91–114), but of the borders becoming incorporated into a much larger canvas of political economic transformation and capital accumulation. The political geographies of the borderlands are increasingly incorporated into a larger mosaic of political economic transformation, wherein capitalist primitive accumulation and resource extraction are becoming primary political issues in many parts of the country, and not just in the former conflict zones. In this sense, it is as vital to understand relations forged by different investment projects, land encroachments, land-use changes, and other economic processes, as it is to appreciate complex ethnic politics in the borderlands.

Our focus is primarily on a case study of Karenni refugees along the Mae Hong Son borderline with Kayah State, and upon certain aspects of the changing political and economic landscape of Kayah State. Figure 14.1 shows the location of Ban Nai Soi in relation to Mae Hong Son Province, Thailand, and Kayah State, and it is in this zone where we have been conducting much research on the Karenni refugees. This zone has been particularly sensitive to cross-border geopolitical change, and to the recent transformations in the political landscape on the Myanmar side of the border. In this sense we perceive this study as one segment of a much bigger story that is unfolding. These changes are happening quickly and require monitoring because they relate to a political economy and political ecology of change that has fundamental implications for the resident and returnee populations of Karenni/Kayah State. However, what is happening within this area of borderland is far from exceptional, and is in fact a reflection of much broader political economic processes of change affecting many other places and people in the vast borderlands of Myanmar. The next section provides a brief examination of the geopolitics of forced migration, which generated conditions of great insecurity and non-freedom for many people. The rest of the chapter will then focus upon the nature of current developments affecting freedoms and engagements for both refugees and resident populations of Kayah/Karenni State.

CROSS-BORDER GEOPOLITICS AND LANDSCAPES OF FEAR

Without notice
Suffering came quick to greet us
Soldiers
Rapid
They burnt our houses
An annihilated place.

Rice barns to ashes
Our food lost

FIGURE 14.1
Part of the Mae Hong Son — Kayah (Karenni) Borderland where We Carried out Our Research

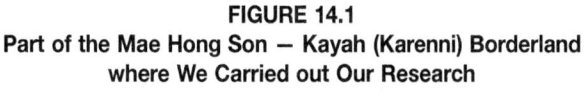

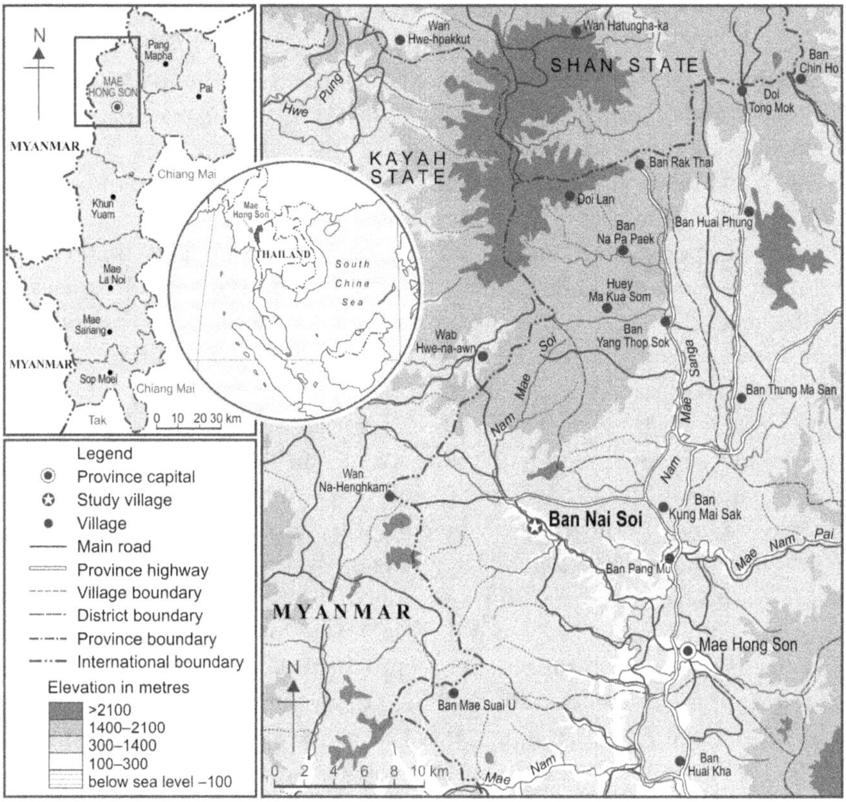

Source: Author's Own.

Inhabiting the forest deep
From my house of ashes
As the enemy searched for us
In the basket, my father took me away
My village
I can never see again.
(Tee Noe 2014)

This excerpt from a longer poem *I Do Need Peace* by Karen writer Tee Noe aptly describes a situation faced by a great many Karen and Karenni forcibly displaced persons for much of the 1990s and first decade of the new millennium. Displacement was a chronic condition that deeply impacted on almost every aspect of life in the borderlands. Meanings of displacement take on many guises. Perhaps the best way to understand it for any interested outsider and observer is to read through the tens of thousands of testimonies carefully recorded by groups such as the Karen Human Rights Group (KHRG) over many years, or to read the moving reports of roving Free Burma Rangers (FBR) meeting with groups of hungry, anxious and needy internally displaced persons in the mountains and jungles of Karen and Karenni territory.

It is important to understand the cumulative impacts that forced relocation and coerced displacements have had on the human landscape of the borderlands over time. As Kevin Heppner observed in *A Village on Fire, the Tatmadaw* (Burma Army) sought to establish a militarized version of national security by imposing strict restrictions on everyday life, which was "destroying the very fabric of ... agrarian society and the viability of the farming as an economic and social unit" (Heppner 2000, p. 16), making normal life a virtual impossibility for hundreds of thousands of people inhabiting border areas where insurgent non-ceasefire groups were still active. Many farmers were essentially operating on a subsistence level, yet they also faced demands for forced labour, food, money, and materials by army battalions in and around their village locations. Those villagers who were relocated to supposedly secure areas were often not permitted to return to their fields and they still had to give up supplies and labour to serve the Army. For the military, these rural areas provided opportunities to confiscate and sell rations, cut bamboo, collect rice, and obtain forced labour. As Heppner (2000, p. 15) reported:

> In the thousands of interviews conducted by the Karen Human Rights Group with villagers who have fled their homes, approximately 95 percent say they have not fled military battles, but rather *the systematic destruction of their ability to survive*, caused by demands and retaliations inflicted on them by the SPDC (former State Peace and Development Council) military (our emphasis).

For many years territorial geopolitics between the *Tatmadaw* and so-called insurgency groups meant that life was full of anxiety and cruelty. As one founding member of the Karenni National Women's Organization (KNWO) recalls:

> We were constantly on the move and in fear: The Burmese Army used to come to our village once a week; sometimes one month four to six times. Many villagers were afraid because the Burmese soldiers destroy homes (burn rice paddies, house) and kill villagers. Call people and kill. Sometimes they put landmines [around the village] and villagers step on them. If they found resistance soldiers [then] they would question villagers about it. I [used to] stay near the borderline. Burmese soldiers came and we run. We run every year. We build tents to stay. Last time, the army came with aeroplanes and shoot at us when we were located in the borderland. [After that] we moved into camp 3 [located in Thailand] (interview with Ah Mu Doh, Founder of KNWO, 2013).[3]

The brutal political economy of militarized existence within the borderlands generated conditions of severe economic vulnerability and human insecurity, which directly contributed to massive internal displacement, and for others, cross-boundary escape into Thailand either as undocumented irregular migrants or into the so-called "temporary shelters" (refugee camps) along the border. The former State Law and Order Restoration Council (SLORC, 1988–97), SPDC (1997–2011), sought to extend their own version of internal security, "national integrity" and martial rule into the borderlands, either through ceasefire arrangements with ethnic armed groups or by use of the "Four Cuts" (*Pya Ley Pya*) strategy of cutting off sources of food, funds, intelligence and recruits to the armed insurgency groups. This deliberate strategy turned extensive border zones into a

> vast chessboard under the *Tatmadaw*'s ... regional commands and shaded in three colours: black for entirely insurgent-controlled areas; brown for areas both sides still disputed; and white was "free", meaning under SPDC control (Smith 1999, p. 259).

Thus, consideration of the underlying geopolitics and history of forced displacement should be part of analyses of contemporary conflict resolution and peace processes.

If an area was deemed "black" or "brown" there was no such thing as "neutral villages" in a geography dominated by military security strategies, and so people living in "black" areas were automatically perceived to be siding with insurgent forces even though many of them were poor farmers often with little direct involvement in armed resistance. In "brown" areas all villagers were viewed with suspicion and many villages were relocated to so-called secure settlements near army barracks. Distinction between civilians and combatants was often vague in conflict-affected zones (Lang 2002, p. 12). Within these landscapes of fear, many people experienced periods of time when they went into hiding to avoid arrest or army demands, living close to villages subjected to military surveillance, living off hidden stores and by foraging in hilly forested areas (Grundy-Warr 2004, p. 231). Thus the geographies of displacement were extremely complex, often relating to specific localized military conditions, and for many people spells of displacement were just part of everyday life within zones subject to low intensity warfare, counter-insurgency operations, and ad hoc martial law.

Research by The Border Consortium (TBC) (2013, p. 18) documented "the destruction, forced relocation or abandonment of more than 3,700 villages between 1996 and an average annual rate of 75,000 people displaced during the past decade", with an estimated 400,000 internally displaced persons (IDPs) in the rural areas of thirty-six townships of southeast Myanmar at the end of 2012. For every person displaced there is a critical story that directly relates to a human landscape that was fractured and damaged by decades of political instability and military violence. It would be a terrible irony if within a reforming political landscape the very people who suffered the most from conflict are the last to receive or experience "freedom's possibilities".

BORDER DEVELOPMENT AND DISPARITY

Borderlands are not "margins" or marginal spaces in terms of processes of capital accumulation and economic investment. Capitalists and investors seeking out resources to exploit (such as in teak wood, hydropower, agribusiness, and property development) do not discriminate in terms of spatial location. Rather, the borderlands, particularly conflict-prone zones, have now become more amenable to inward investments, and it is the notion of them as potentially lucrative resource frontiers that seems to be driving certain economic alliances and underlying infrastructure developments. In fact, the "marginal" characteristics of borderlands lies primarily in relation to the idea of nation state (or military regime) centres, which had much more currency before Myanmar embarked on a process of partial political reform and relative geo-economic openness after 2011. If we consider borderland spaces much like any other spaces open for economic exploitation and forms of "development", then the situation in the last few years of political reform seems to have shifted to one in which there is a tendency to view the borderlands as an open landscape for economic investment as opposed to the former "mosaics" of control and development characterising much of the period from the end of the 1980s through to the early 2000s (see Maclean 2008). Whilst in specific conflict-prone areas there remain intense concerns over basic human security (TBC 2013), and there is uncertainty about the emerging economic landscape in ceasefire zones, key drivers of change are likely to be increasingly political economic ones as opposed to primarily military ones. Hence, any analysis of what is happening in the borderlands needs to focus on the manner in which land, resources and space is being opened up for economic gain, control and access in a transitional period between open military conflict and relative (yet unstable) peace.

Since the late 1980s, ceasefire politics have been influential in the changing political economic landscape of Myanmar's borderlands, although the social and economic consequences of ceasefires have been geographically highly uneven in terms of their benefits to local populations (Buchanan et al. 2013, pp. 1–8). By 1997 there were approximately twenty-two ceasefire groups and armed militias with ceasefire arrangements covering much of the borderlands. For instance, whilst the Karenni National Progressive Party (KNPP) remained for most of the time a non-ceasefire party, other Karenni groups signed ceasefires with the military junta, including the Karenni Nationalities People's Liberation Front (KNPLF) and Kayan New Land Party (KNLP).

Karenni territory had some areas that were open to border development projects whilst other areas, particularly nearer to the Thai border remained as effective "free fire zones" where it was dangerous for civilians to cross and where any economic activity was precarious. Thus, the human landscape was being simultaneously impacted by military security and human insecurity on the one hand, and patchy economic development and resource exploitation enabled by ceasefire arrangements on the other. During the 1990s the military under the SLORC and from 1997 renamed SPDC — sought forms of "development" (read, economic advantage for military-related agents) through myriad ceasefire arrangements with different ethnic political parties and militia organizations in the borderlands. These forms of development were basically partnerships between the *Tatmadaw*, military-linked enterprises, overseas companies, and specific partners in the ceasefire zones. Such forms of development were associated with the Program for the Progress of the Border Areas and National Races Development or *Na Ta La* (Burmese acronym) which generated what Curtis Lambrecht (2004, pp. 150–81) called "oxymoronic development", ostensibly to bring progress to border areas and ethnic groups, but in reality benefiting certain military players, ethnic elites and foreign investors.

Geopolitical ideology underlying development was linked to notions of "non-disintegration of the Union" with the Burmese military viewed as "the bulwark of the nation" (Lambrecht 2004, p. 153) and regime-centred ideas about maintaining "national sovereignty". Whilst the rhetorical goal of border development was to bring the border areas out of "darkness" and to allow all "national races" to enjoy "the fruits of progress" (Lambrecht 2004, p. 150, citing The New Light of Myanmar 1994), in reality there were underlying geopolitical goals relating to the *Tatmadaw*'s obsession with securing national integrity by "bringing into the national fold" (Lambrecht 2004, p. 154) various ceasefire groups. According to a report entitled *Developing Disparity* by the Transnational Institute (2013, p. 15):

> The lack of economic development in the resource-rich ethnic areas is one the primary grievances among ethnic communities, along with historical resistance to military state-building efforts in their territories. Despite the investments in resource extraction in the borderlands, local activists complain that the profits have not been reinvested in promoting local development. There is little physical and communication infrastructure, and most communities lack electricity. Many investments take place in the absence of community leaders. Even when community leaders do take part, they are often ineffective in representing the interests of the communities. There is also widespread disregard for the social and environmental impacts of investment projects. Moreover, the profits benefit only the local elites, government and military officials, businessmen and members of armed groups, who do not represent local communities.

In generic terms the pattern of border development has tended to embolden and reward military participants, specific ethnic elite leaders, participating local business groups, and foreign investors (Buchanan et al. 2013, pp. 8–14). The result of two decades of ceasefire developments in border zones produced a complex political economic landscape with massive socioeconomic disparity between those who benefited from resource exploitation and those who did not, including dispossessed and economically displaced communities. Economic investments under quasi-military rule, including localized armed groups with the *Tatmadaw*, and improvised ceasefire arrangements led to forms of differentiated political economic sovereignty (Maclean 2008, pp. 141–44).

Official junta-sanctioned border development did place more of the country under centralized control than at any previous period since the country's independence, it did so under forms of patchwork authority and control based upon different amalgams of power within each ceasefire zone. In what Ken Maclean (2008, pp. 141–42) termed as Myanmar's "entrepreneurial turn", he reveals "the rapid conversion of previously contested spaces into commodified ones" with the creation of militarized "extractive enclaves" primarily based on joint ventures made possible due to ceasefire arrangements. Indeed, Grundy-Warr and Dean (2011) identified the political geographies of the borderlands in terms such as partially securitized, semi-autonomous, non-compliance, resistance, and state evasion. These categories reveal that the borderlands were under mosaics of control, political authority, ceasefires and non-ceasefires, making knowledge of context, localities and the historical geopolitics of place central to any analysis of the current peace process and political economic change.

Ultimately the military's "entrepreneurial turn" and it's ideological quest for national reconsolidation led to a highly complex and fragmented political landscape, with some areas "vacillating" between peace and conflict as specific ceasefire groups disagreed with certain conditions imposed by the SPDC or with regional *Tatmadaw* commanders, such as the Kachin Independence Organization (KIO) controlled zones. Indeed, the outbreak of fighting and attacks on the KIO near the Chinese border reveal the fragility of ceasefires and deeply held tensions between government, military and ethnic players over critical issues of territorial, resource and trade control (Wai Moe 2014). Beyond ceasefires, other border areas have long been subjected to intensive militarization, such as much of eastern and southern Kayah State, until very recently (Grundy-Warr and Dean 2011, p. 96). There is a lasting legacy of conflict in all border zones, but especially in those where even the former military regime's notion of border development hardly took off at all. A couple of basic indicators are health and electricity. Kayah State has a shortage of proper health care and doctors beyond the capital Loikaw (*Kantarawaddy Times* 2013*b*), and in spite of the development of hydropower plants such as Lawpita, much of the state has no access to electricity (*Kantarawaddy Times* 2013*a*). As The Border Consortium (TBC) (2013, p. 1) noted:

> Decades of military rule, conflict and abuse have left rural communities impoverished, lacking basic infrastructure, struggling to cope with shocks to livelihoods and with limited access to social services. The vast majority of villagers are subsistence farmers with insufficient access to agricultural land to meet the threshold of self-reliance.

Even before the intensive military campaigns of the mid-1990s when many villages were destroyed or forcibly relocated, the average size of landholdings in Kayah State was a meagre 370 acres (1.5 square kilometres) and a large proportion of the population were landless (Bamforth et al. 2000, pp. 8–14). There were relatively few off-farm employment opportunities for many rural dwellers. Intensive militarization of the state coupled with the loss of villages and access to land has further complicated the business of post-conflict development. Key resource developments such as mining and hydropower are primarily in the hands of the state and businesses allied with the military. For many Karenni refugees there is a concern that they will have little access to land or resources or livelihood opportunities in the post-conflict era.

POST-CONFLICT POLITICAL COMPLEXES AND ECONOMIC DEVELOPMENT

As we enter what can be tentatively called a post-conflict phase, with almost all ethnic organizations entering into some kind of ceasefire arrangement, it is necessary to appreciate many of the forced and violent transformations to space and resources that leave lasting legacies. Not least of all are the huge numbers of people who have been forcibly displaced at one time or another. Numerous sources document widespread fear and insecurity engendered by low intensity warfare, counter-insurgency operations, and military demands being made upon civilian populations (various reports by the Karen Human Rights Group (KHRG) and TBBC over the years; as well as many academic studies, such as Grundy-Warr 2002; Lang 2002; Decha Tangseefa 2007, to mention but a few). Contemporary surveys and testimonies of village people in various border districts reveal alarming indicators of poverty, such as lack of basic infrastructure, inadequate shelters, unprotected and insufficient water supply, vulnerability to waterborne disease, poorly provisioned or absent health clinics, highly restricted access to cultivable land, and periodic food insecurity (TBC 2013). Clearly, basic needs, services and infrastructure are key priorities in the large border zones of southeast Myanmar.

Myanmar is opening up to massive foreign direct investment and international donor aid. Schroeder and Saw U (2014, p. 199) have suggested that the international donor community needs to understand the long history of protracted conflict as well as the "emerging political complexes" (Callahan 2007, pp. 18–24) that are influencing investment strategies and targets inside the country. In part, these political complexes offer new spaces of engagement between former adversaries, including non-state armed groups and ethnic political bodies. However, if we examine the political complexes that emerged from earlier ceasefires under military rule we can see that neo-patrimonial type linkages emerge, offering profit opportunities between motley crews of military, business and ethnic elites, whilst causing loss of land, resource access and various forms of exclusion for large sections of the local communities.

Schroeder and Saw U (2014, p. 212) caution us: "From the very beginning the motives of the government to conclude ceasefires have been all about business and profit-making projects." Business interests come ahead of "any grand strategy to find a solution to political problems". In similar vein, Petrie and South (2014, p. 226) urge us to consider carefully the myriad connections between "business interests and the peace process". However, they also strike a more optimistic note, arguing that the peace process is deepening and widening within Myanmar, particularly through initiatives such as the Myanmar Peace Support Initiative (MPSI), supported by Norway's Ministry of Foreign Affairs, and various international donors, and covering a variety of grassroots projects, including issuing of identity cards to remote and conflict-affected communities in the borderlands. Such initiatives are incredibly important for people who have never had identity documents and for others who have been effectively stateless, for documentation not only increases their visibility but may also enhance legal rights in relation to resource access, land registrations, and protection of human rights in future.

MPSI initiatives are penetrating into previous conflict-affected areas of the borderland. Medical supplies, rice and clothing are being sent into some areas supported by the Committee for Internally Displaced Karen People (CIDKP) with international donor support. In spite of this, some border NGOs and community-based organizations (CBOs) have voiced concern that the peace process is too closely aligned with central Myanmar agencies and the Japanese-funded Myanmar Peace Center. Peace- and confidence-building are extremely sensitive issues, requiring full transparency and deep understanding of local contexts. Political and cultural geographies really matter in the development of trust, particularly amongst alienated groups living in deprived war-ravaged zones. The borderlands, even within one territory, have been affected differentially by displacement and conflict, and there exist different non-state agents and actors who should be part of the interactions and negotiations of peace-building. Some pockets of the borderlands have contested political authority, and in these zones there is a need for third parties and peace-building agencies to engage with CBOs and local leaders from conflict-affected communities. In turn, such non-state and affected community representatives need assistance in order for connections to be made with "donors and diplomats seeking to support the reform and peace processes" (Petrie and South 2014, p. 242).

Critically land remains central to political economic developments in the borderlands and elsewhere inside Myanmar. As Woods (2014, p. 1) wrote in a short piece entitled *The Political Anatomy of Land Grabs*, "this seemingly two-word phrase is in fact very complex and opaque", partly because we are dealing with a palimpsest landscape being over-written with new land-related laws and policies. According to Woods (2014, p. 1), "the new land-related laws are haphazardly and improperly applied to legally turn farmers into 'squatters' and their farm fields into 'vacant wastelands' for corporate investment". In a report by the KHRG (2013) entitled *Losing Ground* they argue that the land "is governed by a patchwork of overlapping, and sometimes contradictory, land laws", some allowing "substantial Government authority to expropriate land" (KHRG 2013, p. 18). In particular, "farmland", especially "fallow land" and "wasteland" (KHRG 2013, pp. 18–24) are malleable categories open to re-allocation and expropriation to private or quasi-state companies for agri-business, livestock or aquaculture, and mining deemed to be in the national interest.

Land issues within development are undoubtedly nationwide, and not just confined to ethnic areas or borderlands, for new national land-use legislation and farmland laws have come under critical scrutiny (Franco 2014, p. 1). However, it does appear that land issues are particularly central to human and livelihood security in former conflict areas. One report in *Mizzima* by Phyu Phyu Zin (2014) argued that there are no measures in the National Land Use Policy draft dealing with historic land-grabs by the military in many areas, and "it does not legally recognise and guarantee freedom of customary collective land ownership, land use and land management of ethnic groups." Thus, for many poorer upland farmers who traditionally practised shifting cultivation techniques, there is a lack of legal protection for customary practices and land access rights are vulnerable to land expropriations backed up by new laws. For IDPs who lost land to military expropriation or conflict, and returnee refugees, the lack of access to land is a severe constraint on "freedom's possibilities".

Land-grabbing and development-induced displacements are often associated with specific mega-projects, especially hydropower dams, cash crop plantations and infrastructure. Indeed, some observers have called these "development invasions" (*Karen News* 2014b). Oftentimes villagers would be notified that land would be transferred to other purposes or that they would no longer be able to use it as it was previously used, and in almost all cases military backing supported the confiscation or targeting of land (Transnational Institute (TNI) and Burma Centre Netherlands (BCN) 2013). As the KRHG (2013, p. 7) reported: "Villagers consistently report that their perspectives are excluded from planning and implementation of these projects, which often provide little or no benefit to the local community or result in substantial, often irreversible, harm." One of the key issues preventing collective action in cases of dispute about land confiscation or poor compensation is the "fear of military actors" (KHRG 2013, p. 44). On the bright side, there are numerous instances of village committees reporting to authorities about land confiscations, petitioning for fair compensation, and reporting on developments, which would have been virtually impossible under the old regime of full military rule.

ANXIETIES WITHIN LANDSCAPES OF CHANGE

One of the major socio-psychological obstacles confronting the peace process is the fact that many people remain deeply anxious about the ultimate goals of development initiatives. One MPSI senior consultant with long experience implementing participatory projects in the borderlands, Alan Smith observes that "however much people want and welcome peace, there is not yet confidence that it can be sustained" (*Karen News* 2014*a*). Referring to Karen displaced persons, Smith noted that people want to return to their lands and orchards, but "they are struggling to find the confidence to do so" (*Karen News* 2014*a*). Such ideas relate to a much larger political economic landscape whereby key decisions are being made at a distance by transnational, national and state decision-makers, with underlying goals aimed at accumulating capital and national-level development, whereby in the process, border areas are viewed as having underdeveloped resources. This scalar dynamic is a norm of capitalist uneven development (Smith 2010), but within former conflict-prone zones of Myanmar, socioeconomic disparities are further deepened due to unresolved issues of gross insecurity and the stuttering pace of conflict resolution. Any inward investment decisions and economic planning are played out in an already fragile landscape scarred by violence, and where ordinary people are struggling to get their lives back together.

For IDPs the situation within zones of recent conflict remains precarious.

> The IDP situation is still the same. Medical care and education are still the same, as the Burma Army does not provide any of these. Even in the city, there is no good medical care service. How can they care for the people in the jungle? (interview with Doh Say, Free Burma Ranger, 2012).[4]

This statement is based on the respondent's active life for a decade as somebody who risked life and limb taking in medical supplies to IDPs, and whilst access to former war zones is much easier under ceasefires, many people remain living on very basic means and without proper homes.

One direct legacy of decades of conflict that is going to take a long time to remove are large swathes of land affected by the presence of landmines (see Figure 14.2). A *Kantarawaddy Times* (2011*b*) report entitled *No More Land for Civilians to Set Foot On* recounted a story about an explosion

FIGURE 14.2
Map Showing Estimated Areas of Kayah State Most Likely Affected by Landmines. There are still Many Unexploded Ordinances and Landmines after Decades of Conflict.

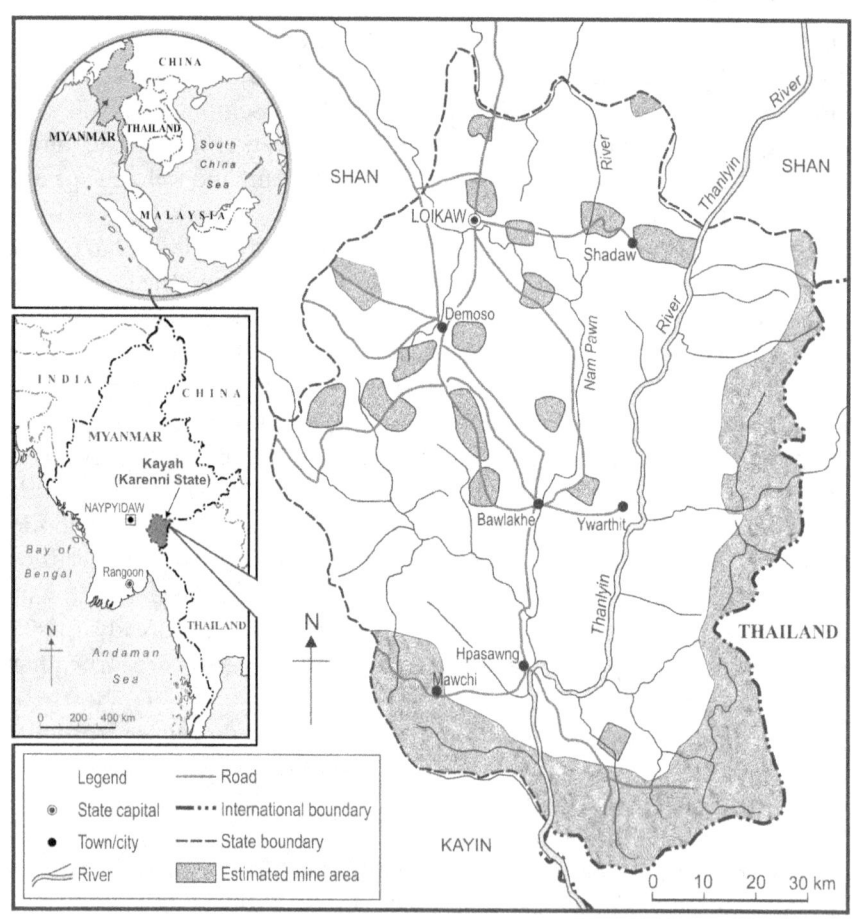

near a Baptist church on a hillside near Mawchi town. Such stories remind us that the decades of conflict have a constraining effect on the spaces of development even in a period of relative peace. Mines were laid by the *Tatmadaw* to dissuade people from returning to their native villages after forced eviction during the "Four Cuts" counter-insurgency campaigns. Many mine casualties occurred when people sought to return to their villages to collect food or other items, or in nearby forests when they went to forage for food, or during travel to nearby villages or agricultural plots. However, ethnic armies have also been planting mines. Indeed, it has been estimated that 40 per cent of Karen National Liberation Army (KNLA) mine injuries and deaths were self-inflicted whilst soldiers were laying, lifting or moving mines, or by stepping on mines already laid by comrades (Moser-Puangsuwan 2008, p. 2). In border states there has still to begin a systematic effort to de-mine areas prone to mines. Many mines were laid in the border region immediately near the Thai borderline to prevent easy border-crossings and to target routes known to be used by the Karenni Army. But even well inside Kayah/Karenni State territory the *Tatmadaw* placed mines around battalion camps, around key installations to protect them from sabotage, such as Lawpita Hydropower Plant in Loikaw Township, and around electricity poles. Unfortunately, the Burma and ethnic armies did not always keep accurate maps of mines being laid. It is not only a problem for people. A Mawchi resident reported: "Cows and buffalos from Kaw Tudoh, Bulaw Pei, Leh Lawhti, Lo Hkarlo, Maw Hser Khe villages in Mawchi Township used to step on landmines every 2 or 3 days. Local people can not do anything (to stop it)" (*Kantarawaddy Times* 2011a). Mine clearance is clearly a major priority in order to prevent needless injuries, deaths and loss of productive land for many years to come.

CHANGING GOALPOSTS AND THE DILEMMAS OF RELATIVE PEACE

Over the years, attempts were made to establish peace within Karenni/Kayah State. A series of ceasefire agreement discussions started at the state level on 7 March 2012 with the KNPP. The peace process represents the best opportunity in many decades to begin resolving Myanmar's complex ethnic and state-society conflicts. Additionally, one of the efforts includes the formation of the United Nationalities Federal Council (UNFC) in February 2011. Twelve of the sixteen major armed groups currently active in Myanmar are members of this umbrella organization. Since its inception the UNFC has been exerting pressure on the government to initiate talks with the body so that the demands of the ethnic groups can be coordinated and decisions taken abided by the members. Such initiatives are central to the political, economic and social shifts occurring within Myanmar and play a vital role in reshaping meanings attached to the borderlands. For exiled ethnic political parties like the KNPP there has been a reluctance to sign nationwide ceasefire agreements due to the slow progress with government troop withdrawal from the ethnic areas (*Kantarawaddy Times* 2013c). The fact is that decades of armed resistance and militarization mean that peace-building has to navigate a terrain of mistrust between key political agents. There is also a need for the KNPP leaders to be more transparent and to explain their policies relating to ceasefire agreements to the broader constituency of citizens, refugees and returnees (*Kantarawaddy Times* 2014).

While the peace agreement is slowly making progress, valid concerns by many communities were raised and this includes the unregulated incursion of business interests, such as natural resource extraction projects and land grabbing into previously inaccessible, conflict-affected areas. The problem is that decades of conflict have generated considerable mistrust within the leaders, activists and organizers of ethnic and refugee organizations. This has not been ameliorated by the mere transferral of authority from largely military to civilian forms of governance. In the countryside, and in many ethnic areas, the continued dominance of military control within administrative and economic sectors (Myanmar Peace Monitor 2013) until recently was viewed as a "trans-legal" force in some respects (interview with David Eubank, Founder of Free Burma Rangers, 2012).[5] This is a critical historical, ethical and moral issue in that the political landscape cannot simply be made clean just through relative democracy after years of brutal military rule. Many who struggled for decades against previous military juntas remain sceptical of the political transformation of Myanmar, at least in respect to Karenni territory.

> KNPP [had] requested for the military to withdraw the military outpost in the border and those near to the villagers to their barracks. But this did not happen (interview with Khu Hte Bu, Director of Karenni Social Welfare and Development Centre (KSWDC), 2013).[6]
>
> From time to time, the [political] situation differs. Sometimes, we are okay with the State government, sometimes we are okay with the military government and sometimes we are not. It is difficult to trust. [For example in] 1996 [there was a] big fight after ceasefire agreement broke down in June. [We actually] started talking in 1993 but ceasefire agreement

only lasted three months. I cannot jump into conclusion that there are changes in the country [now]. We are just trying to negotiate the talk agenda (interview with Khu Oo Reh, Vice-Chairperson of KNPP, 2013).[7]

Myanmar's transforming political situation requires a long period of stability in order to enable conditions for many refugees to return. Long periods of conflict and even uncertain ceasefires generated considerable insecurity and anxiety amongst refugee populations.

> Before the ceasefire, there is less danger for us because we cannot go "inside" at all. Now, we can go in but there are no safeguard at all. Some of the member of the Burmese Army can also come and visit around the area [refugee camp]. This situation is difficult to say and it is dangerous for both sides (interview with Aung Sun Myint, Founder of Karenni Social Development Centre (KSDC), 2013).[8]
>
> It is just ceasefire now, not peace yet. Just stopped fighting for a while and they have to negotiate to get the political settlement. When there is one political settlement, then we can go back. But now the situation can break down anytime. It is just ceasefire. So that's why people in the camp, they go back illegally. They just go and come again, just for visit (interview with Theh Myar, Secretary of the Karenni Religious and Culture Development Community, 2013).[9]

Frequently, when referring to Kayah (Karenni) State, refugees use the term "inside", and "going inside" means crossing the border back to Kayah State.

> They just go back inside because they want to see their villages, and some people want to have a little farm, something like that. They stayed in the camp for many years and they long for their villages now. Now the situation has changed and there are no more Burmese army checks near the border; that's why some of them go back (…). (interview with Theh Myar, Secretary of the Karenni Religious and Culture Development Community, 2013).[10]

Following the ceasefire there is increasing connectivity between "inside" and "outside", between different Karenni groups (refugee and non-refugee), between groups within Kayah State (non-state armed groups, non-state civilian, businesses, NGOs) and Myanmar authorities, as well as a steady increase in cross-border contact. This has potentially productive social and political implications for the future.

> Families on the borderline are able to meet each other. There is trust building. For example, one of my uncles works in the parliament. Before, I did not get to know him or trust him. But now we are able to see each other and we are able to talk, understanding each other's situation a little more (interview with Minyou, Director of KNWO, 2013).[11]

Others working within CBOs see this opportunity to increase their efforts to reach people "inside", providing the less fortunate in Kayah State with much required assistance such as healthcare, women's welfare, and education. Ironically perhaps, former refugee groups under the auspices of political organizations like the KNPP have become very active in the post-ceasefire health, education and social welfare landscape slowly emerging "inside" Kayah State. Even more important for freedom's possibilities to strengthen and evolve is the removal of the blanket of fear that prevented people from talking with one another.

> People are more open to speak up, [and discuss] what their challenges are. More freedom to speak and to travel [are big changes]. Being able to talk about politics is a big change. Before the ceasefire, many would not talk about politics. But now, people recognize the need of having one party being representative for them. People had been under the control of the military regime. Most of them did not get involved in politics, and they just start to get involved now. Hence, much time is required (interview with Khu Oo Reh, Vice-Chairperson of KNPP, 2013).[12]
>
> Most of the funders are interested in the "inside". Previously, priority is provided to the cross-border programme. But it is more attractive to go "inside" and help the people there. It poses a problem for the refugees in Thailand because practically most of the NGOs are shifting "inside" now (interview with Khu Hte Bu, Director of CBO, 2013).[13]

With the political changes taking place within Myanmar, international donors and foreign NGO humanitarian and relief organizations have, over the last few years, shifted attention from refugee populations towards developmental, human rights and welfare issues within different parts of Myanmar. This shift affected the flow of aid and international links to the Karenni people and refugee communities of Mae Hong Son province.

> Aid decreased a couple of years ago. They are more focused in working inside the country (Karenni), as they think that there are more people inside who suffer, not wanting to place their focus on the refugees. (...) Burma shows signs of change which may take place soon. If it really takes

effect, there are more needy people in Burma. For the moment, it is not the right time for them to go into the country but they could initiate programmes. They cannot run their activities freely in the country anyway. The country has just started opening up and there are many (new) laws and regulations imposed. Also, there are no rules or law in certain places, sometimes even in big city as well. People are just beginning to rebuild the country. They should also understand that these changes take time and that they should make slow moves and not rush into things (interview with Khu Oo Reh, Vice-Chairperson of KNPP, 2013).[14]

Other interviewees have suggested that there is relief fatigue in relation to the protracted and long-term refugee situation along the border. "They [foreign NGOs] want the refugees to stand on their own feet" (interview with Elizabeth, Education Coordinator, 2013).[15] Thus, the cross-border Karenni CBOs are beginning to see scope for funding activities inside Karenni/Kayah State.

They heard that there is no more fighting in Myanmar, so they are more interested to fund projects "inside". [Everyone is] excited about Burma. This is our strategy, to show some activity from "inside", to be able to get more funding for the refugee camp. The peace process is not completed yet, so we think it's better to rent houses (in Kayah State) and keep it small for the first year. If everything is fine, we will start later. But if we solely focus on the refugee camp, they (the funding support) might leave us. Even if the peace process is not over yet, there is something we could do, we should try to do (inside Kayah State) (interview with Elizabeth, Education Coordinator, 2013).[16]

Some projects are being initiated in Kayah State territory by Karenni refugee groups, such as by the KNWO, albeit with caution due to uncertainty over the ceasefire holding and deep-seated mistrust of the Myanmar State's intentions.

According to situation, it is easy to get into but not easy to implement activities, not easy to stay in Loikaw. When KNWO was set up, we had based our initiatives on the borderland. According to our activities, we have very close relations with Thailand and also the NGOs operating here. But when we move into Karenni State, we stay in Loikaw, we don't have our office and we don't have a place to stay. Also, the culture and daily lives of the people are a little different from here (in Nai Soi). Even language communication is a little different.

> KNWO might set up a branch office in Karenni State [in the future]... According to the political situation and the whole of Burma's situation, we are not sure how much we can trust the government. (...) If you set up your main office in Loikaw, it means that you are under the control of the Burmese Government. If anything happens, you cannot move out. So we have to have two different plans. So if anything happens, we can shout, and we can speak out outside the country (interview with Minyou, Director of KNWO, 2013).[17]

The very fact that refugee organizations can see opportunities to be active within their former homeland is a vital sign of improved security and basic peace. Figure 14.3 shows the uneven dirt football pitch in a Karenni refugee camp nestled near the mountain scenery of the borderland, which for so long has been an alienated border space full of stark choices and sometimes a razor's edge of life and death. But much has changed in the last five years, and the geopolitical goal posts and the ground itself have completely altered, and so too have the prospects for politically displaced youngsters who have new possibilities for freedom and development.

> I wish for freedom for everyone, no matter what ethnic race you are. Ten years ago, the country had a lot of problems because the ethnic races see themselves as diverse independent groups. If we all continue to see that way, we can never become united (interview with Doh Say, Free Burma Ranger, 2012).[18]

These words were spoken by somebody who has long sought to provide direct and personal help to IDPs, and who only recently has visited his hometown after more than two decades in exile. They are simple yet profound words, for they relate to an appeal for distinct ethnic groups to put down their political differences and to forge a stronger unity, and they relate to Myanmar's peace process within which former enemies and various ethnic groups, including all Burmese identities to be viewed as equals. These words warn us that divisions are still to be overcome. For "freedom's possibilities" to be met there is a need for inclusive and grounded forms of development that recognize the historic legacies of decades-long conflict, and also include people who have been forcibly (internally and externally) displaced and politically exiled. Whilst new political goalposts have been erected in Myanmar, and the geopolitical football game no longer involves junta rule, decades of conflict cannot be easily dismissed, and many displaced people remain deeply anxious about their security within a changing political economic landscape. Many villagers living

FIGURE 14.3
Playing Football at a Border Refugee Camp near Ban Nai Soi

Note: Photograph courtesy of Kok Wenying.

within former conflict-prone areas of the borderland are now facing new challenges generated by inward investment, resource exploitation and land conflicts. Within this new political economy there are numerous ongoing disputes and battles ahead, and it is vital that different ethnic and community leaders, NGOs, CBOs and cross-border agencies continue to forge spaces of engagement to protect social and environmental security for years to come. Freedom's possibilities can only be met with continual struggle for an all-inclusive peace regardless of past political, ethnic and cultural differences.

Notes

1. We use "Kayah State" (official Myanmar designation of the territory where most of our respondents came from) and also "Karenni State" (as a term preferred by political leaders of the Karenni National Progressive Party (KNPP) and activist refugee organizations).
2. We use Karenni when we discuss refugees throughout this chapter due to its

common use amongst most of our refugee respondents, rather than refer to Kayah refugees, which is a reference to the dominant ethnic group of Myanmar's "Kayah State". "Karenni" is a bit of a catch-all term as there are several ethnic groups who reside within the Kayah State. Sometimes we refer to "Karenni State" as a politicized term indicating a "nation-of-intent" and this term is widely used amongst our respondents, and it also relates to the national aspirations of the KNPP.

3. Interview with Ah Mu Doh, Founder of Karenni National Women Organization (KNWO). Interviewed by Carl Grundy-Warr and Chin Wei Jun, Dokita, Mae Hong Son, Thailand, 5 June 2012.
4. Interview with Doh Say, Free Burma Ranger. Interviewed by Carl Grundy-Warr and Chin Wei Jun, Mae Hong Son Town, Thailand, 25 May 2012.
5. Interview with David Eubank, Founder of Free Burma Rangers. Interviewed by Carl Grundy-Warr and Chin Wei Jun, David Eubank's home, Chiang Mai, Thailand, 15 June 2012.
6. Interview with Khu Hte Bu, Director of Karenni Social Welfare and Development Centre (KSWDC). Interviewed by Carl Grundy-Warr and Chin Wei Jun, Dokita, Mae Hong Son, Thailand, 29 May 2013.
7. Interview with Khu Oo Reh, Vice-Chairperson of KNPP. Interviewed by Carl Grundy-Warr and Chin Wei Jun, Nai Soi Town, Mae Hong Son, Thailand, 9 June 2013.
8. Interview with Aung Sun Myint, Founder of Karenni Social Development Centre (KSDC). Interviewed by Carl Grundy-Warr and Chin Wei Jun, Dokita, Mae Hong Son, Thailand, 23 May 2013.
9. Interview with Theh Myar, Secretary of the Karenni Religious and Culture Development Community. Interviewed by Carl Grundy-Warr and Chin Wei Jun, Dokita, Mae Hong Son, Thailand, 2 June 2013.
10. Ibid.
11. Interview with Minyou, Director of KNWO. Interviewed by Carl Grundy-Warr and Chin Wei Jun, Dokita, Mae Hong Son, Thailand, 28 May 2013.
12. Interview with Khu Oo Reh, Vice-Chairperson of KNPP. Interviewed by Carl Grundy-Warr and Chin Wei Jun, Dokita, Mae Hong Son, Thailand, 9 June 2013.
13. Interview with Khu Hte Bu, Director of KSWDC. Interviewed by Carl Grundy-Warr and Chin Wei Jun, Dokita, Mae Hong Son, Thailand, 29 May 2013.
14. Interview with Khu Oo Reh, Vice-Chairperson of KNPP. Interviewed by Carl Grundy-Warr and Chin Wei Jun, Nai Soi Town, Mae Hong Son, Thailand, 9 June 2013.
15. Interview with Elizabeth, Education Coordinator. Interviewed by Carl Grundy-Warr and Chin Wei Jun, Nai Soi Town, Mae Hong Son, Thailand, 5 June 2013.
16. Ibid.
17. Interview with Minyou, Director of KNWO. Interviewed by Carl Grundy-Warr and Chin Wei Jun, Dokita, Mae Hong Son, Thailand, 28 May 2013.
18. Interview with Doh Say, Free Burma Ranger. Interviewed by Carl Grundy-Warr and Chin Wei Jun, Mae Hong Son, Thailand, 25 May 2012.

References

Bamforth, Vicky, Steven Lanjouw, and Graham Mortimer. *Conflict and Displacement in Karenni: The Need for Considered Responses*. Chiang Mai: Burma Ethnic Research Group, 2000.

Buchanan, John, Tom Kramer, and Kevin Woods. *Developing Disparity. Regional Investment in Burma's Borderlands*. Amsterdam: Transnational Institute (TNI) and Burma Centre Netherlands (BCN), 2013.

Callahan, Mary P. *Political Authority in Burma's Ethnic Minority States: Devolution, Occupation and Coexistence*. Singapore: Institute of Southeast Asian Studies (ISEAS), 2007.

Cheeseman, Nick, Monique Skidmore, and Trevor Wilson, eds. *Myanmar's Transition: Openings, Obstacles and Opportunities*. Singapore: Institute of Southeast Asian Studies (ISEAS), 2012.

Decha Tangseefa. "Temporary Shelter Areas and the Paradox of Perceptibility: Imperceptible Naked Karens in the Thai-Burmese Border Zones". In *Borderscapes: Hidden Geographies and Politics at Territory's Edge*, edited by Prem Kumar Rajaram and Carl Grundy-Warr. Minneapolis: University of Minnesota Press, 2007, pp. 231–62.

Franco, Jennifer. "The Draft Land Use Policy: Putting Big Business First". In *Mizzima*, 9 December 2014 <http://farmlandgrab.org/post/view/24314> (accessed 18 December 2014).

Grundy-Warr, Carl. "Lost in Sovereign Space: Forced Migrants in the Territorial Trap". *Asian and Pacific Migration Journal* 11, no. 4 (2002): 437–61.

――――. "The Silence and Violence of Forced Migration: The Myanmar-Thailand Border". In *International Migration in Southeast Asia*, edited by Aris Ananta and Evi Nurvidya Arifin. Singapore: Institute of Southeast Asian Studies (ISEAS), 2004, pp. 228–72.

―――― and Karin Dean. "Not Peace, Not War: The Myriad Spaces of Sovereignty, Peace and Conflict in Myanmar/Burma". In *Reconstructing Conflict. Integrating War and Post-War Geographies*, edited by Scott Kirsch and Colin Flint. Farnham: Ashgate, 2011, pp. 91–114.

Grundy-Warr, Carl and Elaine Wong Siew Yin. "Geographies of Displacement: The Karenni and Shan across the Myanmar-Thailand Border". *Singapore Journal of Tropical Geography* 14, no. 1 (2002): 42–56.

Heppner, Kevin. "A Village on Fire: The Destruction of Rural Life in Southeastern Burma". *Cultural Survival Quarterly* 24, no. 3 (2000): 15–18.

Kantarawaddy Times. "Danger with Every Step: Land Mines Killing and Wounding", 14 July 2011*a* <http://www.bnionline.net/index.php/news/kantarawaddy/11153> (accessed 5 November 2013).

――――. "No More Land for Civilians to Set Foot On", 19 August 2011*b* <http://www.bnionline.net/index.php/news/kantarawaddy/11426> (accessed 5 November 2013).

――――. "Still No Electricity for Karenni State Residents", 11 October 2013*a* <http://www.bnionline.net/index.php/news/kantarawaddy/16332> (accessed 5 November 2013).

———. "Shortage of Doctors Outside Karenni Capital", 12 October 2013*b* <http://www.bnionline.net/index.php/news/kantarawaddy/16336> (accessed 5 November 2013).

———. "KNPP won't Sign Nationwide Ceasefire", 14 October 2013*c* <http://www.bnionline.net/index.php/news/kantarawaddy/16341> (accessed 5 November 2013).

———. "Karenni Women's Groups Want Mega Projects Stopped During Ceasefire", 12 September 2014 <http://www.bmionline.net/index.php/news/kantarawaddy/17990> (accessed 19 December 2014).

Karen Human Rights Group (KHRG). "Losing Ground. Land Conflicts and Collective Action in Eastern Myanmar", 5 March 2013 <http://www.khrg.org/2013/03/losing-ground-land-conflicts-and-collective-action-eastern-myanmar> (accessed 14 November 2014).

Karen News. "Despite Norway's Best Efforts, Peace Remains Elusive", 5 March 2014*a* <http://karennews.org/2014/03/despite-norways-best-efforts-peace-remains-elusive.html> (accessed 1 August 2014).

———. "Caught in a Two-Front War in Post-Ceasefire Karen State", 18 July 2014*b* <http://karennews.org/2014/07/caught-in-a-two-front-war-in-post-ceasefire-karen-state.html> (accessed 1 August 2014).

Lambrecht, Curtis T. "Oxymoronic Development: The Military as Benefactor in the Border Regions of Burma". In *Civilizing the Margins. Southeast Asian Government Policies for the Development of Minorities*, edited by Christopher R. Duncan. New York: Cornell University Press, 2004, pp. 150–81.

Lang, Hazel. *Fear and Sanctuary: Burmese Refugees in Thailand*. New York: Cornell University Press, 2002.

Maclean, Ken. "Sovereignty in Burma after the Entrepreneurial Turn: Mosaics of Control, Commodified Spaces, and Regulated Violence in Contemporary Burma". In *Taking Southeast Asia to Market. Commodities, Nature and People in the Neoliberal Age*, edited by Joseph Nevins and Nancy Lee Peluso. New York: Cornell University Press, 2008, pp. 140–60.

Moser-Puangsuwan, Yeshua. "Anti-personnel Landmines in Myanmar: A Cause of Displacement and an Obstacle to Return". *Humanitarian Exchange Monitor* 41, December 2008.

Myanmar Peace Monitor (MPM). "Economics of Peace and Conflict". Chiang Mai: Burma News International, 2013.

Petrie, Charles, and Ashley South. "Peace-building in Myanmar". In *Burma/ Myanmar. Where Now?*, edited by Mikael Gravers and Flemming Ytzen. Copenhagen: Nordic Institute of Asian Studies (NIAS) Press, 2014, pp. 223–49.

Phyu Phyu Zin. "NGOs Fear Land Use Policy Fails to Deal With Land Grabs, Farmers' Rights". In *Mizzima*, 7 November 2014, <http://farmlandgrab.org/post/view/24185> (accessed 14 November 2014).

Schroeder, Tim and Alan Saw U. "The Karen in Myanmar's Southeast — Great Hopes and Many Unresolved Issues". In *Burma/ Myanmar. Where Now?*, edited by Mikael Gravers and Flemming Ytzen. Copenhagen: Nordic Institute of Asian Studies (NIAS) Press, 2014, pp. 198–216.

Sen, Amartya. *Beyond the Crisis: Development Strategies in Asia*. Singapore: Institute of Southeast Asia (ISEAS), 1999.
Smith, Martin. *Burma. Insurgency and the Politics of Ethnicity*. London: Zed Books, 1999.
Smith, Neil. *Uneven Development. Nature, Capital and the Production of Space*. London: Verso, 2010.
The Border Consortium (TBC). "Poverty, Displacement and Local Governance in South East Burma/Myanmar". Bangkok: The Border Consortium, November 2013.
Transnational Institute (TNI) and Burma Centre Netherlands (BCN). "Access Denied. Land Rights and Ethnic Conflict in Burma", 11 May 2013 <http://www.tni.org/briefing/access-denied> (accessed 20 February 2014).
Wai Moe. "The Struggle for Peace in Northern Myanmar". In *Burma/ Myanmar. Where Now?*, edited by Mikael Gravers and Flemming Ytzen. Copenhagen: Nordic Institute of Asian Studies (NIAS) Press, 2014, pp. 262–78.
Woods, Kevin. "A Political Anatomy of Land Grabs". In *Myanmar Times*, 3 March 2014 <http://farmlandgrab.org/post/view/23224> (accessed 14 December 2014).

Section VI

Institutionalized Identity and Border Practices

15

The Chin State-Mizoram Border: Institutionalized Xenophobia for State Control[1]

BIANCA SON AND N. WILLIAM SINGH

In Mizoram State of India, a popular weekly television programme, *Lamtluang* (Mizo Lyric Blog 2014), reports on different cultures, lifestyles, religious institutions, transport systems as well as other facets of daily life abroad. In 2013, journalists from the programme travelled to the Chin State of Myanmar. In an interview of Chin elders, the topic that arose was the close ethnic relations between the Chin and the Mizo[2] (interview with Chin elders at Aizawl 2014).[3] The elders maintained that while Chin State was part of another country, they were not different from the Mizo in any significant way. They explained that the Chin and the Mizo shared a culture and language and that in many cases, even had kin living across the border. Although the border was drawn during the colonial period, the people have always considered themselves, "wrongly divided; they are brethren" (comments by Mizo Elders during the *Lamtluang* television programme, 12 February 2014 at Aizawl).[4] This was not a new concept. Numerous arguments for this shared ethnicity, history and the wrongly imposed division of the Chin and the Mizo can be found in Vumson (1986, p. 32) and Son (2013, p. 56). In fact, most Chin and Mizo accept that they are the "same people", yet, the television show emphasized that the Chin are from a "different" country. Chin interviewees did not accept this position and further commented on how badly most Chin are treated by their Mizo "brothers" when they cross the border from Myanmar to escape poverty in search of a better livelihood in the Indian state of Mizoram.

INTRODUCTION

In addressing the border separating the Chin Hills of Myanmar from Mizoram of India, this chapter has two aims. It is a study of border exchanges: illegal and legal, licit and illicit, and the dire situation of the Chin in Mizoram. We argue that the intense xenophobia against the Chin is not only fostered but also institutionalized by the Youth Mizo Association (YMA), the largest civil society organization in Mizoram. The social science term, xenophobia was chosen due to the obvious marginalization of the Chin in Mizoram (as well as toward other non-Mizo). In its most basic definition, "[x]enophobia is the intense or irrational dislike or fear of people from other countries" (Oxford English Dictionary 2012). While the YMA does not have any official or legal role in the government of Mizoram or of India, it has much power and control within Mizo society. That is to say, given that every single Mizo person over the age of fourteen becomes a member of this civil society organization, its power reaches beyond the government, the law and the church. Xenophobia is exercised to supress the shared knowledge that the Chin and the Mizo, before the colonial era, were and continue to be brethren. Thus, this chapter addresses the border trade between these two nation states and the plight of the Chin in Mizoram as victims of xenophobia. Xenophobia of minority ethnic groups in Mizoram is socially constructed by Mizo society based on the notion of an ideal Christian way of life. This is a non-political way of looking at xenophobia and identity formations as it is not based on the struggle for power over resources, or claims for power and legitimacy. Instead it has arisen solely as a result of the so-called anti-social practices of a few Chin migrants within Mizoram. Also, most of the Mizo civil society organizations and the powerful Presbyterian Church of Mizoram usually condemn any unwelcoming acts as un-Christian; they overlook mitigating factors such as poverty and livelihood issues of the Chin in Mizoram. The dominant Mizo ethnic group often views Chin migrants in Mizoram as bootleggers who brew liquor illicitly and sell drugs to the God-fearing Mizos.

A bridge spanning the Chin Hills of Myanmar to the northeastern Indian state of Mizoram is used to move goods and products from one nation state to the other. The border town on the Indian side, Champhai, enjoys a thriving economy in legal trade. Chin traders sell their wares in Mizoram's markets including in its capital, Aizawl. The Mizo of India rely on these goods, some being brought all the way from China via Mandalay and Kalemyo. Goods from India are also brought across the border into Myanmar. Hence, both sides rely on products from across the border. The official trading zone is between the Mizo district of Champhai and the

Tedim township of Myanmar. Border crossings do occur at other areas but the rugged terrain of the mountains proves challenging for the transport of goods. During the monsoon, crossing the border south of Champhai is nearly impossible.

HISTORICAL CONTEXT OF THE BORDER OF MIZORAM

To understand this border, the context of the political, economic and sociocultural circumstances must be addressed. Unlike other borders, this fifty-kilometre stretch of the Indo-Myanmar border is not only porous but is open, albeit nominally, and only occasionally controlled. The Indo-Myanmar "Friendship Bridge" spans the Tiau River between the Mizoram village of Champhai and Zokhawthar town in Chin State of Myanmar. Another bridge links the Chin Hills village of Tamu to Manipur's border town of Moreh. Thus, there are two border crossings in this area. However, given that this chapter addresses xenophobia in Mizoram, the Manipur-Myanmar border is not addressed.

The political border separating the Chin and the Mizo (Zo people) has been contested since the colonial era when it was first drawn. Before and at independence, neither group fully recognized this political border although it was understood that it created two separate nation states. These were only "paper agreements" (van Schendel and Abraham 2005, p. 5) and did not correspond to or deter the activities in the borderland. Thus, early border crossings for trade and migration were illegal, but very much licit (van Schendel and Abraham 2005, p. 10).[5] It provided the people in the borderlands viable income out of the reach of either government. Until the 1980s, there was no proper taxation by both the Mizoram and Myanmar authorities on individuals and groups who crossed the border. This border economy, however, only grew in the 1980s after much political turmoil in both nation states had reached the borderlands.

While the Chin in Myanmar were struggling with basic survival, the Mizo of the former Lushai Hills had their own political and economic difficulties. After the massive bamboo famine of 1959, the Mizo National Famine Front (MNFF) was born (Thanga 1978, p. 174). This famine was caused by the bamboo, *Melocannabaccifera*, also referred to as *Mautum* (bamboo death) (a Mizo term), which wreaks havoc once a generation. Bamboo has a life cycle of forty-eight years at the end of which it flowers, bears plentiful fruit and then dies. Rats devour these fructose-rich fruit, temporarily increasing their fertility rates. This results in an explosion of the rat population. Once the bamboo fruit are exhausted, plagues of rats turn to the crops in the fields. The result is a serious and devastating famine across the whole of the northern Arakan mountain range in Chin State as well as in Mizoram (Pachau 2014, p. 8).

These famines have played a significant role in the history of the highlanders.[6] During the colonial era, the famine caused mass migrations. Three such massive famines are found in the historical records (*The Times* 1892; Gougin 1984, pp. 95–96). There are references to a large-scale famine at the turn of the century and another massive famine occurred in 1959 (Nag 2001, pp. 24–30; Lalnunmawia 2005, pp. 317–22). The last famine to occur was in 2006. The 1959 famine, however, had the most impact on the relations between the people of Mizoram and the Chin Hills. India's slow response in 1959 resulted in the formation of the Mizo National Front (MNF) led by Pu Laldenga, who realized that the central government would not send famine relief. Thus, Laldenga resolved to fight for separation from the nation state of India. The year 1960 marks the beginning of a brutal insurgency that lasted for twenty years. Crossing the border during this time proved dangerous as rebels hid and fought in the jungles against the Indian Army. Rebels also hid behind the borders in Myanmar. Thus, traders were often mistaken for rebels and many lost their lives.

The Indian Government learned that Laldenga planned to rise against the government in Delhi. Hence, six years after the formation of the MNF, in 1966, they responded to the insurgency with a series of air strikes. After the air strikes — the only attack to ever occur against an insurgency group in India — many Mizo were displaced, others were killed and the villages were regrouped. This caused additional havoc and mistrust toward the Indian Government. The MNF continued with insurgency activities for another twenty years, making the border unsafe for crossing.

The MNF under the leadership of Laldenga formed itself into an armed separatist movement and waged war against India for two decades from 1966–86. Before 1986, MNF occupied much of the borderlands making crossing the border dangerous for traders, smugglers and migrants. Although crossings still occurred, it was illegal. After the MNF and the Indian Government's Ceasefire Agreement of 1986, however, the border was effectively opened. The border's infrastructure was constructed to be sufficient for anyone spending time in this border heartland. There are plenty of cafes and hostels, which provide lodging and other services for border-crossers. Many Chin from Myanmar cross the border into Mizoram for a day to trade and return to their villages in the evenings. The Chin who cross the border to smuggle contraband rely on cooperatives living in Mizoram, whether Mizo or Chin. Sometimes they have agreements and relationships with border guards who allow them passage for a bribe. Other collaborations may be kin related. These kin also provide lodging, food, and safety to Chin smugglers. It must be noted that there are no real or significant language issues between the Zo of Myanmar and the Zo of India. They speak mutually intelligible Tibetan-Burmese languages and exercise similar cultural practices. Moreover, the MNF, now a political party, insisted on a special clause in the Mizoram Peace Accord and Ceasefire Agreement stipulating that the trading of goods should be made legal. It was signed by Laldenga and by the Government of India (Directorate Office 2008, p. 1). This is just one of the connections between the Chin and the Mizo, which is historical as well as progressive for the future.

In fact, as is mentioned above, there is a pervasive narrative that these two groups of people (as well as others in Manipur, Assam and Bangladesh) all belong to the same ethnic group called Zo. After the ceasefire agreement, numerous Zo reunification movements were formed. These movements campaigned for separatism and demanded their own nation state made up of the areas known as the Chin Hills and Mizoram. These movements are named "*R*eunification" because it is a widely shared belief that before the colonial era, the Zo were one and the same "race" of people. Thus, the border is considered primarily a political construct created by the British and adopted by the central governments of India and Myanmar.

HISTORICAL CONTEXT OF THE BORDER OF MYANMAR

After the 1962 military coup in Burma and a set of new declarations, Ne Win's government instituted the Burma Socialist Programme Party (BSPP). Its philosophy was an amalgamation of communism and Buddhism. It rejected the previous doctrines of Marx and Engels, insisting that the new regime would ensure that every citizen had a decent standard of living with special emphasis on basic sustenance. In order to achieve this end, the BSPP argued, all capitalist endeavours had to be nationalized. This way, Burma's resources could be appropriated across the nation for the purpose of self-reliance. The promises of the BSPP, however, were not realized. The ethnic minorities, especially, suffered under Ne Win's regime. The Chin began relying on previous relationships and economic opportunities across the border in Mizoram. Mizoram was a hill district during colonial times. It was known as Lushai Hills and is now a state of the Indian union. The Chin took refuge in Mizoram in order to survive and to earn their livelihood.[7]

This interdependence is not a new phenomenon. During the precolonial era, the border did not exist. After it was officially drawn by the British in 1892, trading continued. Eventually, some trading was made legal. Items such as auto parts, clothing, foodstuffs and tea are welcome commodities in Mizoram. Over several years Myanmar and Mizoram signed a number of treaties promising cooperation in border trade.[8] In fact, the infrastructure in the Myanmar border town, Zokhawthar, was funded by the Indian Government (Ministry of Development of the Northeastern Region Report 2011, pp. 50–54). However, there is also a subversive illegal economy in existence. The smuggling of jade, diamonds, gold, silver and other precious stones and metals, as well as illegal substances has been a profitable business which has existed for decades. Both types of economies have steadily grown ever since the Mizoram Ceasefire Agreement of 1986. It was a peace accord that had the express purpose of improving the lives of the people on both sides of the border as well as furnishing both governments with tax revenue (Rajagopalan 2008, pp. 4–6).

After signing the peace accord, the governments of Mizoram, India and Myanmar agreed on initiatives to develop this border crossing as an officially recognized international trading zone. They have taken the previously subversive border economy, which had relied on local networks and long-standing relationships between the Chin and the Mizo and brought it into the government's fold by making it legal, with the primary beneficiary being the two governments.

The trading of goods by the Chin from Myanmar via the officially recognized trading zone is encouraged. The illegal economy benefits both the Chin and the Mizo. It is an interdependent relationship between both legal and illegal trading. Despite this interdependence, the Mizo perceive the Chin as taking advantage of the trade between Myanmar and Mizoram. The Mizo may like the products that are brought across the border, but they do not like the people who deliver them to the markets and towns of Mizoram, despite their being "brothers". This larger consensus felt by the Mizo traders is propagated through the media in Mizoram as well as by the Mizo elite and civil society organizations like the YMA. These entities object strongly to the Chin crossing over to find work as migrant workers and actively try to expel these "illegal" immigrants.[9]

As of 1986, the border crossing from Champhai has become an official and protected "Special Economic Zone". Still, the YMA continues to campaign for the expulsion of the Chin to Myanmar on a regular basis. Upon return to the Chin Hills of Myanmar, the Chin often face punitive actions by the Burmese Government. The Burmese military often forces the Chin into forced labour as punishment, a practice that is rampant throughout the Chin Hills. Most of the migrants manage to evade border laws and often stay longer than the prescribed number of days in Mizoram. At the same time, in recent months, some Mizo have opted to migrate to Myanmar to sell their Indian-made products in Mandalay and Kaleymo. It is likely that they will eventually move farther to Rangoon. That is, despite their apparent trade agreements and migrations from both sides, there continues to be intense xenophobia exercised by the Mizo towards the Chin in Mizoram, but not towards the Mizo by Chin in the Chin Hills.

In 1988, the government of India and the government of Mizoram set up makeshift camps in Champhai and elsewhere for Chin asylum seekers on humanitarian grounds. By 1994, Chin refugee camps were closed down when the Indo-Myanmar border trade talks began. One of the main reasons for shutting down the Chin refugee camps was the request by the Myanmar authority which believed that the Chin National Front (CNF) fighting for independence for the Chin State in Myanmar was operating anti-national activities within Mizoram.

People in Mizoram initially (1962–93) had a soft spot for the Chin refugees who migrated to Mizoram as a result of close ethnic ties. Many churches in Mizoram and voluntary organizations initially helped and welcomed the Chin. However, later the attitude changed due to the anti-social and anti-national activities of the CNF within the Mizo Hills. The Mizo attitude towards the Chin transformed from "convivial to hatred". Such negative sentiments toward the Chin in Mizoram became prevalent by 1998. Treatment of the Chin became resilient and uncompromising with stereotypical notions of the Chin as "others" or "outsiders" polluting the harmonic nature of Mizo society. This remains the major factor for shunning the Chin who take refuge in Mizoram. Chin scattered across Mizoram are stereotyped as anti-Mizo and considered anti-Christian. There is a feeling that the Chin are becoming more of a burden to the host community.

Chin economic migrants remain confined to the informal sector of the Mizoram State economy because of their undocumented status and they earn meagre wages. Men do manual labour and work in farms, quarries and construction sites while women work in farms, quarries, markets, hotels and restaurants and as housemaids and weavers. The Chin provide manual and low-skilled work in essential jobs that locals do not want to be employed in. Hence, there is usually no competition for the same scarce jobs. Nonetheless, the Mizo look down on the Chin, labelling them as impoverished economic migrants — and are perhaps unaware of the widespread ethnic, religious, and political persecution they face in Myanmar.

PRESENT BORDERLAND AND THE YOUNG MIZO ASSOCIATION (YMA)

Myanmar instituted a strict nationality law in 1982. Under this law, the Mizo could not apply for Myanmar citizenship. However, they (and the Chin) are able to cross the border legally without a passport, using a contemporary pass issued at the border check post. This is because it is believed that the Mizo only cross the border to visit the legendary *Rhi Dil* Lake located in the Chin Hills and to trade Indian-made goods. Given the dire economic situation in Myanmar, Mizo crossing into the Chin Hills was not a real issue. Generally, people and goods such as foodstuffs move from east to west, while medicine, clothing and auto parts move from west to east. Only a few people move west to east to settle in Myanmar.

Although a significant number of people move from east to west, the Young Mizo Association (YMA) actively attempts to limit Chin migrants from entering Mizoram. The YMA is occupied with the preservation of Mizo identity and culture. It has been in existence since 1935 when Welsh Christian missionaries along with Mizo elite formed the association with three stipulations: firstly the good use of leisure time, secondly good Christian life, and thirdly preserving and fostering Mizo culture and society. While these mottos sound inclusive and constructive, the YMA plays a central role in the marginalization of Chin in Mizoram. They also marginalize other ethnic minority groups such as the Chakma and Mara further south in Mizoram State, of whom many are Buddhist or Muslim.

Marginalization manifests not only as discriminatory practices in relation to housing, wages and education, but also as violence and expulsion. Unfortunately, research on the YMA, both historical and anthropological, is still in its infancy. Thus, very specific questions in terms of the rise of xenophobia have yet to be addressed. This may have been a consequence of Myanmar's separation from British India in 1935–37, during which time the YMA was founded. It may also have been a consequence of the devastating air strikes by the Indian Government against MNF rebels. Perhaps the Mizo realized that unlike their neighbouring states in India, insurgencies would only cease if a unified Mizo state was created. The Mizo allow the YMA to control the aspects of their society that are bound to maintain peace and a decent standard of living for those who reject all other memberships by claiming only the Mizo identity and along with it, YMA mottos, which are essentially Christian with a strong element of exclusivity towards "outsiders". The YMA is the mirror of Mizo society. It remains the foremost agency that connects Mizo society and the Mizoram

State. The role that the YMA plays in Mizo society has been acknowledged by Mizo society as well as the Mizoram State. So far, there have been no disputes between the YMA and the Mizoram State. The YMA have only been flexing their muscles within Mizo society. However, human rights activists and journalists outside of Mizoram are critical towards it for taking the law into its own hands. Nevertheless, it would be rare to find a Mizo individual who is critical towards the YMA and its activities.

> Chins do not follow border rules and regulations. Based on the border regulations and movement of people across Myanmar and Mizoram, Chins can move only up to sixteen kilometres from the point of border checkpoints. Chins have to deposit an identity card to the border checkpoints to get the border pass. Chins on rare occasions deposit their identity card, pays fees and move inside Mizoram. Many of the Chins move beyond the sixteen-kilometre ceiling limit. Sometimes they move up to Aizawl, Guwahati and Delhi (interview with YMA Leader 2014[10]).

The Indian Passport Entry Rules, 1950 framed under the Passport Entry Act, 1920 made relaxations with regard to Citizens of India or a Citizen of the Union of Burma (Myanmar), who ordinarily resided in any area within forty kilometres on either side of the Indo-Myanmar border (see *The Mizoram Gazette* 2003, p. 2). Further notification in 1968 by the Ministry of Home Affairs, Government of India continues with the 1950 Indian Passport Entry Rules. The entry rule on Indo-Myanmar was changed on 21 July 2010. The notification from the Ministry of Home Affairs, Government of India shortened the distance from forty kilometres to sixteen kilometres (see *The Gazette of India* 2010, p. 4) and the entry permit to the borders remains valid for only one month. The permit seekers have to deposit their identity card at the border check posts. The point that we would like to make here is that the Mizo from Mizoram and Chin from Myanmar rarely abide by the prescribed distance limit of sixteen kilometres. Also, most Chin economic migrants do not renew their permits. This provides us with an idea of what "legal" and "permit" mean on both sides of the Indo-Myanmar border.

The central government of India tolerates the existence of Chin in Mizoram but does not offer any legal protection. It allows the Mizo state government to manage its own "illegal immigration problem of Chin within Mizoram". Moreover, India does not officially recognize the Chin as refugees although numerous refugee camps exist in New Delhi. In Mizoram, however, refugee camps do not exist as they are not permitted.

Instead, Chin migrant workers and refugees live in communities around the borderland, eking out a living. Because of the extreme xenophobia in Mizoram, they often have to do so illegally. One way to do so is by distilling alcohol. Given that Mizoram is a dry state, there is a demand for alcohol-based products including illegally manufactured beer.

Many Chin who settle on the outskirts of Aizawl brew illegal yet much desired commodities like beer and alcoholic drinks. The Mizoram Liquor Total Prohibition Act (MLTP) 1995 penalizes sellers and brewers of liquor in Mizoram. The Mizoram State believes that MLTP is successful due to the effective dictums of the YMA and never questions YMA crackdowns against illicit liquor brewers and sellers. Mizoram newspapers report that up to 75 per cent of the homes in villages such as Rangvamual and Phunchhwang are in the alcohol-brewing business. This has stigmatized the Chin community. Brewing or consuming alcohol is not in line with YMA mottos; it is considered neither "Christian" nor a valuable way of spending leisure time. Hence, this is even more reason for the Chin to be stigmatized and marginalized (Chakma 2003*a*).

The Chin also engage in other illegal activities causing the Mizo, or rather, the YMA grave cause for concern. In August 2013, the government of India's Right to Information (RTI) organization reported that the Directorate of Health Services furnished numerous drug licences to an under-aged son of Mizoram Health Minister Lalrinliana Sailo. Wholesale and general licences are meant for the selling and trading of drugs at Zokhawthar village on the Indo-Myanmar border in eastern Mizoram's Champhai district. According to RTI documents obtained by the MNF, these drug licences were used for smuggling pseudoephedrine into neighbouring Myanmar where they are manufactured into dangerous party drugs such as crystal meth. The MNF disclosed that the drug licence was used by a drug peddler, Rampanmawia, a Chin man from the township of Falam in Myanmar. Earlier, Rampanmawia had been arrested by Mizoram State's Excise and Narcotic police on 21 August 2012 in connection with the smuggling of pseudoephedrine. What was striking in this incident, however, was that the YMA locked up what was believed to be the house of Rampanmawia in Aizawl and even expelled the alleged drug peddler from the locality. The YMA did not attack or ask the Health Minister to step down. Rather, it attacked Rampanwawia, who is Chin (*Z News* 2013).

That is to say, the Mizo and the Chin ignore the laws and regulations of either nation state and behave as they see fit. The Chin try to survive by any means necessary including engaging in illegal activities, the Mizo react without government consent to punish only Chin perpetrators, thereby shielding the Mizo from the law. Although both the Chin State and Mizoram State are primarily managed by central governments in the plains, the people in both states manage the borderland as they believe is best, sometimes adhering to government regulations, and ignoring them at other times by engaging in illegal bribing and illegal punishment, as the above case illustrates.

There are numerous reasons for the Chin to seek life in Mizoram. For instance, although not recognized as refugees and having no official status in Mizoram, some Chin are able to gain access to the hospitals and send their children to Mizo schools, even without proper documentation. Their shared language makes it relatively easy for the Chin to integrate into Mizo communities. These Chin, however, tend to have close kin ties to Mizo or Chin who are established in Mizoram. Many of these established and settled Chin are able to integrate into the Mizo community by changing their names and pretending to be Mizo. Without such connections, the Chin are openly discriminated against. The border economy, however, continues to exist since the Mizo rely on goods brought across the border from Myanmar. These goods are staples such as pigs, rice and tea. Other products include Chinese-made goods such as clothing, small electronic items and tobacco. The Burmese also rely on goods being brought from India via Mizoram. Medication, clothing, and auto parts among other products, are much sought after in Myanmar. These are brought in by the Mizo or by the Chin from India and sold in Myanmar's markets of Mandalay and Kalemyo. Despite this mutual reliance however, the Chin in Mizoram continue to be very much discriminated against.

In 2003 a rumour spread around Aizawl that a Chin man had raped a Mizo girl. The girl who was a minor was said to have been raped on 17 July 2003 by a Chin immigrant in Aizwal. Angered by this "ghastly crime", the YMA vowed to "clean up foreigners". All Chin were asked to leave Mizoram immediately. Adding fuel to the controversy, Peace Accord MNF Returnees Association (PAMRA) — a splinter group of the Mizo National Front (MNF) returnees — stated in a press release on 22 July 2003 that it would take action against foreigners who remained in the state. They insisted that the state and its agencies take action against crimes and punish the rapist under relevant provisions of the Indian Penal Code (Chakma 2003*b*). Yet, neither the YMA nor PAMRA have jurisdiction or legal power to enforce the forcible repatriation of the Chin "refugees". Moreover, it is wholly unlawful to punish the entire Chin population for a crime committed by one person.

Still, YMA members took to the streets armed with sticks and axes to drive all the Chin out of Mizoram and back across the border into

Myanmar. The expulsion of the Chin was announced via the dozens of loudspeakers lining the streets of Aizwal. The YMA vowed to "clean up" the city of "foreigners" (Chakma 2003b). Some 600 Chin were repatriated to Myanmar, many of whom faced serious punitive actions by the Burmese Government including jail time, heavy fines and worse, execution.[11] Since most of the Chin seeking refuge in Mizoram stay beyond the permissible time limit given to them, and they rarely renew their permits to extend their stay, the Myanmar authorities use this information to oppress and punish them when they return to the Chin Hills. In 2009, Human Rights Watch issued a public report entitled, "We Are Like a Forgotten People". It detailed several cases of torture and even executions of returned Chin by the Burmese military regime. The Mizo, together with the YMA, were outraged again by the consequent flight of asylum seekers to Mizoram after the pro-democratic reform movements in Myanmar. The YMA voluntarily expelled hundreds of Chin, which in turn forced the Chin either to return to Myanmar or in some cases, to escape to New Delhi or Calcutta, where their marginalization equals that in Mizoram (McDui-Ra 2012, p. 35). The Chin were blamed for the Human Rights Watch report. Some Chin civil societies and non-governmental organizations (NGOs), including the Women's League for Chinland, left Mizoram in fear of retaliation by the Mizo.

As recently as April 2013, the YMA burned down forty houses in the border town Saikhumphai of the Champhai district. Mizo authorities, all of whom are YMA members, reported that the houses were torched due to the increasing number of undocumented Chin migrants. The Chin are trapped in a catch-22 situation as they are not recognized as illegal migrants or refugees and are therefore unable to obtain documentation. Either way, the YMA had ordered the Chin to leave the border town some months earlier. The Chin did not comply given their precarious circumstances in Myanmar (Khonumthung Chin News Group 2013). Thus, the YMA torched the houses of the entire Chin community living in the village.

Given the many promises made by the Burmese Government in the past, the Chin continue to be suspicious of the current regime. Thein Sein and Aung San Suu Kyi's many speeches and promises for change have not had a positive impact on most of the ethnic minority states on the periphery. Although almost all of the ethnic minority states have now agreed to a ceasefire, the marginalization of these minorities continues in Myanmar. Therefore, the Chin continue to cross the border, both for illegal as well as legal trade. Others continue to migrate to Mizoram to work as labourers, domestic helpers and construction workers. Chin and Mizo also cross the border from Mizoram into Myanmar bringing sought-after goods to the Chin Hills and eventually to Mandalay and Kalemyo. In fact, a recent development is that some Mizo have migrated to the Burmese town of Kalemyo where they are able to sell goods in the markets out of reach of the central Burmese government in Naypyitaw as well as their own central government in India.

CONCLUSION

The purpose of this chapter was to highlight cross-border trading between the Chin Hills of Myanmar and the Indian state of Mizoram. While illegal trading has existed since the establishment of colonially drawn borders, the people of the borderlands have managed the border as they see fit. As numerous scholars have argued, the border has its own economic realities which do not always fall in line with the laws and regulations of the central government. The Champai-Zokhawthar border that crosses the Tiau River is a very good example of two simultaneous economies, one legal the other illegal. Yet both are licit. That is, much of the trading that occurs is under the guise of official economic treaties that furnish central governments with revenue. However, illegal trading also occurs with actors participating on both sides of the border. Given the recent changes in Myanmar's government, more regulations in the borderlands in the form of customs houses and immigration offices may be set up. At the time of this article, these regulations are in their infancy.

This chapter also illustrates Mizoram civil society through the YMA, which exercises much power in the state of Mizoram. While it is not a governmental, legal or official institution, it wields power and much clout in the state and among its citizens. This is especially true for the Chin who eke out livelihoods in Mizoram. By way of the YMA, the Chin are often expelled — forced to repatriate to Myanmar where they may face dire circumstances. In Champai, they are often jailed and fined for acts committed against Mizoram laws as well as YMA mottos. It is the YMA that metes out punishments, not the legal system. Hence, while border crossing continues, the YMA will continue to exercise institutionalized xenophobia by forcing the state to act against the Chin, who, it is understood, are brethren of the Mizo.

The Chin are arrested and deported as undocumented foreigners, when there have been anti-foreigner campaigns initiated by the YMA. With their undocumented status, the Chin do not go to the police or courts for help because they fear arrest and deportation. Chin women are least likely to go to the authorities for help since they report being harassed, arrested and detained for selling goods without a permit. The future of the Chin depends on earning an adequate livelihood in Mizoram's economy, which would better enable them to support their families and contribute to Mizo community. Their prospects depend on building positive working relations with non-governmental groups in Mizoram, namely with groups like Mizo Hmeichhe Insuihkhawm Pawl (Mizo Women's Association, MHIP), Mizo Zirlai Pawl (Mizo Students' Association, MZP) and the YMA.

The YMA often claim that Mizoram is the land of the Mizo. Non-state actors like the YMA remained conscious of such identity issues. They have been serving "quit Mizoram" notices to Chin and non-Mizo migrant workers in Mizoram. The reasoning behind this is that outsiders tear apart the social fabric and rich tapestry of the God-fearing Mizos. The stark reality in Mizoram today is that Mizoram state authorities have never challenged YMA Quit Mizoram Notices.

Chin future in Mizoram is gloomy and it all depends on the Indian and Mizoram State finding a creative way of addressing Chin humanitarian concerns as they did for the Chin seeking refuge in 1988 and as they continue to do for Chin seeking refuge today in New Delhi.

Notes

1. We would like to acknowledge the Indian Council of Social Science Research (ICSSR) for funding this research. We would also like to acknowledge the respondents in Mizoram and the Chin Hills of Myanmar for their hospitality.
2. The nomenclature of "Chin" and of "Mizo" is argued to have been constructed by colonials and later by the native elite. It is commonly accepted by scholars that the umbrella term for both (as well as other groups) is Zo (see Son 2014).
3. Interview of Chin elders in Aizawl. Interviewed by William Singh and Bianca Son, Mizoram, India, 14 February 2014.
4. Lamtlung, series no. 4. Zonet Cables, Mizoram, 12 February 2014.
5. Van Schendel and Abraham (2005, p. 20) have explored, in depth, the relationship between legal and licit border trading. The relationship between these terms is shown in the table below by the authors:

	Legal	Illegal
Licit	Ideal State	Underworlds
Illicit	Crony Capitalism/Failed State	Anarchy

6. Pachau only refers to the famine in the state of Mizoram, but it occurs all across the northern Arakan Mountains including some areas of Kachin State.
7. Mizoram became the 23rd state of India in 1971.

8. The first treaty was the *Treaty of Friendship* in 1951. In 1994, the governments of India and Myanmar signed a *Border Trade Agreement* to foster formal trade. In fact, the agreement was designed to promote trade and listed sixty-two items from agricultural products, clothing to hardware, which were legal items of trade. To foster this legal trade, the government of India implements a schedule to provide assistance to states for developing export infrastructure and allied activities (ASIDE).
9. The term illegal is used here somewhat loosely. There are no clear laws about the Chin in Mizoram State. They are not recognized as refugees, yet are not considered wholly illegal under Mizo law either. They, for the most part, are not members of the YMA.
10. Interview with YMA leader in Aizawl. Interviewed by William Singh and Bianca Son, Mizoram, India, 14 February 2014.
11. It is currently nearly impossible to determine the number of Chin refugees who were returned to Myanmar and what punishments, including death, they faced. There are a handful of verbal accounts but these remain anonymous for fear of reprisals.

References

Chakma, Suhas. "Complaint to Stop Forcible Eviction of the Myanmarese Chin Refugees from Lunglei Areas of Mizoram by a Private Organisation, Mizo Joint Action Committee from 20 June 2003, Their Arrest and Imminent Deportation to Myanmar". In *Asian Centre for Human Rights*, 23 June 2003*a* <http://www.achrweb.org/countries/india/mizoram/CR0103.htm> (accessed 27 February 2014).

———. "Complaint to Stop Forcible Repatriation of the Myanmarese Chin Refugees from Aizwal by Young Mizo Association and Peace Accord MNF Returnees Association (PAMRA)". In *Asian Centre for Human Rights*, 28 July 2003*b* <http://www.achrweb.org/countries/india/mizoram/CR0203.htm> (accessed 22 February 2013).

Department of Personnel and Training, Ministry of Personnel, Public Grievances and Pensions, Government of India. "Right to Information: A Citizen Gateway", August 2013 <http://rti.gov.in/> (accessed on 13 April 2014).

Directorate Office. *Mizoram Statistics and Economics Report: Trade with Myanmar, Trade and Commerce in Mizoram*. Delhi: Government of India, 2008.

Gougin, Thangkhanpao. *History of the Zomi*. Manipur: Zomi Press, 1984.

Khonumthung Chin News Group. "Mizoram Authorities Burn Down 40 Houses of Chin People", 1 May 2013 <http://www.khonumthung.org/?p=1435> (accessed 10 October 2013).

Lalnunmawia, Fanai, Lokesh Kumar Jha and Fanai Lalengliana. "Preliminary Observations on Ecological and Economical Impacts of Bamboo Flowering in Mizoram (North East India)". *Journal of Bamboo and Rattan* 4, no. 4 (2005): 317–22.

McDuie-Ra, Duncan. *Northeast Migrants in Delhi: Race, Refuge and Retail*. Chicago: University Chicago Press, 2012.

Mizo Lyric Blog. "Krismas Nang Nen" [Christmas with You] and "Lamtluang"

[Travelogue], 6 October 2013 <mizolyric.blogspot.com/2013/10/krismas-nang-nen.html> (accessed 14 February 2014).

Gazette of India (The). "Extraordinaire, New Delhi". 21 July 2010, p. 4.

Nag, Sajal. "Tribals, Rats, Famine, State and the Nation". *Economic and Political Weekly* 36, no. 12 (2001): 24–30.

Oxford English Dictionary. Oxford: Oxford University Press, 2012.

Pachau, Joy L.K. *On Being Mizo: Identity and Society in Northeast India*. New Delhi: Oxford University Press, 2014.

Rajagopalan, Swarna. *Peace Accords in Northeast India: Journey over Milestones*. Washington D.C.: East-West Centre in Washington, 2008.

Son, Bianca. "The Making of the Zo: The Chin of Burma and the Lushai and Kuki of India through Colonial and Local Narratives 1826–1917 and 1947–1988". Doctoral dissertation, School of Oriental and African Studies, 2013.

Thanga, Lal Biak. *The Mizos: A Study in Racial Personality*. Gauhati: United Publishers, 1978.

Times (The) Issue 3363, Column A. "Latest Intelligence — Burmah". 9 May 1892, p. 5.

Government of Mizoram. *The Mizoram Gazette: Extraordinary, Aizawl Vol. XXXII*. Mizoram: Government of Mizoram, 2003.

Ministry of Development of the Northeastern Region (M/o DONER), Government of India Report. *Expansion of North East India's Trade and Investment with Bangladesh and Myanmar: An Assessment of the Opportunities*. New Delhi: Government of India, 2011.

van Schendel, Willem, and Itty Abraham, eds. *Illicit Flows & Criminal Things: States, Borders & the Other Side of Globalisation*. Bloomington: Indiana University Press, 2005.

Vumson. *Zo History*. Aizawl, Mizoram: Published by the Author, 1986.

Z News. "MNF Demands Mizoram Health Minister's Ouster", 27 August 2013 <http://zeenews.india.com/news/north-east/mnf-demands-mizoram-health-ministers-ouster_872105.html> (accessed 27 February 2014).

16

Tăi Buddhist Practices on the China-Myanmar Border[1]

Takahiro Kojima

INTRODUCTION

This chapter explores the relationship between the local Buddhist practices of Tăi people who cross the border between China and Myanmar and the religious policy of the two countries, in which these movements are situated.[2] It explores the question of how the monks and *holu*, experts in Buddhist rituals, migrate from Myanmar to revive their local religious practices after the Cultural Revolution in China. The next question is how the local people across the border perceive the Buddhist practices which originated from Myanmar. Answering these questions will shed light on the practices of the border area between China and Myanmar, and disclose an aspect of Myanmar Buddhism which is invisible from the viewpoint of national religious institutions.

The research field, Dehong Dai and Jingpo Autonomous Prefecture, Yunnan Province, China, is located on the China-Myanmar border (see Figure 16.1). One of the main groups in this area is the Tăi people. Han Chinese call them Dai, and the Burmese call them Shan. The Tăi people typically live in the basin valley areas, called *məŋ* in the Tăi language. The area where the research was conducted is called Məŋ Mau. After the end of the nineteenth century, the Qin Dynasty and British colonial rulers started the process of boundary demarcation. As a result, Məŋ Mau was divided, finding itself located in two countries — China and Myanmar. Nowadays, the Chinese side of Məŋ Mau is part of Ruili city, while the Myanmar side forms the Muse and Nanhkan townships (see Figure 16.2).

FIGURE 16.1
Map of Dehong Prefecture

Most of the Tăi people follow Theravāda Buddhism. Theravāda Buddhists mainly live in mainland Southeast Asia and share a relatively homogeneous Pali canon. But their practice of precepts and the manner of rituals may differ a little. Groups sharing the same practices have developed into sects.

Historically, among lay Buddhists it was the kings — being the greatest donors and benefactors — who protected Buddhism. However, some kings also drove out monks who were regarded as heretics. These practices legitimized the Buddhist kings. Previous studies point out that the Sangha was institutionalized in each country during nation building, the objective of which was the standardization of Buddhist practices (Ishii 1986 (1975); Tambiah 1976, p. 240).

Although their numbers are much smaller than in Myanmar, Theravāda Buddhists are found in Dehong and Xishuangbanna in China's Yunnan Province as well. The way in which Buddhism spread to Dehong and to Xishuangbanna differs. In the case of Xishuangbanna, Theravāda Buddhism entered via northern Thailand from the end of the second half of the fifteenth century to the first half of the sixteenth century (Liew-Herres et al. 2012,

FIGURE 16.2
Map of Məŋ Mau Basin

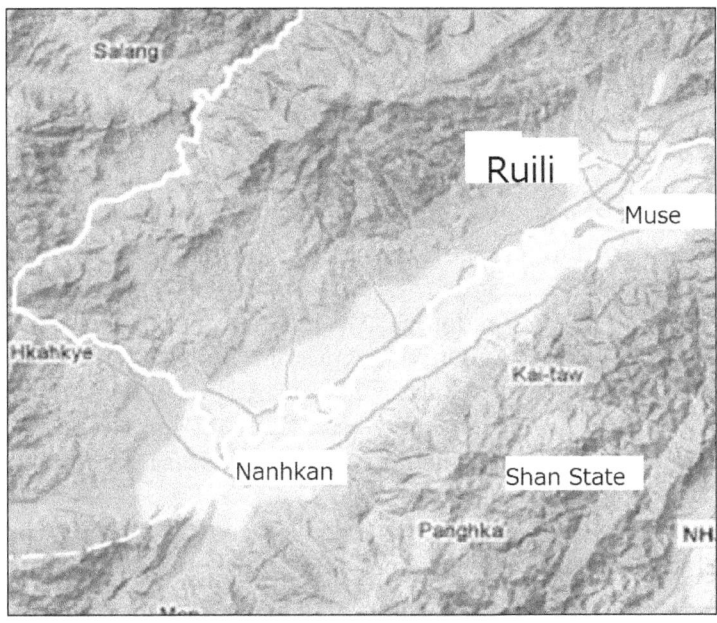

Source: Adaptation of image downloaded from Google Maps.

p. 48). Because of this historical process, characteristics of northern Thai Buddhism are found in Xishuangbanna as well.

In the case of Dehong, there are four major sects, or *kəŋ* (Burmese: *gaing*). The Pɔitsɔŋ, Tsoti, and Tole sects came from Myanmar between the fifteenth and nineteenth centuries and the Yon sect came from northern Thailand in the fifteenth century (Jiang 1983, p. 345; Yan 1986, pp. 457–58; Liu Yangwu 1990, p. 425; Liu Yan 1993, pp. 87–90; Zhang 1992, pp. 116–23; Zhang 1993, p. 75). As three of the four sects entered Dehong via Myanmar, the practices in Dehong show strong influences from Burmese and Shan Buddhism. While the Pɔitsɔŋ and Yon sects are relatively loose in keeping precepts, the Tole sect is stricter and the Tsoti sect is the strictest of all.

The Pɔitsɔŋ and Tsoti sects were originally based in the centre of Myanmar, but they moved to the region around Dehong after the Burmese kings judged them as being heterodox (Yan 1986, pp. 457–58). On the other hand, the traditional lords of each basin in Dehong, *tsău fa*, did not exclude any specific sect but rather, protected each sect (Hasegawa 2009, p. 147). This situation allowed various sects to develop their own practices.

In the case of Myanmar, the Sangha organization was established in 1980 by the government. As the Sangha organization in Myanmar recognized only nine sects, the local sects in Məŋ Mau were not recognized as official sects and so were absorbed into them. This policy was aimed at institutionalizing the innumerable local sects of Buddhism.

In the case of China, the institution of *tsău fa* was abolished after the founding of the People's Republic of China, and the Buddhist Association of Dehong started to manage Buddhism in China in 1957. However, only a year later, the Great Leap Forward (1958–60) began and the Buddhist Association stopped functioning. During the period of the Cultural Revolution (1966–76), Buddhist practices in Dehong were suppressed because of China's less tolerant policy on religion. After the Cultural Revolution, religious freedom was revived. Now the Ethnic and Religious Affairs Commission and the Buddhist Association manage Buddhism under the guidance of the Communist Party.

The study of Theravāda Buddhist societies started in the 1960s. However, except for Thailand, it was very difficult to conduct research in Theravāda Buddhist societies during the Cold War period, and our understanding was limited to a small sample of the region. With the opening of societies around the region and increased access to the field in recent years, some scholars started working in the border areas and focused on the migration of monks across the border (see Hayashi 2009).

In the process of religious revival after the Cultural Revolution, the Buddhist practices in Xishuangbanna were restored due to the relationship with the Sangha in northern Thailand (Hasegawa 1995, p. 68; Davis 2003, p. 99).

In the case of Dehong, previous studies (Zhang 1992, pp. 22–24; Hasegawa 2009, pp. 152–55) pointed out that the monks from Shan State in Myanmar have played an important role in the recovery of Buddhism after the Cultural Revolution. However, they did not refer to the specific networks of local sects which cross the national boundary. Furthermore, they did not pay attention to the migration of *holu* who play important roles in Buddhism in Dehong.

This chapter introduces this new movement using data gathered by the author during more than a year of fieldwork in villages around Ruili city. The main research was conducted from 2006 to 2007 in TL village, with some preliminary trips in 2005 and supplementary work from 2009 to 2011 in 118 temples and pagodas of Ruili city.[3]

FEATURES OF BUDDHIST PRACTICES IN DEHONG

Low Number of Monks and Novices

The local religious practices in Dehong have many things in common with Buddhist practices in Southeast Asia, as they share the same Pali canon. However, the practice in Dehong differs from other Theravāda Buddhist societies in the small number of monks and novices it has there (see Table 16.1). This is in contrast to their increased numbers in Xishuangbanna, where Buddhists also experienced the Cultural Revolution's impacts on their religion. Even when compared with Cambodia, where Buddhist monks were murdered by the Pol Pot regime, the number of monks and novices in Dehong is much lower.

Although all the villages in Dehong have a temple as in the rest of Southeast Asia, most of the temples are uninhabited. According to this author's field survey in 2009, of the 118 religious buildings in Ruili — 112 temples, three pagodas, and three footprints of Buddha — twenty-nine (25 per cent) were inhabited by monks, novices, or women lay practitioners and eighty-nine (75 per cent) were uninhabited. These figures raise the question of why the number of monks and novices is so much lower in Dehong than in other Theravāda Buddhist societies. To answer this question we must look at men who are ordained as well as the villagers who accept them.

A local historian, Mr G (sixty-eight years old) who was familiar with the cultures of both Ruili and Xishuangbanna explained that the number of monks and novices in Xishuangbanna increased again after the Cultural Revolution because "they [people in Xishuangbanna] have the idea that

TABLE 16.1
Number of Priests and Monasteries

	Monasteries	Monks	Monks per monastery	Novices	Novices per monastery	Year
Myanmar	56,839	242,891	4.3	305,875	5.4	2007
Thailand	35,244	258,163	7.3	70,081	1.9	2007
Laos	4,140	8,055	1.9	11,740	2.8	2007
Cambodia	4,237	24,929	5.9	32,421	7.7	2007
Xishuangbanna	577	828	1.4	3,998	6.9	2005
Dehong	602	90	0.1	101	0.2	2007

Source: The Myanmar data was collected by Ryosuke Kuramoto, Thailand by Yukio Hayashi, Laos by Kayoko Yoshida, Cambodia by Satoru Kobayashi. Xishuangbanna and Dehong data by the author from interviews with the Buddhist association in each prefecture.

every boy should become a novice. However, this idea didn't exist in Dehong, even before the Cultural Revolution."[4] Previous studies state that it is believed in Xishuangbanna that boys should become novices in order to be considered adults (Zhongyang Dangxiao Minzu Zongjiao Lilunshi 1999, pp. 453–54). From this evidence, we see that to become a novice is a kind of rite of passage in Xishuangbanna, as in other Buddhist societies. In the central part of Myanmar, for example, it is normal for parents to have their sons ordained as novices so that they acquire an understanding of moral standards in addition to making merit. Parents also make merit from having their sons ordained as novices. But almost all novices disrobe after a certain designated period.

In Dehong, however, one hardly hears of parents having their sons ordained in order to gain merit for the child or themselves. By no means does this signal that Buddhists of Dehong are not enthusiastic about making merit. For example, people actively maintain the cleanliness of temples even if there are no monks. They also participate enthusiastically in Buddhist rituals in order to accumulate merit. However, they believe that they should think twice before making their sons ordain. If the sons wish, they may be ordained. Once they are ordained, it is generally considered that they should not take the decision to disrobe lightly. Thus, the basic thinking in Dehong regarding ordination is different from that in Thailand and the central part of Myanmar.

When I interviewed an elderly villager, Mr J (seventy-five years old) in TL village, he explained to me, "Many villagers hoped to invite a monk before the Cultural Revolution, but the young generation born during or after the Cultural Revolution prefer not to invite monks."[5] This indicates that before the Great Leap Forward, TL village had practices similar to those of other Theravāda Buddhist societies in that it needed monks and novices. The point of difference is that few boys in TL village became novices even before the Cultural Revolution. Therefore, TL villagers had to invite an abbot from another temple of the same sect if the abbot was absent. However, the interruption of the practice for around twenty years took away TL villagers' enthusiasm to invite abbots. Therefore, without resident monks, Buddhist rituals are performed by virtue of the direct relationship between the lay community and their Buddhist texts, Buddha images, and pagodas.

The Role of *Holu*

In particular, *holu* play important roles as mediators in this relationship. *Holu* are basically lay specialists in the recitation of Buddhist texts, with their main function being to represent the lay community in their merit-making activities. *Ho* means "leader", and *lu* means "donation". In Ruili every temple has one *holu*, and all of them are men. In 2009, the *holu* of TL village lived in another village but came to TL village when rituals were held. Eighty-six per cent of *holu* in Ruili were from other villages.

When there is a ritual, *holu* will lead the villagers in reciting the five or eight precepts to the Buddha statue in the temple. In the case of a wedding ceremony, house-warming ceremony, funeral, or incident of misfortune, *holu* recite in front of the shelf of Buddhist texts (*seŋ tala*) in each house. In the afternoon on the days of important ceremonies — such as the Water Festival, the festival to donate *kathina* robes (*pɔi kan thin*), and the special holy days (*van sin*) during the rainy season retreat (*va*) — *holu* recite the Buddhist texts (*tala*) for lay people. The content of the *tala* recited by the *holu* consists of stories of the Buddha's past lives (*tsat to*), precepts that should be upheld by Buddhists, and the proper ways of making offerings. These are recited first in short Pali verses, followed by Tăi translation delivered in story-telling style, so as to make the content easily accessible to followers. People acquire an understanding of the Dhamma (*dănma*) and also gain merit from listening to these recitations. When there are no rituals, *holu* copy the *tala* as requested by villagers. After the *holu* have recited the *tala* in the temple, the villagers would keep the actual texts in the *seŋ tala*. Most *holu* are farmers, but some of them have another job, for example, such as typing invitation letters in Tăi.

MIGRATION FROM MYANMAR TO CHINA

Migration of Monks

The Buddhist rituals are preformed mainly by *holu* in ninety-nine temples (84 per cent) of the 118 temples, but nineteen villagers (16 per cent) have felt the need for monks and novices in the villages. Why do the villagers invite them? The reasons for doing so are varied.

In the case of MA village, when there are funerals, or rituals to be conducted for building new houses, the villagers would invite a monk from Myanmar to their own temple rather than invite one from other neighbouring temples. In LP village, after many villagers and domestic animals died consecutively, the villagers were very fearful of the evil spirits, *phi hai*, and invited a monk from Myanmar. In the case of VM village, when they built a new temple, the villagers decided to invite the monks to keep the temple clean.

Once these villagers have decided to invite a monk, they would go to a temple on the Myanmar side of the border — usually a temple of the same sect (*kəŋ*) — and invite a monk to come and take up the abbotship. The advantage of staying in a temple on the Chinese side is that the monks can collect more donations than on the Myanmar side. Some monks hope to study Chinese because they regard it as a major language.

It is a common practice for monks to be invited from Myanmar. According to the author's 2009 research, of the 116 monks and novices in Ruili, nineteen (16 per cent) were from China and ninety-seven (84 per cent) were from Myanmar, especially Shan State.

These monks become novices mostly in their native villages. They then go on to the central area of Myanmar, for example, Yangon or Mandalay, to study the doctrine of Buddhism and take the examination of Buddhism held by the Myanmar Government (see Figure 16.3). This trend became popular after the road connection was improved in Shan State after the 1970s.

This is a sample case of Ven. V, the abbot of TS temple (see Figure 16.4). He was born in LM village, Mansi township, Kachin State in 1972.[6] When he was seven years old (1979), he became a novice in MV village,

FIGURE 16.3
Migration of 38 Monks and 78 Novices in Ruili from 2004 to 2009

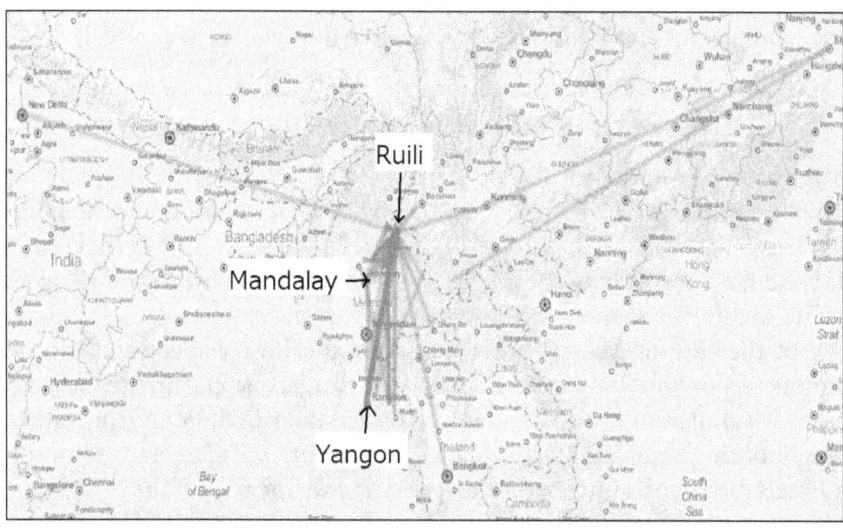

Source: Researched by Takahiro Kojima at 118 temples and pagodas of Ruili city, in August 2009. The image was downloaded from Mapquest Open.

FIGURE 16.4
Migration of Ven. V, Abbot of TS Temple

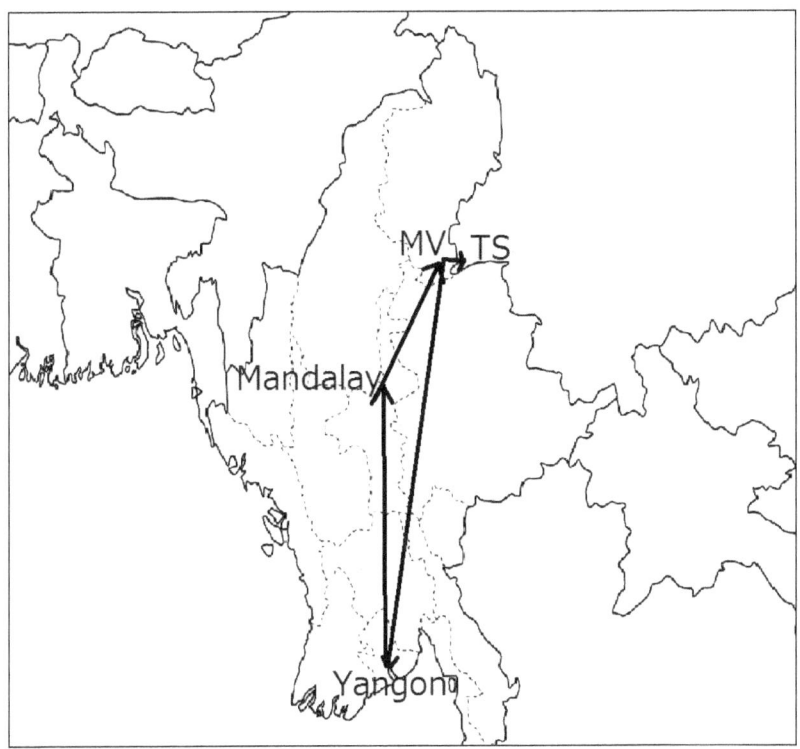

Kachin State. He became a monk in MV village when he was twenty years old, and subsequently stayed in Yangon for three years, Mandalay for two years and then went back to MV temple in Kachin State. In 1999, he moved to TS village on the Chinese side of the border.

The trigger for the TS villagers to invite him was the construction of a new temple in 1994. The villagers thought that it was appropriate to invite an abbot to manage the new temple. They tried to invite a monk of the neighbouring temple to serve as the abbot but the proposal was rejected by the monk because the temple belongs to a different sect, the Pɔi tsɔŋ sect. So the villagers went to MV temple in Kachin State, which belongs to the same sect. The monks and novices of the Pɔi tsɔŋ sect move to the central area of Myanmar to receive Burmese education in Buddhism, but cross the border and move to temples on the Chinese side according to the network of local sects.

The other circumstances under which monks move from the Myanmar to the Chinese side occur when they are invited by monks to whom they are known or when invited by lay people. Figure 16.5 shows the case of Ven. S, the abbot of HS temple.[7] He was born in MT village, Thibaw township, Shan State in 1957. When he was nine years old (1966), he became a novice and stayed in the temple of his native village for four years. He then moved to another temple in Thibaw city (1970). When he was fifteen years old (1972), he moved to a Burmese temple in Monywa. Subsequently, he stayed in Monywa for eight years, Mandalay for eight years and passed the middle class of the Pali examinations held by the Myanmar Government. When he was thirty-seven years old (1994), he met the abbot of HS temple on the Chinese side by chance in Mandalay. This was because many Burmese merchants in Ruili go to HS temple to make donations. Even though the previous abbot was not proficient in Burmese,

FIGURE 16.5
Migration of Ven. S, Abbot of HS Temple

he requested Ven. S to move to HS temple. After the previous abbot passed away, he became the abbot of HS temple.

Migration of *Holu*
Next, how are *holu* recruited after the period of the Cultural Revolution? Some case studies from TL village are described below.

The previous *holu* of TL village, Mr J (seventy-five years old), recalled:

> Before the Great Leap Forward, more people in the village became *holu* than now, because more people had the knowledge of reciting Buddhist texts compared to now. If there was not a suitable person to become a *holu* in the village, the villagers invited someone from another village.[8]

Even if a man has been a novice or monk, he cannot become a *holu* if he does not have a good voice for reciting Buddhist texts.

After the Cultural Revolution, Mr J became a *holu* in TL village. The following is his personal story, focusing on his career as a ritual practitioner. Mr J was born in TL village in 1932. When he was seven years old, he became a novice in the temple of TL village. When he was seventeen years old, he disrobed and got married in TL village. After the Cultural Revolution, the TL temple was rebuilt in 1984. At the time, Mr J was fifty-two years old. As he had had experience of being a novice and his recitation voice was good, the villagers let him become a *holu*. He quit the practice in 1995 because his eyesight had deteriorated.

The *holu* of TL village from 1995 to 2011 was Mr S.[9] In 1967 he was born in LX village of Muse township, Shan State. When he was twenty-one years old, he became the *holu* of LX village at the suggestion of the villagers because he had been a temple boy, *kappi*, and had basic knowledge of Buddhist texts. However, he did not know how to recite the *tala*. He listened to the recitations of other *holu* and learned from them. In 1990 he was invited to KL village, on the Chinese side, as the previous *holu* had retired. In 1992 he married a woman who lived in KL village and took up Chinese nationality. In 1995, however, he quit being the *holu* of KL village because his relationship with the villagers had soured. At that time, the TL villagers invited him to be a *holu* because Mr J had retired.

The situation in TL village is a common one in the aftermath of the Cultural Revolution. My research in 2009 shows that out of the 112 *holu* in Ruili city, eighty (71 per cent) *holu* were natives from the Myanmar side of the border. Only thirty-two (29 per cent) of the *holu* were from the Chinese side. Older people who had the experience or were ordained before the Cultural Revolution were not able to continue as *holu* because of their advanced age. Most of the young men replacing this older generation had become monks or novices in Myanmar, and then moved to the Chinese side as *holu*. Especially after the 1990s, local economic development has taken off on the Chinese side, but on the Myanmar side conflict continued and economic levels remain low. Therefore, the number of *holu* who hope to move to the Chinese side is increasing.

The Networks of Local Sects

The third *holu* of TL village is Mr T (see Figure 16.6).[10] He was born in a village of Kutkaing township, Shan State in 1993. When he was thirteen years old, he was inducted by the Kachin Independent Army (KIA). He escaped from the KIA soon after and became a novice when he was fourteen years old, as the KIA did not induct novices in the temples. The temple where he was ordained was the main temple of the Tsoti sect in Mohnyin (Tăi: Məŋ Yaŋ), Kachin State. After staying at the temple for two years, he disrobed and moved to Ruili in Dehong because his brother lived there as a *holu*. Soon after he moved to Ruili, the senior *holu* of the Tsoti sect introduced him to the TL villagers and he became a *holu* in the village.

The temple of TL village belongs to the Tole sect. Nevertheless, the reason that TL villagers invited the *holu* of the Tsoti sect is that the skill of reciting the texts by *holu* who have been ordained at the temple of the Tsoti sect is highly valued by the people of Məŋ Mau. If they are not a member of the Tsoti sect, many *holu* in Məŋ Mau would attend classes for the Tăi verse of Buddhism which is held every year. All teachers of these classes have been ordained in a Tsoti temple. As this case shows, the network of the Tsoti sect is important for the practice of the *holu*.

Zhang (1992, pp. 149–52) describes the features of the Tsoti sect as follows. Firstly, monks and novices are led by one abbot and live together in one temple. Their temple of residence is not fixed; they move to other temples after a certain period of time. The most senior monk of the Tsoti sect at the time of the 2009 research lived in Mohnyin. In fact, the temple of the Tsoti sect in Dehong had not had a resident monk since 1915, when the most senior monk moved to Shan State. Secondly, monks and novices are required to obey the precepts very strictly. For example, they are not allowed to ride in cars but have to walk when they go out. Not only monks and novices, but laypeople as well are expected to obey the precepts. For example, followers are not allowed to raise livestock, and they cannot eat meat if they have witnessed the slaughter of the animals. Furthermore, laypeople are prohibited from drinking alcohol.

FIGURE 16.6
Migration of Mr. T, *Holu* of TL Village

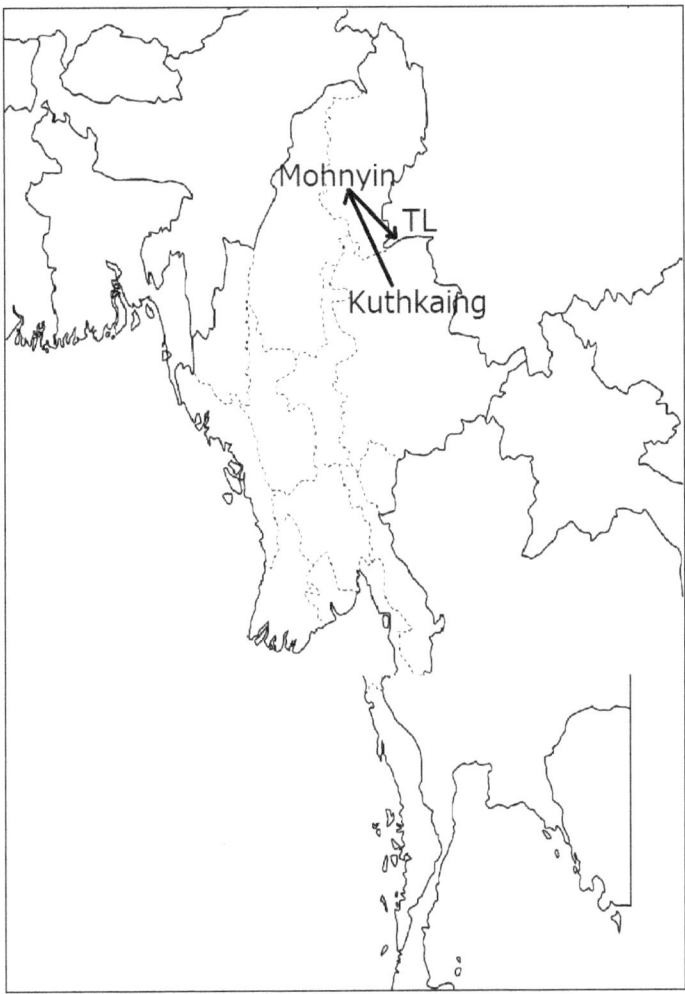

According to this author's field surveys, villagers still adhered to these practices, except that some now raised livestock. There was no Tsoti monk in Dehong, but followers made donations to Mohnyin three times per year — during the Water Festival (*pɔi sɔn lăm*), the beginning of the rainy season retreat (*xău va*), and the end of the rainy season retreat (*ɔk va*). Donations from Dehong were collected at the Tsoti temple in Muse, and representatives took them to Mohnyin. When the ordination ceremony is held in the central temple of Mohnyin every three years, many villagers attend and some boys become novices as well.

A different feature of the monks of the Tsoti sect is that they do not take an examination of Buddhism held by the Myanmar Government because their practices follow the Tăi tradition. They are educated in the ways of reciting and creating the Tăi verse of Buddhism (lăŋ ka).

As explained above, these sects in Dehong, Tsoti, Pɔi tsɔŋ, Tole and Yon are not recognized by the Sangha organization in Myanmar which was established in 1980. It is also said that all the sects in Dehong were united after 1982 in China. Despite the institutionalization of Buddhist sects in the two countries, local networks of the sects continue to exist and play important roles in the practices of local Buddhists. The monks and novices move to the central area of Myanmar to take examinations, but move to temples and cross the border according to the networks of local sects.

CHANGE AND CONTINUITY OF BUDDHIST PRACTICES

As described above, the monks and *holu* who migrated from Myanmar are indispensable to the practice of local Buddhism in Ruili. As a result, the religious practices of Myanmar are brought over to the Chinese side. How do local people view these practices? This is elaborated upon using TL village on the Chinese side as a case study.

Practices of the Monks

The TL villagers did not invite a monk to take up position as an abbot. However, whenever they need a monk, they go to Ven. S from HS village. For example, the villagers invite him when they hope to exorcise evil spirits by reciting the texts of protection (*palit*) and other chants like the *kămpava* as part of the rituals of the whole village. Or when they are faced with difficulties in everyday life, or are not in good health and cannot be treated in the hospital, they go to HS temple to meet Ven. S. He is well-known for his skills in fortune-telling and treating diseases caused by evil spirits in the body.

As mentioned, Ven. S had studied the doctrine of Buddhism in Mandalay. However, he also learned the methodology of fortune-telling and treating diseases from the specialists among laypeople and monks when he was in Mandalay and Thibaw. Ven. S brought these new practices with him when he crossed over to China.

When he is invited to exorcise evil spirits through rituals, he also preaches to the villagers. But he has never been invited to TL village just to preach. This is in contrast to the case in Myanmar. The laypeople in Myanmar often invite monks in order to listen to talks on the Dhamma, which is based particularly on the Abhidhamma. Furthermore, the laypeople in Myanmar invite the monk specialists of Vipassanā meditation which is regarded as an important practice and has become popular in recent years. Ven. S is experienced in promoting the education of Abhidhamma and practising Vipassanā in the central area of Myanmar. However, the laypeople on the Chinese side do not demand the practices usually recognized as being orthodox in Myanmar. Rather the villagers request monks to perform rituals that are important for their own everyday lives.

The Sangha organization in Myanmar regards the practices of fortune-telling and treating diseases as something that monks should not be involved in. When I asked Ven. S why in such a situation he practised fortune-telling and the exorcism of evil spirits, he answered, "these practices are needed for socializing with the laypeople." This explanation suggests that the monks also adjust their practices depending on the preferences of the villagers.

Another factor affecting this phenomenon is the difference in policy of the two countries. As described above, after the Sangha institutions were established in Myanmar, the standardization of Buddhist practices has been the aim and the monks are not allowed to practise fortune-telling or treat diseases. In Dehong, while the Chinese Government manages temples and monks, it does not try to manage the details of actual Buddhist practice. These political circumstances allow the monks to develop the practices depending on the demands of the local people, a practice which is prohibited on the Myanmar side.

Practices of *Holu*

So, how did the villagers perceive the practice of *holu* who migrated from Myanmar? To answer this question, I will focus on the change and continuity of practices concerning Buddhist texts.

Firstly, the Tăi phrases recited in rituals have been changed to the Shan style. The phrases recited in the Pali language are basically the same in every Theravāda Buddhist society, but the phrases in the local language are different in each area. Shan phrases were standardized in 1993 at the Shan monks' conference in Muse. New *holu* such as Mr S learned the standardized forms. Mr S brought them to TL village when he became *holu* in 1995. Moreover, the script of the *tala* also changed from the old

Dehong script to the Shan script because Mr S was used to transcribing and reciting in the Shan script.

On the other hand, the way in which Buddhist texts were recited did not change. When Mr S became *holu* of TL village, he recited Buddhist texts using the intonations of the Tsoti sect (*seŋ kaloŋ pɛn, seŋ peu tɔn*, and *seŋ phi la*). Later he learned the intonation of traditional Məŋ Mau style (seŋ Thuŋ Mau) from previous *holu* and used this form for his recitations.

Why did the script of the *tala* change, while the way of reciting did not? To analyse these phenomena, we must understand the practices in which they occur. For the villagers, the *tala* is not something to read but something to listen to. Moreover, most of the villagers cannot read the Shan script themselves, but they believe that if there is a *tala* in the *seŋ tala* of each house, the household will be safe and sound.

On the other hand, why did Mr S have to change his way of reciting? When asked about his reasons, he replied, "TL villagers were not used to the *seŋ kaloŋ pɛn* and requested me to recite using *seŋ Thuŋ Mau*." Listening to the recitation of the *tala* by the *holu* is an important practice in making merit for TL villagers. The Buddhism of TL villagers is woven into the story and recited melodiously by the *holu*. Except for Mr J, only three men have had the experience of being novices in TL village. They knew the Shan scripts and how to recite them, but they could not become *holu* because their voices were not good enough. This implies that the voice for reciting Buddhist texts is very important for the Buddhist practices in Dehong, and new styles from across the border are not easily accepted.

CONCLUSION

After the Cultural Revolution, the monks and *holu* migrated from the Myanmar side of the border because there were few specialists on the Chinese side for the particular way they practised Buddhism. Furthermore, because local economic development occurred at a faster rate on the Chinese side after the 1990s, monks and *holu* also hoped to move there. The Chinese side is a good place for the monks to collect donations and study Chinese, and the *holu* can improve their economic standing as well.

When they move to the Chinese side, local networks of the sects take on an important role. These local sects had officially disappeared, insofar as the Myanmar and Chinese governments had regulated and controlled these sects by constructing the Sangha organization in Myanmar or a Buddhist association in China. Nevertheless the local networks of Buddhism, which cross the border between China and Myanmar, still exist and play a significant role for the local practice of Buddhism.

The migration of monks and *holu* from Myanmar brought the dynamics of the practice to the Chinese side. The local villagers recognize the ability of the monks and *holu* from Myanmar, but they do not feel the need to adopt all matters of orthodox knowledge or doctrine authorized by the Sangha in Myanmar. Instead they are led by their need for services in the practice of fortune-telling or exorcising evil spirits, in which these monks are knowledgeable and skilled. *Holu* are recognized for their ability in reciting the texts of Buddhism, but they must adjust their intonation of reciting texts in accordance with the preferences of the local villagers. This means that the local people accept the Buddhist practices from Myanmar partially, but they keep their on-the-ground practices intact to a significant degree.

This case suggests the following. As some previous studies pointed out, the institutionalization of Theravāda Buddhism has progressed even in the border area between China and Myanmar. On the other hand, we must pay attention to the interaction between political power and the practice of local people to understand the religious dynamics of border areas.

Notes
1. The other chapters in this volume use "Tai" but I use "Tǎi" in this chapter following the transliteration method by Meng (2007).
2. Some of the description of Tǎi people's practices overlap with my paper (Kojima 2012), but the points of discussion in this chapter are different.
3. The name of the villages, for example TL, MA, LP and VM villages are pseudonyms.
4. Interview in Ruili city. Interviewed by Takahiro Kojima, Ruili city, China, 4 February 2007.
5. Ibid., 27 January 2007.
6. Ibid., 18 November 2006.
7. Ibid., 19 March 2005.
8. Ibid., 27 January 2007.
9. Ibid., 25 March 2007.
10. Ibid., 10 August 2011.

References

Davis, Sara. "Premodern Flows in Postmodern China: Globalization and the Sipsongpanna Tais". *Modern China* 29, no. 2 (2003): 176–203.

Hasegawa, Kiyoshi (長谷川清). "Shukyo Jissen to Rokariti: Unnansho, Tokkou Chiiki Munmao (Zuirei) no Jirei (宗教実践とローカリティー雲南省・徳宏地域ムンマオ（瑞麗）の事例)" [Religious Practices and Locality: The Case of Munmao

(Ruili), Dehong, Yunnan Province]. In *'Kyoiki' no Jissen Shukyo: Tairikubu Tonan Ajia Chiiki to Shukyo no Toporoji* <境域>の実践宗教―大陸部東南アジア地域と宗教のトポロジー) [Practical Religions in Mainland Southeast Asia: Topology of Religion from the Region and 'In-betweeness'], edited by Yukio Hayashi (林行夫). Kyoto: Kyoto University Press, 2009, pp. 131-70.

———. "'Shukyo' Toshite no Jozabukkyo: Sipsonpanna, Tairuzoku no Bukkyo Fukko Undo to Esunishiti (「宗教」としての上座仏教―シプソーンパンナー, タイ・ルー族の仏教復興運動とエスニシティ)". [Theravāda Buddhism as 'Religion': The Revival of Buddhism and Ethnicity of Tai Lu in Sipsonpanna]. In *Shukyo, Minzoku, Dento* (宗教・民族・伝統) [Religion, Ethnicity and Tradition], edited by Yoshio Sugimoto (杉本良男). Nagoya: Institution of Anthropology, Nanzan University, 1995, pp. 55-82.

Hayashi, Yukio (林行夫), ed. *'Kyoiki' no Jissen Shukyo: Tairikubu Tonan Ajia Chiiki to Shukyo no Toporoji* (<境域>の実践宗教―大陸部東南アジア地域と宗教のトポロジー) [Practical Religions in Mainland Southeast Asia: Topology of Religion from the Region and 'In-betweeness']. Kyoto: Kyoto University Press, 2009.

Ishii, Yoneo. *Sangha, State, and Society: Thai Buddhism in History*. Translated by Peter Hawkes. Honolulu: University of Hawaii Press, 1986 [1975].

Jiang, Yingliang (江应樑). *Daizu Shi* (傣族史) [The History of Dai People]. Chengdu: Sichuang Minzu Chubanshe, 1983.

Kojima, Takahiro. "Tai Buddhist Practices in Dehong Prefecture, Yunnan, China". *Southeast Asian Studies* 1, no. 3 (2012): 395-430.

Liew-Herres, Foon Ming, Volker Grabowsky and Renoo Wichasin. *Chronicle of Sipsòng Panna: History and Society of a Tai Lü Kingdom, Twelfth to Twentieth Century*. Chiang Mai: Mekong Press, 2012.

Liu, Yangwu (刘扬武). "Dehong Daizu Xiaocheng Fojiao de Jiaopai he Zongjiao Jieri (德宏傣族小乘佛教的教派和宗教节日)" [The Sects and the Religious Days of Theravada Buddhism among the Dehong Dai People]. In *Beiye Wenhualun* (贝叶文化论) [Discussing the Culture of Palm-leaf Manuscript], edited by Wang Yi Zhi and Yang Shi Guang. Kunming: Yunnan Renmin Chubanshe, 1990, pp. 425-31.

Liu, Yan (刘岩) *Nanchuan Fojiao yu Daizu Wenhua* (南传佛教与傣族文化) [Theravāda Buddhism and Dai Culture]. Kunming: Yunnan Renmin Chubanshe, 1993.

Meng, Zunxian (孟尊贤), ed. *Dai Han Cidian* (傣汉词典) [Tǎi-Chinese Dictionary], Kunming: Yunnan Minzu Chubanshe, 2007.

Tambiah, Stanley Jeyaraja. *World Conqueror and World Renouncer*. Cambridge: Cambridge University Press, 1976.

Yan, Sijiu (颜思久). "Yunnan Xiaocheng Fojiao Kaocha Baogao (云南小乘佛教考察报告)" [Report of Research on Theravāda Buddhism in Yunnan]. In *Zongjiao Diaocha yu Yanjiu* (宗教调查与研究) [Research and Study on Religion] 1 (1986): 394-469.

Zhang, Jianzhang (张建章), ed. *Dehong Zongjiao: Dehong Daizu Jingpozu Zizhizhou Zongjiaozhi* (德宏宗教―德宏傣族景颇族自治州宗教志) [Religion in Dehong: Religions in Dehong Dai and Jingpo Autonomous Prefecture]. Mangshi: Dehong Minzu Chubanshe, 1992.

Zhang, Jianzhang (张建章) *Yunnan Bianjiang Zongjiao Wenhualun* (云南边疆宗教文化论) [Discussing the Religious Culture in the Border Area of Yunnan]. Mangshi: Dehong Minzu Chubanshe, 1993.

Zhongyang Dangxiao Minzu Zongjiao Lilunshi, ed; (中央党校民族宗教理论室编). *Xinshiqi Minzu Zongjiao Gongzuo Xuanchuang Shouce* (新时期民族宗教工作宣传手册) [Handbook for the Promotion of the Scheme of Nationalities and Religions in Recent Times]. Beijing: Zongjiao Wenhua Chubanshe, 1999.

Index

Note: Page numbers followed by "n" refer to endnotes.

A

Abrams, Philip, 148, 149
activist groups in Myanmar, 227
Adnan, Shapan, 155
Adventist Development and Relief
    Agency (ADRA) Myanmar, 176
Ahmed, Boshir, 299
Ahmed, Imtiaz, 164
Alaung Hpaya, 101
All Burma Students' Democratic Front
    (ABSDF), 73
Alternative ASEAN Network on Burma
    (ALTSEAN), 48
Andaman Sea
    maritime boundary, 70, 74
    sea nomads, 6, 10
animal husbandry in Yunnan, 239
Animist groups, 179
Anti-Access and Anti-Denial (A2/AD)
    concept, 90
Anti-Fascist Peoples Freedom League
    (AFPFL), 288
anti-Muslim campaign, 185
Arakan, 124, 139n2
Arendt, Hanna, 300
armed conflict, 11–13
    in Myanmar, map of incidents of, 60
The Art of Not Being Governed (2009),
    164
Association of Southeast Asian Nations
    (ASEAN), 39
Aung San Suu Kyi, 64, 226, 288, 292,
    307, 364
Ayeyarwady Delta, 106, 108

B

Back Packers, 181
Back Pack Health Worker Team, 175, 180
Bamar
    cultural identity, 5
    population, 62
Bangladesh
    maritime disputes with, 75–76
    Ministry of Disaster Management
        and Relief, 159
    national projects of, 148–57
    refugee camps, 299
Bangladesh, Rohingya refugee identity
    politics in, 283–84
    along the borderline, 290–301
    colonial period, 286–88
    historical construction and
        representation of Rohingya
        ethnic minority, 285–86
    methodology, 285
    state-imposed boundaries in shaping
        identity, 288–90
baselines in Myanmar territorial waters,
    76–80
Bjornberg, Anders, 22
Blae Koh, 265–67, 270, 277n2
Bodawpaya in 1785, 123
border
    development, 11–13
    economies, 22
    practices, 26–28
    regions, physical and social
        landscapes in, 11
Border Guard Force, 177

borderland constituencies, 51–54
  characteristics of, 41–42
  map of, 40
  Myanmar 2010 general election results in, 45–47
  People's Assembly 2010 election results, map of, 44
borderlands
  introduction of, 39–49
  politics, 64–66
  of Rakhine State, 57
  territorialization of, 105, 106–12
Border Trade Agreement, 367n8
boundaries, 1–3
British
  colonization, 287
  military force, 302n3
Brodsky, Joseph, 295, 300
Buddhism, 100–102
Buddhist
  of Dehong, 374
  nationalist unity, 151
  non-marriage law, 185
  Rakhine, 122
  refugees, 173
  rituals, 375
  Sangha, 103, 186
Buddhist practices
  change and continuity of, 382–84
  in Dehong, features of, 373–75
Burma Citizenship Law (1982), 289
Burma Socialist Programme Party (BSPP), 289, 357
Burma Update Conference, 306
Burman identity, 99–100
  cultural, 4
  hegemonic, 105
  insular, 110, 111
Burmanization process, 21, 99, 100, 104
Burmese
  Army, 11, 174, 329
  cult of Thirty-Seven Lords, 132
  economy, 308
  exile-based resistance activities, 225–26
  language, 100
  migrants, 192, 306, 203
  nationalism, 151
  practices of Buddhism, 100

C

caravans
  mule. See mule caravans
  muleteer communities, 245
  network, intensity of, 254
Carians, 276n1
  see also Karens
Ceasefire Agreement, 356, 357
ceasefires, 14–16
Chao Phraya Delta, 106
charismatic kingship, 107
Chatichai's buffet government, 116n10
Chavalit Yongchaiyudh, 81, 89
Cheung, Samuel, 162
Chiang Mai, Kachin youth in, 227
Child Development Centre, 208n11
Chin economic migrants, 359
Chin Hills of Myanmar, 354
Chin National Front (CNF), 359
Chin refugee camps, 359
Chin spirit domains, 132
Chin state-Mizoram border, 353
  historical context of, 355–59
  Young Mizo Association (YMA), 354, 360–65
Chin Wei Jun, 26
China
  Anti-Access and Anti-Denial (A2/AD) concept, 90
  migration from Myanmar to, 375–82
China-Myanmar border, Tăi Buddhist practices on, 369–72
  change and continuity of Buddhist practices, 382–84
  features of Buddhist practices in Dehong, 373–75

INDEX

migration from Myanmar to China, 375–82
Chinese border, 7, 17, 27
Chinese Jingpo, 223
Chittagong Hill Tracts, 154, 155
Christian consortium, 177
Christian Sgaw Karen, 178
collective identity, exile and formation of, 298–300
Commission of Enquiry on Violence, 125
Committee for Internally Displaced Karen People (CIDKP), 335
communal violence, 283
community-based organizations (CBOs), 198–202, 206
community mobilization, 230
comparative national-level approach, 48
contemporary cross-border network, 223
contentious place-bound politics, 216
Coral Sea, 80
counter-insurgency
  operations, 6
  strategies, 12
cross-border networking, mule caravans and, 251–53
"Cross-Boundary Marriage", 223
cultural production, 3
cultural reproduction for border work, 204–206
Cultural Revolution, 372, 374, 379, 380
Cyclone Nargis crisis, 80

D
Dali Kingdom, 239
Dehong, features of Buddhist practices in, 373–75
Dehong Prefecture, map of, 370
Democratic Karen Benevolent Army (DKBA), 11, 13, 176
Democratic Karen Buddhist Army (DKBA), 262, 276n1

Department of Fisheries (DoF), 80–81
Developing Disparity, 332
"divide-and-rule", 286
Dudley, Sandra, 179
Du Wenxiu, 246

E
East India Company in 1886, 150
electoral sovereignty, 54
  ethnic complexity, 57–58
  military deployments, 58–62
  population and voter distribution, 55–56
Embryo Buddha, 101
English Immersion Programme (EIP), 201, 208n6
English programme, 205
ethnic complexity, 57–58
ethnic *nat*, 132–33
Ethno-nationalism, 185
Eubank, David, 340
European Commission (EC), 179
Exclusive Economic Zone, 75, 84, 85

F
famines in Mizoram, 355–56
Fast Attack Crafts (FACs), 84
Feld, Steven, 270
fishing, political economy of, 80–85
forced relocation policy, 318
Fortify Rights, 157–58
Foucault, Michel, 266
Four Cuts campaign, 28n2
Free Arakan, 294
Free Burma Rangers (FBR), 180–82, 328
Friendship Bridge, 5
frontiers of Burma, 50

G
Gandharva, 267, 279n13
gendered representation of territorialization, 103–105

Geographic Information System
  calculations, 53
geopolitics, 85–90
Giersch, Patterson, 238
global mobility regime, 264
Great Leap Forward, 372

H
hegemonic Burman/Bamar identity,
  24–26
Heppner, Kevin, 328
Heqing Chamber of Commerce, 246
holu, 385
  migration of, 379–80
  practices of, 383–84
  role of, 374
horse caravan, 237
Hui Muslim caravan muleteers, 249
Human Rights Watch, 364
humanitarian agencies, 172–76
humanitarian engagement on the
  Thai-Burmese border, history of,
  177–80
humanitarian landscape, 177
humanitarianism, 171
  operating in southeast Myanmar,
  182–87
  operating on Thai border, 180–82
hydrocarbon extraction, 85–90
hypermobility, 231

I
identified territories, conflicting
  identities in, 112–13
identity construction, 24–26
idiom of Buddhism, 126
  importance of, 127
illegal Bengali group, 102
illegal Bengali migrants, 157
imagined boundaries, 20–22
imagined political community, 4
Independent Mon News Agency, 82
Indian Government, 65

Indian Passport Entry Rule, 360
Indian Penal Code, 363
India's Right to Information (RTI), 362
institutionalized identity, 26–28
internal boundaries, in Myanmar, 11
internally displaced persons (IDP)
  camps, 224
international donor community, 334
international humanitarian agencies,
  173
International Rescue Service, 181
International Tribunal for the Law of
  the Sea (ITLOS), 72, 75
Irish Centre for Human Rights, 153
Irrawaddy blog, 228
Irrawaddy Delta, 106
Islam, 126–27
Islamic Bengaliness, nationalist project
  of, 146

J
Jesuit Refugee Service, 181
Jinghpawkasa, 228
Journal of Refugee Studies, 162

K
Kachin
  communities, 216
  conflict, 23
  in China, 223
  kinship system, 218, 222, 234n3
  political mobilization, 216
  social network, 224
Kachin Baptist Convention (KBC), 231
Kachin Independence Army (KIA), 48,
  224, 230
Kachin Independence Organization
  (KIO), 6, 215, 224
  in northern Myanmar, 11
Kachin mobilities
  contentious politics and relevance of
  spatiality, 215–17
  as continuity, 217–23

INDEX 393

networks and assemblages of power, 225–32
spatial politics, 223–25
Kachin News Group (KNG), 227–28
Kai Liang, 243
kala nat, 132–33
kala spirits, 21, 122, 126, 133, 135, 140n8
  at margin of Rakhine state, 127–29
  throughout Rakhine history, 123–26
Karen Affairs Committee, 183, 184
Karen Education Department (KED), 201
Karen Human Rights Group (KHRG), 180, 328
Karen National Liberation Army (KNLA), 11, 72, 173, 177, 180, 339
Karen National Union (KNU), 6, 13, 116n9, 152, 174, 178–79, 198, 274, 276n1
Karenni
  groups, 331, 341
  refugee groups, 26, 324, 326, 334, 343
  territory, 331
Karenni National Progressive Party (KNPP), 324, 331, 340
Karenni National Women's Organization (KNWO), 328, 344
Karens
  blood, 183–84
  Buddhism, 176
  Burmese nationals, 180
  Carians, 276n1
  civil population, 177
  communities, 188, 201, 264
  conflict, 175
  humanitarianism, 184
  nationalism, 176
  refugees, 173
Kawthoolei, 271, 272
Kawthoolei Karen Baptist Churches, 179
Kayah–Mae Hong Son borderland, 323–24

anxieties within landscapes of change, 337–39
border development and disparity, 330–34
changing goalposts and dilemmas of relative peace, 339–44
cross-border geopolitics and landscapes of fear, 326–30
freedom's possibilities, 324–26
post-conflict political complexes and economic development, 334–37
Khin Nyunt, 109
King Bodaw Hpaya, 101
King Man Phalaung, 156
King Naramithla, 156
Kyauk Taw, 101

L
labour migrants, 310
Lady of Pegu, 103
Lalrinliana Sailo, 362
Lamtluang, 353
landscape plasticity, 188
landscape transformation, 172–76
Laotian-Burmese frontier, 16
Law of the Seas (1982), 79
Law Relating to the Fishing Rights of Foreign Fishing Vessels, 81
Leach, Edmund, 49–50
Leadership and Management College (LMTC), 264, 267–70
Leider, Jacques, 124, 155, 156
Lewa, Chris, 158
local sects, 372
  networks of, 380–82
local traditional livestock husbandry, 253
local Yunnan muleteer, 253
longue durée mobilities, 219

M
Ma Caiting, 247

Macdonaldization, 204
Madjya, 131
Mae Hong Son, 327
Mae La refugee camp, 178, 200
Mae Ra Ma Luang, 179
Mae Sot, 173
   political activism in, 199
   schooling and training in, 200–204
Mae Sot-Myawaddy borderland, 191
   neoliberal and humanitarian economies in, 192–95
Maha Muni Buddha, 101
Maitreya, 104
Malaysian Kachin community, 228
Malkki, Liisa, 25, 146, 161
mandala pattern, 105
maps
   borderland constituencies, 40
   concentration of military installations in Myanmar, 59
   Dehong Prefecture, 370
   grey areas between Myanmar, Bangladesh and India, 77
   incidents of armed conflict in Myanmar (2011–13), 60
   islands under dispute, 74
   Məŋ Mau Basin, 371
   Myanmar's border and coastal trade zones, 61
   Myanmar's claimed territorial waters, 78
   natural resources in Myanmar's border regions, 15
   People's Assembly 2010 election results in borderland constituencies, 44
   upland, lowland and maritime Myanmar, 9
Mara Ma Gri, 101
Maran Tu Ring, 221, 222
marine Zomia, 10
maritime border regions, 7–16

maritime borderscapes, 19–20
maritime disputes
   with Bangladesh, 75–76
   with Thailand, 74
maritime frontier, challenges in, 71–80
Maritime Zones Law in 1977, 70
Maung Aung Myoe, 20
Maung Zarni, 158
Mayu Island, 76
Mekong River, 50
Melocannabaccifera, 355
Məŋ Mau Basin, map of, 371
migrants, 195–97
   community, 309
migration, from Myanmar to China, 375–82
militarization, 11–13
military deployments, 58–62
military installations in Myanmar, map of, 59
Ming Dynasty, 245, 246
Minmahaw, 201
Mizo civil society organizations, 354
Mizo National Front (MNF), 356, 363
Mizoram
   Ceasefire Agreement of 1986, 358
   Chin state border, 353–65
   economy, 359
   employment and learning trajectory, 197–98
   famines, 355
   Peace Accord, 357
Mizoram Liquor Total Prohibition Act (MLTP), 362
Mizzima, 228
Mobile Kachin, 221
mobile practices, 23–24
mobilities, 217
   Kachin. *See* Kachin mobilities
Moken society, 112
Mon Buddhism, 113
Mon/Karen Theravāda Buddhism, 175

monks
  migration of, 375–79
  practices of, 382–83
Monthathip, Krishna, 279n15
motoshiri, 130
Mrauk U, 121, 124, 135, 136–37, 141n15, 286
mule caravans, 237–39
  and cross-border networking, 251–53
  as form of local politics, 245–48
  rearing and training of, 239–42
  social boundaries, 248–51
  in Yunnan, 242–45
Muslim Arakan State, 157
Muslim-Buddhist violence, 50
Muslim Rohingya, 122, 146, 296
Myanmar
  borders of, 7, 49, 61
  Electoral Commission, 48
  ethnic group, 101
  first election in, 43
  Fisheries Federation, 84
  Fishery Law, 80
  frontiers, 2, 7
  internal boundaries in, 11
  Marine Fisheries Law on 1990, 81
  military, 28n2
  modern political geography, 56
  mountain, 7–16, 19–20
  nation, 3–7
  Navy, 80, 82–84
  ongoing political reorganization, 39
  political transformation, 283
  upland, lowland and maritime, 7–11
  waters, 71
Myanmar Armed Forces (MAF), 224, 226
Myanmar-Bangladesh borderlands, 50, 75
Myanmar National Democratic Alliance Army (MNDAA), 12

Myanmar Peace Support Initiative (MPSI), 335
Myanmar's border regions, 2–3
  map of natural resources in, 15
  practice theory in, 4
Myanmar-Thailand frontier, 50
Myawaddy border, 13
Myeik Archipelago, 108–109, 111–15

N
9/11 World Trade Center attack, 126
1982 Law of the Seas, 79
Na Ta La, 331
nat, 130, 134
Nat Pwe, 136–37
National Democratic Front, 151
National Land Use Policy, 336
national "mainstream," 43
national projects of Myanmar, 148–57
"national reconciliation" processes, 325
"nationwide" ceasefire agreement, 17
natural resource in Myanmar
  in border regions, map of, 15
  extraction, 14–16
Nayapara Refugee Camp, 285, 298
Ne Win, 261, 289, 357
  Operation Dragon King, 152
  Revolutionary Council, 150
neoliberal market economy, 191
"new mobilities paradigm," 217, 218
non-governmental groups in Mizoram, 366
non-governmental organizations (NGOs), 160, 173, 202, 206
  employment, 198–200

O
offshore basins, 85
Operation Mone-Daing, 72
Operation Nagamin, 297
Order Restoration Council, 153
Oyster Island, 76

P

padi states, 8
Pakchan River, 74
pan-Tai transborder Buddhist network, 221
"paper agreements", 355
Passport Entry Act, 360
patron-client networks, 106–12
P'doh Ba Thin Sein, 274
Peace Accord MNF Returnees Association (PAMRA), 363
pentecostalism, 185
People's Assembly 2010 election results, 44
People's Republic of China, 220
Permanent Court of Arbitration, 75–76
Phyu Phyu Zin, 336
pioneer Christian consortium, 178
Pɔitsɔŋ, 371
Political Anatomy of Land Grab, The, 336
political economy of fishing, 80–85
political repression in Myanmar, 22
politics of belonging, 24–26
population and voter distribution, 54–56
practice theory, 2, 3
  in Myanmar's border regions, 4
"pre-Kachin period", 219
Production Sharing Contract (PSC) agreement, 85, 87
  blocks, 85
Pu Laldenga, 356
Pwa K' Nyaw, 275
Pyithu Hluttaw, 51, 52, 66n1

Q

Qing Dynasty, 252

R

Rakhine community, 296
Rakhine identity, 102
Rakhine society, "ethnification" of, 127
Rakhine State, 21
  borderlands of, 57
  conflict in, 121
  context of violent situations in, 129
  kala, 123–29
  at margins of Myanmar studies, 122–23
  Muslims of, 122
  population in, 147
  rituals and spirit cults, 130
  social and political situation in, 136
  during World War II, 125–26
Rakhine topography, 133–34
Rakhinization process, 102
Rampanmawia, 362
refugee camps, 173, 361
regional political-economic elite band, 248
rituals, in Rakhine sprit cults, 129–130
  since 2012, 136–38
roadmap to democracy, 302
Rohingya, 22, 25, 122, 124, 125, 139n3, 140n9, 283
  of Arakan, 289
  community, 290, 292
  construction of *Desh* (Homeland), 290–91
  ethnic minority, historical construction and representation of, 285–86
  minority group, 146, 284, 287
  Muslim Arakanes, 287
  refugee identity politics, 290–301
  Refugee Resettlement Commission, 159
  refugees, 284, 299, 301
  resistance movements, 303n13
Royal Thai Navy, 74
Ruili, 373

S

Saffron Revolution, 261

Sangha organization, 372
  in Myanmar, 383
scepticism, Myanmar Government, 62
Schofield, Clive, 79
Scott, James, 8, 293
Self-Administered Zones, 47
Sen, Amartya, 285, 325
Seventh-Day Adventist Church, 176
Seventh-Day Adventist movement, 176
Shan migrant community, 307, 310–12
  "myth of return," 312–18
  in Thailand, 308–10
shihuang mineral, 245, 246
Shwe project, 88
Sittwe, 137–38
Skinner, William, 238
social-cultural networks, 239
social marginalization, 155
social organization, 22
social practices theory, 3–7, 135
sociohistoric formations, 4
sociohistoric production, 3
socio-spatial connectivities, 216
Southeast Asia, seas in, 10
southeast Myanmar, humanitarianism operating in, 182–87
sovereignty
  electoral. *See* electoral sovereignty
  spatial boundaries and, Myanmar, 22
  Westphalian concept of, 5
spatio-economic strategy, 14
special economic zones (SEZ), 14–16, 358
spirit cults, 130
State Law and Order Restoration Council (SLORC), 81, 89, 151, 276n1, 329
State Peace and Development Council (SPDC), 81, 262, 276n1
state policy, Burmese, 288
Straight Baseline in 1968, 70

T

2010 general election results in borderland constituencies, 45–47
Tabin Shwei Hti, 105
Tăi Buddhist practices on China-Myanmar border, 369–84
Tangbau Naw Seng, 228
Tanintharyi coastal area, 82
Tanintharyi Division, 109
Tatmadaw, 12, 72–73, 80, 172, 177, 274, 276n1, 289, 331, 333, 339
"temporary shelters", 329
territorial autonomy, 215
territorial claims, 20–22
territorial cults, 130–31, 134
  political use of, 135
territorial waters, baselines in, 70, 76–80
territorialization
  of borderlands, 106–12
  gendered representation of, 103–105
  strategies, 12
territory in Burman representations, 100–102
Thai-Burmese border, 13, 16, 22, 171, 173
  Burmese migrants in, 306
  economy, 195, 203
  humanitarianism operating on, 180–82
  maritime disputes with, 74
  Shan migrant community in, 308–10
  trawlers, 84
  warship, 92n1
Thailand Burma Border Consortium (TBBC), 173, 177, 189n2
The Border Consortium (TBC), 174, 177–78, 181, 182, 189n2, 330, 332
Thein Sein, 39, 43, 53, 364
Theravāda Buddhism, 185, 370
  society, 372, 383
Tibetan refugee community, 295
topographic effect, 160
traditional seasonal migrants, 252
"translocal assemblage" concept, 226

transnational scholars, 317
"transnational social fields," 317
transnationalism, 310
Tsoti sects, 371, 380, 382

U
Ullah, Anser, 295, 296
Union of Myanmar Economic Holding Limited (UMEHL), 81
Union Solidarity and Development Party (USDP), 43, 57, 63, 66
United Nationalities Federal Council (UNFC), 339
United Nations Convention on the Law of the Sea (UNCLOS), 70, 77, 79
United Nations Convention on the Status of Refugees, 154
United Nations High Commissioner for Refugees (UNHCR), 147, 154, 159, 161, 179, 198, 285, 306
  Bangladesh programme, 162
  intervention in Bangladesh, 157–63
U Nu's policy, of instituting Buddhism, 100
U Thammanya, 184

V
van Schendel, Willem, 28n3, 154
Ven. S, 382, 383
  migration of, 378
Ven. V, migration of, 376, 377
Vipassanā meditation, 383

voters
  density by party contesting 2010 general election, 56
  distribution and population, 54–56

W
Weapons of the Weak, 293
Westphalian concept of sovereignty, 5
Wide Horizons programme, 201
World Education project, 201

X
Xishuangbanna, 370, 373

Y
Yadana Gas Project, 86, 87–88
yakhine kala, 124
Yang Yuke, 246
Yetagun gas field, 87
Yhome, Khriezo, 151
Young Mizo Association (YMA), 18, 26, 354, 360–65
Yunnanese caravans, 254
Yunnanese jade trade, 220
Yunnan, mule caravans in, 242–45

Z
Zahau, Cheery, 306
Zawtika project, 87, 88
Zaw Tun, 57
Zhao Zhongqi, 246
Zomia, 10, 28n3

www.ingramcontent.com/pod-product-compliance
Lightning Source LLC
Chambersburg PA
CBHW072117290426
44111CB00012B/1694